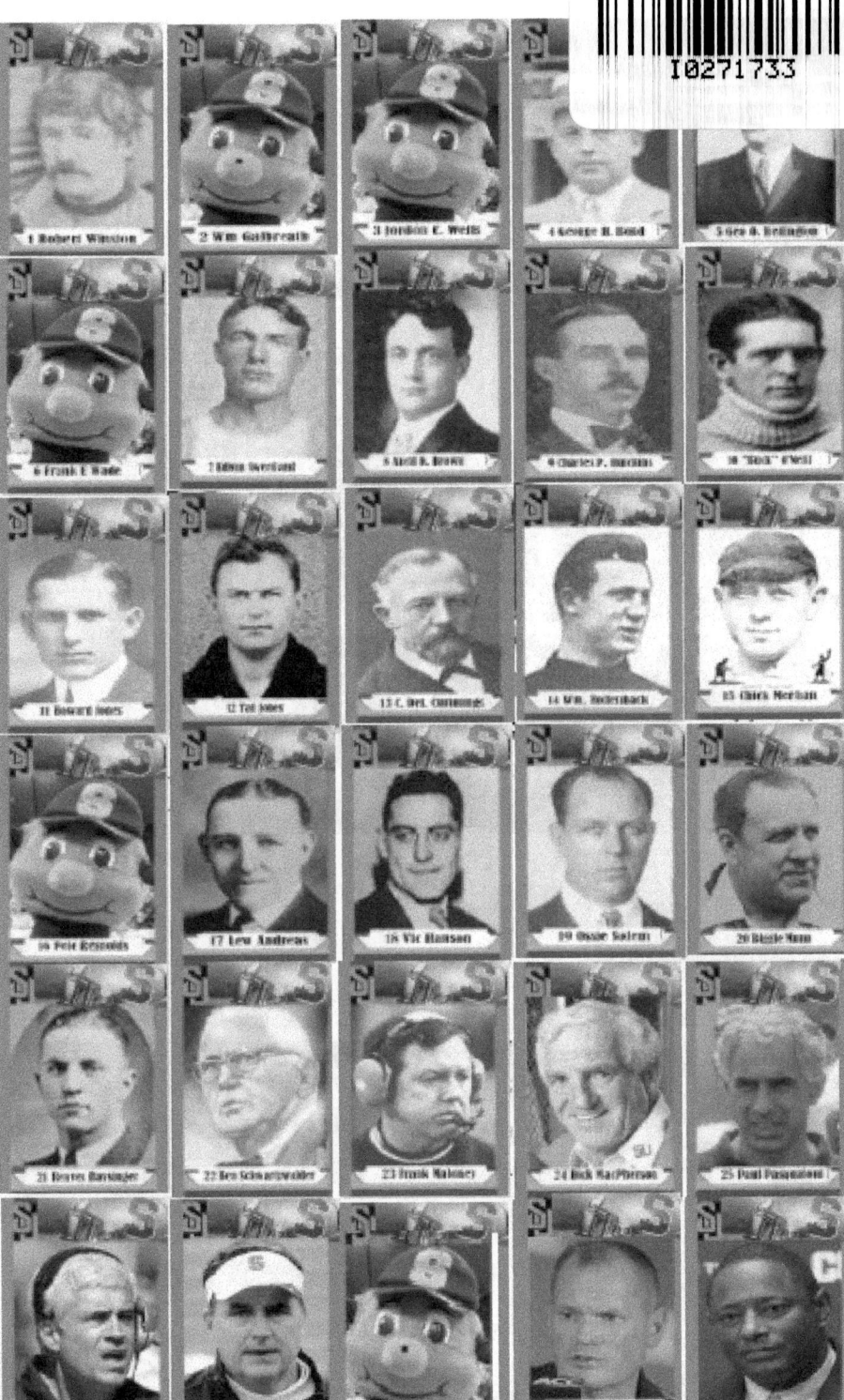

Great Moments
in
Syracuse Football

This book begins at the beginning of Football and goes to the Dino Babers era.

> This book is written for those of us who love Syracuse University and especially love the Syracuse Orange Football Team. You'll like all the stories from the University's founding in 1870, just about 150 years ago, to the beginning of the football program, through the great coaches to Syracuse as an annual National Champion contender and as a National Champion. This is a must-have book for Syracuse fans by providing a leg up on the facts missing from the bookshelves of those who do not have this book.
>
> You will learn that the Syracuse Orange, once known as the Orangemen, are fierce and passionate competitors. From the stadium to the classroom to the research lab, the Syracuse Orange always play to win.
>
> The book first tells the story about Syracuse's founding in 1870 and quickly gets to the first football game in 1867. From there, the progression leads, to Syracuse's first football game in 1889, then to the first Syracuse coach in 1890, and of course to the great immortal Syracuse coaches—Frank Buck ONeill, Chick Meehan, Ben Schwartzwalder, Dick MacPherson, and Paul Pasqualoni, all the way to the current season with Coach Dino Babers.
>
> This book captures the great moments in Syracuse Football. It takes the reader through stories about the Orange's 29 coaches to great stories about 129 seasons worth of great games (1306 games) with 720 great wins. The book often stops in time and talks about a particular great player such as Jim Brown, Ernie Davis, Larry Csonka, Floyd Little, Donovan McNabb, Marvin Harrison, Art Monk, John Mackey, Don MacPherson, or Dwight Feeney to add to your reading enjoyment.
>
> This book is your finest source for a great read on your favorite college football team. It is the closest thing to an all-encompassing, full-blown encyclopedia of Syracuse Football—a blow by blow history with tales of the great moments. We capture all the action and all the memorable moments of Orange football. This book is for your reading pleasure but also is a great reference for when you want to see how a particular Syracuse game in any year happened to turn out.
>
> You cannot ever get enough of Syracuse greatness, but we do give it a try in this can't miss book. You will not be able to put this book down.

Brian Kelly

LETS GO! PUBLISH

Great Moments in Syracuse Football

Author: Brian W. Kelly
Copyright © 2018 Brian W. Kelly
Publisher/ Editor, Brian P. Kelly

All rights reserved: No part of this book may be reproduced or transmitted in any form, or by any means, electronic or mechanical, including photocopying, recording, scanning, faxing, or by any information storage and retrieval system, without permission from the publisher, LETS GO PUBLISH, in writing.

Disclaimer: Though judicious care was taken throughout the writing and the publication of this work that the information contained herein is accurate, there is no expressed or implied warranty that all information in this book is 100% correct. Therefore, neither LETS GO PUBLISH, nor the author accepts liability for any use of this work.

Trademarks: A number of products and names referenced in this book are trade names and trademarks of their respective companies.

Referenced Material: *The information in this book has been obtained through personal and third-party observations, interviews, and copious research. Where unique information has been provided or extracted from other sources, those sources are acknowledged within the text of the book itself or at the end of the chapter in the Sources Section. Thus, there are no formal footnotes nor is there a bibliography section. Any picture that does not have a source was taken from various sites on the Internet with no credit attached. If resource owners would like credit in the next printing, please email publisher.*

Published by: LETS GO PUBLISH!
Publisher & Editor: Brian P. Kelly
Mail Location: P.O. Box 621, Wilkes-Barre, PA
Email: info@letsgopublish.com
Web site www.letsgopublish.com

Library of Congress Copyright Information Pending
Book Cover Design by Michele Thomas, Editing by Brian P. Kelly

ISBN Information: The International Standard Book Number (ISBN) is a unique machine-readable identification number, which marks any book unmistakably. The ISBN is the clear standard in the book industry. 159 countries and territories are officially ISBN members. The Official ISBN For this book is on the outside cover:

978-1-947402-35-5

The price for this work is : $19.95 USD

10   9   8   7   6   5   4   3   2   1

Release Date: April 2018

LETS GO PUBLISH!

Syracuse Season Records from 1889 through 2017

Year	Coach	W	L	T	Year	Coach	W	L	T
1889	No Head Coach	0	1	0	1954	Ben Schwartzwalder	4	4	0
1890	Robert Winston	7	4	0	1955	Ben Schwartzwalder	5	3	0
1891	William Galbreath	4	7	0	1956	Ben Schwartzwalder	7	2	0
1892	Jordon C. Wells	0	8	1	1957	Ben Schwartzwalder	5	3	1
1893	George H. Bond	4	9	1	1958	Ben Schwartzwalder	8	2	0
1894	George H. Bond	6	5	0	1959	Ben Schwartzwalder	11	0	0
1895	George O. Redington	6	2	2	1960	Ben Schwartzwalder	7	2	0
1896	George O. Redington	5	3	2	1961	Ben Schwartzwalder	8	3	0
1897	Frank E Wade	5	3	1	1962	Ben Schwartzwalder	5	5	0
1898	Frank E. Wade	8	2	1	1963	Ben Schwartzwalder	8	2	0
1899	Frank E Wade	4	4	0	1964	Ben Schwartzwalder	7	4	0
1900	Edwin Sweetland	7	2	1	1965	Ben Schwartzwalder	7	3	0
1901	Edwin Sweetland	7	1	0	1966	Ben Schwartzwalder	8	3	0
1902	Edwin Sweetland	6	2	1	1967	Ben Schwartzwalder	8	2	0
1903	Ancil D. Brown	5	4	0	1968	Ben Schwartzwalder	6	4	0
1904	Charles P. Hutchins	6	3	0	1969	Ben Schwartzwalder	5	5	0
1905	Charles P. Hutchins	8	3	0	1970	Ben Schwartzwalder	6	4	0
1906	Frank "Buck" O'Neill	6	3	0	1971	Ben Schwartzwalder	5	5	1
1907	Frank "Buck" O'Neill	5	3	1	1972	Ben Schwartzwalder	5	6	0
1908	Howard Jones	6	3	1	1973	Ben Schwartzwalder	2	9	0
1909	Tad Jones	4	5	1	1974	Frank Maloney	2	9	0
1910	Tad Jones	5	4	1	1975	Frank Maloney	6	5	0
1911	C. Def. Cummings	5	3	2	1976	Frank Maloney	3	8	0
1912	C. Def. Cummings	4	5	0	1977	Frank Maloney	6	5	0
1913	Frank "Buck" O'Neill	6	4	0	1978	Frank Maloney	3	8	0
1914	Frank "Buck" O'Neill	5	3	2	1979	Frank Maloney	7	5	0
1915	Frank "Buck" O'Neill	9	1	2	1980	Frank Maloney	5	6	0
1916	William Hollenback	5	4	0	1981	Dick MacPherson	4	6	1
1917	Frank "Buck" O'Neill	8	1	1	1982	Dick MacPherson	2	9	0
1918	Frank "Buck" O'Neill	5	1	0	1983	Dick MacPherson	6	5	0
1919	Frank "Buck" O'Neill	8	3	0	1984	Dick MacPherson	6	5	0
1920	Chick Meehan	6	2	1	1985	Dick MacPherson	7	5	0
1921	Chick Meehan	7	2	0	1986	Dick MacPherson	5	6	0
1922	Chick Meehan	6	1	2	1987	Dick MacPherson	11	0	1
1923	Chick Meehan	8	1	0	1988	Dick MacPherson	10	2	0
1924	Chick Meehan	8	2	1	1989	Dick MacPherson	8	4	0
1925	Pete Reynolds	8	1	1	1990	Dick MacPherson	7	4	2
1926	Pete Reynolds	7	2	1	1991	Paul Pasqualoni	10	2	0
1927	Lew Andreas	5	3	2	1992	Paul Pasqualoni	10	2	0
1928	Lew Andreas	4	4	1	1993	Paul Pasqualoni	6	4	1
1929	Lew Andreas	6	3	0	1994	Paul Pasqualoni	7	4	0
1930	Vic Hanson	5	2	2	1995	Paul Pasqualoni	9	3	0
1931	Vic Hanson	7	1	1	1996	Paul Pasqualoni	9	3	0
1932	Vic Hanson	4	4	1	1997	Paul Pasqualoni	9	4	0
1933	Vic Hanson	4	4	0	1998	Paul Pasqualoni	8	4	0
1934	Vic Hanson	6	2	0	1999	Paul Pasqualoni	7	5	0
1935	Vic Hanson	6	1	1	2000	Paul Pasqualoni	6	5	0
1936	Vic Hanson	1	7	0	2001	Paul Pasqualoni	10	3	0
1937	Ossie Solem	5	2	1	2002	Paul Pasqualoni	4	8	0
1938	Ossie Solem	5	3	0	2003	Paul Pasqualoni	6	6	0
1939	Ossie Solem	3	3	2	2004	Paul Pasqualoni	6	6	0
1940	Ossie Solem	3	4	1	2005	Greg Robinson	1	#	0
1941	Ossie Solem	5	2	1	2006	Greg Robinson	4	8	0
1942	Ossie Solem	6	3	0	2007	Greg Robinson	2	#	0
1944	Ossie Solem	2	4	1	2008	Greg Robinson	3	9	0
1945	Ossie Solem	1	6	0	2009	Doug Marrone	4	8	0

1946	Clarence Biggie Munn	4	5	0	2010	Doug Marrone	8	5	0
1947	Reaves Baysinger	3	6	0	2011	Doug Marrone	5	7	0
1948	Reaves Baysinger	1	8	0	2012	Doug Marrone	8	5	0
1949	Ben Schwartzwalder	4	5	0	2013	Scott Shafer	7	6	0
1950	Ben Schwartzwalder	5	5	0	2014	Scott Shafer	3	9	0
1951	Ben Schwartzwalder	5	4	0	2015	Scott Shafer	4	8	0
1952	Ben Schwartzwalder	7	3	0	2016	Dino Babers	4	8	0
1953	Ben Schwartzwalder	5	3	1	2017	Dino Babers	4	8	0

Total Games   1306
Total Wins   720
Total Losses   537
Total Ties   49   * Prior to Overtime Rules
Stats from   1889 * Through Nov 2017

Dedication

I dedicate this book

To my wonderful brothers and sisters:

Angel Edward J. Kelly, Jr.

Carol & Amelia Kelly

Nancy "Ann" Flannery & Angel Jim Flannery

Mary A. Daniels & Bill Daniels

Joseph A. Kelly & Diane Kelly

I surely am a lucky person to have

Such a great family

Edward J Kelly and Irene McKeown Kelly

.

Acknowledgments:

I appreciate all the help that I have received in putting this book together as well as all of the other 151 books from the past.

My acknowledgments were so large at one time that readers complained that they had to go through too many pages to get to page one.

And, so I put my acknowledgment list online, and it continues to grow. Believe it or not, it would cost about a dollar more to print my books with full acknowledgments.

Thank you and God bless you all for your help. Please check out www.letsgopublish.com to read the latest version of my heartfelt acknowledgments updated for this book.

In this book, I received some extra special help from many fine American patriots including Dennis Grimes, Gerry Rodski, Wily Ky Eyely, Angel Irene McKeown Kelly, Angel Edward Joseph Kelly Sr., Angel Edward Joseph Kelly Jr., Ann Flannery, Angel James Flannery Sr., Mary Daniels, Bill Daniels, Angel Robert Gary Daniels, Angel Sarah Janice Daniels, Angel Punkie Daniels, Joe Kelly, Diane Kelly, Brian P. Kelly, Mike P. Kelly, Katie P. Kelly, Angel Ben Kelly, and Budmund (Buddy) Arthur Kelly.

Thank you all!

Table of Contents

Dedication ix

Table of Contents xiii

Chapter 1 Introduction to the Book 1

Chapter 2 History of Syracuse Football "Stadiums" 21

Chapter 3 The Founding of Syracuse University 33

Chapter 4 SU's Mission Statement & Vision Statement 39

Chapter 5 Syracuse Launches its First Football Team 41

Chapter 6 The Evolution of Modern Football 45

Chapter 7 Syracuse Football – From 1889 to 1902 63

Chapter 8 Syracuse Football – From 1903 to 1915 85

Chapter 9 Syracuse Football – From 1916 to 1929 107

Chapter 10 Vic Hanson Era From 1930 to 1936 137

Chapter 11 Coach Ossie Solem et al From 1937 to 1948 145

Chapter 12 Coach Ben Schwartzwalder From 1949 to 1973 167

Chapter 13 Coach Frank Maloney From 1974 to 1980 235

Chapter 14 Coach Dick Macpherson From 1981 to 1990 245

Chapter 15 Coach Paul Pasqualoni From 1991 to 2004 281

Chapter 16 Coach Greg Robinson From 2005 to 2008 329

Chapter 17 Coach Doug Marrone From 2009 to 2012 337

Chapter 18 Coach Scott Shafer From 2013 to 2015 355

Chapter 19 Coach Dino BabersFrom 2016 to ???? 363

Chapter 20: What Is the Future of Syracuse Football? 379

Other books by Brian Kelly: (amazon.com, & Kindle) 396

References

I learned how to write creatively in Grade School at St. Boniface. I even enjoyed reading some of my own stuff.

At Meyers High School (HS Diploma) and King's College (BS Data Processing), and Wilkes-University, (MBA Accounting & Finance) learned how to research, write bibliographies and footnote every non-original thought included in my writings. I learned to hate ibid, and op. cit., and I hated assuring that I had all citations were written down in the proper sequence. Having to pay attention to details took my desire to write creatively and diminished it with busy work.

I know it is necessary for the world to stop plagiarism, so authors and publishers can get paid properly, but for an honest writer, it sure is annoying. I wrote many proposals while with IBM and whenever I needed to cite something, I cited it in place, because my readers, IT Managers, and company management, could care less about tracing the vagaries of citations. I always hated to use stilted footnotes, or produce a lengthy, perfectly formatted bibliography. I bet most bibliographies are flawed because even the experts on such drivel do not like the tedium.

I wrote 151 books before this book and several hundred articles published by many magazines and newspapers and I only cite when an idea is not mine or when I am quoting, and again, I choose to cite in place, and the reader does not have to trace strange numbers through strange footnotes and back to bibliography elements that may not be readily accessible or available.

Yet, I would be kidding you, if in a book about the great moments in Syracuse Football, I tried to bluff my way, so you would think that I knew everything before I began to research and write anything in this book. I spent as much time researching as writing. I might even call myself an expert of sorts now for all the facts that I have uncovered.

Without any pain on your part, you can read this book from cover to cover to enjoy the stories about the many great moments in Syracuse Football.

This book is not intended for historians per se, but it does teach a lot of history. It is for regular people of all levels of intelligence. It is for people that want to have a fun read, who like smiling when Syracuse Football is the topic. It is fun reading about each of SU's 720 wins. This book is for people who love Syracuse and perhaps it is also for some Syracuse detractors who want to have command of the facts.

There are lots and lots of facts in this book. This book is not for sticklers about the mundane aspects of writing that often cause creative writers to lay bricks or paint houses instead of writing. It is for everyday people, like you and I, who enjoy Syracuse because it is Syracuse and who enjoy football because it is football. It is that simple.

When Syracuse plays a team and wins or loses, that is a historical fact, but to discover such facts, it does not require fundamental or basic research. The University itself copyrights its material but only so it can say "no" if somebody else's creativity affects the University negatively. Even Syracuse does not own well-known facts that are readily available about legacies such as Dick MacPherson, Ben Schwartzwalder, and championship seasons.

The championships and the coaches and the great players are well known and well defined, though some may think Jim Brown is an Actor and not the greatest Syracuse and Cleveland Browns football player of all time. So, what? As the author of this book, I care but it is a sports book. I use a judicious approach to assure that I am not throwing the bull when I am presenting the facts.

Nonetheless, this is not a book about heavy math algorithms, or potential advances to the internal combustion engine, or space travel, or the eight elements necessary to find a cure for cancer. So, I refuse to treat this book 100% seriously. If you find a fault, I will fix it. This is a book about sports and sports legends and stories about sporting events that have been recorded seven million times already someplace else. Though I tried for sure to get it all right and I used the work of others to assure so, I bet I made a mistake or two.

What is my remedy for the *harmed* if I have made a mistake? I did not write this book to harm anybody. If I did not write this book, would the *harmed individuals* from the book be unharmed. So, at the very least, I can *unpublish* those parts of the book. If any reader is harmed, let me know, and I will do whatever must be done for all to be OK.

Preface:

"It was not a competitive program when we came here, and now everything about it is competitive. We can stay at this level, because Syracuse is that kind of team. But it's not enough. This program and this area deserves a legitimate top 32 team, when you're going to a bowl every year." Quote by Dick Macpherson, a great SU coach

The late Dick Macpherson is one of the more quoted of Syracuse's past coaching masters. It is no wonder why. In his ten great years at Syracuse, Big Mac called it as he saw it.

Everything that is—can be made better. When Clemson came to town in 2017, having had a *much-too-easy* victory against the Orange in 2016, they were planning to leave Syracuse with another big win. But, because everything came together from the pregame to the game, it did not happen.

With Dino Babers as coach, even as it is rebuilding, Syracuse is again a team with a heart. It is a team that cannot be messed with. To get the fans stirring for the Clemson Friday game last fall, the fans planned a big splash. The Orange were back in the Carrier Dome on this Friday for one of the most highly-anticipated games of the season versus the reigning national champion Clemson Tigers. Kickoff between the Orange and the Tigers was at 7:02 p.m. for a game viewable across the world on ESPN.

Syracuse has had many other games like this but none with such meaning and hype as undefeated Clemson was the one and only reigning national championship team in the fall 2017. The Clemson encounter was the 1,300th in the illustrious 128-year history of the Syracuse football program. Lots was happening all day from individually planned trips to the great bookstore and a number of pep filled events leading up to the game including pregame festivities on the Quad that started at 4 p.m. A Quad pep rally featuring the "Pride of the Orange" marching band began at 5:30 p.m. The band performed on the steps of Hendricks Chapel. It was a grand scene.

The band's pregame performance inside the Dome began at 6:48 p.m. and Coach Dino Babers led the Orange team onto the field at 6:57 p.m. It was like clockwork and full precision. This particular week in the ACC was Fall Sportsmanship Week. To showcase their continued dedication to sportsmanship and fair play, the Orange and Tigers met at midfield to shake hands just prior to kickoff.

The following is a complete listing that shows the key times of interest for the Orange on this magical Friday. This was a great pre-game for a great history making game:

- 3:30 p.m. – Parking lots open
- 4 p.m. – Quad opens
- 4:30 p.m. – Student gates open
- 5 p.m. – "Orange Gameday" radio show begins 99.5 FM (TK 99)
- 5 p.m. – Carrier Dome gates open to the public
- 5:30 p.m. – Quad Pep Rally featuring the Syracuse Marching Band
- 6 p.m. – "Orange Pregame" begins -- IMG Sports Network
- 6:43 p.m. – Marching Band takes the field -- pregame performance
- 6:48 p.m. – Alma Mater
- 6:50 p.m. – National Anthem
- 6:53 p.m. – Syracuse intro video
- 6:56 p.m. – Tunnel Walk
- 6:57 p.m. – Syracuse takes the field
- 6:59 p.m. – Clemson takes the field
- 7 p.m. – Coin Toss
- 7:01 p.m. – ACC Sportsmanship Handshake
- 7:02 p.m. – Kickoff
- End of 1st Quarter – Hometown Hero Presentation
- Halftime – Marching Band performs

The last few years, and now with an exciting coach like Dino Babers, Syracuse is looking for the same magic formula for all games including pep rallies and for tailgating festivities. The objective is team spirit and the notion is to bring out the fans in major numbers to help rev the team up for a great game. The Clemson formula worked against Clemson in 2017. Would that not be nice to see a lot more pep and spirit in 2018 and beyond. Look at the results from 2017:

Dungey has 3 TD passes, Syracuse stuns No. 2 Clemson 27-24

"Eric Dungey threw for 278 yards and three touchdowns, Cole Murphy kicked a tiebreaking field goal in the fourth quarter, and Syracuse stunned #2 Clemson 27-24 on Friday night to put a damper on the Tigers' chances to repeat as national champions."

Syracuse was at its best. Thank you, Coach Dino Babers, and a spirited group of Orange.

The Syracuse University Bookstore is outstanding for on campus shopping and it is also as good as it gets online at http://shop.und.com/. You can acquire a host of relics and memorabilia and some nice SU wear from the bookstore, plus you can buy books that are all about Syracuse University. I bet the store will also be pleased to sell you some great textbooks about your favorite subjects.

The bookstore is located in the Schine Student Center, 303 University Place, Syracuse, NY 13210: https://bookweb.syr.edu -- 315-443-9900. Give them a call to order this new book for your many Syracuse friends. Of course, you can reach them online at https://bookweb.syr.edu/

This new book by Brian Kelly, which highlights the Great Moments in Syracuse Football is one of the items that is expected to be available all 52 weeks and in fact all 365 days each year except in LEAP YEAR where the University adds an extra day for your shopping pleasure. The Bookstore is there to add to your Syracuse Orange football experience. Once you get this book, it is yours forever unless, of course you give it away to one of the many SU fans, who will be in awe of your new possession.

Whether you get to the pep rallies and home games on campus or not, this book and its nearly 500 pages brings the glory of Syracuse football right to your bookshelf, your pocket, or right to your hands. Reading this book is like reliving the last game, the last football season, and / or all the seasons before last season without ever having to get on or off a plane. Seeing a game in the Dome, however, is an exhilarating experience, I've done it many times. This book will help you relive that experience over and over. Besides the great read, with this book in your hand at your private venue, there is no limit on the hours for book-tailgating. Moreover, there is no charge, as long as you have stocked up before the read.

The book examines more than just great moments. There are some moments that are not so great in every team's football seasons and Syracuse offers no excuses for those times. Your author shows the bad with the good to get the proper perspective for those great moments.

Not all Syracuse coaches, for example, are named Schwartzwalder or MacPherson or Pasqualoni, so not all games are in the W column. However, all teams, no matter who the coach is, were Syracuse tough, nonetheless. That means they all fought hard for wins as the Syracuse Orangemen. I hope you enjoy the contrast.

Opening with its first story at the very beginning of Football as a sport in America, this book goes all the way to Coach Dino Babers' last game in 2017. Then, it presents the 2018 season schedule and the outlook for 2018 and the future of the program.

It is written for those of us who love Syracuse Football as played in either Archbold Stadium or the Carrier Dome. The book first tells the story about Syracuse University's founding in 1870. Then, in story-telling mode, it recounts the events leading to the first college football game in America in 1867, and it continues to the first Syracuse Football Game (without a coach) in 1889. It then advances to the games, mostly victories, of the first Syracuse Football Coach in 1890, and the book moves onward to the great immortal Syracuse Coaches of historical fame—O'Neill, Meehan, Schwartzwalder, MacPherson, and Pasqualoni. What a book!

Predicting that another future immortal great may be in our midst, the book then takes us up to the current season with Coach Dino Babers. Finally, to sum it all up, Brian Kelly, your author, caps off the experience with a unique perspective on the future of Syracuse Football in Chapter 20: "What Is the Future of Syracuse Football" It is an honest look at what Syracuse University must do to remain vital to the institution. It also offers some other options that are "out of the box."

This book is all about the great moments in Syracuse Football. It touches every aspect of the historical and mythical Syracuse Football Teams. It tells exhilarating stories about SU's 29 coaches and its 129 seasons worth of great games. The book stops every now and then, and it takes the reader on a side excursion in time to learn about a particular event or a great player. The player list always begins with the living immortal, Jim Brown, then moves to the heavenly immortal, Ernie Davis, and on to Floyd Little, Qadry Ismail, Eric Dungey, and a slew of SU All-Americans who have made Syracuse Football a bright light experience for the program's many years and many fans.

In my role as Editor in Chief of Lets Go Publish! and Syracuse fan, as I have been at many games with my dad, your author, I predict that you will not be able to put this book down

You are going to love this book because it is the perfect read for anybody who loves Syracuse University and Syracuse Football and who wants to know more about one of the most revered athletic programs in the Northeast.

Few sports books are a must-read but Brian Kelly's Great Moments in Syracuse Football will quickly appear at the top of Americas most enjoyable must-read books about sports. Enjoy!

Who is Brian Kelly?

Brian Kelly aka Brian W. Kelly, is one of the leading authors in America with this, his 152nd published book. Brian continues as an outspoken and eloquent expert on a variety of topics. Moreover, Kelly also has written several hundred articles on other topics of interest to Americans.

Most of his early works involved high technology. Later, Brian wrote a number of patriotic books and most recently he has been writing human interest books such as *The Wine Diet* and *Thank you, IBM.* His books are always well received. If I could get the pen out of Dad's hand for just awhile, I might be able to write a few books of my own, but my editing chores at Lets Go Publish always come first.

Brian Kelly's books are highlighted at www.letsgopublish.com. They are for sale at Amazon, Kindle, and Amazon.com/author/brianwkelly, as well as Barnes & Noble and other fine booksellers.

The best!

Sincerely,

Brian P. Kelly, Editor in Chief
I am Brian Kelly's eldest son

About the Author

Brian Kelly retired as an Assistant Professor in the Business Information Technology (BIT) Program at Marywood University, where he also served as the IBM i and Midrange Systems Technical Advisor to the IT Faculty. Kelly designed, developed, and taught many college and professional courses. He continues as a contributing technical editor to a number of technical industry magazines, including "The Four Hundred" and "Four Hundred Guru," published by IT Jungle.

Kelly is a former IBM Senior Systems Engineer. His specialty was problem solving for customers as well as implementing advanced operating systems and software on his client's machines. Brian is the author of 151 books, including 23 Sports Books, and hundreds of magazine articles. He has been a frequent speaker at technical conferences throughout the United States.

Brian was a candidate for the US Congress from Pennsylvania in 2010 and he ran for Mayor in his home town in 2015. Kelly loves Syracuse and he became a big fan in the 1980's when he was with IBM and he ran many bus trips from Scranton to Syracuse to watch Pennsylvania Teams such as Penn State and Pittsburgh, play the Orangemen.

When PSU stopped playing the Orange, the annual PSU game, which once alternated between PSU and Pitt continued to be billed for Scranton IBMers as the Annual Penn State Game. However, the game itself would feature Army or another appropriate team against the Orangemen of Syracuse. Sometimes our bus parked right alongside the Army busses and our kids loved watching the cadets. This is Brian's seventh "Great Moments" book about major College Football Teams and writing about Syracuse has been a special treat.

Chapter 1 Introduction to the Book

Syracuse celebrates its 129th year of football

Dino Babers, Syracuse Football Coach Leading the Orange

In 2019, Syracuse will celebrate its 130th year of collegiate football. This book celebrates Syracuse Football; its founding; its struggles; its greatness; and its long-lasting impact on American life. People like me, who love Syracuse from way back when they were the Orangemen, will love this book. Syracuse Haters will want their own copy of this book just for additional ammo. Yet, it won't help them! Hah!

We begin the rest of the Syracuse story in Chapter 3 with the founding of the Syracuse institution and we continue in subsequent chapters right into the founding of the football program in 1889.

In defining the format of the book, we chose to use a timetable that is based on a historical chronology. Within this framework, we discuss the great moments in Syracuse Football History, and there are many great moments. No book can claim to be able to capture them all, as it would be a never-ending story, but we sure try.

Jim Brown, Ernie Davis (RIP), Floyd Little, and other Syracuse greats have great reverence for the University for which they played the game of football. Nearly a half century after he left Syracuse to embark on his NFL career, Floyd Little returned to his alma mater in 2011 Thursday, quoting lines from a Robert Frost poem to describe why he decided to give up a cushy retirement to be back at school. "I have promises to keep and miles to go before I sleep," said the Hall of Fame running back, who was introduced as Syracuse's special assistant to the athletic director. The most famous of them all is Jim Brown, who literally is the greatest.

Ernie Davis is one of God's angel's today and surely, he shines on Syracuse University a light that will never be extinguished. Like Brown and Little, Ernie Davis was a Syracuse phenomenon who got sick before the good things happened and he died but his memory lives on.

Every NFL team wanted Ernie Davis to play for them. It was the most lucrative contract for an NFL rookie up to that time. He chose the Cleveland Browns where he would have been teamed with the great Jim Brown. The Browns' dream of pairing Davis with Jim Brown took a tragic turn when Davis was diagnosed with leukemia.

Following his death, the Browns retired his number 45 jersey. Davis was a great man in his short life and we know he is still showering blessings on Syracuse. If asked, by the Browns, I would bet that he would have said that ND jerseys and Syracuse jerseys should not be retired because with all of the history of these great teams, there would be no numbers left.

I use my feelings about Ernie Davis as a great human being as an idea to help promulgate the notion that nobody can write a book about Syracuse Football History that is all inclusive, because even if it can be written, it would be too big to ever be read. I hoped this book would come in at a little over 200 pages, but if it had, you would not have liked it. Read what you can when you can. It will be a fun experience.

I capture all the great Syracuse moments in this book. OK, I get most of them! If I missed any and you tell me, then we'll do a second edition. The great moments naturally include a lot of great people, including players and the 27 great coaches that over time would make or break Syracuse University.

If Syracuse were ever to break because of a coach, as some believe it has at times, simply because it is Syracuse, the University not only would continue, it will always continue.

Syracuse has been able to survive a number of coaches who could not survive themselves, while the university and the football program have both grown in acceptance and popularity.

We all as individuals and as honest institutions, such as Syracuse do our best in life and sometimes it is just enough. Sometimes it is just not enough. Even if we survive and become more than OK, detractors may suggest our success is not enough. I disagree. Let the naysayers say "nay," and go away!

Let me please assure you that I have done my best to portray an accurate depiction of Syracuse Football History, displayed in a properly summarized format so that none of us are reading this book forever. There are a ton of great stories for sure. More importantly, none of us should need to search further than this book for the truth about many of the depictions in this book. Let's talk about some Syracuse football moments and some great athletes and coaches now, before we close out the first chapter of this book highlighting the Great Moments in Syracuse Football.

Brief Overview

Ya just gotta love Syracuse University and the Syracuse Orangemen Football Team, who now—those in recent years call the Syracuse Orange. I know I do from way back. I have been to the Carrier Dome and Manley Field more than I have been in any college stadium in the country. And, I love College Football and the Syracuse Orangemen.

After many years as an independent, the Orange Football Team joined the Big East in 1991 and then, in 2013, in another change for the better, all of the Syracuse athletic teams joined the Atlantic Coast Conference (ACC). The ACC is part of the National Collegiate Athletic Association (NCAA) Division I conference that is part of the Football Bowl Subdivision (FBS). Syracuse, for all of its great play over the years has one national championship, along with an awful lot of close calls.

Their big championship season was earned under coach Ben Schwartzwalder, a Syracuse coaching immortal during the 1959 season. Currently, The Orange are coached by Dino Babers, who was hired on December 5, 2015, to succeed Scott Shafer. Home games are played at the Carrier Dome, located on the school's beautiful campus in Syracuse. Regardless of what the temperature is outside, the magnificent Carrier Dome facility is always a toasty 69 degrees.

Syracuse opened as an institution in 1870 and it took just nineteen years to begin a football program that became one of the nation's best. They played on what they called the Old Oval Athletic Field. It was deployed by the University from 1898 to 1907. Check it out on the next page:

The Old Oval athletic field, Syracuse University, *circa* 1898–1907

Syracuse played its first football game on November 23, 1889. The score was 0-36 in a game played against Rochester. Things changed for the better, and quite rapidly from 1890 on. In 1890, for example with First coach Robert Winston, the Orangemen put forth a highly respectable season at 7-4, for a team operating in just its second year.

National success was achieved not too long after this first game in the 1890s and 1900s. With the construction of the "state-of-the-art" Archbold Stadium in 1907, Syracuse rose to national prominence under College Football Hall of Fame coach Frank "Buck" O'Neill. O'Neill could not get enough of Syracuse as he kept leaving and coming back. He always produced great teams. His 1915 squad got itself a Rose Bowl invitation, but the administration declined because the team had already played on the West Coast that season. Times have changed.

The 1920s brought on continued success with teams featuring star end Vic Hanson, one of only two individuals who are members (Amos Alonzo Stagg—not from Syracuse being the other) of both the Basketball Hall of Fame and the College Football Hall of Fame. Hanson later coached the team.

Back then, there were a lot of football teams from schools we heard little about in the national spotlight. From 1891 to 1961, Colgate University was Syracuse's biggest rival. Despite how powerful the Orangemen were, Colgate held the edge during this period, 31–26–5.

From 1937–1945, Ossie Solem served as Syracuse's head coach, compiling a 30–27–6 record. Though a winning record, things had slowed down a bit for the Orange on their path to football glory. Ben Schwartzwalder would change that as he put in 25 years and is responsible for modern Syracuse football for being a mainstay on the US college and university football map.

Ben Schwartzwalder era (1949–1973)

Coach Schwartzwalder with quarterback Dick Easterly at the Los Angeles Coliseum, 1959

When Ben Schwartzwalder took over as coach in 1949, it was a breath of fresh air for the program, which had been neglected and had stagnated during the 1930's and 1940's. Army dominated the national scene at this time as did Notre Dame with Frank Leahy at the helm.

A number of special teams during this period benefitted by service academy personnel in attendance, or their universities were part of a service academy, prospered while a lot of other one-time fine teams, including basketball great Gonzaga could not find enough players to field a quality football team during the war years. Syracuse was affected in 1943 and did not field a team that year.

The Orangemen made their first bowl appearance in the 1953 Orange Bowl under Coach Schwartzwalder, in his fifth year. They followed this in 1957 with an appearance in the Cotton Bowl, and then the 1959 Orange Bowl.

The 1957 Cotton Bowl Classic team featured Hall of Fame running back Jim Brown who my dad and many others believe is the best "living" football player of all time. When Jim Brown passes on in another 75 years, I suspect, the adjective "living" will be deleted and he will be known simply as the best running back of all time. Rumor has it that to stay as fast and as powerful as he wanted to be, Brown chose not to wear hip pads. Perhaps the lack of those extra inches on his width helped him slip through smaller openings. However, from having watched Jim Brown on our brand new black and white Admiral TV, I have a feeling his record would be the same even if his bones were that big.

In 1959, Syracuse was undefeated. Because the team played the best in the nation, they were awarded their first national championship following this undefeated season and their Cotton Bowl Classic victory over Texas. Though Jim Brown was playing pro football for the Brown's that year, a phenomenal sophomore running back named Ernie Davis, assured the championship season for Syracuse and Ben Schwartzwalder. Davis was great. He went on to become the first African American to win the Heisman Trophy, a major milestone in Syracuse football history.

in 1961, Syracuse All-American tackle Ron Luciano, who eventually become a prominent Major League Baseball umpire was a bulwark on the team. Tragedy hit Ernie Davis, who with today's medicine would be alive and offering commentary with Jim Brown. He was slated to play for the Cleveland Browns in the same backfield with Jim Brown.

Can you imagine the agony of the defensive lines with that combo pounding them play after play. Ernie Davis, a great young man, died of leukemia before being able to play one game professionally. Syracuse remained competitive through the 1960s with a series of All American running backs, including the great Floyd Little and one of the best fullbacks ever, Larry Csonka.

Ben Schwartzwalder retired as Syracuse's head coach following the 1973 season, which was Syracuse's third-consecutive losing season. Whether Schwartzwalder had lost his fight, or the Syracuse administration chose not to work hard to receive scholarship athletes is a question for the ages. Ben Schwartzwalder left Syracuse with a proud 153-91-3 record. Regardless, the great one, Ben Schwartzwalder chose to pack it in.

Frank Maloney era (1974-1980)

There was only one Ben Schwartzwalder though many times school administrations think that it was some other magic than the coach, that brought in all the wins. Michigan assistant coach Frank Maloney was hired as Schwartzwalder's replacement. Giving the benefit of the doubt, the best one could say about Maloney's tenure at Syracuse was that it was marked by inconsistency. The fan base turned on him as the Orange failed to achieve the national status they had enjoyed under Schwartzwalder. It is always better to replace a coach who is a bum than a great coach. Maloney learned this lesson.

Maloney had a problem with racial unrest among other things. Many who look at it objectively saw that the administration's lack of financial support for the program was a large part of the blame. Few coaches would have done well in similar circumstances. Maloney's program had a tough go with the limitation of archaic facilities.

Archbold Stadium, Syracuse's home field since 1907, had had its best days and it was in need of replacement. Despite adversity, Maloney was able to recruit a number of future NFL stars such as Joe Morris and Pro Football Hall of Fame member Art Monk.

Maloney was the subject of criticism, not only from the fans and alumni, but also from the 1959 national championship team, who had forgotten that Ben Schwartzwalder had losing seasons before he finally left the program. Members of this elite championship team wanted more championships regardless of university resources. They began a campaign calling for Maloney's ouster.

Ironically enough, this call from program alumni came during the 1979 season, which was Coach Maloney's best season at Syracuse. The Orangemen qualified for the Independence Bowl, beating McNeese State. After coaching the Orangemen for seven seasons and presiding over the opening of a new stadium, the Carrier Dome, in 1980, Maloney resigned. When somebody who knows the inside scoop writes a factual article about what really happened to Syracuse for ten years, beginning the last three years of the Schwartzwalder era, in a second edition, we will be pleased to tell the full story.

Dick MacPherson era (1981–1990)

When visiting Syracuse's Carrier Dome on my many bus trips, I always thought Dick MacPherson was a great coach and I thought Don McPherson was his son. I later learned they spelled their names differently.

Dick MacPherson was hired as the head coach in 1981 and after several mediocre seasons, fans wanted MacPherson fired. They coined the phrase, "Sack Mac." Once a team tastes national success as Syracuse did under Schwartzwalder, the alums and the fan base want nothing less. Syracuse is no different than other universities across the country. After losing to Clemson in 2016, I bet we could find a number of feint calls for Alabama's Nick Saban's head out there in the ethosphere.

Fans are fickle once the winning begins. The fans' opinion of Coach MacPherson changed when the program returned suddenly to national prominence in 1987 with an undefeated 11-0 regular season record. Dick was OK then by the fans. That team featured Maxwell Award-winning quarterback Don McPherson and fullback Daryl Johnston. Before the BCS times, luck had a lot to do with whether a great undefeated national team could even get into a national championship bowl game.

And so, the team missed an opportunity to play for the NCAA Division I-A national football championship, but not because they were not good enough. It was because both Oklahoma and Miami also finished undefeated that year and finished higher in the polls.

Consequently, the Orangemen were scheduled to face Southeastern Conference Champion Auburn University in the Sugar Bowl. In a nail-biter, the game ended in a tie. Auburn managed to kick a late field goal rather than trying for a game-winning touchdown.

Dick MacPherson resigned after the 1990 season to accept the position of head coach for the NFL's New England Patriots. MacPherson coached the Patriots in 1991 and 1992 and received strong consideration for Coach of the Year honors in 1991. The Pats were 1-15 in 1990 and with five more wins, McPherson led them to a 6-10 record in his first season.

Things were looking bright but then in his second season the team struggled like in the past, starting four different quarterbacks and the Pats finished a dismal 2-14. MacPherson was subsequently fired at the end of the season. Later, he took a spot as assistant coach with the Denver Broncos and then the Cleveland Browns.

Paul Pasqualoni era (1991-2004)

Syracuse had gotten its mojo going again with McPherson and continued to do well under his successor, Paul Pasqualoni. Coach Pasqualoni had previously been the team's linebackers' coach, as head coach, his teams appeared in 11 bowl games (including three major bowls) and they won 9 of the 11 games. Syracuse also captured or shared three Big East football championships during the Pasqualoni period.

Big name players under Pasqualoni included Donovan McNabb, Marvin Harrison, Dwight Freeney, Keith Bulluck, Rob Moore, Donovin Darius, Qadry Ismail, Kevin Johnson, Rob Konrad, Tebucky Jones, and Marvin Graves.

Coach Pasqualoni

Pasqualoni had good talent and he made the most of it.

For years, every other year, IBM took a trip to Syracuse from Scranton to see the Penn State v Syracuse game at the Carrier Dome. It was great football. Every other year, it was Pitt. In the early 1990's Penn State ended its series with Syracuse and joined the

Big Ten. After I had left IBM, I brought a busload from Scranton every year for many years.

Meanwhile, fewer and fewer independents, such as Penn State, were finding it advantageous to go it alone. Syracuse chose to join the newly formed Big East football conference with traditional rivals University of Pittsburgh, West Virginia University, and national power Miami. In 2004, Miami and Virginia Tech left the Big East to join the Atlantic Coast Conference (ACC). In 2004, Syracuse gave up its nicknames Orangemen and Orangewomen, and settled on being the Syracuse Orange in all sports.

In 2005, Boston College left the Big East for the ACC. Syracuse felt this threatened the stature of the Big East. Syracuse had been originally invited to leave the Big East and join the ACC, but politics entered the fray. The Governor of Virginia pressured the ACC, which then decided to invite Virginia Tech to join the conference, instead. Thus, Syracuse for a number of years reluctantly remained in the Big East.

Syracuse and Pittsburgh together left the Big East on July 1, 2013. They each had to find the cash. Each team paid the Big East $7.5 million to depart on that date. Notre Dame joined the ACC on July 1, 2013, while Louisville left for the ACC on July 1, 2014. The ACC, with Clemson winning the national championship last year has certainly become a super conference.

Syracuse's streak of winning seasons ended in 2002 when they went 4–8. This was followed by consecutive 6–6 seasons. Although the Orange won a share of the Big East title in 2004 and competed in the Champs Sports Bowl, the teams from 2002–2004 were considered mediocre by Syracuse new standards. This prompted new athletic director Dr. Daryl Gross to fire Pasqualoni after a mostly-successful 14-years at the helm.

Greg Robinson era (2005–2008)

In 2005, Syracuse hired Greg Robinson as the new head coach. He had been the defensive coordinator for Texas. Robinson changed the style of Syracuse football by installing a new West Coast offense scheme. This replaced the option run style of offense previously run by Pasqualoni, and he added new defensive schemes.

Former football head coach Greg Robinson "chases" the last of his players onto the field before the kickoff of his inaugural 2005 season. It was the first game played on the Carrier Dome's new FieldTurf.

The 2005 season started very positively as Syracuse had an upset going over eventual Big East and Sugar Bowl champion West Virginia. They forced five turnovers but did not capitalize. They lost the game 7-15.

They came right back with a 31–0 blowout over Buffalo and another near upset win to #25 Virginia. Bad luck prevailed as the Orangemen lost 27–24 on a last-second field goal.

The good news was over for the season as the squad lost its final eight games. Syracuse finished the year 1–10, the worst season in school history and they won only 10 games while Robinson was running the program.

The team showed some signs of life with a 4–8 record in 2006 but skidded to 2–10 in 2007. On the high side, they did get the best of

#18 Louisville in a great road game nail-biter, W (38-35), but finished with only two wins. The team continued to struggle in 2008, and fired Coach Robinson, after a dismal 3–9 season which ended with a loss against Akron on November 29. The season high point was a 24–23 upset of Notre Dame. Pundits suggest the game that best represented this low period in Robinson's tenure was a 55–13 loss to long-time rival Penn State.

Doug Marrone era (2009–2012)

Less than two weeks after McPherson got his final notification, on December 12, 2008 Doug Marrone, a former Orangeman and offensive coordinator for the NFL's New Orleans Saints, was announced as the replacement for Robinson as SU head coach. Marrone was the first Syracuse alumnus to serve as head football coach since Reaves H. Baysinger in 1948.

It was reported that he had some powerful alums rooting for him. Tim Green and Floyd Little wanted Marrone from the moment the previous coach Greg Robinson was fired, and when interviewed by Green, Marrone was found to have kept a folder of current high-school players in the Syracuse area to get a head start in recruiting. The program seemed to improve immediately in 2009, as the Orange, despite only a marginal improvement in their win-loss record. looked much better on the field. The team record was 4–8 under Marrone for his first year, including a 28–7 loss at number-seven Penn State.

In 2010, the Orange finished the regular season with a winning record for the first time since the 2001 season at 7–5, including road wins against number-19 West Virginia and two-time defending conference champion Cincinnati. The team earned its first bowl bid since 2004 and along with second-ranked Oregon and 10th-ranked Boise State, the five road wins were the best in 2010 of all FBS teams. December 30, 2010, Syracuse defeated Kansas State in the inaugural Pinstripe Bowl at Yankee Stadium. In 2011, the Orange slipped again to 5-8, but came right back to 8-5 in 2012. In 2012, the Orange defeated West Virginia in the 2012 Pinstripe Bowl. This would be Marrone's last season

On January 7, 2013, Marrone left Syracuse, accepting the head-coaching position of the NFL's Buffalo Bills. He was a fine coach.

Scott Shafer era (2013–2015)

Instead of going out with a national search, the day after Marrone's departure, Syracuse promoted defensive coordinator Scott Shafer to head coach. His first season was marked by inconsistency from the team.

In his first game at the helm, Coach Shafer nearly guided the team to an upset of Penn State, with the Orange eventually losing 23–17. The Orange got their first win under Shafer in a 54–0 rout of Wagner, and followed it up with another blowout win, beating Tulane 52–17.

<< Coach Shafer

However, the first season under this new coach also produced blowouts the other way with a crushing 14-49 defeat at home to fourth-ranked Clemson, and road losses to unranked Georgia Tech 0-56 and eventual national champions Florida State 3-59. These huge losses were hard to take.

Syracuse faced off against Boston College in the season finale, needing a victory to become bowl eligible. They got it with a great finish. The Orange were down 31–27 with 2:08 remaining. Quarterback Terrell Hunt pulled off a spectacular 75-yard, game-winning drive, capped off with a 25-yard touchdown pass to tight end Josh Parris with six seconds remaining.

This victory gave the Orange a bowl bid for the third time in four years. Syracuse finished the season with a nice 21–17 victory over Minnesota in the 2013 Texas Bowl to finish above 500 at 7–6. The next season, the Orange would make its debut in the ACC.

Things did not go so well in 2014 despite the Orange starting the season 2–0. The season began with a spectacular double-overtime, 27–26 victory over FCS power Villanova, marked by a Syracuse extra point that was called good, but replays later showed that it was just wide left. Nonetheless the Orange got the V. In the next game, the Orange beat Central Michigan W (40-3) but that was the end of the good times. Syracuse lost 9 of its last 10 games to finish the season a disappointing 3–9.

In 2015, fans and media noticed a significant uptick in the team's performance after they started with three wins 3–0. In game four, they played tough with eighth-ranked LSU at home, barely losing 34–24. Then, the Orange, which had been having trouble finishing seasons positively, lost eight of their last nine games, though they played closely with multiple ranked teams. The team finished 4–8, and on November 23, 2015, and after three losing seasons, it was announced that Shafer would be fired after the last game of the 2015 campaign.

Dino Babers Era (2016–present)

This time, in finding a new coach, the administration took its time and chose to look across the country before they committed to anything.

After an extensive search, the University announced that it had hired Bowling Green head coach Dino Babers, as the new Syracuse head football coach. Babers is the first African-American head football coach in Syracuse University history. He brought with him a very exciting, up-tempo offense that he had employed in the past both as a head coach and as an assistant coach.

In Babers' first season in charge, Syracuse started the year at 4–4. The highlight of the first eight games was a 31–17 upset of # 17 Virginia Tech at home. The Orange kept it going after this upset as they beat rival Boston College on the road, 28–20. Their next game was against the #3 Clemson who soon would be National

Champions. DeShaun Watson was unstoppable running the Tigers' offense. Clemson got the best of the Orange to say the least L (0-54).

In the final game of the season, Syracuse lost to ACC rival Pittsburgh by a score of 76–61. The game was the highest scoring in FBS history with a combined score of 137. Syracuse finished 4–8 for the second consecutive year.

In 2017, the Orange started 4-3, including a great win over defending Champion, #2 Clemson. However, as in the past, the team had a tough time finishing. They lost their final five games to finish 4-8 for the third straight year.

Despite two 4-8 records in his brief tenure, Coach Dino Babers thinks he's got the formula ready for 2018. We all hope he is right. Babers stopped looking back and he has his eye right on the prize for 2018. He made what is being called an "unvarnished statement" that is building up a new set of expectations for his third season.

"I think this is the beginning," Babers said. "I really believe that the 2018 season is going to be something that we're going to be talking about here for a long, long time."

Let's start talking now!

Syracuse has a rich tradition of football greats. Let's take a look at the Syracuse College Football Hall of Fame members that we will read about in this book.

Syracuse Orange Hall of Famers

Inductee	Pos.	Class	Career
Biggie "Smalls" Munn	HC	1959	1946
Frank "Buck" O'Neill	HC	1951	1906–1919; 1936
Ben Schwartzwalder	HC	1982	1949–1973
Joe Alexander	G	1954	1917–1920
Larry Csonka	FB	1989	1965–1967
Ernie Davis	HB	1979	1959–1961
Vic Hanson	E	1973	1924–1926
Floyd Little	RB	1983	1964–1966
Jim Brown	RB	1995	1956–1958
Tim Green	DT	2002	1982–1985
Don McPherson	QB	2008	1984–1987
Tad Jones	HC	1958	1909–1910
Howard Jones	HC	1951	1908
Dick MacPherson	HC	2009	1980–1990
Art Monk	WR	2012	1976–1979

Syracuse football athletes in the Pro Football Hall of Fame below:

- Jim Brown – Pro Football Hall of Fame Class of 1971
- Jim Ringo – Pro Football Hall of Fame Class of 1981
- Larry Csonka – Pro Football Hall of Fame Class of 1987
- John Mackey – Pro Football Hall of Fame Class of 1992
- Al Davis – Enshrined as a coach and not a player. Pro Football Hall of Fame Class of 1992
- Art Monk – Pro Football Hall of Fame Class of 2008
- Floyd Little – Pro Football Hall of Fame Class of 2010
- Marvin Harrison – Pro Football Hall of Fame Class of 2016

In the next chapter, let's take a quick peak at the Syracuse University Football facilities from over the years. I think you'll agree that like most things in the modern era, Syracuse may be your father's university, but it is much better.

Chapter 2 History of Syracuse Football "Stadiums"

The Oval Field

The Oval Field being built with horse-power

The first Syracuse football game in 1889 was played in between some nice new buildings (at the time) in a field called the Old Oval. On the south side of what is known as University Place, the Holden Observatory was built in 1887, followed by two Romanesque Revival buildings – von Ranke Library (1889), now Tolley Administration Building, and Crouse College (1889). Together with the Hall of Languages, these first buildings formed the basis for what is called the "Old Row," a grouping which, along with its companion Lawn, established one of Syracuse's most enduring images.

The emphatically linear organization of these buildings along the brow of the hill follows a tradition of American campus planning which dates to the construction of the "Yale Row" in the 1790's. At

Syracuse, the Old Row continued to provide the framework for its growth well into the twentieth century. Not everything endures, and initial ideas are often superseded by better ideas. The first exception to the linear development pattern was the placement of the Gymnasium (1891) in the hayfield behind the Hall of Languages.

At the same time, a portion of that open land was graded and placed into service as an athletic field, together with a vegetable garden for the faculty. Loosely framed by buildings on two sides, the "Old Oval," as the field was known, joined the Lawn as a campus open space where football was played until a new plan was developed in 1906. The Oval's modest beginnings belied its later significance to the University's physical development. Seven years later, the construction of Steele Hall (1898), the University's first science building, gave definition to another new open space, located to the west of the Gymnasium and to the south of Crouse College.

There was lots of activity in this campus space in the 1880's. In the historical picture below, you can see the tools of the day as workers used horses to grade the "Old Oval," circa 1880s; the baseball field was located in this area, and it was where football was played for the first ten years. It is on the south side of today's Quad

Oval Athletic Field When In service

After playing on the oval for years, it was a big treat for Syracuse's football team to move to Archbold Field, a state of the art stadium for its day.

1906 Picture of the construction of Archbold Stadium

Archbold Stadium in its heyday was a multi-purpose stadium in Syracuse, New York. It opened in 1907 with an original capacity of 23,000, and was home to the Syracuse University Orangemen football team prior to the Carrier Dome opening in 1980. It was the third concrete football stadium built in the United States. Considering the Oval had a tough time with crowds over a couple thousand, Archbold Stadium not only gave Syracuse great room for expansion, it made it so that many of their competitors would rather play away games at Archbold than made, than home games on their own patches of grass.

The stadium was named for John D. Archbold, who donated $600,000 for the project. He was also responsible for funding towards the building of Archbold Gymnasium, located just to the east overlooking the stadium.

The stadium was occasionally used to stage Syracuse Stars minor league baseball games, such as in 1920 while the Stars were awaiting the completion of Star Park.

Originally this was an 800' x 475' stadium that like most football fields was built in an oval shape with a running track as part of the design. The running track was originally a dirt area carved out for long track meet runs such as the mile (4 laps). The playing area was carved out and lined-out with a natural grass football field. The west end zone, the stadium's main entrance, was magnificent. It had a grand castle-like façade with turrets framing its gateway arch. There was originally a wooden roof over the central section of the south grandstands for the reserved seating. Soon, even Archbold Stadium was too small for the needs of the institution.

In the 1950s, the stadium was expanded to the north and south, bringing the capacity up to 40,000. However, by the 1970s, stricter fire codes forced a reduction in capacity to 26,000. This made it tough to attract the type of teams needed to keep the program running as one of the nation's finest.

In many ways, this was the stadium's undoing. By the mid-1970s, because of its limited capacity, Syracuse faced the prospect of being demoted to Division I-AA unless it was able to respond with a more modern stadium to fit the times. Knowing this was due or die, the university had this historic grand stadium razed following playing the 1978 season. The Carrier Dome now occupies Archbold Stadium's former footprint.

One of the most interesting historical facts about Archbold field is that until its last season, the Orangemen had never had a season in which they did not win at least one game at Archbold Field. In 1978, the teams were not doing so well and there was a lot of concern that this record from 1907 to 1977 might be broken. In the Final game at Archbold Stadium, on November 11, 1978, the Orangemen were playing nationally ranked Navy. So, it looked like this would be the end of Archbold and the end of that long-standing record. However, the Orangemen put it together late in the game and they beat Navy by a hair, 20-17.

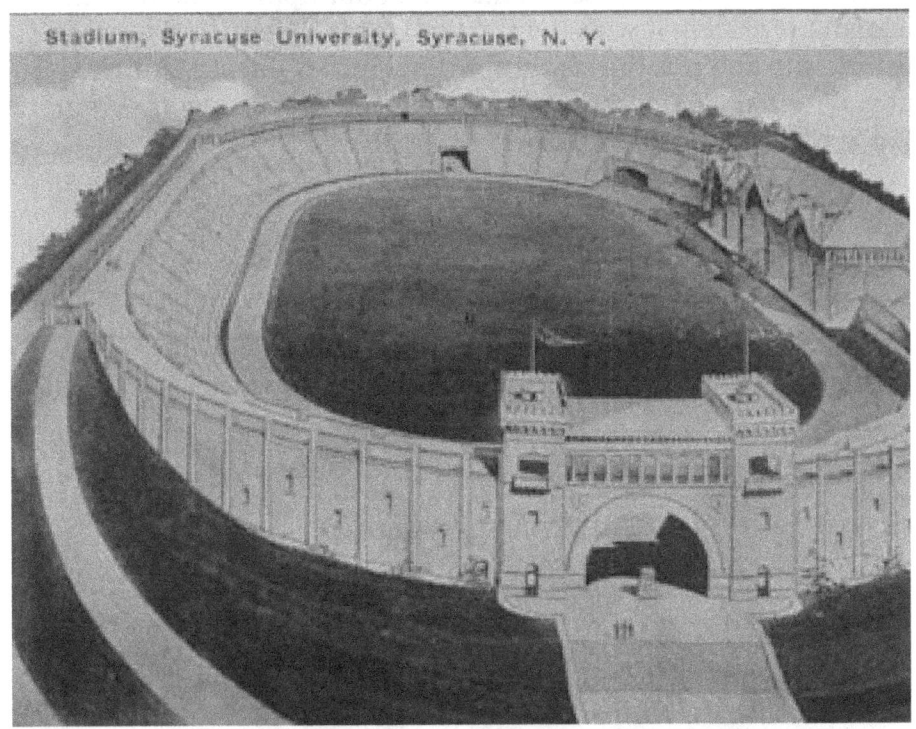

Archbold Stadium, Syracuse University

During its history, Syracuse compiled a 265-112-20 record at Archbold. Archbold Stadium is no longer there but right next to the Carrier Dome, which replaced it is the Archbold Gymnasium. If you park in the CARN lots, which have a few spots available on game day, you'll pass it on the way into the Carrier Dome

The Carrier Dome, where great SU football is played

Since 1980, the Syracuse Orange football team plays its games at the Carrier Dome. The Dome is used for several sports at the university and seats 49,250 for football. It is the largest domed stadium of any college campus and the largest domed stadium in the Northeastern United States. The field was dedicated in 2009 to Ernie Davis, the first African American Heisman Trophy winner. The field now reads "Ernie Davis Legends Field" between the 45-yard lines on the home side. Davis's number forty-four was also placed along that yard line. The dedication took place at the Syracuse vs. West Virginia game October 10, 2009. Davis won the award in 1961.

There had to be a lot of consternation about ripping down Archbold field and replacing it with the Carrier Dome. After all, it was a historic site and it is the stadium from which Syracuse launched its only National Championship—while being coached by the immortal Ben Schwartzwalder.

The Carrier Dome.

Syracuse is not a suburban University. It is in fact, a neighborhood university. Consequently, it is a great place to live and to go to school if you can deal with parking and traffic congestion. Most of the parking for sports games is by Manley and SkyTop field houses, on a newer part of the campus, well separated from the main-campus. So, even parking is no excuse for the potential student who is thinking about matriculating at 'Cuse.

It is a twenty-minute or so walk to the stadium, which many in my bus from Scranton did for many years after they had stuffed their faces with Phillies Phinest Hoagies from Carey Avenue in Wilkes-Barre, PA. They loved the walk as the university section of the City is simply beautiful. Many of my group stayed behind rather than walk to the field.

They lit a few grills and had a few beers before catching one of the many shuttle busses that are provided free of charge for those who park in these traditional lots. You just need to leave about fifteen minutes to one half hour ahead

It is again a very pleasant walk and the walkways on the SU campus are very wide.

In the last five to ten years that we were taking the trip from Scranton every year, we found a few bus parking areas that are about two blocks from the Carrier Dome. I checked a campus map and they are still there. When I bought the game tickets, I would buy the bus parking passes. That way, those who wanted to stay tailgating longer, could do so without missing any of the game action.

It was just a two-block walk to the stadium and most pleasant. Many of our group would stop at one of the many refreshment stands in the stadium and get a container of gold beverage. The concessionaires served a number of varieties of this beverage until the end of halftime as I recall. Syracuse was always a great place to see a game.

As adults are more and more childrenized by the current gendarme who promise to keep us all safe by removing our adult privileges, this may change. I think it started to change when seventy became the new sixteen, but I digress.

When the Orange joined the ACC, there was a lot of concern about the Dome's beer policy. Some thought it would have to change but did not want it to change. I suspect that if every seat were sold every game, this could quickly revert back to a romper room beverages and food deal pretty quickly. Dome Dogs might not be served with mustard if mustard is ever deemed hazardous or intoxicating.

So, before I discuss Manley Field, I will give you all the prevailing thought on the matter of the golden elixir served at the games. One thing that you can be sure of, adults or not, nobody will be walking out of the Carrier Dome post-game with a nice Dome beer and a fine Dome Dog in their hands any time soon. If they are permitted, at a minimum, the carrier will have to endure a very warm beverage.

Some of Syracuse University's cherished sports rivalries are in jeopardy but one tradition at least for now, thanks to the ACC speaking out, seems safe: Carrier Dome beer sales.

SU's decision to move to the Atlantic Coast Conference has not affected the school's decision to sell beer at home games, as the ACC leaves it up to the schools to sell beer during athletic events or not.

SU has long been unusual among colleges in that the on-campus Dome has sold beer during football and basketball games since the facility opened in 1980. Only a handful of other colleges do the same and many of those only serve at off-campus facilities.

For regular season games, the NCAA leaves it up to the schools to make the decision, as does the Big East.

The ACC's policy is the same.

The University of Maryland, the University of North Carolina, Wake Forest and Florida State University, all ACC schools, sell alcohol in areas such as club seats, suites or booster areas of their athletic facilities for either football or basketball games.

Alcohol is sold to the general public at Florida State basketball games and University of Miami football games, which are played off campus.

Representatives of many schools say they choose not to sell beer at on-campus games to avoid problems with underage drinking by students.

ACC schools Boston College, Duke University and Clemson University athletic department officials said those campuses do not sell alcohol at any athletic events, on campus or off, but the decision was the school's.

The concessions manager at the Dome said many people were asking him if beer sales would continue after SU joined the ACC. He said he had not heard otherwise. We cannot blame Trump for that as it is reported he has never even tasted a beer. Poor Donald!

The athletic communication head at SU, said she too had fielded questions about the subject but said it wasn't a priority given the complexity of the major conference change.

The general manager of TJ Sheehan, one of the beer distributors to the dome, said he hadn't heard if the ACC allegiance would affect sales to the Dome, which he said have declined over the years.

"I think beer sales aren't what they used to be anyway," a spokesperson for the company said. "They reduced the time when sales are available. Football they reduced it to halftime and basketball it used to be with 10 minutes left and they reduced that to halftime."

"It's nice to have it in (the Dome)," he said, "but it's not what it used to be."

I know my crew from Scranton PA enjoyed their quaffs at the stadium as much as the game and when they were cut off at the end of the third quarter in the early days, they were fine with it. There was a lot of snoring on the bus ride home. My suggestion would be to increase the price of the ticket as it seems to grow on its own anyway without any fan benefit at all. Hire an extra force of boozer watchers, and let adults be adults.

The Dome is shown on the right of the circle in the campus map.

Since teenage drinking ought to be stopped anyway, I would recommend that at each post where the golden nectar is sold, one or two gendarmes can check the cards and give them a special symbol that they are of age. Better yet, when game tickets are purchased, anybody thinking they look too young, should pay for an I'm OK pass if they plan to have a nip. The gendarme at the beverage stops will still be able to check them and they better have their special ribbons or markings. If I can figure out how to do it, Syracuse can figure out how to do it without having to childrenize the adults.

Syracuse University, North Campus Map

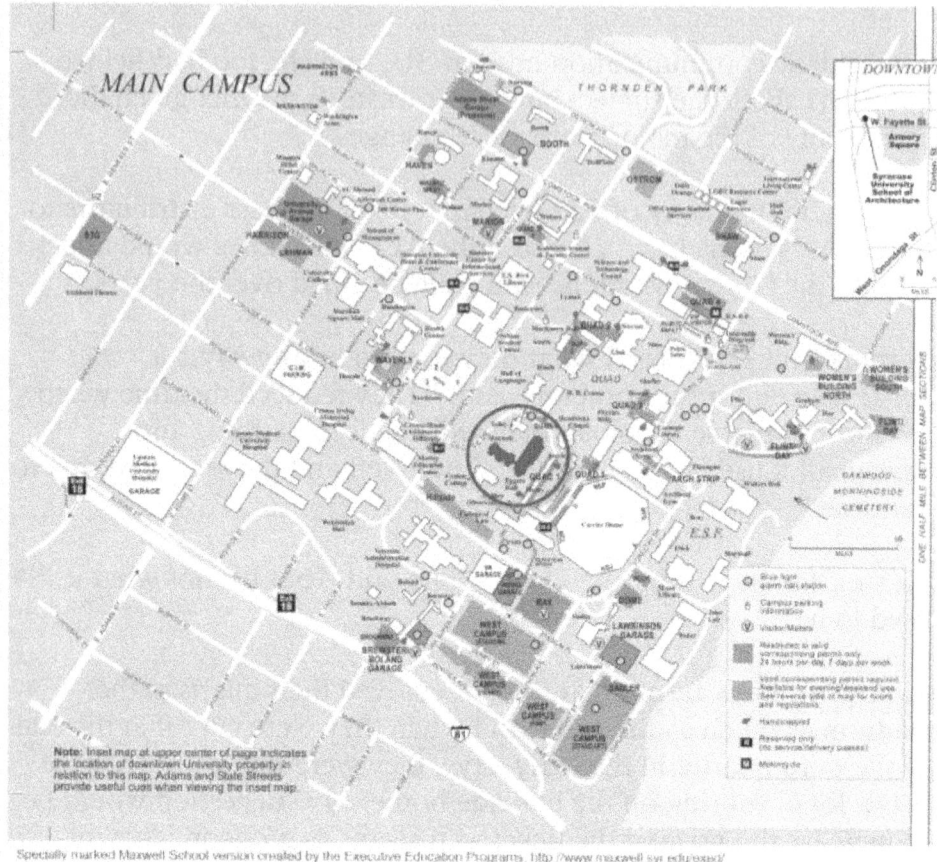

If you do not like the idea of beer being sold at fun events, then don't buy any!

Manley Field House—on the newer campus

This giant athletic complex was built in 1962. It is known as the Manley Field House complex and it houses many of the offices of SU Athletics. It also contains academic rooms and two weight rooms strictly for Syracuse athletes only. Since the main campus is within the City, there is not much room to play.

So, adjacent to the complex there are a variety of fields used for softball, soccer, field hockey, as well as a track for the track and field team. Manley was initially intended as an indoor training facility for the football team but was soon utilized as a home court for men's basketball.

Manley Field House

However, upon completion of the new Carmelo K. Anthony Basketball Center, which houses practice courts, weight rooms, locker rooms and offices for both the men's and women's basketball teams, the original plans for Manley have come full circle. Syracuse was able to spend more than $2 million to renovate it and create a new state of the art indoor practice facility. Manley now features an indoor FieldTurf practice area, complete with three-lane running track. The original land benefactors to Syracuse never had any idea how grand and successful their university would become.

Chapter 3 The Founding of Syracuse University

Syracuse University Famous Hall of Languages

Our History

Then. Now. Always.

The history of Syracuse University may date back to 1870, but that doesn't mean we're caught in the past.

In fact, we've always been ahead of our time and original in our outlook. We were the first to adopt one official color—a proud orange. We were the first in the nation to offer a bachelor of the fine arts degree, and were founders of the nation's first iSchool.

We opened doors for women as far back as 1870, from pioneers that include Karen DeCrow (women's rights activist) to Eileen Collins (the first female commander of a Space Shuttle). Building on the leading role we played in the first G.I. Bill, we're recognized as the #1 private school for military service members, veterans, and their families—a commitment that will soon expand with the construction of the National Veterans Resource Complex (NVRC). And that's just where we are today.

Today, as in our past, the University's commitment to access honors every individual's potential—and that enriches us all. From the development of an oral insulin to the discovery of gravitational waves, Syracuse's future is bright—and our students, even brighter.

We have been an inclusive and welcoming place since our beginning. At the 1870 inauguration of Syracuse University, Dr. Jesse Truesdell Peck (a founder and first chair of the Board of Trustees) charged the faculty to remember that the University was to be impartial and general. "The conditions of admission shall be equal to all persons... there shall be no invidious discrimination here against woman.... brains and heart shall have a fair chance..."

Syracuse University Early History:

It all began to move in February 1870, at the Methodist State Convention in Syracuse, NY. Like many other great colleges and universities, a new college was conceived from the kind hearts of a religious group. They passed a resolution to create a university in the City of Syracuse, not in the New York wilderness or the suburbs. They immediately got to work on implementing their ideas.

Measures were quickly taken to raise $500,000 to endow the university, with the city of Syracuse putting in its own funds totaling $100,000. subscribing $100,000. The Rev. Jesse T. Peck, who was elected president of the Syracuse University Board of Trustees, suggested purchasing fifty acres of farmland in southeastern Syracuse City. The Board of Trustees of Syracuse University signed the University charter and certificate of incorporation on March 24, 1870.

Fifty acres is a lot of room for a college for sure but as time would tell, like most colleges within a city. It would eventually need more space.

There was a theory that Genesee College in Lima, Livingston Co., NY, was a predecessor of Syracuse University. Starting in 1866, and that attempts were made to move Genesee College to Syracuse, a more central location in the state. The truth is that it such a move never got underway. There was strong opposition from the residents of Lima which prevented this from happening. The Board of Trustees of Genesee College even obtained permission from the state to move the school to Syracuse in 1869; however, an injunction obtained by Lima residents made such a move impossible. As a result, Genesee College remained in Lima until 1875, when it was dissolved under New York State law by petition of its Board of Trustees.

The cornerstone for the Hall of Languages had just been laid in August of 1871, when the Syracuse University Board of Trustees decided to open the College of Liberal Arts in September, just one month later, with no structures supporting the institution.

Nonetheless, the Hall of Languages was the first building built on campus. Prior to its construction classes were held in a block of rented buildings known as the Myers Block, located on E. Genesee and Montgomery Streets in downtown Syracuse.

The Hall of Languages building still is spectacular. It was primarily an H-shape with recesses in the front and rear walls on either side of the central section. The rear recesses were partially occupied by coal houses (needed for heating the entire campus for years). The east and west towers were part of the original construction; the central tower was not added until 1886. The east and west towers held large water tanks capable, it was believed, of flooding the entire structure in the event of fire.

The west tower also held an awesome 600-pound bell. The building originally rose 3½ stories in the central section and 2½ stories in the wings and was topped by a slate-covered mansard roof. Molded metal cornices sported stone brackets and the exterior walls had a "pecked" finish. The building was the home of the College of Liberal Arts from its beginning, although other schools and departments have also occupied the edifice, including the Registrar and the Chancellor. A section of the eastern wing is said to have been used as a natural science museum. There was so much fear that the University might not endure in the panic of 1880 that no more buildings were built for years. This magnificent building with some gifted people as the keepers of the institution managed to run the entire university from this one major building on campus.

During the 1979, renovation, long after the building had made Syracuse a university, very few alterations were made to the exterior. It was already a historically beautiful edifice. Glass-enclosed vestibules were added to the rear of the building and the first floor was graded so that an elevator could be accommodated.

The upper floors of the Myers Block of rented rooms in downtown Syracuse, were rented as a temporary campus. Applicants underwent a series of written examinations, after which forty-one students, including seven women, were admitted to either four-year programs of classical study or three-year programs in a scientific field.

Faculty of the University met several times during this first year to determine adequate courses of study. By 1872 the University devised a set of programs for three fields of study, each four-years long. In

February 1873, Alexander Winchell was inaugurated as Syracuse University's first chancellor.

SU Chancellor Kent Syverud Touring Campus Towers

In May the Hall of Languages, the first building on the new campus, was dedicated and in use.

From its first days, Syracuse University has grown and prospered all for the many students who have gained a superior education from a dedicated administration and faculty. Today, there are over one hundred buildings, facilities, stadiums, and fields which comprise the entirety of Syracuse University. There was never any doubt that SU would be something special and it sure is.

Chapter 4 SU's Mission Statement & Vision Statement

Crouse College, above, Instagram photo by @nora_keefe, was home to the first College of Fine Arts in the United States, now known for both its College of Visual and Performing Arts and the Rose, Jules R., and Stanford S. Setnor School of Music.

Syracuse University's mission:
To promote learning through teaching, research, scholarship, creative accomplishment and service.

Syracuse University Vision:
In 1992, the Syracuse University Senate adopted a mission focused on promoting learning and a positive campus culture. Syracuse

University continues to embrace those goals and is guided by the principles contained in the statement. In building on that foundation, the University recognizes that its greatest strength is based on the interactive and collaborative nature of its many programs. Through active engagement with practitioners and communities around the world, Syracuse University faculty and students learn, discover, and create. We are dedicated to faculty excellence and scholarly distinction, attracting and supporting enterprising students, and a close interaction and engagement with the world—locally, nationally, and globally.

Chapter 5 Syracuse Launches its First Football Team

Many of these 1890 players also were on the 1889 team.

1889: Just 19+ years from the founding

On Nov. 23, 1889, nearly 20 years after the big meeting that formed Syracuse University, the first Syracuse team, a rag tag group put together by captain John Blake Hillyer, played its first football game. It was the one and only game played that season. The Orangemen were defeated 0-36 in a game played against The University Rochester. There was one problem with the Orangemen that day besides the loss. They were not yet the Orangemen. In fact, for this game, Syracuse wore pink and blue uniforms. Rochester had already played most of its 1889 season, its first and were pretty well accustomed to playing gridiron, rugby-like football as American football was being defined.

There are very few records of this game or how things got going for the football team but more than likely it was because students demanded it after playing hither and yon on the streets of Syracuse for several years in an intramural style.

There are reports that students had been playing the evolving game of American football for some time before this game in November 1889, but this was the first intercollegiate game in Syracuse's long football history. There is also a reported game, though not at an intercollegiate level that was played by a football team from Syracuse University in 1884 against the Medical College of Syracuse.

Syracuse students began playing football long before there were football helmets and protective gear of any kind. In this devastating 0-36 loss to the University of Rochester, the game was painful even without enduring the big loss. There were a few broken bones during the game to match the bruised egos of the Syracuse players who then had to make it home by locomotive, licking their wounds After the lopsided loss. It had to be a tough ride back to Syracuse that night.

Shortly after the first game began the day before Thanksgiving 1889, the rain fell in torrents. The football field was a quagmire. There ae no accounts of how the scoring went after the opening kick-off, but Syracuse University's uniform pants were caked with mud and blood. John Blake Hillyer, who founded the team and served as its captain for two years, was forced to leave the game and watch from the sidelines as he sustained a dislocated elbow. Shortly after Hillyer left the game a fellow player suffered a fractured collarbone. Football with no helmets and no padding was a tough sport for sure pre-1920's.

The more experienced Rochester team was also playing in its first intercollegiate season. The difference was that Rochester had played almost a full season before their ninth game, which was Syracuse. Their record was 4-4 record entering the game. Unlike Syracuse which began play in late November, Rochester had played teams such as Trinity and Amherst and a number of other teams from New York State from September on.

Syracuse knew what to expect but had never played a game before their whipping by Rochester in their first game ever, 0-36. It was demoralizing but it got the program rolling nonetheless. Then,

Hillyer and the rest of the team took the locomotive back to Syracuse and were mentally ready for a much better 1890 season. Rochester played one more game after this—a scoreless tie against Union on November 28. The following year, Syracuse would have a full season with a real coach.

Looking back from the 100th anniversary, as the Syracuse players piled off the train after that ignominious debut on Nov. 23, 1889, they were understandably disappointed. But they weren't crushed. Like so many schools wanting to engage in football at the time, the players and Captain Hillyer were pioneers. They overcame many obstacles to get their program started and the Syracuse Orange Football program of today owes them a huge debt of gratitude.

The university, like many at the time considered football a violent sport. They did not believe that it was in synch with the school's academic mission. Consequently, they offered little financial or moral support. So Hillyer and Co. had to scrape together money to buy uniforms and a football. There was no such thing as equipment. Out of their persistence a football program was born. The Syracuse campus and the college game would never be the same.

In the 1890's besides the Oval field, some games were also played at Star Park where the baseball team *The Syracuse Stars* played for years. These games normally attracted 200 to 700 spectators, some of whom (not kidding) occasionally would wander onto the field to help tackle opposing ball-carriers. The game was rough and tumble and to assure their own safety, referees often turned their backs on the shenanigans of the fans. Coach Winston could handle just one year, and he left after his one year of directing the team. He had done a fine job and his absence was felt immediately. The 1890 team had an 8-3 record. However, in 1891, the Orangemen slipped to 4-6 but soon Syracuse would reconstitute its football team and the future was bright. We'll pick the stories of Syracuse's prowess in football in Chapter 7.

Chapter 6 The Evolution of Modern Football

Lots of playing before playing became official

The official agreed upon date for the first American-style college football game is November 6, 1869. If you can find a replay of this game someplace in the heavens, however, you would find it would not look much like football as we know it. But, it was not completely soccer or rugby either.

Before this game, teams were playing a rugby style similar to that played in Britain in the mid-19th century. At the time in the US, a derivative known as association football was also played. In both games, a football is kicked at a goal or run over a line. These styles were based on the varieties of English public-school football games. Over time, as noted, the style of "football" play in America continued to evolve.

On November 6, 1869, the first football game in America featured Rutgers and Princeton. Before the teams were even on the field it was being plugged as the first college football game of all time.

Syracuse University opened in 1870, the year after the first college football game.

The first game of intercollegiate football was a sporting battle between two neighboring schools on a plot of ground where the present-day Rutgers gymnasium now stands in New Brunswick, N.J. Rutgers won that first game, 6-4.

There were two teams of 25 men each and the rules were rugby-like, but different enough to make it very interesting and enjoyable.

Like today's football, there were many surprises; strategies needed to be employed; determination exhibited, and of course the players required physical prowess.

1st Game Rutgers 6 Princeton 4 College Field, New Brunswick, NJ

At 3 p.m. the 50 combatants as well as 100 spectators gathered on the field. Most sat on a low wooden fence and watched the athletes discard their hats, coats and vests. The players used their suspenders as belts. To give a unique look, Rutgers wore scarlet-colored scarfs, which they converted into turbans. This contrasted them with the bareheaded boys from Princeton.

Two members of each team remained more or less stationary near the opponent's goal in the hopes of being able to slip over and score from unguarded positions. Thus, the present day "sleeper" was conceived. The remaining 23 players were divided into groups of 11 and 12. While the 11 "fielders" lined up in their own territory as defenders, the 12 "bulldogs" carried the battle.

Each score counted as a "game" and 10 games completed the contest. Following each score, the teams changed direction. The ball could be advanced only by kicking or batting it with the feet, hands, heads or sides.

Rutgers put a challenge forward that three games were to be played that year. The first was played at New Brunswick and won by Rutgers. Princeton won the second game, but cries of "overemphasis" prevented the third game in football's first year when faculties of both institutions protested on the grounds that the games were interfering with student studies.

This is an excerpt of the Rutgers account of the game on its web site. A person named Herbert gave this detailed account of the play in the first game:

"Though smaller on the average, the Rutgers players, as it developed, had ample speed and fine football sense. Receiving the ball, our men formed a perfect interference around it and with short, skillful kicks and dribbles drove it down the field. Taken by surprise, the Princeton men fought valiantly, but in five minutes we had gotten the ball through to our captains on the enemy's goal and S.G. Gano, '71 and G.R. Dixon, '73, neatly kicked it over. None thought of it, so far as I know, but we had without previous plan or thought evolved the play that became famous a few years later as 'the flying wedge'."

"Next period Rutgers bucked, or received the ball, hoping to repeat the flying wedge," Herbert's account continues. "But the first time we formed it Big Mike came charging full upon us. It was our turn for surprise. The Princeton battering ram made no attempt to reach the ball but, forerunner of the interference-breaking ends of today, threw himself into our mass play, bursting us apart, and bowing us over.

Time and again Rutgers formed the wedge and charged; as often Big Mike broke it up. And finally, on one of these incredible break-ups a Princeton bulldog with a long accurate, perhaps lucky kick, sent the ball between the posts for the second score.

It was at this point that a Rutgers professor could stand it no longer. Waving his umbrella at the participants, he shrieked, "You will come to no Christian end!"

Herbert's account of the game continues: "The fifth and sixth goals went to Rutgers. The stars of the latter period of play, in the memory of the players after the lapse of many years, were "Big

Mike" and Large (former State Senator George H. Large of Flemington, another Princeton player) …

Syracuse did not get into the football act until the late 1880's. At this time, the rules of rugby kept changing to accommodate the infatuation for the Americanized style of "football" play that would ultimately become the American game of football.

Walter Camp: the father of American football?

Walter Camp was a very well-known rugby player from Yale. In today's world, he would have been characterized as a rugby hero. It was his love of the game, his knowledge of the game as it was played, and his innovative mind that caused him to take the evolution of football even further. He pioneered the changes to the rules of rugby that slowly transformed the sport into the new game of American Football.

The rule changes that were introduced to the rugby and association style of play were mostly those authored by Camp, who was also a Hopkins School graduate. For his original efforts, Walter Camp today is considered to be the "Father of American Football". Among the important changes brought to the game were the introduction of a line of scrimmage; down-and-distance rules; and the legalization of interference (blocking).

There was no such thing in those days as a forward pass and so the legalization of interference in 1880 football permitted blocking for runners. The forward pass would add another dimension to the game that made it much different than rugby or association football.

Soon after the early football changes, in the late nineteenth and into the early twentieth centuries, more game-play type developments were introduced by college coaches. The list is like a who's who of early American College Football. Coaches, such as Eddie Cochems, Amos Alonzo Stagg, Parke H. Davis, Knute Rockne, John Heisman, and Glenn "Pop" Warner helped introduce and then take advantage of the newly introduced forward pass. College football as well as professional football, were introduced prior to the 20th century. Fans were lured into watching again and again once they saw the game played.

College football especially grew in popularity despite the existence of pro-football. It became the dominant version of the sport of football in the United States. It was this way for the entire first half of the 20th century. Bowl games made the idea of football even more exciting in the college ranks. Rivalries grew and continued, and the fans loved it! This great football tradition brought a national audience to college football games that still dominates the sports world today.

For those who would like to read more about American College Football and Walter Camp's role in helping form the rules, I am pleased to say that I have a solution There are now two-new book available. One is titled: American College Football: The Beginning, and the other is titled, The Birth of American Football. If you think you'd like to trace the roots of American College Football, I think you'll love those books.

This book, however is about Syracuse Football, and this chapter is the one and only chapter about the origins of football. This book has little to do with pro-football or any other sport.

However, there is no denying that the greatest college football players more often than not eventually found their fortunes in professional football. Pro football can be traced back to the season that Syracuse's third full football season after a two-year lapse from what I will call its first half-Rugby season in 1889. It was 1892 when William "Pudge" Heffelfinger signed a $500 contract to play for the Allegheny Athletic Association against the Pittsburgh Athletic Club.

Twenty-eight years later, the American Professional Football Association was formed. This league changed its name to the National Football League (NFL) just two years later. Eventually, the NFL became the major league of American football. Originally, just a sport played in Midwestern industrial towns in the United States, professional football eventually became a national phenomenon. We all know this because from August to February, in America, many of us are glued to our TV sets or chained to our seats in some of the most intriguing pro-football stadiums in America.

Rules and Penalties

The big problem players from different teams and different geographies had when playing early American-style football in college was that the style of play was not standardized. The rulebooks were not yet written or were at best incomplete and disputable.

A rule over here, for example, would be a penalty over there. And, so in the 1870's there was a lot of work to try to make all games to be played by the same rules. There were minor rule changes such as team size was reduced from 25 to 20 but of course over the years, this and all other rules continued to evolve. For years, there was no such thing as a running touchdown. The only means of scoring was to bat or kick the ball through the opposing team's goal.

Early rugby rules were the default. The field size was rugby style at 140 yards by 70 yards v 120 X 53 1/3 (including end zones) in today's football game. There was plenty of room to huff and puff and almost get lost. There were no breaks per se for long periods. Instead of fifteen-minute quarters, the game was more like Rugby and Soccer with 45-minute halves played continuously.

In 1873 to put some order to the game, Columbia, Princeton. Rutgers, and Yale got together in a hotel in New York City and wrote down the first set of intercollegiate football rules. They changed a few things along the way; but the end product was a much more standard way of playing football games. Rather than use the home team's rules, all teams then were able to play by the same rules

Harvard did not to comply with rules

For its own reasons, Harvard chose not to attend the rules conference. Instead, it played all of its games using the Harvard code of rules. Harvard therefore had a difficult time scheduling games. In 1874, to get a game, Harvard agreed to play McGill University from Montreal Canada. They had rules that even Harvard had never seen. For example, any player could pick up the ball and run with it, anytime he wished.

Another McGill rule was that they would count tries (the act of grounding the football past the opponent's goal line. Since there was no end zone, which technically makes a football field of today 120 yards long, a touchdown gave no points. Instead, it provided the chance to kick a free goal from the field. If the kick were missed, the touchdown did not count.

In 1874 McGill and Harvard played a two-game series. Each team could play 11 men per side. This was in deep contrast to the even earlier days of college football before standard rules when games were played with 25, 20, 15, or 11 men on a side.

The first game was played with a round ball using what were known as the "Boston" rules (Harvard). The next day, the teams played using the McGill rules, which included McGill's oval ball which was much like an American football, and it featured the ability to pick up the ball and run with it. Harvard enjoyed this experience especially the idea of "the try" which had not been used in American football. Eventually, the try evolved into the American idea of a touchdown and points were given when a try was successful.

Not all the rules lasted the duration, and some were very strange by today's standards. One of the most perplexing rules was that a man could run with the ball only while an opponent chose to pursue him. When a tackler abandoned the ball-carrier, the latter had to stop, and was forced to kick, pass or even throw away what was called "his burden."

McGill has a great account of this match on their web site. Type *Mcgill web site football against Harvard* into your search engine.

Their players wore no protective pads. Woolen jerseys covered the torso, while white trousers encased the players' legs. Some trousers were short, and some were long. It did not seem to matter for the game. A number of the men wore what they called black "football turbans" which were the ancestors of the modern helmet; others chose to wear white canvas hats.

The Harvard players wore undershirts made of gauze. Think about that for a while. They also wore what were called *full length gymnasium costumes*. They also wore light baseball shoes. Most of the team wore handkerchiefs, which were knotted about their heads.

The gauze undershirts were a trick. There was strategy in this choice of top uniform. When a player was first tackled, the gauze would be demolished, and the next opponent would have nothing to grab other than "slippery human flesh." Harvard won this game by a score of 3-0

The next go at playing by the rules was when Harvard took on Tufts University on June 4, 1875. This was the first American college football game played using rules similar to the McGill/Harvard contest. Tufts won this game. Despite the loss, Harvard continued pushing McGill style football and challenged Yale.

The Bulldog team accepted under a compromise rule set that included some Yale soccer rules and Harvard rugby rules. They used 15 players per team. It was November 13, 1875 for this first meeting of Harvard v Yale. Harvard won 4-0. Walter Camp attended the game and the following year he played in the game as a Yale Bulldog.

Camp was determined to avenge Yale's defeat. Onlookers from Princeton, who saw this Harvard / Yale game loved it so much, they brought it back to Princeton where it was quickly adopted as the preferred version of football.

Once Walter Camp caught onto the rugby-style rules, history says he became a fixture at the Massasoit House conventions. Here the rules of the game were debated and changed appropriately. From these meetings, Camp's rule changes as well as others were adopted.

Having eleven players instead of fifteen aided in opening the game and it emphasized speed over strength. When Camp attended in 1878, this motion was rejected but it passed in the 1880 meeting. The line of scrimmage and the snap from center to the quarterback also passed in 1880. Originally the snap occurred by a kick from the center, but this was later modified so the ball would be snapped with the hands either as a pass back (long snap) or a direct snap from the center.

It was Camp's new scrimmage rules, however, which according to many, revolutionized the game, though it was not always to increase speed. In fact, Princeton was known to use line of scrimmage plays to slow the game, making incremental progress towards the end zone much like today during each down.

Camp's original idea was to increase scoring, but in fact the rule was often misused to maintain control of the ball for the entire game. The negative effect was that there were many slow and unexciting contests. This too would be fixed with the idea of the first down coming into play.

In 1982, at the rules meeting, Camp proposed that a team be given three downs to advance the ball five yards. These rules were called the down and distance rules. Along with the notion of the line of scrimmage, these rules transformed the game of rugby into the distinct sport of American football.

Among other significant rule changes, in 1881, the field size was reduced to its modern dimensions of 120 by 53 1/3 yards (109.7 by 48.8 meters). Camp was central to these significant rule changes that ultimately defined American football. Camp's next quest was to address scoring anomalies. His first cut was to give four points for a touchdown and two points for kicks after touchdowns; two points for safeties, and five points for field goals. The notion of the foot in football /rugby explains Camp's rationale.

In 1887, game time was fixed at two halves of 45 minutes each. Additionally, college games would have two paid officials known as a referee and an umpire, for each game. In 1888, the rules permitted tackling below the waist and then in 1889, the officials were given whistles and stopwatches to better control the game.

An innovation that many list as most significant to making American football uniquely American was the legalization of blocking opponents, which back then was called "interference." This tactic had been highly illegal under the rugby-style rules and in rugby today, it continues to be illegal.

The more those who know soccer and football find rugby to be more like soccer.

Though *offsides* is a penalty infraction today, *offsides* in the 1880's in rugby was very much the same as *offsides* in soccer. The prohibition of blocking in a rugby game is in fact because of the game's strict enforcement of its *offsides* rule. Similar to soccer, this rule prohibits any player on the team with possession of the ball to loiter between the ball and the goal. Blocking continues as a basic element of modern American football, with many complex schemes having been developed and implemented over the years, including zone blocking and pass blocking.

Camp stayed active in rule making for most of his life. He had the honor of personally selecting an annual All-American team every year from 1889 through 1924. Camp passed away in 1925. The Walter Camp Football Foundation continues to select All-American teams in his honor.

With many rule changes as noted, as American style rugby became more defined as American football, more and more colleges adopted football as part of their sports programs. Most of the schools were from the Eastern US. It was not until 1879 that the University of Michigan became the first school west of Pennsylvania to establish a bona-fide American-style college football team.

Back then, football teams played whenever they could in the fall or the spring. For example, Michigan's first game was in late spring, near the end of what we would call the academic year. On May 30, 1879 Michigan beat Racine College 1–0 in a game played in Chicago. In 1887, Michigan and Notre Dame played their first football game, which did not benefit from Camp's rules. In 1889, Syracuse played its first game.

The first night time game

It was not until September 28, 1892 that the first nighttime football game was played. Mansfield State Normal played Wyoming Seminary in Mansfield, Pennsylvania. These schools are close to where I live. The game ended at a "declared" half-time in a 0–0 tie. It had become too dark to play.

Wyoming Seminary was not a college and to this day it is not a college. I live about five miles from the school. It is a private college preparatory school located in the Wyoming Valley of Northeastern Pennsylvania. During the time period in which the game was played, it was common for a college and high school to play each other in football—a practice that of course has long since been discontinued.

The reason that it got too dark to play, ironically was not because the game began at dusk. Mansfield had brought in a lighting system that was far too inadequate for game play. This historical game lasted only 20 minutes and there were only 10 plays. Both sides agreed to end at half-time with the score at 0-0. Though it may seem humorous today, for safety reasons, the game was declared ended in a 0-0 tie after several players had an unfortunate run-in with a light pole.

Mansfield and Wyoming Seminary are thus enshrined in football history as having played in the first night game ever in "college football." History and football buffs get together once a year to celebrate the game in what they call "Fabulous 1890's Weekend." This historic game is reenacted exactly as it occurred play by play just as the actual game is recorded in history. Fans who watch the game are sometimes known to correct players (actually actors) when they deviate from the original scripted plays. Now, that shows both a love of the game and a love of history.

Mansfield and Wyoming Seminary's game added additional fame to both schools when the 100th anniversary of the game just happened to occur on Monday, September 28, 1992. Monday Night Football celebrated "100 years of night football" with its regularly scheduled game between the Los Angeles Raiders and the Kansas City Chiefs at Arrowhead Stadium. The Chiefs won 27–7 in front of 77,486 fans. How about that?

More football history was recorded when Army played Navy in 1893. In this game, we have the first documented use of a football helmet by a player in a game. Joseph M. Reeves had been kicked in the head in a prior football game. He was warned by his doctor that he risked death if he continued to play football. We all know how tough the Midshipmen and Black Nights (Cadets) are regardless of who they may be playing. Rather than end his football playing days prematurely. Reeves discussed his need with a shoemaker in Annapolis who crafted a leather helmet for the player to wear for the rest of the season.

Football conferences

Things were happening very quickly in the new sport of football. Organization and rules became the mantra for this fledgling sport. It was being defined while it was being played. Formal college football conferences were just around the corner. In fact, the Southeastern Conference and the Atlantic Coast Conference both got started in 1894.

The forward pass

None of Camp's rules for American Football included the most innovative notion of them all – the forward pass. Many believe that the first forward pass in football occurred on October 26, 1895 in a game between Georgia and North Carolina. Out of desperation, the ball was thrown by the North Carolina back Joel Whitaker instead of having been punted. George Stephens, a teammate caught the ball.

Despite what most may think or surmise, it was Camp again when he was a player at Yale, who executed the first game-time forward pass for a touchdown. During the Yale-Princeton game, while Camp was being tackled, he threw a football forward to Yale's Oliver Thompson, who sprinted to a touchdown. The Princeton Tigers naturally protested and there appeared to be no precedent for a referee decision. Like many things in football including a game-beginning coin-toss, the referee in this instance tossed a coin, and then he made his decision to allow the touchdown.

Hidden ball trick

Dome one-time tricks have not survived football. For example, on November 9, 1895 Auburn Coach John Heisman executed a hidden ball trick. Quarterback Reynolds Tichenor was able to gain Auburn's only touchdown in a 6 to 9 loss to Vanderbilt. This also was the first game in the south that was decided by a field goal.

The trick was simple but would be illegal today. When the ball was snapped, it went to a halfback. The play was closely masked and well screened. The halfback then thrust the ball under the back of the quarterback's (Tichenor) jersey. Then the halfback would crash into the line. After the play, Tichenor "simply trotted away to a touchdown."

The end of college football?

Football was never a game for the light of heart. You had to be tough physically and tough mentally to compete. Way back in 1906, for example complaints were many about the violence in American Football. It got so bad that universities on the West Coast, led by California and Stanford, replaced the sport with rugby union. At the time, the future of American college football, a very popular sport enjoyed by fans nationwide was in doubt. The schools that eliminated football and replaced it with rugby union believed football would be gone and rugby union would eventually be adopted nationwide.

Soon other schools followed this travesty and made the switch. Eventually, due to the perception that West Coast football was an inferior game played by inferior men when compared to the rough and tumble East Coast, manhood prevailed in the West over the inclination to make the game mild. The many tough East Coast and Midwest teams had shrugged off the loss of the few teams out West and they had continued to play American style football.

And, so the available pool of rugby union "football" teams to play remained small. The Western colleges therefore had to schedule games against local club teams and they reached out to rugby union powers in Australia, New Zealand, and especially, due to its proximity, Canada.

The famous Stanford and California game continued as rugby. To make it seem important. The winner was invited by the British Columbia Rugby Union to a tournament in Vancouver over the Christmas holidays. The winner of that tournament was rewarded with the Cooper Keith Trophy. Nobody in America cared. Eventually the West Coast came back to football.

Nonetheless the situation of injury and death in football persisted and though there was a lot of pushback, it came to a head in 1905 when there were 19 fatalities nationwide. President Theodore Roosevelt, a tough guy himself, is reported as having threatened to shut down the game nationwide if drastic changes were not made. Sports historians however, dispute that Roosevelt ever intervened.

What is certified, however, is that on October 9, 1905, the President held a meeting of football representatives from Harvard, Yale, and Princeton. The topic was eliminating and reducing injuries and the President according to the record, never threatened to ban football. The fact is that Roosevelt lacked the authority to abolish football but more importantly, he was a big fan and wanted the game to continue. The little Roosevelts also loved the sport and were playing football at the college and secondary levels at the time.

Meanwhile, there were more rule changes such as the notion of reducing the number of scrimmage plays to earn a first down from four to three in an attempt to reduce injuries. The LA Times reported an increase in punts in an experimental game and thus considered the game much safer than regular play. Football lovers did not accept the new rule because it was not "conducive to the sport."

Because nobody wanted players injured or killed in a game, on December 28, 1905, 62 schools met in New York City to discuss major rule changes to make the game safer. From this meeting, the Intercollegiate Athletic Association of the United States, later named the National Collegiate Athletic Association (NCAA), was formed.

The forward pass is legalized

One rule change that was introduced in 1906 was devised to open up the game and thus reduce injury. This new rule introduced the legal forward pass. Though it was underutilized for years, this proved to be one of the most important rule changes in the establishment of the modern game.

Because of these 1905-1906 reforms, mass formation plays in which many players joined together became illegal when forward passes became legal. Bradbury Robinson, playing for visionary coach Eddie Cochems at St. Louis University, is recorded as throwing the first legal pass in a September 5, 1906, game against Carroll College at Waukesha.

Later changes were in the minutia category, but they added discipline and safety to the game without destroying its rugged character. For example, in 1910, came the new requirement that at least seven offensive players be on the line of scrimmage at the time of the snap, that there be no pushing or pulling, and that interlocking interference (arms linked or hands on belts and uniforms) was not allowed. These changes accomplished their intended purpose of greatly reducing the potential for collision injuries.

As noted previously, great coaches emerged in the ranks who took advantage of these sweeping changes. Amos Alonzo Stagg, for example, introduced such innovations as the huddle, the tackling dummy, and the pre-snap shift. Other coaches, such as Pop Warner and Notre Dame's Knute Rockne, introduced new strategies that still remain part of the game.

Many other rules changes and coaching innovations came about before 1940. They all had a profound impact on the game, mostly in opening up the passing game, but also in making the game safer to play without diminishing its quality.

For example, in 1914, the first roughing-the-passer penalty was implemented. In 1918, the rules on eligible receivers were loosened to allow eligible players to catch the ball anywhere on the field. The previously more restrictive rules allowed passes only in certain areas of the field.

Scoring rules also changed which brought the scoring into the modern era. For example, field goals were lowered from five to three points in 1909 and touchdowns were raised from four to six points in 1912.

Star Players

Star players emerged in both the collegiate and professional ranks including Jim Thorpe, Red Grange, and Bronko Nagurski and other stars. These three in particular were able to move from college to the fledgling NFL and they helped turn it into a successful league. Notable sportswriter Grantland Rice helped popularize the sport of football with his poetic descriptions of games and colorful nicknames for the game's biggest players, including Notre Dame's

"Four Horsemen" backfield and Fordham University's linemen, known as the "Seven Blocks of Granite".

Jim Thorpe, Circa 1915

The Heisman

Jay Berwanger (on prior page) was the 1st Heisman Winner. In 1935, New York City's Downtown Athletic Club awarded its first Heisman Trophy to University of Chicago halfback Jay Berwanger (left).

He was also the first ever NFL Draft pick in 1936. The trophy continues to this day to recognize the nation's "most outstanding" college football player. It has become one of the most coveted awards in all of American sports.

As professional football became a national television phenomenon, college football did as well. In the 1950s, Notre Dame, which had a large national following, formed its own network to broadcast its games, but by and large the sport still retained a mostly regional following. Other teams began their own networks as time went by.

New formations and play sets continued to be developed by innovative coaches and their staffs. Emory Bellard from the University of Texas, developed a three-back option style offense known as the wishbone. Bear Bryant of Alabama became a preacher of the wishbone.

The strategic opposite of the wishbone is called the spread offense. Some teams have managed to adapt with the times to keep winning consistently. In the rankings of the most victorious programs, Michigan, Texas, and Notre Dame are ranked first, second, and third in total wins.

And so that is as far as we will take it in this chapter about the early evolution of football. With so many conferences and sports associations as well as pro, college, high school, and mini sports, something tells me we have not yet seen our last rule change.

Chapter 7 Syracuse Football – From 1889 to 1902

Coaches #1 to #7

Finishing the 1890's—with a coach)

Year	Coach	Record	Conf
1889	No coach	0–1	Ind
1890	Robert Winston	7-4-0	Ind
1891	William Galbreath	4-7-0	Ind
1892	Jordon C. Wells	0-8-1	Ind
1893	George H. Bond	4-9-1	Ind
1894	George H. Bond	6-5-0	Ind
1895	George O. Redington	6-2-2	Ind
1896	George O. Redington	5-3-2	Ind
1897	Frank E Wade	5-3-1	Ind
1898	Frank E Wade	8-2-1	Ind
1899	Frank E Wade	4-4-0	Ind
1900	Frank Sweetland	7-2-1	Ind
1901	Frank Sweetland	7-1-0	Ind
1900	Frank Sweetland	6-2-1	Ind

Circa 1890 Syracuse Fans Getting Ready to Tailgate

The Oval Field Used until 1907 as SU Home Football Field

Intro to SU 1890's Football

After the 1889 inauguration year with one game at Rochester the Wednesday before Thanksgiving, it seemed like it would be all downhill. SU got the program going with a great coach in 1890 but Head Coach Winston left right after the season. With a new coach, 1891 was a mediocre season. Then, with another new coach, in 1892, Syracuse had what would become known as the worst season in the school's first 100 years of football. The team was shut out eight times and outscored, 218-4, finishing with a 0-8-1 record. That team poorly executed on both sides of the ball, but its offensive ineptitude contrasted starkly with a much improved 1904 club, which averaged an astounding 45 points per game. Syracuse was back in business.

The phenomenal scoring average in 1894 was bolstered by a 144-0 victory against Manhattan College half way through the season. The Orangemen scored more points in that contest alone than they did in 32 of their first 100 seasons.

Eleven years later, with Frank "Buck" O'Neill coaching, defense became the trademark of Orange football. The 1915 team recorded nine shutouts and limited the opposition to a meager total of 16 points and 16 first downs in 12 games. That year, the Orangemen finished 9-1-2 but for its own reasons, turned down a bid to play Washington in the Rose Bowl. The rationale given was that they had already traveled more than 10,000 miles by rail in playing their regular season games. It was no pleasure traveling days on a train for a football game.

Back to 1890

An English boxer named Robert Winston became the school's first football coach in 1890. He was a no-nonsense coach and lorded over the team with an iron fist. Under Winston, in its second year on the intercollegiate scene, SU compiled a nice 7-4 record. Uniforms and equipment were not a priority. That season, during a game at Hamilton College, SU players were mocked for their pink-and-blue uniforms.

Worse than that, the team lost 4-6 away in Clinton, NY. When they returned to Syracuse, they urged the student council to change the school colors. Their plea was taken seriously. Orange became the dominant color from then on, thus sparing subsequent generations from having to chant, "Let's go, Pink!"

Like all football teams that are starting out, the early football years of the new Orangemen were primitive at best. There was no huge alumni pool ready with contributions to buy as much as a pair of socks for a needy player. Players dressed for home games and practices in the basement of the school library and bathed one at a time in an old washtub filled with cold water.

At the 100th anniversary celebration, the pundits wrote: A century from the beginning of SU football, "under the stewardship of peripatetic Coach Dick MacPherson, the football team that had problems getting off the ground is in full flight. SU ranks among the top 20 teams nationally and is rekindling memories of previous successes under legendary coaches such as Ben Schwartzwalder, Buck O'Neill and Chick Meehan."

1889 No coach: Syracuse's football program began in 1889 with its first official intercollegiate game against the University of Rochester on November 23. The soon-to-be Orangemen were defeated 0-36. The team wore their pink and blue uniforms without incident.

1890 Robert Winston Coach # 10

Orange was adopted as the school color and Syracuse athletic teams henceforth were known as "Orange" or "Orangemen". SU defeated Rochester 4-0 on Nov 15, to make up for the 36-0 shellacking from Rochester in SU's first and only game in its first season (1889). The season record was very respectable at 7-4. Bobby Winston was the program's first head coach.

First Football Victory Ever for SU

On September 26, 1890, SU managed to win its first game ever against the Syracuse Athletic Club W (14-0). It was only the second game in the second season in the history of the program. They followed this up with another win against the same club W (32-0) on Oct 2. In the 1890's and for about thirty more years, college teams would play just about any group to get a game.

<< Coach Bobby Winston

There were many athletic clubs, such as the Syracuse Athletic Club, and The Scranton Athletic Club, that sponsored athletic teams, especially football at that time. They normally gave the fledgling college teams a good run for their money. Some colleges and universities also played well-formed high-school clubs when the alternative was to not play a game.

On Oct 18, Syracuse faced off against St. John's Military Academy and won their third straight. W (26–6). The first loss came at home on Oct 27 against Union NY L (0-26). This was followed by a home win on Nov 1 against Hamilton in a nail-biter W (14-12). Next up was Union in a game played on Nov 8 at Schenectady. Syracuse was defeated for loss #2 of the year L (0-28).

The following week the big locomotive took the team to Rochester for a rematch from their first game and this time SU prevailed W (4-0). However, when Rochester came to Syracuse the following week on Nov 22, they beat Winston's squad L (0-11). Syracuse then made the trip to Clinton, NY on the day before Thanksgiving Nov 24, and were humiliated about their pink and blue uniforms, and they were also beaten on the field by Hamilton L (4-6). That was the last loss of the season

On Nov. 27, Syracuse beat the athletic association again W (16-14) and followed it up a few days later with another victory over St. John's Military Academy at home W (16-14).

Famous Coaches (From the Past) by SWC75.

This is from a blogger known as SWC75. The idea of including a piece of his post in each new coach's section is fully explained right before the Ben Schwartzwalder Era (Chapter 12) and within the section after the 1948 games of the season. The full blog URL is:

Part I or Part II of https://syracusefan.com/threads/famous-coaches-part-1.60694/, and
https://syracusefan.com/threads/famous-coaches-part-2.60695/

For each coach that SWC75 writes about, we offer his blog piece with the same title as this" Watch for inserts tiled:
Famous Coaches (From the Past) by SWC75

> (This is even longer that my "Facilities" post, so I'm posting it in two parts to make it look a little less intimidating.)
>
> Whenever the SU football program takes a dip, the same suggested cure always makes its appearance on internet boards, radio shows and letters to the editor: The University ought to

pony up and hire (fill in name of a famous unemployed coach). He'll be the answer. I think it's another issue that needs some historical perspective. I thought I'd go over the history of SU head football coaches and see what it can tell us. My intention was to be brief but, well, you know me. I like a good story.

Syracuse' first head football coach was Bobby Winston, an English rugby player and boxer who had immigrated to this country in 1883 and was Syracuse' athletic trainer. The school had played its first football game the previous year, losing 0-36 to Rochester. Winston led the team through its first full season, winning 8 and losing 3. (The schedule, such as it was, included two games against Rochester, both victories, a split with Hamilton, two one-sided losses to Union, two wins over St. John's. later Manlius, Military Academy and ended with three straight wins over the Syracuse athletic club.).

Ken Rappoport, in "The Syracuse Football Story", in a chapter entitled "The Stone Age," quotes a contemporary observer:

"Winston's services were timely. He instilled an enthusiasm and love of the game into the players, which, though it has sometimes dwindled in times of poor support and defeat, has never left the team. His odd English ways and London songs made him a great favorite and, when he left, the team had the principles of the game as played at that time well in hand." He left for other jobs after that and was also the first head coach at the University of Georgia in 1894.

One more note on facilities: "The players dressed in a tiny room in the basement of the school library and after practice bathed one after another in an old wash tube filled with cold water. (Bob Snyder's "Orange Handbook" says that "the players took postgame baths by raising a trapdoor and dropping into icy water beneath the library". At least they had hydrotherapy.

The campus playing field was no better that a stone quarry. The ground was hard as diamonds, uneven in spots and punctuated by boulders the size of watermelons. Stones filled the area. Miniature craters abounded." One player recalled: "We had to spend a day or two raking and picking off the stones, filling up the holes with dirt and sawdust." Syracuse undoubtedly had some of the worst facilities in the nation at that time. They were a mess.

1891 William Galbraith Coach # 2

After Coach Winston left the University, the 1891 Syracuse Orangemen football team in their third season were managed by head coach William Galbraith, coaching his first season with the Orangemen. William Fanton was the team captain.

Stephen Crane, author of the Civil War classic, "Red Badge of Courage," was a member of the SU squad that finished 4-7.

On Sept 26, a tough Cornell team defeated the Orangemen at Cornell. After a few weeks break, and some more practices, Cornell came to Syracuse on Oct 17, and barely beat the Orangemen L (6-12) before 800. On Oct 22, SU played the Syracuse Athletic Assoc. and won the game W (22-0). Two days later on Oct 24, SU lost a close on to St. John's Military Academy L 0–4. Then on Oct 30 at Hamilton in Clinton, NY, the Orangemen lost another L (4–22).

On Nov 7 at Colgate in Hamilton, NY, SU lost to its new rival L (16-22) On Nov 11 in a game at Union in Schenectady, NY, the Orangemen were overpowered L (0–75). Things were not going good after that blowout and the disappointed Orangemen lost for the first time to the Syracuse Athletic Assoc. (L (0–28). This was followed with a nice win at home against Rochester on Nov 21, W (18-6)

On Nov 26, the Orangemen came back to beat the Syracuse Athletic Assoc. in a nice match W 22–10 before 1,000 onlookers. Then, on Nov 28 SU defeated St. John's Military Academy at home W (22-4)

Famous Coaches (From the Past) by SWC75.

Winston was replaced by William Galbraith, who became the first SU head coach to get fired- I think. He had played center for Cornell and doubled as the team manager. Rappoport's book shows

Galbraith as the coach for the whole season but "Syracuse University Football: A Centennial Celebration" by Michael Mullins says that Galbraith was replaced by Jordan Wells after an opening 0-68 loss to Cornell. They didn't waste time in those days. SU's second game was a 6-12 loss to Cornell's "second team", (I assume this was a JV squad). According to Mullins it was coached by William Galbraith! Bum Phillips used to say of Don Shula: "He can take his'un and beat your'un or he can take your'un and beat his'un". Like most coaches, Galbraith needed to have better material than his opponent. That was Galbraith's only year as a collegiate head coach.

1892 Jordan C. Wells Coach # 3

The 1892 Syracuse Orangemen football team was led by head coach Jordan C. Wells, in his first season with the Orangemen. This was the fourth season in school history for football and it would be the worst in Syracuse's history of sporting a football team. Here we are in 2018, and this was the only season that Syracuse was ever winless.

Syracuse began the year again Sept 28, against Cornell in Ithaca, NY, and were subjected to a major blowout L (0-58). On Oct 12, it was the Syracuse Athletic Assoc. L (0–24). Then again on Oct 21, it was the Syracuse Athletic Assoc. L (4–18). These were the only points SU scored all season long.

On Oct 29, it was Union at home L (0–52) On Nov 5, it was Hamilton at home L (0–12). On Nov 9, it was the Syracuse Athletic Assoc. The Orangemen played them to a scoreless tie T (0-0). Next SU traveled to Rochester NY L (0–22). Again, came the Syracuse Athletic Assoc. for another loss L0–4). Then, on Nov 23, St. John's Military Academy at home L (0–28). It was a tough year. A year such as this would thankfully never come again.

Famous Coaches (From the Past) by SWC75.

Jordan Wells "coached as well as he could" but 1892 was SU's only winless campaign, (despite all of G-Rob's efforts). That was his only year on the official records as anybody's head coach, although, if Mullins' account his correct he should be credited with the four victories from the prior year. But it seems a shame to spoil a spotless record, (although the 1892 team did tie Syracuse Athletic club 0-0, one of four games with them). The next year we tried not having a coach and that was actually an improvement, as we went 4-9-1, beating Hamilton, tying Rochester and ending the season with a three game winning streak over "Syracuse High School", Onondaga Academy and Cazenovia. Those Lakers are tough to beat!

1893 George H. Bond Coach # 4

Officially, SU had no coach this year but George H Bond, captain of the team served as captain and coach. "Without a coach," the Orange finished the season with a 4-9-1 record with wins against Syracuse High School, Hamilton, Onondaga Academy and Cazenovia.

The 1893 Syracuse Orangemen football team competed in their fifth season of intercollegiate football. They were led by stand-in head coach and team captain George H. Bond in his first of "two" years as head coach of the Orangemen. This season was a big improvement over 1892 but nobody was making big smiles yet. In fact, the beginning of this season for the first six games were as winless as 1892. It was frustrating for the team and the fans.

Here are the six quick losses to begin the season:
Sept 21 Syracuse Athletic Assoc home L (0–22)
Sept 27 Cornell home L (0–44)
Oct 7   St. John's Military Acad. L (16–24)
Oct 14   Syracuse Athletic Assoc. home L 0–28
Oct 21   St. John's Military Acad. Home L 4–18
Oct 26   at Colgate L (0–58)

It was getting so nobody thought the Orangemen would win again.

Oct 31, the Orangemen played Syracuse High School and finally won a game W (20–0). Then, on Nov 4, the Orangemen played Hamilton in Clinton, NY for a close win W (16–14).

Union was always tough and on Nov 11 in Union pitched a blowout shutout L (0–66). On Nov 15 at Syracuse Athletic Assoc. field, SU lost L (4–28) with just 75 fans in the stands. On Nov 18, at Home SU tied Rochester T (10-10). Then, after a locomotive to Rochester on Nov 30, SU was defeated L (0-6). Two late season games were scheduled, and they added to the win column. On Dec 2, Onondaga Academy at home W 30–0 and Dec 9 Cazenovia at home W 24–0.

Things were getting better, but nobody was passing out cigars yet. Coach Winston had spoiled everybody for wins.

Famous Coaches (From the Past) by SWC75.

At this point James Roscoe Day became Chancellor. He was a big man who loved sports and football; Under him the first athletic department was organized, a gymnasium built and a special training table for athletes established. (We catch up to other schools eventually.) Also, George Bond, one of Winston's players, became our fourth coach and led the team to a 6-5 record. "Fighting against defeat and hoping against hope, (we) knew that the dawn of better days was breaking." One of his players said that "the father of Syracuse football was George Bond. He was an uncanny diagnostician of the offense, a great teacher, mean as the devil on the football field but a fine chap off." But that was also his only year as a college head coach.

1894 George H. Bond Coach # 4

The 1894 Syracuse Orangemen football team competed in their sixth season of intercollegiate football. They were led by George H. Bond in his second as official head coach of the Orangemen. Robert Adams was the team captain. The team record was above five hundred with a record of 6-5. This season was another big improvement over 1892 and there were some who were smiling that the bad days might be over.

<<George Hopkins Bond (August 10, 1873 – May 8, 1954) was an American football player, coach, and lawyer. He served as the head football coach at Syracuse University for one season in 1894, compiling a record of 6–5. He was captain of the team in 1893 and served as its head coach, unofficially.

Bond was born in Syracuse, New York on August 10, 1873. He graduated from Syracuse University with a bachelor's degree in philosophy in 1894 and from Syracuse University College of Law in 1897. Bond was a senior partner in the law firm of Bond, Schoeneck & King until his resignation in 1953. In 1937 he served as president of the New York State Bar Association. He was also an organizer and president of the New York State Association of District Attorneys.

Bond was the fourth coach in SU football history; in 1893, the team played without a formal coach after Jordan C. Wells couldn't muster a win the prior year. The team entrusted Bond and he led it on a school-record winning streak with victories over Cazenovia, St. John's Military Academy, Rochester and Hamilton. The streak began and ended with shutouts while the Orange also set a mark for points scored in a season, with 188.

Even teams that previously had whooped Syracuse had a more difficult time this year. For example, on Sept 26 at Cornell in Ithaca, NY, the Orangemen narrowed the margin but still did not score L (0–39). On Sept 29, SU defeated Hobart at home W 18–4. On Oct 6, the feast day of St Bruno (also Brian), SU fell to Hamilton College at Hamilton L (8-32). On Oct 13, Syracuse had recovered from the opening day pasting by Cornell enough to shut them out at home W (22-0). This was a very good sign for the program to beat Cornell.

The Syracuse Athletic Assoc. was getting tougher and on Oct 20, Syracuse suffered its third loss of the season L (6–10). SU then beat

Cazenovia on Nov 3 W 20–0. They followed this on Nov 6 with a win v St. John's Military Acad. W (20–12) and a win on Nov 10 at the University of Rochester W 28–18. Feeling pretty good about itself, the Orangemen pounded Hamilton at Syracuse W (50–0). Union no longer had its way with Syracuse, but they won the game on Nov 21 at home L (10-20). Syracuse let down on the last game of the year and were beaten on Nov 24 by St. John's Military Academy L 6–22

1895 George O. Redington Coach # 5

The 1895 Syracuse Orangemen football team competed in their seventh season of intercollegiate football. They were led by George O. Redington in his first of two years as head coach of the Orangemen. Robert Adams was again the team captain. The team record was the best ever with a record of 6-2-2. This season was another big improvement over 1892 and there were some who were smiling hard knowing the bad days from 1892 were over.

<<< George O Redington

The Orange secured its first real home field as SU went from playing in parks throughout the city of Syracuse to playing at The Oval, which was a space located behind the Hall of Languages. The Orange recorded its first victory against rival Colgate, by what appears to be an unusual score of 4-0. However, in 1895, a touchdown was worth just four points.

Syracuse even began to play away tough games quite well. In the away opener at Cornell on Sept 26, played in Ithaca, NY, SU came really close but could not score and lost the game L (0–8). Even Scranton, PA got in the act. This coal town was huge back then and big in mining with a lot of tough players. On Oct 5, at

Scranton Athletic Assoc, the Orange prevailed in a tough match W (12–0).

On Oct 10, the Orangemen had clearly regained their moxie a the finally beat what was once their easiest foe, the Syracuse Athletic Assoc. at home W 24–0. On Oct 19, SU traveled out of state to Maryland and played Williams in Williamstown MA but did not have enough for the win L (10–28). This was SU's first opponent from outside of New York State. On Oct 26, SU played to a tie with St. John's Military Academy at home T (6–6).

Finishing up a fine season with no more losses, SU beat Hobart at home W (46-0) on Nov2. On Nov 9, in a squeaker, with a TD worth just four points, they shut-out Colgate at home W (4-0). Then they finished a fine season with another win on Nov 13 against the Syracuse Athletic Assoc. W 18–0, followed by a home win v Rochester on Nov 16 W (30-0). After such a fine season, they capped it off with a hard-fought tie on Nov 23 at St. John's Military Acad. T (4–4).

Famous Coaches (From the Past) by SWC75.

Another former Winston player was George Redington, who would coach the team for the next two seasons, winning 11, losing 5 and tying 4 (there were lots of ties in those low-scoring days). He was noted for being very strict about training rules and keeping schedules. He was the first SU coach to last two full seasons. But like Galbraith, Wells, and Bond, those were his only seasons as a collegiate head coach. He had spent the 1896 commuting from his New York City law office to coach the team, (no mean feat in those days), and decided to stick with the law.

1896 George O. Redington Coach # 5

The 1896 Syracuse Orangemen football team competed in their eighth season of intercollegiate football. They were led by George O. Redington in his second of two years as head coach of the

Orangemen. Robert Adams was again the team captain. The team record was great with a record of 5-3-2. This season found fans no longer thinking about the big disappointment from 1892. Syracuse was on its way to greatness. Wunderbar!

1896 Syracuse Football Team

This year, SU played the Clyde Athletic Association at home on Nov 26 as another great association that wanted to kick the pants off college teams. They did not but SU finished the season with a tie because the Athletic Associations were getting stronger, having picked up a lot of college graduates who knew how to play great football.

On Sept 29, a tough Syracuse HS team was defeated by SU W (24-0). Still not able to begin a season with a win v Cornell at Ithaca, the Orangemen want down in the season opener again L (0-22). Elmira got itself an Athletic Association in 1896 and they played a close game Oct 10m v SU but lost W (20-6). Williams then beat SU at home on Oct 17, L (6-24). In a road trip to Hamilton, NY on Oct 24, SU lost to Colgate L (0-6).

Never forgetting the 1889 first loss to Rochester, Syracuse hammered them om Cot 27 W (62-4). On Oct 31, it was the

Syracuse Athletic Assoc. and SU prevailed W (26–0). Then, on Nov 7 at Buffalo at the Buffalo Baseball Park, SU played to a tie T (6–6). Rebounding again, on Nov 14, SU whooped St. John's Military Acad. At home W 40–0, and after an OK season, on Nov 26 at Clyde Athletic Assoc., they tied in the season finale, T (10–10)

Famous Coaches (From the Past) by SWC75.

Redington was followed by Frank Wade, who became our first three-year coach, going 17-9-2. He was our first coach who had been a head football coach anywhere else before getting the job here, having spent one-year coaching DePauw in Indiana to a 3-3-1 record. He was attending law school here. He was credited with upgrading the athletes in the program: "Not only were they smarter about the game: they were also faster and in better condition." I wonder if he did what we would now call "recruiting"? His great accomplishment was considered to be a near-upset of Army in 1899. Wade then began a long career as a lawyer and businessman in the Syracuse area and Syracuse began a new century.

1897 Frank E. Wade Coach # 6

The 1897 Syracuse Orangemen football team competed in their ninth season of intercollegiate football. They were led by Frank E. Wade in his first of three years as head coach of the Orangemen. Robert Adams was again the team captain. The team record was great with a record of 5-3-1.

A major rule changed occurred in 1807 as a touchdown, which had previously been worth four points was upgraded to five points.

On Sept 25, SU defeated Cazenovia in the home opener W 36–0. On Oct 2 at Cornell, SU was shut out L (0–16). Then, the Orangemen came back on Oct 7 against Hobart at home for another win W (20-6). Next was a tie against rival Colgate on Oct 16 in Hamilton, NY T (6-6)

The Colgate "Hoodoo" was born when a newspaper reporter sympathetic to the Red Raiders' cause, tackled an SU player who was on his way to scoring the winning touchdown. The game ended in a 6-6 tie.

Syracuse then blew out Union on Oct 23 at home W (40-0). This was followed by a win against neighboring Cortland at home W (24-0). The following week Rochester came to town and were defeated by the Orangemen W (36-0). The season ended in two disappointing losses against Buffalo. The first was a shutout on Nov 6 at Buffalo's Baseball Park L (0–16) before 800 fans and the second was at home on Nov 13 L (0-10).

1898 Frank E. Wade Coach # 6

The 1898 Syracuse Orangemen football team competed in their tenth season of intercollegiate football. They were led by Frank E. Wade in his second of three years as head coach of the Orangemen. Morgan Wilcox was the team captain. The team record was great posting a record of 8-2-1. They outscored opponents 192-69. It was a fine season indeed.

Syracuse had a tough first game this season against Cornell on Sept 21 in Ithaca, NY were shut out by the Big Red L (0-28). On Sept 21, SU came right back and shut-out Rochester at home W (35-0). Cornell then came to Syracuse on Oct 5 and shut out the Orangemen again L (0-28). This would be the last loss of the season.

On Oct 12 at Hobart in Geneva, NY, SU prevailed W 46–5. Travelling to Cleveland Ohio on Oct 22 to play the Case School of Science, SU won its third game of the season in a shutout W (10-0). At home on Oct 26, the Syracuse Athletic Assoc. fell to the Orangemen W 28–0. Then, on Oct 29, the Orangemen traveled way up NY state to Ogdensburg, right across the St. Lawrence from Brockville Canada, and the Orangemen came home with the win (17–6). The next game was on Nov 5 at Ohio Field in New York against NYU for another victory W (17-0)

On Nov 9 SU beat the Syracuse Athletic Assoc. W (28–0). Then on Nov 12, Syracuse traveled down through Scranton, and Wilkes-Barre PA to Kingston for a victory of a tough prep school, Wyoming

Seminary W (11-0). On Nov 19, SU finished the season with a tie at home against Trinity T (0-0).

1899 Frank E. Wade Coach # 6

The 1899 Syracuse Orangemen football team competed in their eleventh season of intercollegiate football. They were led by Frank E. Wade in his third of three years as head coach of the Orangemen. Carl Dorr was the team captain. The team finished with a season record of 4-4-0.

The Orangemen played just eight games in 1899, cutting back by about three games from its average season. The team, regardless of the coach, had settled into a negative tradition of losing its opener to Cornell and this year was more of the same. The game was played in Ithaca, NY on Sept 27 L (0-17). On Oct 7, Syracuse shut out the Syracuse Athletic Assoc. at home W 6–0. This was followed on Oct 14 by another home win against NYU W (10-5).

On Oct 28, Syracuse lost at home to Williams L (0-6) and the following week on Nov 4, lost to Buffalo at home L (0-16) On Nov 11 at Rochester, the Orangemen pitched a shutout W (23-0). Then, on Nov 18, at Army's "The Plain" at West Point NY, Syracuse fell in a close match L (6–12). The Orangemen wrapped up the season on Nov 22 at Dickinson in Carlisle, PA NY with a nice victory W (18–7)

Famous Coaches (From the Past) by SWC75.

Our first 20th century coach was Edwin R. Sweetland, still another Cornellian who had played for Pop Warner there and coached Hamilton College, (Mullins reports it as Colgate, which is in Hamilton, New York). At Syracuse he stressed speed. His 1900 team averaged 163 pounds per man. "Syracuse, light almost to frailty, compensated for a clear lack of brute force and achieved success through the sheer rapidity of its play." Mullins calls Sweetland "a Vince Lombardi type: tough, aggressive, intelligent, a disciplinarian". (We have had a Vince Lombardi type here, after all.) He was the first Syracuse coach who made coaching a profession: he was also the University's crew coach and later became Kentucky's first basketball coach.

The team was also accused of dirty play and brawls with Cornell and NYU caused an interruption in those series. At the same time, Syracuse upgraded its schedule and was now playing the top teams in the East, giving their records more meaning. Sweetland's teams were up to the task, going 20-5-2 in his three years here. Sweetland wanted more money and returned to Hamilton. From there he went to Ohio State, then came back to coach Colgate, moved on to Kentucky, (one observer said his team "fought like Wildcats", which became their official nickname), then Miami of Ohio, West Virginia and Tulane, finally winding up at Alfred, finishing his mercurial career in 1918 with an even 100 football wins vs. 41 losses and 10 ties. He retired to become a farmer and part-time lawyer.

1900 Edwin Sweetland Coach # 7

From the 1899-1904 Alumni Record: "On Sept. 4 Coach Sweetland began his work with the football team. An excellent showing was made this Fall. As a football coach Mr. Sweetland is a genius. St. Lawrence was defeated by a score of 70 too, New York University 12 too, Amherst, 5 too, Dickinson 6 too, Rochester 68 to 5. and the game with Brown was a tie, 6 to 6. The Cornell game resulted in a score of 6 to 0 in favor of Cornell. It was the last game with that College to the present time."

<< Coach Sweetland<<

Edwin Sweetland was a Cornell grad, hired as head football coach and to start the crew program. He later coached against SU as the head coach at Colgate

After a mediocre 1899 football season, the 1900 Syracuse Orangemen football team rebounded in their twelfth season of intercollegiate football. They were led by Edwin Sweetland in his first of three seasons as head coach of the Orangemen. Haden Patten was the team captain. The team finished with a season record of 7-2-1. Sweetland had two more fine seasons for SU before he moved on. He was a great coach and under his direction Syracuse became a powerhouse.

SU went back to a ten-game season for 1900. On Sept 22 at home SU shut-out Cortland W (35–0). The following week, SU traveled to Ithaca to play Cornell and just about pulled it off this time. L (0–6). On Oct 6, SU beat St. Lawrence W (70-0). On Oct 13, the Orangemen beat NYU in Geneva, NY W (12–0).

In the early days of football, the Ivy League schools were especially strong. Syracuse decided to test Princeton on Oct 17 at University Field New Brunswick, NJ, and suffered a blowout from the Tigers L (0-43. SU came right back and beat Amherst at home on Oct 20. On Nov3, at Oberlin Ohio, SU shut out Oberlin W 6–0. On Nov 10, it was Dickinson at home W (6-0). Then on Nov 17, the Orangemen laid a big hurt on Rochester at home W 68–5. SU finished the season with a tie, on Nov 24 against another IVY League school, Brown in Providence, RI T (6–6).

1901 Edwin Sweetland Coach # 7

The 1901 Syracuse Orangemen football team were again playing great football in their thirteenth season of intercollegiate football. They were led by Edwin Sweetland in his second of three seasons as head coach of the Orangemen. Lynn Wycoff was the team captain. The team finished with a season record of 7-1-0. Sweetland had two more fine seasons for SU before he moved on. If it were not for a close loss (0-5) to Lafayette, Syracuse would have had its first undefeated season. Sweetland was a genius and a fine football coach.

In the home opener on Sept 21, Cortland came to Syracuse and were shut-out W (35–0)/ Next, on Sept 28, RPI played at the Oval and Syracuse prevailed in a shutout W (26-0). On Oct 5, it was at Brown in Providence, RI. The Orangemen won again, W (20–0) before 500 fans. On Oct 12 in a home contest at the Oval, SU lost to Lafayette

L (0–5) before 3,000, Clarkson came down from the North Country to take a shutout beating from the Orangemen on Oct 19, W (27–0).

In another home game on Oct 26 SU beat Amherst at Syracuse, W (28–17) before 5,000. In a road trip on Nov 9 at Columbia's South Field in NYC, Syracuse hung on for the win W (11–5) On Nov 20, Vermont was shutout by the Orangemen W (38–0) before 1,000 fans.

1902 Edwin Sweetland Coach # 7

The 1902 Syracuse Orangemen football team competed well in their fourteenth season of intercollegiate football. They were led by Edwin Sweetland in his third of three seasons as head coach of the Orangemen. Ancil D. Brown was the team captain. The team finished with a season record of 6-2-1.

As I slowly go through each and every season of each and every team when I write Great Moments books, I get to take notice of the records of all the coaches. It is a labor of love. I love writing about wins, however, much more than I like wiring about losses. Having a long-time affinity for Syracuse, having lived in Utica as a 21-23year old and having run many bus trips to the Carrier Dome in my day, I root for Syracuse. As I encounter 1902, for example, I am rooting for Syracuse to win it all and then as I research further I find they lost two and had a tie. For me, it's like being at the games. So, now what I know the record and I am about to write the game summaries, I sure wish Edwin Sweetland, one of the great coaches of Syracuse had another few more years. But, I am most appreciative for all the good work that he did as football was becoming more accepted in the USA.

On Sept 20, 1902, in the home opener, Syracuse shut out Cortland W 21–0. On Sept 27 at home the Orangemen pitched another shutout—this time against the Onondaga Indians W (34–0). The Onondagas were a tough and gritty bunch of football players from the turn of the last century who loved their education and they loved the game of football. Below is a picture of the 1902 team. They also played Syracuse in 1903. Onondaga, is a big name in the areas outside

Syracuse. Like the Carlton Indians from PA who had the famous Jim Thorpe on their squad, these folks were tough football players.

The Onondaga Indians – A Tough Team

On Oct 4 at home Syracuse beat Clarkson W (34–0). On Oct 11, SU pitched another shutout against Colgate at home on the Oval, W 23–0. On Oct 18, SU shut out Amherst W (15–0). Testing the Ivy League again, on Oct 25, Syracuse traveled to Yale at Yale Field in New Haven, CT to put up a good fight but lose the game in a shutout L 0–24. Williams came down from Massachusetts on Nov1 and Syracuse just got the win with little to spare W (26–17).

One of the toughest teams in the nation until the 1950's was Army. Syracuse made the trip across NY state to play on Nov 15 at Army at The Plain in West Point, NY. It was a lopsided loss L (0–46). Army often decimated opponents. On Nov 27 at Columbia's South Field in NYC, SU played Columbia to a hard-earned tie T (6–6)

Chapter 8 Syracuse Football – From 1903 to 1915

Coaches # 8 to #13

Year	Coach	Record	Conf
1903	Ancil D. Brown	5-4-0	Ind
1904	Charles P. Hutchins	6-3-0	Ind
1905	Charles P. Hutchins	8-3-0	Ind
1906	Frank "Buck" O'Neill	6-3-0	Ind
1907	Frank "Buck" O'Neill	5-3-1	Ind
1908	Howard Jones	6-3-1	Ind
1909	Tad Jones	4-5-1	Ind
1910	Tad Jones	5-4-1	Ind
1911	C. Def. Cummings	5-3-2	Ind
1912	C. Def. Cummings	4-5-0	Ind
1913	Frank "Buck" O'Neill	6-4-0	Ind
1914	Frank "Buck" O'Neill	5-3-2	Ind
1915	Frank "Buck" O'Neill	9-1-2	Ind

Syracuse Football Team Practice in Snow at New Archbold Field

1903 Ancil D. Brown Coach # 8

The 1903 Syracuse Orangemen football team competed in their fifteenth season of intercollegiate football. They were led by Ancil D. Brown, his first and only season as head coach of the Orangemen. Brown had been the captain on the 1902 Syracuse football team. Nobody in those days was paid a lot for bringing new football teams into being. Frank H. O'Neill was the team captain. He would soon become one of SU's revered coaches. The team finished with a season record of 5-4-0.

The season home opener on Sept 19 against Cortland resulted in a nice W (23–0) shutout for the Orangemen before 2,000. On Sept 26, Syracuse shut out the Onondaga Indians on the Oval W (35–0). On Oct 3, SU defeated Clarkson at home W (34-0). RPI came to Syracuse on Oct 10 and were shut out W (33-0). With a nice 4-0 record going, it looked like a great season until Oct 17 at home Colgate squeaked a win out against the Orange L (5-10).

Famous Coaches (From the Past) by SWC75.

SU anticipated something the Chicago Cubs would do decades later and used two coaches who alternated, game by game, in 1903. Unlike the Cubs' experiment Jason Parrish and Ancil Brown led the team to a winning record at 5-4. But neither of them were head coaches in any other year. They were replaced by Dr. Charles P. Hutchins, who must have had the right prescription, because the team outscored nine opponents 405-57, including a school record 144-0 win over Manhattan College, (whose facilities were not very good). They stopped the game after 32 minutes. We had 25 touchdowns. They had no first downs. (I'm hoping the Florida State game will be closer.) Hutchins was 14-6 in his two years here, before moving on to coach Wisconsin for two years. He went on to become athletic director at Indiana.

<< Coach Charles P. Hutchins

In the sixth home game of the season, on Oct 24, Syracuse lost to Williams from Massachusetts L (5-17) before 2500. On Oct 31, SU got back its moxie in another home game against Niagara W (47-0). Then, the Orangemen traveled to New Haven Connecticut to the Yale Field where they were beaten by another Ivy League team, Yale, L (0–30) before 5,000. On Nov 4, the Orangemen lost a close match at Brown on Nov 14, in Providence, RI L (5–12) before 3800 fans.

1904 Charles P. Hutchins Coach # 9

Charles Pelton Hutchins (September 10, 1872 – December 28, 1938) was an American football coach. He served as the head football coach at Dickinson College (1902–1903), Syracuse University (1904–1905), and University of Wisconsin–Madison (1906–1907), compiling a career college football record of 31–16–1. From 1904 to 1905, he coached at Syracuse, tallying a 14–6 record. From 1906 to 1907, he coached at Wisconsin, where he compiled an 8–1–1 record. Hutchins was also the athletic director at Indiana University Bloomington from 1911 to 1913.

The 1904 Syracuse Orangemen football team competed in their sixteenth season of intercollegiate football. They were led by Charles P. Hutchins in his first of two seasons as head coach of the Orangemen. This was the ninth different coach in the 16 years since the program was started in 1898. For such constant change in coaching, Syracuse was doing quite well compared to other startups across the nation. Robert Park was the captain on the 1904 Syracuse football team. The team finished with a season record of 6-3-0.

The home opener was played on Sept 24 against Cortland's Red Dragons at the Oval in Syracuse, NY. SU shut out Cortland W (27–0) before 600 fans On Oct1, SU defeated Clarkson in a major blowout at home W (69–0). Colgate came over to play at the Oval from Hamilton, NY on Oct 8 in a rival match and defeated the Orange L (0–11). Traveling to Yale again for another chance, the Orangemen played better than the year before and almost pulled it off on Oct 15, but were defeated despite the close score at Yale Field in New Haven, CT L (9–17)

On Oct 22 SU defeated Niagara at home in a blowout W (52–4). On Oct 29, still feeling mighty after the prior week's blowout, SU did a bigger number against Allegheny at Yale Field in New Haven, CT W (69–0). On Nov 5, SU collected a huge blowout win of W (144-0) at Syracuse. On Nov 12 at Lehigh in Bethlehem, PA, SU prevailed W 30–4. On Nov 19, SU lost at Army to the powerful Cadets in The Plain at West Point, NY (L 5–21).

1905 Charles P. Hutchins Coach # 9

The 1905 Syracuse Orangemen football team competed in their seventeenth season of intercollegiate football. They were led by Charles P. Hutchins in his second of two seasons as head coach of the Orangemen. David Tucker was the captain on the 1905 Syracuse football team. The team finished with a season record of 8-3-0.

In the season home opener on Sept 22, SU took on a new opponent, Alfred University at home, and shut them out W (52–0). On Sept 27, SU defeated Hobart at home W (24–0) In another home game, on Sept 30, the Orangemen defeated Rochester W (16–0). It was back to Yale again on Oct 7 for another unsuccessful try in a game played in Yale Field New Haven, CT L (0–16). Th next road trip was on Oct 14 to Clinton, NY v Hamilton College W (27-0). On Oct 14, SU defeated Hamilton's neighbor Colgate at home in a close match W (11-5).

Next home game was on Oct 28, in which SU defeated Lehigh before 3000 fans W (17-0). Still struggling against Ivy League teams. SU lost to Brown in Providence, RI on Nov 4 L (0–27). On Nov 11, at home, SU beat Holy Cross W (16-4). RPI was next and the Orangemen gave them a big shellacking on Nov 18 W (62-0). Still without a win against Army, SU tried again on Nov 25 at The Plain in West Point, NY but failed L (0–17). This ended the 1905 season.

1906 Frank "Buck" O'Neill Coach # 10

The 1906 Syracuse Orangemen football team competed in their eighteenth season of intercollegiate football. They were led by Frank "Buck" O'Neill in his first of two seasons (on this tour – O'Neill would be back) as head coach of the Orangemen. James Stimson was the captain on the 1906 Syracuse football team. The team finished with a season record of 5-3-1.

The season opener on Sept 22 pitted Hobart against Syracuse at home. The Orangemen grabbed the victory W (28–6) before 800 at

the Oval. On Sept 27 SU defeated Rochester at home in a shutout W (38–0). On Oct 6, Syracuse faced a powerful Yale team at Yale Field in New Haven, CT and lost in a blowout L (0–51). After playing Yale, on Oct 13, SU traveled to Clinton NY to play Hamilton College and pitched a fine shutout W (37-0). At home the next week against Colgate, who happen to be from Hamilton, NY, the SU offense never fired up and the team was defeated narrowly L (0-5). Five points was one touchdown in 1906.

On Nov 3 vs. Carlisle at Buffalo, NY, Syracuse lost a close game L (4–9) before 8,000. On Nov 10, at home SU walloped Niagara W (46–0). Then, after traveling to Lafayette in Easton, PA, the Orange brought home a victory W (12-4). Finishing up a fine season, the Buck O'Neill boys came through with a huge victory against Army played on The Plain in West Point, NY W (4–0)

Famous Coaches (From the Past) by SWC75.

Charles Hutchins was replaced by the first Syracuse coach who would wind up in the Hall of Fame. Frank "Buck" O'Neill had coached at Colgate for three years, going 18-8-2. He was another coaching lawyer, (I'll bet those guys knew the rulebook), and took some years off to tend to his law practice in New York City. He was head coach at SU from 1906-07, 1913-1915 and 1917-19 "and his name was synonymous with Syracuse through that era. Of high intelligence and executive capacity, he was forceful, rigorous and adamant in his system, method and discipline. He knew and loved this great game and was impatient with indifferent, incapable or stupid play or players."

He was a Syracuse native, working in a butcher's shop in Manlius that supplied meat for the St. John's Military Academy. He delivered it and became intrigued by football practice. He volunteered to help out the scrubs when they were short a man and filled his derby hat with straw as protection against concussions, (does the NFL know about this?). He was invited to attend the academy and play football for the team, worked hard in class and became an honor student. He went to Williams College. He played football for them and became team captain.

Colgate hired him in 1902 and he coached them while coaching and playing for a professional team representing the Syracuse Athletic Club, which won something called "The World Series of Football", (a year before the Baseball World Series began), in Madison Square Garden, the first indoor football games ever played. The field was 70 by 35 yards, (Manley Field House's field is bigger). They beat something called "the New York Team", (which was from Philadelphia: it consisted of baseball players from the Phillies and Athletics trying to stay in shape during the off-season: they called themselves that to draw more fans in the Big Apple), 5-0, (a touchdown was worth 5 points then). Syracuse could have made it to 6 points but Pop Warner, who was playing for Syracuse, along with his brother and a couple of Carlisle Indians, missed an extra point. Syracuse then beat the Knickerbockers 36-0 and then a team from New Jersey, the Orange Athletic Club, by the same score.

O'Neill and the coaches who followed him benefited from the opening in 1907 of John D. Archbold's gift to SU, a huge, (by 1907 standards), concrete and steel football stadium named after the benefactor. O'Neill guided Syracuse to a 52-19-6 record, including the 9-1-2 team of 1915 that was invited to the second Rose Bowl, (the first having been held after the 1901 season, to be replaced for 14 years by chariots races), but had to turn it down for financial reasons. And he coached the team that in 1919, crushed Warner's Pittsburgh team that had won 34 straight games against collegiate teams, 24-3. He then became the coach at Columbia, which was much closer to his law offices, from 1920-22, finishing with an 81-42-8 record. He was elected to the College Football Hall of Fame in 1951, primarily for his record at Syracuse.

1907 Frank "Buck" O'Neill Coach # 10

The 1907 Syracuse Orangemen football team competed in their nineteenth season of intercollegiate football. They were led by Frank "Buck" O'Neill in his second of two seasons (on his first tour – O'Neill would be back) as head coach of the Orangemen. Ford Park was the captain on the 1907 Syracuse football team. The team finished with a season record of 6-3-0.

On Sept 25 Syracuse hosted Hobart in its brand new Archbold Stadium before 2000 fans. The Orangemen won their season home opener in their state of the art stadium with a nice shutout W (28–0). Sept 28. See Chapter 3 for information about Archbold Stadium.

On Sept 28, at Archbold Stadium, Syracuse defeated Rochester W (40–6). On Oct 5, SU made their annual trek to Yale Field In New Haven, CT and were shut out by Yale L (0–11). Still licking their wounds from the close Yale defeat, on Oct 12 vs. Carlisle in

Buffalo, NY, the Orangemen suffered another loss. L (6–14). On Oct 19 at Archbold Stadium on the Syracuse campus in Syracuse NY, SU defeated Williams W 9–0 before 6,000 fans.

SYRACUSE (N. Y.) UNIVERSITY.

On Oct 26 Hamilton played SU at Archbold Stadium and were shut out by the Orangemen W (22–0). On Nov 2, Syracuse played Bucknell for the first time. This game was at Archbold Stadium and the Orange grabbed the victory W (20–6). On Nov 16 Lafayette played Syracuse to a tie at Archbold Stadium T 4–4. In the season finale, Army was up for the task after losing the prior year to the Orange. On Nov 23, the Cadets defeated the Orangemen at The Plain in West Point, NY L (4–23). The Orangemen did not lose a game at Archbold Stadium in 1907, their first year playing in this great facility.

Famous Coaches (From the Past) by SWC75.

During this first O'Neill, interregnum the team was coached, successively, by a pair of brothers who would wind up in the Hall of Fame with O'Neill. The 1908 coach [described above] was Howard Jones, who had just finished playing for Yale for three years during which the Elis never lost a game. He directed Syracuse to a 6-3-1 record. This was the year Pop Warner fooled the Orange by stitching a football-shaped decoration on his player's jerseys and bamboozled the Syracuse players in a 0-12 Carlisle win. They the Indians played Harvard. Coach Percy Haughton had the footballs painted Crimson and Harvard won 17-0. But Jones scored a huge victory over Michigan, 28-4, the team rushing for 400 yards to 75 for the Wolverines.

Howard Jones moved onto Ohio State the next year, then went into private business. He coached Yale for a year in 1913. His great fame began when he became the coach at Iowa (1916-23), Duke for one year, (1924), and Southern California (1925-40). He turned the latter school into the national power they have been ever since. His overall record was 194-65-21. Jones was elected to the Hall of Fame in 1951, (both he and O'Neill were part of the first class, which had 54 inductees).

Howard then turned the job over to his brother, Thomas, Albert Dwight, "TAD" Jones. He had been a star quarterback for Yale in 1906-07. This was his head coaching debut, but he didn't have as much success as his brother. His 1909 team had a losing record for the first time since 1909. His 1910 team got back above the line at 5-4-1 but was a very dull team that outscored ten opponents by a combined 53-42. He didn't coach another team until he got the Yale job in 1916. With a break for the war, he coached them until 1927, going 69-24-6 overall and getting elected to the Hall in 1958.

1908 Howard Jones Coach # 11

The 1908 Syracuse Orangemen football team competed in their twentieth season of intercollegiate football. They were led by Howard Jones in his first and only season as head coach of the Orangemen. Marquis Horr was the captain on the 1908 Syracuse football team. The team finished with a season record of 6-3-1.

<< Coach Howard Jones

This year's home opener was on Sep 23 with a nice blowout over Hobart W (51-0) The Syracuse offense was clicking, and the defense was strong again on Sep 26 at Archbold Stadium as SU defeated Hamilton W (18-0). The win streak would end on Oct 3 at Yale in New Haven CT with a close match against the Bulldogs L (0-5). The Carlisle Indians, always tough beat SU the following week on Oct 10 L (0-12) making the Syracuse record 2-2 for the season.

On Oct 17 at Archbold, SU defeated Rochester W (23-12). After a trip to the Ivy League to play Princeton, SU returned home with a hard-fought scoreless tie T (0-0). On Oct 31, SU shut out Williams W (23-0) at Archbold. Colgate then gave the Orangemen their final loss of the season on Oct 31, in a close match L (0-6) On Nov 14, Syracuse shut out Tufts at Archbold W 28 0. For the first time, Syracuse played Michigan. The game was at Archbold and the Orangemen got the best of a very experienced Michigan team W (28-4).

All American Maurice Horr 1908

Marquis Horr was a great tackle for the team and he was the first All American in 1908 for the Orangemen.

Horr was a native of Central Square, New York. He attended Syracuse University from 1905-1908 where he played football, ran track, and graduated with a law degree. As a tackle, Horr anchored a young offensive line on a team that opened the newly built Archbold Stadium with a win against Hobart in 1907. One year later, Horr was honored as a team captain.

<< Maurice Horr He continued his football career as a line coach for Purdue University, Northwestern University, and Syracuse University. A national champion in the shot put, hammer, and discus throws, Horr's success allowed him to become a member of the 1908 U.S. Olympic team. He worked as an attorney for American Liability Insurance until he retired in 1946.

1909 Tad Jones Coach # 12

The 1909 Syracuse Orangemen football team competed in their twenty-first season of intercollegiate football. They were led by Tad Jones in his first of two seasons as head coach of the Orangemen. Herbert Barry was the captain on the 1909 Syracuse football team. The team finished with a season record of 4-5-1.

<<< Coach Tad Jones

Being a Pennsylvanian, I was surprised as I read some of the archives about this season and others. SU had played the very tough Carlisle Indians but some of the accounts such as Wikipedia have the Carlisle Indians playing out of Buffalo, NY. So, I looked for a Carlisle College in Buffalo and there is none.

The Carlisle Indians football team is the one and only and they represented the Carlisle Indian Industrial School in intercollegiate football competition. They were great and well feared as being tough and willing to do what it took to win a game. Their campus was in Carlisle Pennsylvania, not Buffalo NY as some would suggest.

Their program was active from 1893 until 1917, when it was discontinued. During the program's 25 years, the Indians compiled a tough-to-beat 167–88–13 record and 0.647 winning percentage, which makes this group of great men over 25 years to be the most successful defunct major college football program. Teams had to play their best to beat this crew.

At the turn of the 20th century, the college leading the football gridiron in the US was not Harvard or Yale – it was a little-known powerhouse called the Carlisle Indian Industrial School. During the early 20th century, Carlisle was a national football powerhouse. Hey, they were good enough that they got to play national powerhouse Syracuse. They regularly competed against other major programs such as the Ivy League schools. Several notable players and coaches were associated with the team, including Pop Warner and Jim Thorpe, a native American, and an All-American hero in many sports as well as the Olympics. To beat Carlisle was to beat a great team.

The season home opener on Sept 25 featured Syracuse v Hamilton at Archbold Stadium. SU grabbed a nice shutout win W (20–0). Many of the NY teams with smaller stadiums permitted SU to have home games in the larger and nicer Archbold to help more fans see the games. Yale, on the other hand would not play Syracuse unless it was a Yale home game. And, so, again on Oct 2, the Orangemen went off to the Yale Field in New Haven, CT and came back with a loss L (0–15). At Archbold on Oct 9, SU defeated Rochester W (17-0)

Still not ready to beat the Carlisle Indians, especially away, Syracuse licked its wounds coming back home with a loss after a close-in brawl on Oct 16 losing L (11-14). On Oct 23 at Archbold, SU got the best of Niagara W 9–0. On Oct 30, after beating Michigan in the first encounter at Archbold, the Orangemen had to go to Ferry Field, not yet the Big House, but in Detroit Michigan to play the Wolverines. It was a make-up day for Michigan as they had promised themselves never to take Syracuse lightly again. SU lost big that day in a blowout L (0-43).

On Nov 6, at Archbold, SU lost to Bucknell in a close match, L (0-5). For want of an extra point on a five-point TD, on Nov 13, at Archbold, SU lost to Colgate L (5-6). On a losing streak with a new coach, the Orangemen kept the losing streak going against another new team on Nov 20, v Illinois at Archbold Stadium in Syracuse, L (8–17). The best SU could do to wrap up what had become a poor season was to squeak out a tie Fordham in New York, NY T (5-5)

1910 Tad Jones Coach # 12

The 1910 Syracuse Orangemen football team competed in their twenty-second season of intercollegiate football. They were led by Tad Jones in his second of two seasons as head coach of the Orangemen. Harry Hartman was the captain on the 1910 Syracuse football team. The team finished with a season record of 5-4-1.

On Sept 25 in the home opener SU could not take down St. Bonaventure at Archbold Stadium in Syracuse NY and were forced to settle for a scoreless tie T (0–0). On Oct 1, Syracuse made the annual trek to Yale in New Haven CT and were barely defeated L (6–12). On Oct 8 at Archbold, SU defeated Rochester by a slim margin W (6–0). Then, on Oct 15, the powerful Carlisle Indians were ready to take home a big win at Archbold Stadium on the campus in Syracuse, NY, but they were surprised and did not score against the Orangemen who won W 14–0 before 10,000 fans.

On the road again on Oct 19 at Illinois Field in Champaign, IL, the Orangemen endured a close loss to the Fighting Illini, L (0–3). On Oct 22 SU engaged Hobart at their complex in Geneva, NY, and walked away with a close win W (12-5). Knowing Michigan would be tough and that they were coming to town on Oct 29, Syracuse was ready but that was not enough at Archbold Stadium on campus in Syracuse, NY, as SU could not score and lost the game against Michigan L 0–11 before a record crowd of 11,000.

On Nov 5 Vermont played Syracuse at Archbold Stadium but were beaten back in a close game W (3–0). In a NY rival game on Nov 12, a determined Colgate crew came to Archbold Stadium ready to win. They played tough and took home the win L (6–11). In the season finale, on Nov 24, Coach Jones took a chance and went outside the state again to the country's midsection and they played against Saint Louis at St. Louis, MO, and walked away with a very close win after a hard-fought game, W (6–0).

Famous Coaches (From the Past) by SWC75.

The Jones Brothers were replaced by Deforest Cummings. The highlight of his two- year run, (9-8-2) was a 12-11 win over Carlisle's greatest team, coached by Warner and with Jim Thorpe at his peak in 1911. Those two teams were the only ones ever coached by Cummings. O'Neill came back for the next three years after the two years of Cummings.

1911 Charles Deforest Cummings # 13

The 1911 Syracuse Orangemen football team competed in their twenty-third season of intercollegiate football. They were led by C. Def Cummings in his first of two seasons as head coach of the Orangemen. Preston Fogg was the captain on the 1911 Syracuse football team. The team finished with a season record of 5-3-2.

On Sept 30, the Archbold Stadium home opener in Syracuse, NY, the Orangemen defeated Hobart W 6–0. Off to Yale for an annual defeat, which in time would eventually be a victory, on Oct 7 at Yale Field in New Haven, CT, SU lost again by a little bit. L 0–12. It was a loss nonetheless and no matter how good Yale was at the time it was very annoying to Syracuse fans. On Oct 14, away at Rochester in Rochester, NY, the Orangemen hung on to win W (6–5). Then, on
Oct 21   Lafayette, another great academic and athletic school came to Archbold Stadium in Syracuse, NY, and defeated the Orange L (0–10) before. The days of the stands filling up at Archbold were in front of the University at this time.

<< Coach Cummings
On Oct 28, Springfield (from MA) came to Archbold Stadium and beat the Orangemen by a slight margin – the margin of victory L (5–9). On Nov 4 at Michigan's Ferry Field in Ann Arbor, Michigan, SU tied the home team T (6–6) in a tough contest. On Nov 11, SU invited Vermont to play at Archbold Stadium and prevailed against the out-of-staters, W 16–0. The Carlisle Indians, tough on their weakest days came back on Nov 5 to Archbold Stadium in Syracuse, NY and lost by one point to Syracuse W (12–11) In a first time ever match, on Nov 25, SU took on Ohio State in Ohio Field, Columbus, OH and came home with the victory, W 6–0. In the season finale, in the second game ever against St. Louis played on Nov 30 at Saint Louis, St. Louis, MO, the teams squared off for a season ending tie T (6–6)

1912 Charles Deforest Cummings # 13

The 1912 Syracuse Orangemen football team competed in their twenty-fourth season of intercollegiate football. They were led by C. Def Cummings in his second of two seasons as head coach of the Orangemen. Rudolph Propst was the captain on the 1912 Syracuse football team. Team finished with a losing season record of 4-5-0.

In the SU home opener on Sept 28 at Archbold Stadium in Syracuse, NY, the Orangemen defeated Hobart W (12–0). After traveling to Yale, the following week, Oct 5, in a game played at Yale Field in New Haven, CT, Syracuse took a shutout loss L (0–21). In these early years tough Yale Teams rarely gave up any points to the Orangemen. On Oct 12 at Archbold, the Carlisle Indians beat the Orange in a shutout L (0–33). The worst game of the year was the following week on Oct 19 at Princeton's University Field in NJ as the Orange were walloped L (0-62). On Oct 26, SU got its moxie back and defeated Michigan at Archbold Stadium W (18-7)

On Nov 2 at Archbold, Syracuse defeated Rochester W (28–0). Then, on Nov 9 at Lafayette's March Field in Easton, PA, the Orange beat the Tigers W (30–7). On Nov 16, at home, Syracuse lost to Colgate in a close match L (0-7). On Nov 23, Syracuse lost to Army at The Plain in West Point, NY L 7–23. The army team had quite a few notables on the squad such as to-be General Dwight D. Eisenhower, and to-be General Dwight D. Eisenhower. I thought you'd like the picture below:

Part of the 1912 West Point football team.
Cadet Eisenhower 3rd from left; Cadet Omar Bradley 2nd from right

1913 Frank "Buck" O'Neill Coach # 10

The 1913 Syracuse Orangemen football team competed in their twenty-fifth season of intercollegiate football. They were led again by Frank "Buck" O'Neill in the first of three years in his second tour of duty as head coach of the Orangemen. O'Neill was one of the best Army coaches. Martin Hilfinger was the captain on the 19132 Syracuse football team. The team finished with a winning season record of 6-4-0.

In the home opener on Sept 27 at Archbold Stadium on the campus of Syracuse University in Syracuse, NY, the Orangemen toppled Hobart W (41–0). On Oct 4 Hamilton was defeated by SU at Archbold Stadium W (18–0). On Oct 11, SU p traveled to Rochester and won in a close shutout W (6-0). The next week, Oct 18, SU lost to Princeton at Princeton's University Field in Princeton, NJ L (0–13).

On Oct 25, Western Reserve rolled into Archbold Stadium in Syracuse, NY and were shut out by Syracuse W 36–0. On Nov 1, the Orangemen made the trip to Ferry Field in Ann Arbor, MI and were soundly defeated by the Wolverines L 7–43. The following week, Nov 8 NYU was blown out of Archbold Stadium W (48–0). Then Colgate beat the Orangemen on Nov 15 at home   L (13–35). On Nov 22, the tough Carlisle Indians beat the Orange at Archbold L (27–35) before 5,000 fans. SU finished the season with a big win on Nov 27 at St. Louis in St. Louis, MO W 75–0, before 10,000 fans.

1914 Frank "Buck" O'Neill Coach # 10

The 1914 Syracuse Orangemen football team competed in their twenty-sixth season of intercollegiate football. They were led again by Frank "Buck" O'Neill in the second of three years in his second tour of duty as head coach of the Orangemen. 'Neill was one of the best Army coaches. James Schufelt was the captain on the 1914 Syracuse football team. The team finished with another winning season record of 5-3-2.

The season home opener was On Sept 26 featuring Hobart at Stadium on the campus of Syracuse University in Syracuse, NY. The Orangemen dominated the game W (37–0). Next game was on Oct 3 when Hamilton was defeated by SU at Archbold in a blowout W (81–0). After two wins, SU suffered its first defeat on Oct 10, at the hands of Princeton in a game played at University Field, Princeton, NJ -- L (7–12). On Oct 17, SU grabbed win # 3 from Rochester at Archbold Stadium W (19–0).

<<< **Buck O'Neill** later in life. After being beaten badly in 2013, Buck O'Neill's Orangemen were ready on Oct 24 to gain some respect back against Michigan. In this game, the Orangemen made amends at home in Archbold Stadium with a nice win W (W 20–6) before 10,000 fans. O'Neill had the Orangemen on a roll and on Oct 31, they won again v the Carlisle Indians from Carlisle PA. W (24–3).

In the first game ever against Rutgers, aka the State University of New Jersey, on Nov 7, Syracuse played the Scarlet Knights at home to a tie T (14–14) On Nov 14, SU pitched another tie against Colgate at home but this one was scoreless T (0-0) before a packed house of 17,000 fans. On Nov 21, back to the Ivy League at Dartmouth in Hanover, NH, the Orangemen were shut out L (0–40). Working against Jesse Harper, ND Head Football Coach and Knute Rockne, Assistant, Buck O'Neill's team hung in and made it a real game on Nov 26 at Notre Dame's Cartier Field in South Bend, IN L (0–20).

1915 Frank "Buck" O'Neill Coach # 10

The 1915 Syracuse Orangemen football team competed in their twenty-seventh season of intercollegiate football. They were led again by Frank "Buck" O'Neill in his third second of three years in his second tour of duty as head coach of the Orangemen. If you are counting at home folks, at this point O'Neill had coached five years, and this was the most of any coach to that date. This would be a great season for the Orangemen. 'Neill was one of the best Army coaches. The team finished with another winning season record of 9-1-2

For the first year ever, Syracuse was in the running for the national championship with a 9-1-2 record. Cornell, however finished 9-0, and in a season full of contenders, they were the consensus choice for the 1915 mythical national championship and would have run away with #1 had there been an AP poll that season.

The #2 slot was either Pittsburgh or Nebraska or Harvard

In 1915, Harvard would easily have finished 2nd in an AP poll, and that works fine. Their loss came to #1 Cornell, their only loss since 1911. Regarding 8-0 Pittsburgh vs. 8-0 Nebraska is a more difficult prospect. Speculation is that Pitt would have edged Nebraska out for #3, but it isn't clear, and Nebraska had the bigger win, over 7-1 Notre Dame (#9), while Pitt's best came over 8-1-1 Washington & Jefferson, a team that was tied by unrated 5-2-1 West Virginia. And, so they would come in this sequence: Harvard #2, Nebraska #3, and Pittsburgh #4.

#5 slot among Minnesota, Illinois, and Washington State

Coming in next in an AP poll would have been 6-0-1 Minnesota, followed by 5-0-2 Illinois, followed by, (speculation) 7-0 Washington State. Minnesota's wins were all dominating. 5-0-2 Illinois was a defending MNC, and they were also dominating in their wins. 7-0 Washington State was dominating as well, winning all their games by more than a touchdown. The verdict was Minnesota #5, Illinois #6, and Washington State #7.

Princeton, Notre Dame, Syracuse, and Dartmouth

Now you know why in this book, we added this little piece of information about the other national contenders. SU was a contender this year for the first time. Next up for a 1915 AP poll would have been 6-2 Princeton, and though 7-1 Notre Dame had a better relevant record. Princeton will do for #8. They lost 10-6 to #2 Harvard, a game effort, but they also took a loss at 4-5 Yale in their finale, a poor effort, albeit in a rivalry game. Notre Dame didn't take an upset loss, but they also didn't defeat a single top 25 team.

With its record of 9-1-2, Syracuse also played a tougher schedule than 7-1 Notre Dame, but their wins were not as impressive as Princeton's, so their case for being rated higher than Notre Dame is weaker. Syracuse took a pair of upset ties, to 7-1-1 Dartmouth and at 2-2-2 Montana. The Dartmouth tie was damaging for rankings, because like Notre Dame, Dartmouth did not beat a single top 25 team. But unlike Notre Dame, who lost to #3 Nebraska by just 1 point on the road, Dartmouth's loss was ugly, 30-7 at #8 Princeton.

So, 7-1 Notre Dame should be rated higher than 7-1-1 Dartmouth, and therefore Syracuse tying Dartmouth is a problem for them. Still, Syracuse did pile up a nice number of strong wins: 38-0 over 5-1 Colgate (#13), 28-0 at 5-3 Oregon State (#25), 35-0 at 7-1 Occidental, 6-0 at 5-4-1 Brown, and 14-7 at 4-3-1 Michigan. However, they also edged a very bad 2-6-3 Bucknell team 6-0 at home, and those scores against Brown and Michigan were also not impressive. And while Colgate will be rated highly in this top 25, that rating comes sheerly from reputation, as they, like Notre Dame, did not beat a single top 25 team this season.

It's a close call, to be sure, but the pundits went with 7-1 Notre Dame and their lack of an upset loss or tie over 9-1-2 Syracuse and their tougher schedule. And, so the result is Princeton #8, Notre Dame #9, Syracuse #10, and Dartmouth #11.

All American Harold "Babe" White 1915

Harold M. "Babe" White was an All-American football player for Syracuse University. He played at the guard position for Syracuse from 1913-1916. A native of New York, White attended DeWitt Clinton High School. At 6 feet, 6 inches in height and 273 pounds, White was the largest American football player of his time. He was selected as a first-team All-American in 1915. He was also selected as the captain of the 1916 Syracuse football team.

"Babe" White 1915

All American Christopher Peter Schlachter 1915

Christopher Peter Schlachter was an All-American football player for Syracuse. A native of Brooklyn, Schlachter played at the guard position for the Syracuse Orange football team from 1915 to 1916.

He was selected by Walter Camp as a first-team guard on the 1915 College Football All-America Team. In October 1916, he sustained a broken collar bone and missed the remainder of the 1916 season but was still called out for the 1916 All-American Team.

In May 1918, Schlachter was inducted into the United States Navy and assigned to the United States Naval Academy, attaining the rank of lieutenant in 1919. In 1917, while playing for the Newport Naval Reserve team, he was selected for the All Service teams selected by Paul Purman and The New York Times. The Service Academies were special places where former college All-Amaricans could play football legally again. Navy and Army especially enjoyed winning games against teams such as SU when sometimes former SU players were among the opposition.

The games of the 1915 Season

On Sept 25, in a rare occurrence, Syracuse played its season home opener against a group of Syracuse Alumni that had formed a "pick-up" team. The current Syracuse varsity beat the old-timers W (43-0) at Archbold Stadium on campus in Syracuse NY.

On Oct 2, 1915 at Archbold. SU defeated Bucknell W (6-0). The next week at Princeton, Syracuse lost a squeaker L (0-3). O'Neill's squad came right back the next week at home and shellacked Rochester W (82-0). On Oct 23, at Brown Syracuse won in a tight match W (6-0). In a big game on Oct 30, Syracuse traveled to Ann Arbor Michigan and beat the wolverines in a tight match W (14-7).

On Nov6, at home against Mt. Union, Syracuse pitched a big blowout-shutout W (73-0). They grabbed another shutout the following week from Colgate on Nov 13 at Archbold Stadium W (38-0). On Nov 20, the Orangemen tied Dartmouth T (0-0) and then on Thanksgiving they tied Montana at Montana T (6-6). On Wed, Dec 1, Buck's boys shut-out Oregon State W (28-0) and on a Monday, Dec 6 at Occidental, they brought home a nice shutout W (35-0). This great season 9-1-2 was SU's best ever at the time. Just a field goal prevented the Orangemen from being undefeated.

Chapter 9 Syracuse Football – From 1916 to 1929

Bringing excellence to an already great record

Year	Coach	Record	Conf
1916	William Hollenback	5-4-0	Ind
1917	Frank "Buck" O'Neill	8-1-1	Ind
1918	Frank "Buck" O'Neill	5-1-1	Ind
1919	Frank "Buck" O'Neill	8-3-3	Ind
1920	Chick Meehan	6-2-1	Ind
1921	Chick Meehan	7-2-0	Ind
1922	Chick Meehan	6-1-2	Ind
1923	Chick Meehan	8-1-0	Ind
1924	Chick Meehan	8-2-1	Ind
1925	Pete Reynolds	8-1-1	Ind
1926	Pete Reynolds	7-2-1	Ind
1927	Lew Andreas	5-3-2	Ind
1928	Lew Andreas	4-4-1	Ind
1929	Lew Andreas	6-3-0	Ind

There was not one losing season from 1916 to 1929

1923 SU Football Team – great picture with no attributions

Famous Coaches (From the Past) by SWC75.

Bill Hollenbeck, a former Penn all-American who had coached at Missouri and Penn State, going unbeaten in Happy Valley in 1911-12. He was beatable in Syracuse, going 5-4 before retiring from coaching, preferring business and politics. He's in the Hall of Fame but as a player, not a coach. Perhaps if he'd kept at it...

1916 William Hollenback Coach # 14

The 1916 Syracuse Orangemen football team competed in their twenty-eighth season of intercollegiate football. They were led by William Hollenback in his first and only year as head coach of the Orangemen. Harold M. "Babe" White was the team captain. The team finished with another winning season record of 5-4

<<< **William Hollenback**, picture from 1910

All games but two were played at Archbold Stadium on the SU campus in Syracuse NY. Michigan and Tufts were played on the road.

On Sept 30 in the season home opener, the Syracuse Alumni decided to try the varsity one more time but were defeated by the current Orangemen in a blow-out W (57-0). On Oct 7, SU defeated Ohio in a blowout W (73-0). On Oct 14, in another blowout, SU defeated Franklin & Marshall W (60-0). The first loss came against Pit in a shutout L (0-30). After traveling to Ann Arbor on Oct 21, the Orangemen went home disappointed with a one-point loss to the Michigan Wolverines L 13-14). On the road again on Nov 4 in Springfield Mass, SU lost a tough match to Dartmouth L (10-15),

On Nov 11, SU shut out Susquehanna U from Selinsgrove PA W (42-0). The following week on Nov 18, the Orangemen were shut out L (0-15) by Colgate. In the season finale, on Nov 25 # Tufts, the Orangemen found enough steam to win in a close match W (20-13)

Famous Coaches (From the Past) by SWC75.

O'Neill returned for the third time, greatly assisted by Chick Meehan, his quarterback in 1917 and his assistant coach in 1918-19. When O'Neill took the Columbia job.

1917 Frank "Buck" O'Neill Coach # 10

The 1917 Syracuse Orangemen football team competed in their twenty-ninth season of intercollegiate football. They were led by Frank "Buck" O'Neill in his third tour as head coach of the Syracuse Orangemen. This was his first year of three in his third tour, making this his sixth season overall. O'Neill was SU's best coach at this point and they kept bringing him back and he kept winning. The team finished with another great winning season record of 8-1-1.

< Coach Buck O'Neil Pic from 1901

William Hollenback was a fine and respected coach by all parties at the time, but he was no Buck O'Neill. The only thing Buck never brought in to Syracuse was an undefeated season. But, with time like all the great immortals, he would have done so.

As the War approached, more and more men were opting the service over college. The US was gearing up for a major conflict.

The Impact of World War I on College Football

At the beginning of the 1917 football season more Americans were concerned about World War I than were concerned about football or any sport. The country was at war and were in it in a big way. Until the draft, the volunteers for duty were less than 100,000 and as the country was preparing for war, this, plus the small army that existed, simply could not do.

The Selective Service Act or Selective Draft Act (Pub.L. 6512, 40 Stat. 76), was enacted on May 18, 1917. It authorized the United States federal government to raise a national army for service in

World War I through conscription. It was envisioned in December 1916 and brought to President Woodrow Wilson's attention shortly after the break in relations with Germany in February 1917.

The Act itself was drafted by then-Captain (later Brigadier General) Hugh S. Johnson after the United States entered World War I by declaring war on Germany. The Act was canceled with the end of the war on November 11, 1918. The Act was upheld as constitutional by the United States Supreme Court in 1918.

The draft was a major impetus for many to volunteer. By the end of World War, I, some two million men had volunteered for various branches of the armed services, and some 2.8 million had been drafted.

Essay: The impact of service teams on the 1917 and 1918 football seasons and the popularity of the game in the 1920's

There has been a lot of debate about whether (1) the football rule changes to make the game faster and less deadly that were made prior to 1912 or (2) the adoption of football as a training vehicle for the troops, was most responsible for football becoming so popular in the 1920's. In the most extensive analysis of the matter, the conclusion reached was that the armed service's engagement in football was the prime mover for the popularity of football and the acceptance of pro football in the 1920's.

WWI was blazing in 2017 but there was no military draft during the early part of the war. Nonetheless many who otherwise would have gone to college instead enlisted in the military, especially after the draft was called.

On April 6, 1917, the U.S. joined its allies--Britain, France, and Russia--to fight in World War I. Under the command of Major General John J. Pershing, more than 2 million U.S. soldiers fought on battlefields in France. Many Americans were not in favor of the

U.S. entering the war and wanted to remain neutral. However, the U.S. eventually did enter the war.

The "great War" ended at the 11th hour on the 11th day of the 11th month of 1918. At 5 a.m. that morning, Germany, short of manpower and supplies and faced with an imminent invasion, signed an armistice agreement with the Allies in a railroad car outside Compiégne, France. The First World War left nine million soldiers dead and 21 million wounded, with Germany, Russia, Austria-Hungary, France, and Great Britain each losing nearly a million or more lives. In addition, at least five million civilians died from disease, starvation, or exposure.

In the two calendar years tin which he US engaged in the war, (1917-1918) 53,402 died in combat whereas 63,114 died from other causes for a total of 116,516 American deaths. 204,002 Americans were wounded in the conflict.

What made football popular: The US Service or better Football Rules

Below, I have cobbled together pieces of fact about the state of football during the period from 1918 through 2018 and into the 1920's. Rather than tell the story in a later chapter, since the war began for the US in 1917, we will present this essay below. It is a bit light in its theme as it deals with issues of relative unimportance compared with WW I. However, it is very interesting as it sets the stage for Syracuse Football and all other football programs of the day and those to come as it tries to determine why football became so popular when at the time baseball was the national past-time.

A major reference for this short essay come from the Journal of Sport History, Vol. 16, No. 3 (Winter, 1989) *The Service Football Program of World War I: Its Impact on the Popularity of the Game* by James Mennell.

The essence of the argument in Mennell's analysis is that by 1912, only five years before a formal service football program began in both the Navy and the Army, all the rule changes had been made which transformed football into basically the game we know today. Consequently, the evidence to show that service football popularized the game had to be clearly delineated from other evidence proving that the rule changes popularized the game.

The evidence shows that service football was a greater popularizer of football than were the many football rule changes. For example, although criticism of the brutality of the game dramatically declined after the 1912 rule changes, reports of attendance do not show a dramatic rise in the period 1912-1918 with the exception of Yale which had built a new huge stadium in 1914.

Syracuse's 1907 Archbold Stadium did not bring forth a huge increase in fans but for a few games. Though attendance reports are scarce, those that do exist continue to show comparatively low attendance figures for college games during World War I, especially for games not involving service teams.

For example, a crowd of 25,000 watched Harvard play a service team in October 1917. By contrast Penn drew only 18,000 for its last game of the season when a victory over powerful Michigan would have enabled Penn to claim the "national championship."10 One may gain some perspective on these figures by comparing them to the 110,802 English soccer fans who attended the cup final in 1906, only eighteen years after the founding of the professional Football League.

Additionally, only two schools, Penn and Brown, were reportedly considering new stadiums between 1914 and 1918. Nor did any college football program make profits large enough to attract the attention of the New York Times during those same years (although it must be admitted that no sport did well during the war). After the war the situation seemed to change dramatically. The New York Times reported several schools making comparatively big profits since the war. This suggests that attendance did not rise quickly and dramatically after the rule changes, while in the period 1919-1921 there was a dramatic expansion of college football programs and attendance at games.

Thirteen colleges took up varsity football in the first three years after the war. This was a noteworthy increase over the period 1912-1918 just after the rule changes when only three schools adopted varsity football. And while only three new stadiums were considered in the six years immediately after the rule changes, fourteen were considered in the three-year period right after the war. Thus, the sudden dramatic expansion of college football programs immediately after the war seems to suggest that the service football program had significantly stimulated interest in collegiate football.

Walter Camp, *the Father of American Football,* who was responsible for most of the rule changes that created what we know today as American Football, was hired as the Navy's sports coordinator during the 1917 season and beyond. Camp claimed that he and others had developed outside competition to help the game pf football. This is supported by a particular action he took during the 1917 season.

Military teams had begun to play "outside" games with colleges and other camps. But each service played only teams from the same service. Camp realized that service football competition could be taken one step further: the natural rivalry between soldiers and sailors might be used to create an attractive football game (similar to the Army-Navy game) between army camp teams and naval station teams. Camp's attempt to arrange such a game (in this case between the Newport Naval Station and the Maine Heavy Field Artillery) illustrated the perseverance military camp athletic directors around the country had to possess in scheduling games.

First, Walter Camp began this adventure on October 25,1917 by writing to obtain Raycroft's (Army's sports coordinator) approval for the Army team to play. Second, he selected the teams and arranged for the disposal of the game profits. Third, it was necessary to find a suitable football stadium with an open date (the Yale Bowl, built in 1914 had openings on November 3 and 10, 1917); Fourth and finally, he had to publicize the game within only days of its being played. Having reserved the Yale Bowl, Camp had the tickets printed and urged sportswriters to publicize the game, only to have a dispute between the team representatives break out over which charity was to receive the gate receipts.

When the military camp service teams began to compete successfully with established college football programs, service football made a major contribution to the game. Service teams demonstrated that all-star teams playing together over a full season could provide superb entertainment. This quality of play had not been expected when the initial season began. It was assumed that the collections of all-star players (college graduates who had already played four years of major college football) on the service teams would not become as smooth-working as college teams for a year or more, and few believed in mid-1917 that the war would last until the 1918 season.

Therefore, service football's entertainment value was expected to be limited largely to seeing many individual stars on the field at one time. This apparently had limited spectator appeal because at first crowds were small at service games. It was not long, however, before the service teams began to work well together. When that happened sportswriters began to see these teams as the best ever assembled. The public became so enthralled by the best service teams that the highest attendance figures began to be at games involving the military.

The most attendance in the 1917 season, for example, involved a service eleven against Harvard. Not only was service football winning new civilian fans for football, but it also had a significant impact on thousands of soldiers and sailors. They loved it. During the 1917 season some sportswriters noticed this impact which they felt fell into two categories: soldier participation in football play (and all other sports for that matter, but especially football), and participation in the activities surrounding the game, like cheering, singing and half-time activities. It was good for morale and it kept many in top shape.

As early in the season as October 27, 1917, the Philadelphia Inquirer described the football scene at Camp Dix, New Jersey. Plans had been made to mass the regimental bands into a camp marching band of 250 pieces to play at half-time during regimental games at Camp Dix. Thousands of visitors, "equal to the crowds which flock to intercollegiate games came to see these games.

As you can see by examining the schedule of games played the last few years, including 1917, Syracuse played a number of service teams during this time period. As the 1917 football season came to a close it was becoming evident that the war was not likely to end before the 1918 football season began. It was also evident that interest in service camp games had grown so much that service teams clearly rivaled collegiate teams in sharing the interest of sportswriters. Given this new situation it was unclear how football would be organized in 1918.

An unsigned syndicated article datelined Chicago suggested collegiate football in 1918 would be "an unimportant part of the game." Thankfully, that did not happen. The writer suggested that service football was so exciting that it would be "a professional attraction next season." Pro football did come. It is possible that service football provided the impetus to form a professional football league after the war based on the same entertaining foundation of service football: i.e., a team of all-stars who play together for the entire season.

The 1918 service football season no doubt continued to develop popular interest in football in the same way the 1917 season had: by involving even more draftees on military teams in organized play with all the glamor that attached to it.

Presumably family and friends supported the teams representing the draftees and the service volunteers. The relationship between the colleges and the service teams was not cordial in 1918 apparently because many of the service teams were so powerful they threatened to damage college reputations. This seems evident from the 1918 schedule of games. Six leading service teams (Camps Grant, Taylor and Dodge, Great Lakes, Cleveland Naval Station, and the U.S. Army Balloon School) were able to schedule only six of their total of twenty-seven games with colleges; and four of them were the first game of the season when the all-star type service teams would not yet be working well together.

Though 1917 was a great year for service football, there were a number of reasons why it was not as big in 1918. One reason was that the war was winding down and would be over during the 1918 season. Another big reason was that the Spanish influenza epidemic swept the country at the beginning of the football season. So many Americans died that public gatherings were sometimes cancelled to avoid contagion. People walked around in gauze masks to avoid breathing contaminated air. This did not lend itself to packed stadiums. Syracuse was only able to play six games this year and the season did not begin in earnest until late October 1918

Nevertheless, service football most certainly hastened the popularization and full acceptance of collegiate football quite significantly. It did so in three ways: first, service football opened up the number of participants in organized football, thus familiarizing them with a game most had not played in an organized manner before. Second, it gave nonplaying soldiers a chance to experience the music, color and spirit of the game, formerly limited largely to college people. Third, service football gave friends and neighbors of the draftees and service volunteers new exposure to the game when they supported service teams representing their soldiers, thus feeling a sense of belonging at the games.

The experts thus concluded that the exact impact on the popularity of football in the 1920s cannot be accurately measured in comparison to the rule changes. However, it does seem evident from the foregoing description that service football did have a significant impact on the growing popularity of collegiate football. This lasted for a long time afterwards and began again when the US began taking draftees and volunteers for World War II. Service teams were always very competitive even when they lacked talent. They were simply tough.
    --end of essay--

FYI, I wrote a book in 2017, titled, *The Birth of American Football*, which features much of the work of Walter Camp in separating soccer and rugby from his conception of American football. Ironically, this is one of my best-selling sports books; but it sells far better in Europe and the UK than in the US. Go figure.

All American Alfred Russell Cobb 1917

(June 7, 1892 – September 12, 1974) was an All-American for Syracuse University where he played for the Syracuse Orangemen football team and he also played professional football in the NFL.

In 1917 he was recognized as a consensus first-team All-American at the tackle position, having received first-team honors from International News Service (INS), News Enterprise Association (NEA), and Collier's Weekly (as selected by Walter Camp).

Cobb played in the early days of the NFL, when it was still known as the American Professional Football Association (APFA), including for the Akron Pros and the Cleveland Bulldogs. As a member of the 1920 Akron Pros, Cobb was a member of the very first NFL Championship team.

Over three APFA/NFL seasons, Cobb played in 21 games as a lineman, starting 16 of them.

On Sep 29, 1917, SU played the 47th Infantry Division Team, and like most service teams, they were no slouches. They held the Orangemen to zero and they scored zero in a scoreless tie T (0-0). Syracuse was yet to be affected by the war, but the SU team always gave the service the priority and so on Oct 6, 1917, they played the 47th Infantry again and this time, they beat them W (19-0). Nobody laid down for the service teams and in fact, they played tougher against them as it helped both teams. Everybody was concerned about the war and we all wanted America, if Wilson chose to engage the US, to be victorious. Football was good practice for military personnel and it was a lot of fun for the Orangemen.

Moving through their schedule, next was on Oct 13, v Rutgers at home. SU prevailed W (14-10). Then on Oct 20, at Pitt, SU took a big shutout defeat L (0-28) in a game played in Pittsburgh, PA. On Oct 27, SU beat Tufts in a blowout win W (58-0).

On Nov 3, the Orangemen traveled to Brown for a nice but very close win W (6-0). Then, on Nov 10, 1917, SU faced Bucknell in a one-way advantage match for Syracuse W (42-0). Colgate came to Archbold to win on Nov 17 but left with a solid defeat provided by its arch rival SU W (27-7).

Then back to Michigan to play the other team from that State on Nov 24. SU won the match v Michigan State W (21-7). Syracuse had been making a point through many coaches to play the best teams in the country and on Nov 29, another great team invited the Orangemen to play in Nebraska against Nebraska, which was and is one of the finest teams in the nation. SU came home this year with the tough win in 1917, W (10-9).

1918 Frank "Buck" O'Neill Coach # 10

The 1918 Syracuse Orangemen football team competed in their thirtieth season of intercollegiate football. They were led by Frank "Buck" O'Neill in his third tour as head coach of the Syracuse Orangemen. This was his second year of three in his third tour, making this his seventh season overall at the helm. O'Neill was SU's best coach at this point and they kept bringing him back and he kept winning. The team finished with another great winning season record of 5-1-1.

As the war was still in full bloom at the beginning of the season. And the Spanish Flu was in the air, Syracuse began its season late on Oct. 26

On Oct 26, 1918 on a Saturday, after sitting idle practicing and practicing from August through most of October, the Orangemen got their chance to play football again. This game was against the Navy Transport. SU got the W (13- 0). The teams were willing to play anytime, anywhere to get in some games. Some teams canceled their 1918 seasons because they were impacted in one way or another by the war.

On Nov 3, 1918, Syracuse played a Sunday game at Dartmouth, a very tough team and they came away with a nice win W (34-6) Buck O'Neill was a great coach and got all he could out of his players. Brown, another great Ivy League team that had dominated in the past were walloped on Sunday Nov 10 at home in Archbold W (53-0). The Orangemen were off and running. Maybe they were reading their own press clippings, because they failed on Nov 16 at Michigan in a game played at Ferry Field in Ann Arbor, MI against Michigan L (0-15).

The Orangemen were tough, but they were clearly beaten by a team that played tougher on Nov 16. That was the last failure of this season, but it was devastating in its impact on the championship.

On Thanksgiving Day, Nov 28, 1918, SU gave the hometown folks a reason to put more gravy on the turkey with a great shutout win against Columbia W (20-0). Doing anything to have a season, SU played two days later on Saturday Nov 30, 1918 against the best football team in New Jersey, Rutgers. It was a great shutout win W (21-0).

Despite only playing six games in a season when the National Champion played just five games and lost one. It was that one unexplainable loss to Michigan that kept SU out of contention for the mythical national championship. The Orangemen were mentioned but they were dismissed;

The best sports writeup by a pundit explaining the scenario goes like this:

"Michigan went 5-0 and defeated a powerful 5-1 Syracuse team 15-0, and they are the only other team I will be considering for the 1918 mythical national championship (MNC). The 1918 football season barely qualified as a football season at all, and there were plenty of teams that may well have been equal to or better than Pittsburgh or Michigan, but what sets Pitt and Michigan apart from the rest is that each defeated another MNC contending team."

There is a lot of irony in that the 1918 NCAA football season had no clear-cut champion. Syracuse was considered but dismissed. The

NCAA schedule was also affected by the war, which ended right before the season ended that there was little season left to be played. The official NCAA Division I Football Records Book list Michigan and Pittsburgh as national champions.

The highest profile game for all those good enough to even sniff the championship air as the pundits were making the determinations. was a highly pundit publicized War Charities benefit that was staged at Forbes Field in Pittsburgh in front of many of the nation's top sports writers, including Walter Camp.

The game pitted John Heisman's undefeated, unscored upon, and defending national champion Georgia Tech Yellow Jackets against "Pop" Warner's Pittsburgh Panthers who were sitting on a 30-game win streak. Yes, this is the same Heisman that the trophy is named after. In this game, Pitt defeated Heisman's vaunted Georgia Tech team 32-0.

The Spanish flu pandemic of 1918 saw the implementation of quarantines that eliminated much of that year's college football season. Pittsburgh dominated the Yellow Jackets in this game and would have had a clean title if it were not for this. Would you count this:

The Cleveland Naval Reserves were great and tough like most service teams continue to be. They literally came out of nowhere to ruin a clean National Championship for Pitt with the help, some say of some slanted officiating. The final game of the season for Pitt at Cleveland Naval Reserve resulted in "Pop" Warner's first loss at Pitt. It is one of the most controversial losses in school history. Could Warner have really lost this game or was some unknown chicanery involved. Warner was never known as a complainer.

Warner, along with some reporters covering the game, insisted Pitt was robbed by the officials who, claiming the official timekeeper's watch was broken, arbitrarily ended the first half before Pitt was able to score and then allowed the Reserves extra time in the fourth quarter to pull ahead 10–9 before calling an end to the game.

Now, that does not sound fair, does it? Judy Harlan, formerly of Georgia Tech, and Moon Ducote, formerly of Auburn starred for the Cleveland Naval Reserves. Ducote kicked the winning field goal. Warner declared him "the greatest football player I ever saw." Harlan stated: "I intercepted a pass and returned it to midfield in the fourth quarter. I felt I at least had evened up some of the losses we had at Tech."

History normally proves the complaining team wrong. Not this time with Pittsburgh. As Spalding's football guide put it at the time, they were "universally conceded to be the champion team of the country," and if there had been an AP poll in 1918, Pitt would have easily finished out as the highest ranked college team.

Though this is an SU book, Syracuse vied for the same National Championship as Pitt did in 1918. The Cleveland Military, a dirt tough team got credit for the win v Pop Warner's team, but Pitt got the national championship in the opinions of the most important authoritative people in the game at the time--even though Pitt had to share the title with Michigan.

To repeat, this highly controversial loss ended the Pitt season and snapped a 32-game Pitt winning streak, but the Panthers had outscored opponents 140–16 in that short season and thus were retroactively selected as the national champion by the Helms Athletic Foundation and Houlgate System and as a co-national champion with Michigan by the National Championship Foundation.

All American Joe Schwarzer 1918

<< **Joe Schwarzer** (dressed for basketball) was born in the Austro-Hungary Empire, and moved to the United States when he was four. He grew up to be an amazingly talented natural athlete who excelled at multiple sports while he attended Syracuse University. In basketball, he was an excellent ball handler and fine shooter. He was the designated free throw shooter at a time when one player shot all the free throws for a team. Schwarzer was a

Helms Foundation All-American in 1918. He was declared ineligible his senior season in basketball by the university due to a ruling by the Athletic Committee that he had used up his varsity eligibility by starting for three seasons already. Besides starring in basketball, he also lettered in football (four times) and in baseball (and was captain of all three teams). Schwarzer was an All-American End on the football team in 1918, a team that went 8-1-1. He graduated with a law degree from Syracuse in 1919. While practicing law in Syracuse, Schwarzer remained active in sports the rest of his life.

All American Louis Childs "Lou" Usher 1918

Louis Childs "Lou" Usher was born on June 27, 1897 and he passed away on January 1, 1927). He was a pro football player who graduated as an All-American from Syracuse U in 1918. He played professionally as tackle, guard, and center in the National Football League (NFL) for five seasons with the Rochester Jeffersons, Chicago Bears, Hammond Pros, Kenosha Maroons, and Milwaukee Badgers. Usher was killed on January 1, 1927 in an automobile accident near Calumet.

All American Joseph "Doc" Alexander 1918

<< Joseph Doc Alexander
Joseph A. "Doc" Alexander (April 1, 1898 – September 12, 1975) was an all-American football player for Syracuse and a Syracuse Hall of Famer. He played professionally in the National Football League (NFL) for the Rochester Jeffersons and the New York Giants. He was inducted to the College Football Hall of Fame in 1954.

1919 Frank "Buck" O'Neill Coach # 10

The 1919 Syracuse Orangemen football team competed in their thirty-first season of intercollegiate football. They were led by Frank "Buck" O'Neill in his third tour as head coach of the Syracuse Orangemen. This was his third year of three in his third tour, making this his eighth season overall at the helm. O'Neill was SU's best coach at this point and for the longest time SU kept bringing him back and he kept winning for them. This O'Neill team finished with another great winning season record of 8-3-0. After the war and the flu were gone from America. Football went back to normalcy.

In the 1919 season home opener at Archbold Stadium in the center of the campus of Syracuse University in Syracuse NY, all the flurry of the war years was over. From now on, for twenty more years, until WW II, it would be all football. And, so, on **Sep 27,** in this year, the Syracuse Alumni had been bolstered by returning great service players and they put up a fine battle against the varsity but lost anyway because they had no visible offense W (10-0).

On my Wedding anniversary (just 56 years later on Oct 4 to a woman I still love to pieces), Syracuse whooped Vermont at home at Archbold Stadium in a shutout W (27-0). A still very tough Army team invited Syracuse again to the Plain in West Point, NY and SU escaped with a less than TD loss but a loss nonetheless against a tough advantaged army Cadet Squad W (7-3). National Champion Pitt had lost enough of their big guns that the Orangemen knocked them off the national stage with a finishing blow on Oct 18, W (24-3) in a fine, hard-played game.

Working through the season, on Oct 25, SU unexplainably lost to Washington & Jefferson L (0-13). They then came back and beat an ivy leagues fine football power, on Nov 1, at Brown W (13-0) > the wins kept coming after the unexplainable loss on a Tuesday. Nov 4, 1919 v Rutgers W (14-0). Then there was Bucknell on Nov 8 with a close win W (9-0). Not so big on offense this year, on Nov 19, SU beat Colgate, W (13-7) From here, it was at Indiana on Nov 22 and a loss in a close one, L (6-12). On Nov 27, in a season ender, the game was decided by a field goal against Nebraska in a loss L (0-3)

Famous Coaches (From the Past) by SWC75.

After being his QB and then Assistant coach to Buck O'Neill, Chick Meehan took over as coach at Syracuse after this O'Neill stint, and coached some of our best teams in 1920-24. His Syracuse coaching record was 35-8-4, including a 1923 team that was ranked #1 in the country by James Howell:

http://www.jhowell.net/cf/cf1923.htm

I call that team our "other" national champion.

Meehan opted to move to New York City and coach NYU, briefly turning them into a national power, and Manhattan, (who had improved its facilities). He retired in 1937 with a laudable 115-44-14 record. He was famous for saying: 'We learn practically nothing from a victory. All our information comes from a defeat. A winner forgets most of his mistakes.'" But he was never elected to the Hall of Fame, probably because of his involvement in a scheme to sell steel on the black market during the Korean War.

1920 Chick Meehan Coach # 15

The 1920 Syracuse Orangemen football team competed in their thirty-second season of intercollegiate football. They were led by Chick Meehan in his first season of five as head coach of the Syracuse Orangemen. This SU team finished with another great winning season record of 6-2-1. Coach Meehan is recognized as one of the greatest coaches of the Orange though he put in just five seasons. He was a keeper but he moved on nonetheless after five years.

<< Coach Chick Meehan

On Sep 25, SU defeated Hobart in the home opener at Archbold Stadium, on the campus of Syracuse University in Syracuse, NY W (55-7) Then on Oct 2, at home again SU blew out Vermont, W, 49, 0. Oct 9, at home, Syracuse pitched another blowout against Johns Hopkins W (45- 0). The perfect season ended the following week at home on Oct 16, when the Orangemen played Pitt to a tie T (7- 7).

On Oct 23, at Dartmouth, Syracuse prevailed W (10-0). Then, on Oct 30, at Holy Cross, the Orangemen experienced their first defeat of the season against Holy Cross L (0- 3). The following Saturday, on Nov 6, SU beat Washington & Jefferson W (14-0). The second loss of the season came on Nov-13 against Maryland L (7- 10). Syracuse then wrapped up its season on Nov 20 with a nice win at Colgate W (14-0)

All American Bertrand L Gulick 1920

Bertrand L. Gulick, Jr. (March 20, 1898 – December 9, 1972) was an All American football player and businessman. He starred at the tackle position for the Syracuse Orange football team in 1920. He was selected by the United Press, International News Service, and The New York Times as a first-team player on their 1920 College Football All-America Team.

1921 Chick Meehan Coach # 15

The 1921 Syracuse Orangemen football team competed in their thirty-third season of intercollegiate football. They were led by Chick Meehan in his second season of five as head coach of the Syracuse

Orangemen. This SU team finished with another fine winning season record of 7-2-0.

Syracuse played its season home opener on Sept 24, 1921 at Archbold Stadium on the campus of Syracuse University and shut-out Hobart, W (35-0). On Oct 1, SU defeated Ohio, W (38-0) Then, on Oct 8 the Orangemen took on and defeated Maryland, W(42-0). On Oct 15, Syracuse beat (Ivy League) Brown, W, (28-0). As its program grew in strength with great coaches, no longer did SU have to take second fiddle to schools from the Ivy League.

SU played its first away game on Oct 22, against Pop Warner's always-strong Pitt team. Warner was in his seventh season at Pitt and he mentored his team on the way to defeating Syracuse L (0-35) in Pittsburgh, PA. Syracuse lost its second game of the season in a row on Oct 29 against Washington & Jefferson, L (10-17). On Nov 21, the Orangemen traveled to Montreal Canada to defeat McGill University W (13-0). Then, on Nov 12, SU defeated Colgate W (14-0) and they wrapped up the season with a win on Nov 19 at Dartmouth in New York, NY W (14-7).

1922 Chick Meehan Coach # 15

The 1922 Syracuse Orangemen football team competed in their thirty-fourth season of intercollegiate football. They were led by Chick Meehan in his third season of five as head coach of the Syracuse Orangemen. This SU team finished with another fine winning season record of 6-1-2.

Syracuse played its season home opener on Sept 23, 1922 at Archbold Stadium on the campus of Syracuse University and defeated Hobart, W (28-7.). All games were played at Archbold field this years except for Brown and Penn State. On Sept 30, Syracuse defeated Muhlenberg, W (47-0) Then on Oct 7, 1922, Syracuse shut out New York University (NYU) W (34-0). On Oct 14, the Orangemen traveled to Providence Rhode Island to fight Brown University to a scoreless tie T (0-0). For its first loss of the season, Syracuse were defeated by Pitt in a nail biter L (14-21).

Then, on Oct 28, the Orangemen played on a neutral field game against Penn State in the NYC Polo Grounds and fought the Nittany Lions to a scoreless tie T (0-0) It was their second scoreless tie of the season. Then, Syracuse played perennial great Nebraska at home and fought for a tough victory against the Cornhuskers W (9-6)

On Nov 11, McGill from Canada were shut out at home by the Orangemen W (32-0). In the season finale, Syracuse defeated Colgate at home W (14-7)

1923 Chick Meehan Coach # 15

The 1923 Syracuse Orangemen football team competed in their thirty-fourth season of intercollegiate football. They were led by Chick Meehan in his fourth season of five as head coach of the Syracuse Orangemen. This SU team finished with the best record of Meehan's tenure 8-1-0. Again, SU just missed having its first undefeated season.

All American Evander G. "Pete MacRae

Evander G. "Pete" MacRae (January 22, 1902 – March 1965) was an All American football player at Syracuse University on 1923 and he was a basketball star. He first gained note as a football player for the undefeated 1919 Allegheny High School football team from Pittsburgh, Pennsylvania. He then enrolled at Syracuse University where played both football and basketball. He played at the end position for the Syracuse Orangemen football team and was a consensus first-team All-American in 1923.

He also played for three years from 1921 to 1924 on the Syracuse Orangemen's basketball team. After graduating from Syracuse, he played professional basketball with the Syracuse All Stars.

Games of the 1923 season

Syracuse played its season home opener on Sept 29, 1923 at Archbold Stadium on the campus of Syracuse University and defeated Hobart in a shutout, W (33-0). On Oct 6, SU defeated William & Mary, in a blowout, W (61-3). In their first ever matchup against Alabama at home on Oct 13, Syracuse shut out the Crimson Tide W (23-0)). Then on Oct 20, at Yankee Stadium in the Bronx, NY, Syracuse survived Pop Warner's Panthers W (-03). Next up at home was Springfield and the Orangemen made quick work of them W (44-0).

On Nov 3, at home against Penn State, SU shut out the Nittany Lions in a close match W (10-0). Next at home on Nov 10, the Orangemen defeated Boston University, W (49-0). SO far, the Orangemen were undefeated this season until they faced their nemesis Colgate at home and were defeated by the Raiders L (7-16). This would be the only loss of Chick Meehan's otherwise perfect season with the Orangemen. The following week, Meehan's squad took on Nebraska at Nebraska and defeated the Cornhuskers by a close shutout W (7-0).

The loss to Colgate not only kept SU out of contention for the mythical national championship, it kept them from consideration for the top twenty-five, but it did wonders for Colgate which at least was mentioned in pundit write-ups as a potential top-25 team. "Colgate (6-2-1) beat 8-1 Syracuse, and would have been ranked in a top 25," even with two losses. However, the tie really was what hurt their 1923 record.

1924 Chick Meehan Coach # 15

The 1924 Syracuse Orangemen football team competed in their thirty-sixth season of intercollegiate football. They were led by Chick

Meehan in his fifth and last season of five as head coach of the Syracuse Orangemen. This SU team finished with a fine record of 8-2-1.

Syracuse played its season home opener on Sept 27, 1924 at Archbold Stadium on the campus of Syracuse University and defeated Hobart in a shutout, W (35-0). On Oct 4, my Wedding Anniversary, SU defeated Mercer at Archbold Stadium, W (26-0). On Oct 11, the Orangemen defeated William & Mary, at home, W (24-7). On Oct 18 at Archbold Stadium, SU beat Boston College, W (10-0). Then on Oct 25 at New Beaver Field in State College, PA, Syracuse defeated the Nittany Lions, W (10-6).

On Nov, at home SU tied Pitt T (7-7). This was followed by the first loss of the season at home against West Virginia Wesleyan, L (3-7). On Nov 15, the Orangemen beat Niagara, W (23-6). On Nov 22, SU defeated Colgate at home W (7-3). On Thanksgiving Day, Nov 27, at Baker Field in Manhattan, New York, NY, Syracuse beat Columbia in a nail-biter W (9-6). Then in the season finale, the Orangemen sustained their second loss of the season to USC, after traveling to the Los Angeles Memorial Coliseum in Los Angeles, CA, on December 6, 1924, L (0-16).

Famous Coaches (From the Past) by SWC75.

Pete Reynolds took over for one year and did a good job, going 8-1-1. As in 1923, the only loss was to Colgate. It was the beginning of the "HooDoo", when we were unable to beat Colgate for 13 consecutive years, including three where that was the only game we lost, (and that doesn't include '23). Reynolds was back again the next year, going 7-2-1. Vic Hanson was his big star. That was also the year of the "Massacre of the Plains", a big brawl after a game at West Point against Army that terminated the series until 1955. Reynolds was at the end of a long coaching career that began in 1909. His previous stops had been at Hobart, Hamilton and Bucknell. He was from Illinois and he also coached at Knox College in 1935-37. Most sources don't list that period but if that's true, Pete's overall coaching record was 77-58-14. He settled in Oneida, New York, where he died in 1951.

1925 Pete Reynolds Coach # 16

The 1925 Syracuse Orangemen football team competed in their thirty-seventh season of intercollegiate football. They were led by Pete Reynolds in his first of two as head coach of the Syracuse Orangemen. This SU team finished with a fine record of 8-1-1 – almost undefeated.

Syracuse played its season home opener on Sept 26, 1925 at Archbold Stadium on the campus of Syracuse University and defeated Hobart in a shutout, W (32-0). On Oct 3, SU handed Vermont a defat at Archbold Stadium W (26-0). The next week on Oct 10, Syracuse got win #3, a shutout, under their new coach against William & Mary W (33-0). Win number four was through the next door at Indiana on Oct 17 W (14-0). For SU win number five, Providence did not survive the big blowout shutout on Oct 24 at home W (48-0).

On October 31, for win #6, Syracuse fired all its bricks and put down the Nittany Lions of Penn State at home. W (7-0). Looking for seven, on Oct 31, the Orangemen tied Wesleyan W (7-0). Still without a loss, on Nov 14 nemesis Colgate came in and stopped all the rhymes and beat the Orange in a fair tough game, L (7-0). On Nov 21, SU shut out Niagara at home in Archbold Stadium, W (17 0). In the season finale on Turkey Day at Columbia in New York City, the Orangemen grabbed another victory W (16-5). it was a fine season for new coach Pete Reynolds. But those folks from Colgate, they just would not go away easily.

Chris Island wrote a piece about this one-time rivalry several years ago for the Daily orange and it captures the essence of how serious these two teams took each other.

> "All it took was a pact, and then nothing more than a verbal agreement, to try and stop the insanity of it all. It became too dangerous, too raucous. The store owners grew tired of having to board up the windows, and the Syracuse hotels no longer wanted to have to move furniture out of the lobby to avoid having it destroyed.

All this trouble for a football game between Syracuse and Colgate.

The memories will rush back into the minds of alumni who were once a part of the storied past Syracuse-Colgate rivalry weekends, when those weekends were at their peak. Alumni will remember the pep rallies, the poster contests, the — fairly — innocent kidnappings of students, the scalping, and maybe even the games, themselves.

'There were huge displays outside the fraternities and sororities,' said former Colgate player, coach and athletic director Fred Dunlap. 'They all always said, 'Beat Colgate,' and the game always had a sell-out crowd.'

These were just a part of the unending, all-encompassing events of those long-forgotten weekends that have lost their excitement and draw.

Over the first 20 games the Orangemen and Raiders met, Colgate went 13-5-2. From 1925 to 1937, the Raiders took 11 more games from the Orangemen.

But starting in 1951, Syracuse began to take control of the series. Eventually, it became too much for Colgate — and the towns of Hamilton, N.Y., and Syracuse — to bear, and the series was cancelled for 20 years. But before the cancellation, SU expected to defeat the Raiders every year."

In 1925, Colgate surely had destroyed SU's chance at a shot at the National Championship—again. Of course, the tie to Ohio Wesleyan did not help matters either. And so, in all the discussions by the pundits about mythical national champions and the runners up, Syracuse was mentioned as tying and losing to Colgate, but not as a contender for top honors. Dartmouth was crowned mythical national champion in the pundit post-voting.

When the mythical dust settled, writers hailed Dartmouth as the national champions. Grantland Rice: "In the midst of all the noise and excitement, football's main banner for the waning year goes to the peace and far-away restfulness of Dartmouth, the college on the hill."

Dartmouth was invited to the Rose Bowl to play 10-0-1 Washington, but they were already widely considered the national champions, and the players didn't want to give up their Christmas holidays, so they voted to reject the offer. That was critical for Alabama, who would not have emerged decades later as the consensus national champion among retroactive selectors without that game. Only in college football could a championship be given, and a championship be taken away. One thing for sure, Colgate had made sure that the Orangemen were not in consideration. Grrrrrrr!!!

1926 Pete Reynolds Coach # 16

The 1926 Syracuse Orangemen football team competed in their thirty-eighth season of intercollegiate football. They were led by Pete Reynolds in his second of two as head coach of the Syracuse Orangemen. This SU team finished with a fine record of 7-2-1.

Syracuse played its season home opener on Sept 25, 1926 at Archbold Stadium on the campus of Syracuse University and defeated Hobart in a shutout, W (18-0). On Oct 2, SU handed Vermont a blowout defeat at Archbold Stadium W (64-0). The next week on Oct 10, Syracuse got win #3, a shutout, against William & Mary W (35-0). With three wins under their belt, the Orangemen looked forward to tangling with a tough Amery team, but the Cadets prevailed and beat Syracuse in a tough match L (21-27). The Orangemen traveled to New Beaver Field in State College to face the Nittany Lions of Penn State and they carried home all the marbles in a nice game W (10-0).

On Oct 30, SU beat Johns Hopkins at home W (31-0). On Nov 6, the Orangemen lost in a first-time match against Georgetown L (7-13). On Nov 13, nemesis Colgate was at the front door again and they plaid the Orangemen to a tie T (10-10). On Nov 20, SU defeated Niagara W (12-6) at Archbold Stadium. Then, the Orange traveled to New York City to face Columbia and the squad prevailed W (19-12)

All American Victor A. Hanson 1926

Victor A. Hanson (July 30, 1903 – April 10, 1982) was an All American football player and coach for Syracuse University in 1926. He was also a basketball player, and baseball player. He served as team captain in all three sports. The Watertown, New York native was named an Basketball All-American three times—in 1925, 1926, and 1927—by the Helms Athletic Foundation and was a consensus selection to the 1926 College Football All-America Team.

<<< Victor Hanson

Following his college career he played briefly with the Cleveland Rosenblum's in the American Basketball League and then formed a basketball team, the Syracuse All-Americans. He was also signed by the New York Yankees of Major League Baseball upon graduation from Syracuse in 1927 and played one year in their farm system. Hanson served as the head football coach at Syracuse from 1930 to 1936, compiling a record of 33–21–5. He is only player inducted into both the Naismith Memorial Basketball Hall of Fame and the College Football Hall of Fame.

Famous Coaches (From the Past) by SWC75.

Pete Reynolds was replaced by Lew Andreas, more famous as a long-time basketball coach, (it was his school record for victories that Jim Boeheim broke), and athletic director. He hired Vic Hanson to be his assistant. Andreas sort of stumbled along for three years at 15-10-3 before handing the reigns to Hanson.

1927 Lew Andreas Coach # 17

The 1927 Syracuse Orangemen football team competed in their thirty-ninth season of intercollegiate football. They were led by Lew

Andreas in his first of three seasons as head coach of the Syracuse Orangemen. This SU squad finished with a fine record of 5-3-2.

Syracuse played its season home opener on Sept 26, 1927 at Archbold Stadium on the campus of Syracuse University and defeated Hobart in a shutout, W (13-0). Hobart was playing much better football. On Oct13, SU handed William & Mary a shutout shut defeat at Archbold Stadium W (18-0). The next week on Oct 8, Syracuse got win #3, against Johns Hopkins (21-6). On Oct 15, at home, SU defeated Georgetown W (19-6). In a first, Penn State defeated Syracuse on Oct 22 at Archbold Field L (6-9).

After a fine start, and just one loss, in its trip to Nebraska on Oct 29, the Cornhuskers finally won their first game against Syracuse and it was a shutout L (0-21). On Oct 5, Ohio Wesleyan, a proven tough squad tied the Orangemen at Archbold Stadium T (6-6). Those nasty guys from Colgate played Syracuse at Archbold on Nov 12, and the tough play resulted in a tie T (12-12). Niagara was next at Archbold and SU prevailed in a lose match W (13-6). In a rare defeat, Syracuse traveled to Columbia in NYC and were defeated in a close match L (7-14).

1928 Lew Andreas Coach # 17

The 1928 Syracuse Orangemen football team competed in their fortieth season of intercollegiate football. They were led by Lew Andreas in his second of three seasons as head coach of the Syracuse Orangemen. This SU squad finished with a so-so record of 4-4-1.

Syracuse played its season home opener on Sept 29, 1928 at Archbold Stadium on the campus of Syracuse University and defeated Hobart in a close match W (14-6). Hobart continued to play better football and this year scored on the Orangemen. On Oct 6, SU handed William & Mary a shutout defeat at Archbold Stadium W (32-0). The next week on Oct 13, Syracuse got win #3, a blowout against Johns Hopkins (58-0). On Oct 20, at Nebraska, SU lost to the Cornhuskers in a nail-biter L (6-7) On Oct 26, at Penn State tied the Orangemen in a tough battle T (6-6). Then, on Nov 3, at Pitt, SU lost in a shutout L (0-18).

Still having trouble with Ohio Wesleyan, on Nov 10, L (0- 6). On Nov 17, the Orangemen took a tough loss from Colgate L (6-30). Springing back from last year's defeat at home. SU beat Columbia at home in NYC on Nov 29 W (14-6).

1929 Lew Andreas Coach # 17

The 1929 Syracuse Orangemen football team competed in their forty-first season of intercollegiate football. They were led by Lew Andreas in his third and last of three seasons as head coach of the Syracuse Orangemen. This SU squad finished with nice record of 6-3-0.

Syracuse played its season home opener on Sept 28, 1929 at Archbold Stadium on the campus of Syracuse University and defeated Hobart in a blowout W (77-0. On Oct 5, SU handed St. Lawrence a shutout defeat at Archbold Stadium W (55-0). The next week on Oct 12 Syracuse lost against Nebraska at home (6-13). On Oct 19, at home in Archbold Stadium, SU whooped John Hoskins in a major blowout W (85-6). On Oct 29, Black Tuesday, the Stock Market crashed. On Nov 2, at Archbold Field, Penn State beat the Orangemen in a low scoring nail-biter L (4-6).

Then, on Nov 9, at Niagara, SU won the game in a shutout L (20-0. Colgate came into Archbold Field like they owned it on Nov 16 and defeated the Orangemen in a shutout L (0-21). SU went to Columbia in NYC on Thanksgiving, Nov 28, again, and took the close game in a shutout W (6-0).

Chapter 10 Vic Hanson Era From 1930 to 1936

Victor Hanson, Coach # 18

Year	Coach	Record	Conf
1930	Vic Hanson	5-2-2	Ind
1931	Vic Hanson	7-1-1	Ind
1932	Vic Hanson	4-4-1	Ind
1933	Vic Hanson	4-4-0	Ind
1934	Vic Hanson	6-2-0	Ind
1935	Vic Hanson	6-1-1	Ind
1936	Vic Hanson	1-7-0	Ind

Head Football Coach Victor Hanson and Fiancée Dorothy Burns Circa 1931

Famous Coaches (From the Past) by SWC75.

Vic Hanson did somewhat better than his predecessor Pete Reynolds, going 7-1-1 in 1931 and 6-1-1 in 1935. But he couldn't beat Colgate and when the 1936 team fell to 1-7, the old hero was fired. Syracuse was the only head football coaching job Andreas or Hanson ever held. Both were alums of the school.

1930 Victor Hanson Coach # 18

The 1930 Syracuse Orangemen football team competed in their forty-second season of intercollegiate football. They were led by Victor Hanson in his first of seven seasons as head coach of the Syracuse Orangemen. This SU squad finished with nice record of 5-2-2.

Syracuse played its season home opener on Sept 27 at Archbold Stadium on the campus of Syracuse University and defeated Rensselaer (RPI) in a blowout W (55-0. On Oct 5, SU handed Hobart a shutout defeat at Archbold Stadium W (49-0). The next week on Oct 12 Syracuse shut out Rutgers at home W (27-0). On Oct 18, at home in Archbold Stadium, SU lost to Pitt in a shutout L (0-14). On Oct 25, at Archbold Field, SU beat St. Lawrence W (34-6).

Then, on Nov 1, at home, SU tied the game against Brown University from Providence RI T (16-16). On Nov 8, at Penn State in State College PA, the Nittany Lions and the Orangemen finished in a scoreless tie T (0-0). On Nov 15, SU lost big to Colgate at home L (7-36). SU then traveled to Columbia in NYC on Thanksgiving, Nov 27, again, and beat the Lions W (19-7)

1931 Victor Hanson Coach # 18

The 1931 Syracuse Orangemen football team competed in their forty-third season of intercollegiate football. They were led by Victor Hanson in his second of seven seasons as head coach of the Syracuse Orangemen. This SU squad finished with nice record of 7-1-1.

Syracuse played its season home opener on Sept 26, 1931 at Archbold Stadium on the campus of Syracuse University and defeated St. Lawrence in a blowout W (46-6. On Oct 3, SU handed Hobart a shutout defeat at Archbold Stadium W (49-0). The next week on Oct 10 Syracuse blew out Ohio Wesleyan at home W (48-7). On Oct 17, at home in Archbold Stadium, SU beat the Florida Gators W (33-12) Then, on Oct 24, the Orangemen defeated Penn State in a one-TD shutout L (7-0).

On Oct 31, at Spartan Stadium, SU beat Michigan State, W (15-10). On Nov 7, SU shut out Western Reserve W (33-0) at home. Undefeated in seven games, the next team up was the typical spoiler. Still having trouble with Colgate who looked at Archbold Stadium as their own field, SU could not get past Colgate on Nov 14, and were defeated by two touchdowns L (7-21). On Nov 21 SU traveled again to Columbia in NYC and this time the teams played to a scoreless tie T (0-0).

1932 Victor Hanson Coach # 18

The 1932 Syracuse Orangemen football team competed in their forty-fourth season of intercollegiate football. They were led by Victor Hanson in his third of seven seasons as head coach of the Syracuse Orangemen. This SU squad finished with a so-so record this year of 4-4-1.

Syracuse played its season home opener on Sept 24, 1932 at Archbold Stadium on the campus of Syracuse University and defeated Clarkson in a close match W (13-6) On Oct 1, SU handed St. Lawrence a shutout-blowout defeat at Archbold Stadium W (54-0). The next week on Oct 8 Syracuse lost to Ohio Wesleyan at home L (12-19) On Oct 15, at home in Archbold Stadium, SU lost to Southern Methodist (SMU) L (6-16) On Oct 22, at New Beaver Stadium, Syracuse beat Penn State W (12-6)

Then, on Oct 29 at home, the Orangemen were defeated by Michigan State L (13-27) On Nov5, Oglethorpe came to Archbold Stadium and left without a victory as the Orangemen beat these new visitors W (27-6) SU still was on a losing trek against Colgate and extended by a game as Colgate defeated the Orangemen L (0-16). In the season finale against Columbia in NYC, the teams played to a hard-fought scoreless tie T (0-0).

1933 Victor Hanson Coach # 18

The 1933 Syracuse Orangemen football team competed in their forty-fifth season of intercollegiate football. They were led by Victor Hanson in his fourth of seven seasons as head coach of the Syracuse Orangemen. This SU squad finished with a so-so record this year of 4-4-0.

Syracuse played its season home opener on Oct 7, 1933 at Archbold Stadium on the campus of Syracuse University and defeated Clarkson in a bow-out match W (52-0) On Oct 14, SU handed Ohio Wesleyan a shutout defeat at Archbold Stadium W (40-0). The next week on Oct 21 for the first time in years, SU played at Cornell and beat the Big Red in a close match W (14-7). On Oct 28, at Spartan Stadium in Michigan, the Spartans beat Syracuse L (3-27).

On Nov 4, at Archbold, SU defeated Penn State W (12-6). Then, on Nov 11, Brown defeated SU at Archbold Stadium L (7-10) Colgate was next up and they were tough as usual beating the Orangemen in a tough match L (3-13). At Columbia on Nov 25, SU lost its season finale L (0-16)

1934 Victor Hanson Coach # 18

The 1934 Syracuse Orangemen football team competed in their forty-sixth season of intercollegiate football. They were led by Victor Hanson in his fifth of seven seasons as head coach of the Syracuse Orangemen. This SU squad finished with a nice record this year of 6-2-0 . The Orangemen were the 28th nationally ranked team this year.

Syracuse played its season home opener on Oct 6, 1934 at Archbold Stadium on the campus of Syracuse University and defeated Clarkson in a shutout W (28-0) On Oct 13, SU handed Cornell a tough defeat at Archbold Stadium W (20-7). The next week on Oct

20, in a tough match, SU prevailed over Ohio Wesleyan W (32-10) On Oct 27, at Brown, SU beat the Bears in Providence RI in a shutout W (33-0).

On Nov 3, at Penn State's New Beaver Field, SU defeated Penn State W (16-0). Then, on Nov 10, The Orange got the best of Michigan State at Archbold Stadium W (10-0). Colgate was next up, and they were like a cog in the wheel of success for SU that could not be undone. They beat the Orangemen in a tough match as usual L (2-13). At Columbia on Nov 25, SU lost its season finale L (0-12)

All American James Steen

Steen was born March 28, 1913 and passed away November 23, 1983. He was an All American College Football Player. He attended New Rochelle High School and Syracuse University. He played college football for the Syracuse Orangemen football team and was selected by the United Press, Liberty magazine and the Central Press Association as a first-team tackle on the 1934 College Football All-America Team.

Steen also played professional football in the National Football League from 1935 to 1936 with the Detroit Lions. As the story goes, Steen was a tackle for Syracuse's offensive line. He was named captain of the team in 1934. After his career at Syracuse, he was invited to the 1935 East-West Shrine All-Star Game. He then was drafted to play for the Detroit Lions in 1935-36.

1935 Victor Hanson Coach # 18

The 1935 Syracuse Orangemen football team competed in their forty-seventh season of intercollegiate football. They were led by Victor Hanson in his sixth of seven seasons as head coach of the Syracuse Orangemen. This SU squad finished with a very nice record this year of 6-1-1.

This was a nice year…the next year was a disaster as if Syracuse had pulled the plug on scholarships. I will investigate this and if I find something, I will show it in the 1936 season. With one less loss in 1935, SU's ranking was almost top 10 nationally but # 14 was not so shabby.

Syracuse played its season home opener on Oct 5, 1935 at Archbold Stadium on the campus of Syracuse University and defeated Clarkson in a shutout W (33-0) On Oct 12, SU handed Cornell a tough defeat at Archbold Stadium W (21-14). The next week on Oct 19, in a tough match, SU prevailed over Ohio Wesleyan W (18-10) On Oct 26, at Brown, SU beat the Bears in Providence RI in a shutout W (19-0).

On Nov 2, at home SU again beat an eager, tough Penn State Team W (7-3) in a nail-biter. Then, on Nov 9, The Orange got the best of Columbia at NYC W (14-12). Colgate was next up, and they were like rocks preventing Syracuse from championships. As much as I hate to say it, they walloped the Orangemen in an easy match for Colgate. L (2-27). Instead of the last game being at Columbia, SU finished the season at Baltimore Maryland on Nov 28, the teams played tough and finished in a scoreless tie L (0-0).

1936 Victor Hanson Coach # 18

The 1936 Syracuse Orangemen football team competed in their forty-eighth season of intercollegiate football. They were led by Victor Hanson in his seventh and last of seven seasons as head coach of the Syracuse Orangemen. This SU squad finished with one of its worst records ever 1-7-0.

I promised that I would investigate what happened this year, and I did. However, information is hard to come by at Syracuse. I contacted the Sports Information Department and I received no response. If an avid Syracuse fan happens to have the information as to why the team did so poorly in 1936, and also why Victor Hanson was replaced by what appears to be a less-capable coach, I will update this book after it is published so that SU fans can know what happened.

In my second research effort, I did find a great write-up about Hanson, commemorating his placement in the hall of fame that I will share below. It comes from http://www.footballfoundation.org/Programs/CollegeFootballHallofFame/SearchDetail.aspx?id=20054

Victor Hanson Great SU Coach – Member Biography

Called by Grantland Rice, "the best all-around athlete Syracuse ever had," Victor Hanson was a three-sport star for the Orangemen. In addition to playing as an All-America end in football, Hanson was an All-American in basketball and good enough in baseball to be signed by the New York Yankees. Hanson began his collegiate career in 1924 as the only sophomore on the varsity. A teammate on that 1924 team was future Hall of Fame coach Lynn Waldorf. During three varsity seasons Syracuse posted a 23-5-3 record. Hanson, playing end, called the plays for the offense. He captained the football, basketball and baseball teams. After graduation he played one year in baseball's minor leagues. He returned to Syracuse as an assistant coach in 1928 and 1929. In 1930, at the age of 27, Hanson was named head football coach. In seven seasons he posted a 33-21-5 record. He later became a prominent insurance counselor. Hanson was elected to the Basketball Hall of Fame in 1960 and the College Football Hall of Fame in 1973. He was born July 30, 1903 and died April 10, 1982.

Details
Position: End
School: Syracuse
High School: Syracuse, NY (Central HS)
Years: 1924-1926
Inducted: 1973
Place of Birth: Sacramento, CA
Date of Birth: Jul 30, 1903
Place of Death: Minoa, NY
Date of Death: Apr 10, 1982
Height: 5-10
Weight: 174

Games of the 1936 Season

Syracuse played its season home opener on Oct 3, 1936 at Archbold Stadium on the campus of Syracuse University and defeated Clarkson in a shutout W (31-0). This would be the only win of the year. On Oct 10, SU lost to Baldwin-Wallace L (0-19). The next week on Oct 17, in a tough match, SU lost at Cornell L (7-20) On Oct 24, at Brown, SU was shut out by Maryland at home L (0-20).

On Oct 31, at State College, PA, Penn State beat the Orangemen L (0-18). Then, on Nov 7, The Orange lost in a nail-biter at Indiana L (7-9). On Nov 14, at Columbia, Syracuse lost their sixth game in a row L (0-17). Colgate was next up in the season finale and again, the Raiders were like rocks preventing Syracuse from a chance of victory. The Orange lost their seventh game in a row capping a miserable season L (0-13)

Chapter 11 Coach Ossie Solem et al From 1937 to 1948

Ossie Solem, Coach # 19
Biggie Munn Coach # 20
Reaves Baysinger Coach #21

Year	Coach	Record	Conf
1937	Ossie Solem	5-2-1	Ind
1938	Ossie Solem	5-3-0	Ind
1939	Ossie Solem	3-3-2	Ind
1940	Ossie Solem	3-4-1	Ind
1941	Ossie Solem	5-2-1	Ind
1942	Ossie Solem	6-3-0	Ind
1943	No team due to World War II		
1944	Ossie Solem	2-4-1	Ind
1945	Ossie Solem	1-6-0	Ind
1946	Clarence Biggie Munn	4-5-0	Ind
1947	Reaves Baysinger	3-6-1	Ind
1948	Reaves Baysinger	1-6-0	Ind

Crowd in downtown Syracuse, World War II victory parade, September 1945.

Famous Coaches (From the Past) by SWC75.

Hanson was replaced by possibly the most prominent coach at the time of hiring we've ever had, (Bill Hollenbeck might be the exception, but he only lasted that one year and then retired). Ossie Solem has played for Dr. Henry Williams at Minnesota when they were a major national power. Then he went into pro football, coaching a team called the Minneapolis Marines that went on to join the NFL.

By that time, Solem had switched to college coach as well as being an athletic director at Luther College in Iowa, (1920), Drake, (1921-31) and Iowa, (1932-36). Drake was a fairly prominent program at that time and his teams went 7-0-0 in 1922 and 7-1-0 in 1928. Wikipedia, in its article on the Drake Bulldogs, says that they "shared the national championship in some national polls. They were invited to the White House for their accomplishments."

I've checked the various selectors who list rankings for each year online and I couldn't find anyone who rated that team higher than 16th. Usually they are around #30. They were what we would now call a good "mid-major". But it still got Solem some national recognition. Drake was a founding member of the Missouri Valley Conference in 1928 and won its first four championships. .

Solem moved on to Iowa in 1932. The Hawkeyes had just been temporarily suspended by the Big Ten due an athletic department slush fund scandal that dated back to the Howards Jones Era. (They were paying players! Horrors!) Even after the suspension, Solem had a hard time filling out his Big Ten schedule because all the members would rather play Notre Dame. The Depression also hit the University hard and they weren't able to pay Solem his full salary.

Nonetheless, he soldiered on to a 15-21-4 record over five seasons. The period was not without its high points. In 1933 they surprised with a 5-3 record and quarterback Joe Laws was Big Ten MVP. But his greatest player was Ozzie Simmons, "The Ebony Eel" who was named second team All-American in 1934 and first team in 1935. Solem was also able to recruit a strong freshman class in 1936 that included Nile Kinnick, who would win the 1939 Heisman Trophy.

But Solem had a run-in with Simmons, whose teammates resented his notoriety and maybe also his color. They decided not to have a captain of the team his senior year to avoid voting for him. Some even refused to block for him. The coach accused him of "laying down" in a 0-52 loss to Minnesota, even though Simmons played the game with an injured leg. Simmons left the team saying "I've taken too much abuse this season because of Iowa's poor showing. I've taken more punishment than I did in my sophomore year and Solem has been screaming at me. He doesn't scream at the other players, just me." (There was bullying in those days, as well.)

Solem replied "Other players on the team were berated for their play in the Minnesota game but they took it without a word. I made one criticism of Simmons and he couldn't take it." They later made up and Simmons said, "He probably could have been tougher (on the players), but he was the finest gentleman I've ever been around."

Nonetheless, Solem left Iowa to come east and coach Syracuse for the 1937 season. He assembled perhaps the finest football staff ever with two protégés who had also played for Minnesota assisting him, Clarence "Biggie" Munn and Bud Wilkinson. One of their players was Hugh "Duffy" Daughtery, who gave this scouting report for himself:

"He may be small, but he sure is slow."

Duffy joined Solem's staff on graduation. Wilkinson, of course, went on to become coach at Oklahoma, turning them into a dominant program while Munn and then Daugherty coached Michigan State to nearly equal prominence. Despite the quality of the coaching, there were plenty of ups and downs during Solem's tenure, (1937-45), during which he went 30-27-6.

The high points were winning what Grantland Rice called the greatest game he had seen against powerful Cornell in 1938, 19-17, finally breaking the HooDoo against Colgate later the same year, 7-0 and upsetting national power Wisconsin 27-20 in 1941 using the controversial "reverse center" formation which was subsequently banned. (Amos Alonzo Stagg commented that "a time of war was not the time to be showing your backside to the enemy"). The most prominent players were Marty Glickman and Wilmeth Sidat-Singh.

Solem moved on after the war to coach at Springfield College in Massachusetts, (Wikipedia, for some reason, lists it as "YMCA" the first seven years but it was the college). In 1956 his team went 8-0-1 thanks, in part to a center/linebacker named Dick MacPherson , who captained Solem's last team in 1957.

Solem was 44-7-3 coaching the Minneapolis pro team and then 162-117-20 in a 37-season college coaching career, (SU did not field a team in 1943). He had also gone 37-31 in four seasons as the Drake basketball coach. I had thought he was in the Hall of Fame but, in fact, he is not, although his three famous assistants are.

About Coach Ossie Solem

Oscar Martin "Ossie" Solem (December 13, 1891 – October 26, 1970) was an American football player, coach of football and basketball, and college athletics administrator. He served as the head football coach at Luther College in Decorah, Iowa (1920), Drake University (1921–1931), the University of Iowa(1932–1936), Syracuse University (1937–1945), and Springfield College (1946–1957), compiling a career college football record of 162–117–20.

From 1913 until 1920, Solem was the head coach of the Minneapolis Marines, prior to that team's entry into the National Football League (NFL). During his time with the Marines, Solem introduced the team to the single-wing formation, developed by the famed coach, Pop Warner, and used by the University of Minnesota, where Solem had played football. Solem was also the head basketball coach at Drake University for four seasons, from 1921 to 1925, tallying a mark of 37–31. For Syracuse, he was a fine coach, and if it were not for the frustration of fielding a team in the WWII years, Ben Schwartzwalder may not have been needed.

1937 Ossie Solem Coach # 19

The 1937 Syracuse Orangemen football team competed in their forty-ninth season of intercollegiate football. They were led by Ossie Solem in his first of eight seasons as head coach of the Syracuse Orangemen. This SU squad finished with a fine record of 5-2-1.

Syracuse played its season home opener on Friday Oct 1, 1937 at Archbold Stadium on the campus of Syracuse University and defeated Clarkson W (26-6). This would be the first of five wins this year. On Oct 9, SU beat St. Lawrence in-a shutout W (40-0). The next week on Oct 16, at Cornell, in a tough match, SU defeated the Big Red W (14-6) On Oct 23, at Maryland in a game played in Baltimore, Maryland defeated the Orangemen L (0-13).

On Oct 31, at home, SU beat the Nittany Lions of Penn State W (19-13) 0-18). Then, on Nov 6, at home, the Orange defeated Western Reserve W (27-6). The Orangemen then traveled to Columbia in NYC on Nov 13 and tied the Lions T (6-6) Colgate was next up in the season finale on Nov 20, and again, though this time in a very close match, the Raiders defeated the Orangemen L (0-7).

1938 Ossie Solem Coach # 19

The 1938 Syracuse Orangemen football team competed in their fiftieth season of intercollegiate football. They were led by Ossie

Solem in his second of eight seasons as head coach of the Syracuse Orangemen. This SU squad finished with a fine record of 5-3-0.

Syracuse played its season home opener on Friday, Sept 30, 1938 at Archbold Stadium on the campus of Syracuse University and shut out Clarkson W (27-0). This would be the first of five wins this year. On Oct 8, SU beat Maryland in-a shutout W (40-0). The next week on Oct 15, at Cornell, in a tough match, SU defeated the Big Red W (19-17) On Oct 22, at Michigan State the Spartans defeated the Orangemen L (12-19.

On Oct 31, at Penn State, SU lost to the Nittany Lions of Penn State L (6-33). Then, on Nov 5, at home, after ten losses in a row, the Orange finally defeated nemesis Colgate W (7-0) The Orangemen then lost to Duke at home L (0-21). The next week, on Nov 19, the Orange traveled to Columbia in NYC in the season finale and beat the Lions T (13-12).

1939 Ossie Solem Coach # 19

The 1939 Syracuse Orangemen football team competed in their fifty-first season of intercollegiate football. They were led by Ossie Solem in his third of eight seasons as head coach of the Syracuse Orangemen. This SU squad finished with a so-so record of 3-3-2.

Syracuse played its season home opener on Friday, Sept 29, 1939 at Archbold Stadium on the campus of Syracuse University and shut out Clarkson W (12-0). This would be the first of just three wins this year. On Oct 7, SU lost at Cornell L (6-19). The next week on Oct 14, at Georgetown, the teams played to a tie T (13-13) On Oct 21, at Duke, the Blue Devils overpowered the Orangemen L (6-33).

On Oct 28, at home, Penn State and SU played to a tie T (6-6). The Orangemen then lost in a lopsided game at Duke L (6-33). On Nov 4, at home SU lost a close match to Michigan State L (3-14). Then, on Nov 18, at home, the Orange beat nemesis Colgate for the second year in a row and by the same score, W (7-0.). About two weeks later, on Nov 30, the Orange traveled to Maryland in the season finale and beat the Terrapins W (10-7).

1940 Ossie Solem Coach # 19

The 1940 Syracuse Orangemen football team competed in their fifty-second season of intercollegiate football. They were led by Ossie Solem in his fourth of eight seasons as head coach of the Syracuse Orangemen. This SU squad finished with a losing record of 3-4-1.

Syracuse played its season home opener on Friday, Sept 27, 1940 at Archbold Stadium on the campus of Syracuse University and shut out Clarkson W (33-0). This would be the first of just three wins this year. On Oct 5, SU was shut-out at Archbold Stadium by Northwestern L (0-40). The next week on Oct 14, at NYU in the Bronx, NY, SU got its moxie back, W (47-13). On Oct 19, at Cornell, the Red Raiders overpowered the Orangemen L (6-33).

On Oct 26, at Columbia, SU defeated the Lions in a close match W (3-0). On Nov 2, at home SU lost by a bigger score against Georgetown L (6-28). Then, on Nov 9, at home Syracuse & Penn State played to an unlucky tie T (13-13). Then, on Nov 16, after two victories in a row SU lost to nemesis Colgate L (6-7.

1941 Ossie Solem Coach # 19

The 1941 Syracuse Orangemen football team competed in their fifty-third season of intercollegiate football. They were led by Ossie Solem in his fifth of eight seasons as head coach of the Syracuse Orangemen. This SU squad finished with a fine record of 5-2-1.

Syracuse played its season home opener on Friday, Sept 26, 1941 at Archbold Stadium on the campus of Syracuse University and shut out Clarkson W (39-0). This would be the first of five wins this year. On Oct 4, SU was shut-out at Cornell by the Red Raiders L (0-6). The next week on Oct 11, at home against Holy Cross, the Orangemen pitched a close shutout W (6-0). On Oct 18 at NYU in the Bronx, NY, SU threw another shutout W (31-0). On Oct 25, at home, SU defeated the Scarlet Knights of Rutgers in a big win W (49-7).

On Nov 1 at Wisconsin, SU squeaked by the Badgers for the win -- W (27-20). On November 8 at State college, PA, Syracuse lost to Penn State L (19-34) On Nov 15, SU tied Colgate T (19-19) in its season finale.

1942 Ossie Solem Coach # 19

The 1942 Syracuse Orangemen football team competed in their fifty-fourth season of intercollegiate football. They were led by Ossie Solem in his sixth of eight seasons as head coach of the Syracuse Orangemen. This SU squad finished with a fine record of 6-3-0. This was the most wins that SU would get in its eight seasons under Coach Solem.
Syracuse played its season home opener on Friday, Sept 25, 1942 at Archbold Stadium on the campus of Syracuse University and blew-Out Clarkson W (58-6). This would be the first of six wins for SU this year. On Oct 3, SU shut-out Boston University at Archbold Stadium W (25-0). On Oct 9, at home, SU beat Western Reserve W (13-0). The next week on Oct 17, at Holy Cross, the Orangemen pitched a shutout W (19-0). On Oct 18, at home, SU just got past Cornell in a close match W (12-7)

On Oct 31, at home, SU lost to a military team, North Carolina Pre-Flight, L (0-9) The military was in full bloom again with the beginning of WWII in 1939. On Nov 1 at Wisconsin, SU squeaked by the Badgers for the win --W (27-20). On November 7 at State college, PA, Syracuse lost to Penn State L (13-18). On Nov 14, at home, SU lost to nemesis Colgate L (0-14). On Nov 21 @ Rutgers, SU defeated the Scarlet Knights W (12-7). In the season finale.

1943 Season cancelled due to World War II

1944 Ossie Solem Coach # 19

The 1944 Syracuse Orangemen football team competed in their fifty-fifth season of intercollegiate football. They were led by Ossie Solem in his seventh of eight seasons as head coach of the Syracuse Orangemen. This SU squad finished with a poor record of 2-4-1

After the year off for the war, it was a difficult task for college teams to rebuild as many of their best players were in the service of our nation.

The military teams, especially Army, were knocking them all out across the country and the people of America were cheering for their armed services. It was tough being Syracuse this year and the next. Ironically, for Coach Solem, this happened after his most productive season, 1942.

The war played havoc on college teams across the country and teams such as Gonzaga gave up on football for good after the war. So, also with Clarkson, who puttered around for a while but were not ready to play SU in 1945. Clarkson students still like football and they still have homecoming games but not at a Division I level as Syracuse.

Clarkson has not fielded a school sponsored football team since 1951, The Club football notion is alive and well as students form clubs and play intercollegiate football but not NCAA football. The new teams are charter members of the Yankee Collegiate Football Conference, a collection of seven tackle-football club teams across New England and New York. My alma mater King's College from Wilkes-Barre, PA, with one of my best friends, RIP, Frank Kurilla as a star player, with Eddie Brominski, as their dedicated coach, won the Club Football Championship in 1968 in a game at IONA, NY, which I attended. Club Football was and is great for students. And, so, the Friday SU games with Clarkson ended in 1942.

Syracuse thus played its season home opener on a Saturday, Sept 23, 1944 at Archbold Stadium on the campus of Syracuse University and lost big to Cornell L (6-39). On Oct 7, at Columbia, SU lost to the Lions, L (2-26). On Oct 14, at home, SU beat Lafayette for its first win of two this season. The next week on Oct 21, at Temple in Philadelphia, the teams played hard to achieve a tie T (7-7).

On Oct 28, at Boston College SU lost a close game to the Eagles L (12-19). On November 4 at home, Syracuse lost to Penn State in a blowout L (0-41). Then, as a sweet finish to an otherwise dismal season. on Nov 18, at home, SU finally put a good whooping on nemesis Colgate W (43-13), who were still struggling with the war taking all the players. For SU, this was a great season finale.

1945 Ossie Solem Coach # 19

The 1945 Syracuse Orangemen football team competed in their fifty-sixth season of intercollegiate football. They were led by Ossie Solem in his eighth and last of eight mostly fine seasons as head coach of the Syracuse Orangemen. This SU squad finished with another poor record of 1-6-0. After 1943, a year off for the war, SU had not yet come back to full strength as many of their best players were in the service of our nation. Coach Solem looked at it as his fault and he resigned after the completion of the season. He moved on to Springfield and finished off a nice career there.

Syracuse played its season opener on a Monday, Sept 24, 1945 at Archbold Stadium on the campus of Syracuse University and lost to Cornell L (14-26). On Friday, Sept 28, at Temple, SU lost to the Owls in a nail-biter, L (6-7) On Oct 6, at Columbia in NY, the Orangemen lost L (0-32) On Oct 21, at home, SU beat West Virginia for its only win of the season. The games for the most part were not blowouts, but victories were almost impossible to achieve. Coach Solem was a good coach, nonetheless.

On Oct 27, at Home, SU lost a close game to Dartmouth, L (0-8). the Eagles L (12-19). On Nov 3, at Penn State, Syracuse was shut-out by the Nittany Lions. L (0-26). In the season finale against major nemesis Colgate, for want of an extra point SU lost the game L (6-7). It was disheartening for Coach Solem for sure.

Famous Coaches (From the Past) by SWC75.

Biggie Munn took over as head coach in 1946 after Solem had a 1-6 season the previous year. [Syracuse could not stomach losing seasons.] Munn had been assisting Fritz Crisler at Michigan. He improved the team's record to 4-5 but left for Michigan State with most of his staff, an offer "that comes once in a lifetime". It sounds reminiscent of Doug Marrone [explored later in this essay].

State was a large public school that was ambitious to build up its program and try to gain entrance into the Big Ten, which had become the Big Nine when Chicago gave up the sport. Syracuse was not so ambitious. Munn built the Spartans into a national power, winning 28 games in a row from 1950-53, the national championship in 1952 and the Rose Bowl in '53, the first year they were eligible for it. Munn then became athletic director and appointed Daugherty as his successor. Duffy won the Rose bowl with his 1955 team and the coach's version of the national title in 1965. Munn was elected to the Hall of Fame in 1959 and Daugherty in 1984

[Think of all the great coaches that mentored at Syracuse. They were the best of the best. SU officials seemed to take all the talent for granted.]

1946 Clarence "Biggie" Munn Coach # 20

The 1946 Syracuse Orangemen football team competed in their fifty-seventh season of intercollegiate football. They were led by "Biggie Munn in his first and last of one losing season as head coach of the Syracuse Orangemen.

<< Biggie Munn.

This SU squad finished with a so-so record of 4-5-0 but it was a big improvement from the 1-6-0 season in 1945. I can't keep making excuses for 1943, the year off for the war, but SU still had not yet come back to full strength as many of their best players were in the service of our nation or just getting out of the service. Nonetheless the alumni and fans continued to expect victories from their favorite team.

I have not figured out yet why games were being played on Mondays and Fridays as well as Saturdays during the war but now that the war was over, all games this season were played on Saturdays, which to this day is college football day in America. Especially as we move from the War Years in which the survival of our country was assured by brave men, football players some, but not all. With the disrespect to the flag shown by the NFL in 2017, many college football lovers in 2017 were wishing college football were played on Sunday's also. Many were ready to let pro-football come to a graceful end while helping college players excel in a sport played for sport and for the school--Syracuse in our case.

The Orangemen played their season opener on a Saturday, back to normal, Sept 28, 1946 at Archbold Stadium on the campus of Syracuse University and the Orangemen whooped Boston University W (41-6). On Oct 5 at Dartmouth, SU lost to the Big Green in a tough match, L (14-20). On Oct 12 at home Penn State beat Syracuse in a fair contest L (0-9). Then, on Oct 19, at Holy Cross, SU beat Holy Cross W (21-12). Then, on Oct 26, at West Virginia, SU lost in a shutout, L (0-13).

On Nov 2, at home v Temple, the Orangemen got it together to beat the Owls W (28-7). Next at Cornell, the Orangemen kept their sights on the prize and beat Cornell W (14-7) Still trying to figure out nemesis Colgate, this would not be the year for SU to break free from the spell and they were beaten in a fair game L (7-25. SU liked to finish off its seasons at Columbia, a team that had never come to Syracuse to play a football game. This year after the trip to New York for the game, The Orange had to endure an embarrassing licking L (21-59) One might ask, "where was the 'D'?"

Famous Coaches (From the Past) by SWC75.

Next up was Reaves "Ribs" Baysinger, an old SU football hero from the 20's who had been coaching the freshman team. Les Dye: "His success didn't carry on for reasons beyond my knowledge. And then, consequently football kind of petered out at Syracuse in terms of popularity." Dye felt that things might have been different in Munn had stayed. "He was considerably more aggressive in his recruiting tactics than Baysinger when he was head coach.

Baysinger went 3-6 his first year, although he managed to beat Colgate, 7-0. The next year may have been SU's worst team ever. The beat Niagara in their opening game, 13-9, thanks to a fumble at the goal line in the final seconds. Niagara gave up football after that season, the joke going that they decided to give it up since they couldn't beat Syracuse. Then came eight losses in a row by a combined 76-235. That was it for "Ribs".

SU fans had a solution: bring in a famous coach. They were shocked when Lew Andreas chose the head coach at Muhlenberg to be the next coach at Syracuse. In the words of that Muhlenberg coach: "The alumni wanted a big-name coach…and got a long-name coach."

1947 Reaves Baysinger Coach # 21

Coach Reaves Baysinger was the 21st coach for the Syracuse Orange. He was born February 22, 1902 and passed away at 92 years of age on December 4, 1994. He was the head football coach at Syracuse from 1947 to 1948. Despite his strong ties to the university he only produced a 4-14(.222) record. On a higher note, in 1927, he coached the freshman basketball team== undefeated 23-0 record.

Baysinger played college football as a guard and end at Syracuse. During his senior season, he was an honorable mention all-American. He also played basketball as a point guard, and baseball as an outfielder. Baysinger played one game in the NFL as a member of the Rochester Jeffersons in 1924.

The 1947 Syracuse Orangemen football team competed in their fifty-eighth season of intercollegiate football. They were led by Reaves Baysinger in his first of two very poor seasons head coach of the Syracuse Orangemen. This SU squad finished with a so-so record of 3-6-0. It was a worst season than that turned in by "Biggie" in his one season at the helm.

Nonetheless, Baysinger would get another shot at the apple in 1948, though his record was not worthy of such as shot. I'd love to see the coach's salary records for this period.

Anything was a big improvement from the 1-6-0 season in 1945 or so it seemed. No more excuses for 1943 would be accepted by the very tolerant SU faithful. Instead, it was obvious something other than the weather was the problem. The SU administration was simply making poor choices for coaches as other teams with whom SU competed were doing better than Syracuse That is the major measurement.

Not everybody can lose all games in any season as somebody is better than somebody else them—enough to beat them. SU had a tough time at this time being better than anybody and beating anybody. Why? Typically, that is the coach's fault or the administration's fault, for being tight on the purse strings on coach's salary and / or scholarships. SU fans were not ready for excuses. They were looking for results. After such a great fifty some years, it was no wonder why.

The Orangemen played their season opener again on a Friday, on Sept 26, 1947 at Archbold Stadium on the campus of Syracuse University and the Orangemen defeated Niagara University W (14-7). On Oct 4, my wedding anniversary, at Dartmouth, SU lost again to the Big Green L (7-28). On Oct 11 at home, SU beat Temple W (28-12). Then, on Oct 18 at Penn State, SU was shut out in a big way by the Nittany Lions L (0-40).

Then, on Oct 25, at home v Holy Cross, the Orangemen could not bring in the win and in fact, were shut-out L (0-26).

On Nov 1, at Lafayette, SU lost in a close match L (7-14). Next was a tough Cornell team in a game played in Ithaca, NY. Cornell defeated Syracuse L (6-12). Considering fresh air, a win against Colgate, Syracuse got its fresh air on Nov 8 in a nice win against their nemesis W (7-0). Then, it was off to Columbia for the annual encounter. SU were defeated on Nov 22 by nationally ranked # 19 Columbia L (8-28).

1948 Reaves Baysinger Coach # 21

The 1948 Syracuse Orangemen football team competed in their fifty-ninth season of intercollegiate football. They were led by Reaves Baysinger in his second of two very poor seasons as head coach of the Syracuse Orangemen. This SU squad finished with a terrible record of 1-8-0. There was little positive that could be said of the season. Coach Baysinger was gone as soon as it was over.

As I said in the 1947 section, I'd love to see the coach's salary records for this period. I have researched many football programs and often a lapse in victories has to do with a change in the investment and the commitment of the institution. There is little written about Syracuse in the early years but the bare minimum. I do not want to falsely accuse, but the University may have been trying to run a national football program on the cheap, but their record would suggest that they were not getting away with it.

When I got to this point in the book, I was getting frustrated finding quality information about the Syracuse Orangemen other than their record and some good stuff about some of the coaches, but it was tough going. Then, I came across a site called syracusefan.com that had a wealth of information and an especially good story about all the great coaches Syracuse has had over its lifetime. Nothing, however, was easy. Even Wikipedia articles were incomplete. So, I contacted the Syracuse Sports Information Department and the archive department, and they said they had no pictures or anything special to give me. That was that.

Nonetheless I have a lot of good stuff in this book about a great team that has been playing football for about 130 years. This is my seventh "Great Moments" book and without help from the University, it is not as easy as it could be.

With attendance moving to about 30,000 from closer to 50,000, I would have expected SU to have more stuff to link to so that more people can either strengthen their ties to the Orange or learn enough about the great SU football years that the attendance and the fan loyalty can increase. I hope one day Syracuse opens up its archives and makes them more understandable. When this happens, more books will be written about the great Syracuse teams and coaches and players even those before the great Jim Brown. Since Jim Brown was born on February 17, 1936, and right now is age 83 as I write this paragraph,

I know that soon in this book, I will be talking about his escapades and Ben Schwartzwalder's leadership on the Syracuse Gridiron. But, today as I was looking for the real reason why Syracuse fell apart right before Ben Schwartzwalder came to town, I found a great bored historian known as SWC75 who wrote a very interesting two-part essay about SU's finest coaches from 1899 to 2013.

Much of what I have already from some facts and a lot of deductions, and inductions has been proven true in this nice article. Additionally, as of the Reaves Baysinger Era, I went back to what I had written and each time I modified the whole book so that each time I introduce a new coach in a time period, I include the part from Part I or Part II of https://syracusefan.com/threads/famous-coaches-part-1.60694/, and https://syracusefan.com/threads/famous-coaches-part-2.60695/.

When I find who the user SWC75 bored historian is, I promise, I  will change this book to include his name and the bio he provides me. This man whose picture is below, is the epitome of a great sports fan.

He is one of ours. He is a great Syracuse Sports Fan. He is ambidextrous. In fact, he is multi-dexterous with a love of College Football, Pro Football, Basketball, etc. He is a great bored historian in all facets of all games. Thank you WSC75 and I am sure the readers of this book thank you also.

I once said that Anything was a big improvement from the 1-6-0 season Syracuse experienced in 1945 or so it seemed. Well, 1-8 is definitely worse than that. SU fans were not ready for excuses. They were looking for results. After such a great fifty some years, it was no wonder why.

Games of the 1948 Season

The Orangemen played their season opener again on a Tuesday, (I have no explanation for the day of the week in this case) on Sept 28, 1948 at Archbold Stadium on the campus of Syracuse University and the Orangemen defeated Niagara University W (13-9). SU had clobbered Niagara for years, and this year, some might even say they played expecting to lose.

The 1948 pundits reported that without a Niagara fumble in the final seconds, SU would not have won the game. Niagara had enough of the game and sent their football records to the archives and liquidated the team. They gave up football after 1948, the year I was born.

The Niagara Story Continued

My alma mater is Kings College, Wilkes-Barre, Pa. I was a three-year starter on the baseball team and though tempted, I never played Club football. I played catcher and then, as I tell the story, as a sophomore catching batting practice for Coach John Dorish, who had his day in the major leagues, I would (my words not his) throw better curves back to him than he threw to me. Many catchers learn the same tricks as pitchers. As Kings lost its pitchers through graduation in 1967, Dorish asked me to pitch for Kings in the 1968 and 1969 seasons. I graduated in 1969.Dont ask me about my record but I got a lot of innings and I had a good curve.

In 1968-69, Dorish worked for a guy who is the continuation of the Niagara Story. His name is Ed Donahue. Niagara had long given up football, but it had become a national powerhouse in basketball.

I met Ed Donahue about thirty rows away from the main stage in 1968 at an opening assembly when he came to tell us that as he walked across the Susquehanna River that day, before taking the podium, he contemplated his words carefully. The audience immediately broke out in applause.

The reference was that Kings expected Donahue to turn their basketball program into something better immediately like a miracle. There is only one person, or deity, that is documented to have ever walked on Water and his Statue is on top of the Christ the King Building, the main building of Kings College. Donahue knew that if we accepted his story, he would be the second deity

Ed Donohue was a great athlete himself At Poughkeepsie High School, graduating in 1947 (I was born in 1948) Poughkeepsie, NY, he was a four-sport standout in football, basketball, baseball, and track. Donohue was awarded a football scholarship to attend Niagara University, where, after one year on the freshman team, he served in the military (Air Force) in 1950 during the Korean War. In 1952, he would marry his wife Ruth and the two remain together today after many years of marriage.

After completing his duty in the Air Force, Donohue resumed his education at our school, Syracuse University, where he achieved a Bachelor of Arts degree in physical education and a master's degree in 1957

While at Syracuse, Donohue was a classmate of NFL legend Jim Brown who would serve as a babysitter for Ed and Ruth's daughter, Karen. He was a successful HS coach in multiple sports for many years, He was a sports guy's sports guy... and a great one at that.

In 1963, Ed found his way back to Niagara University when he was hired as head coach of the freshman team while also serving as an associate professor of health and physical education. In 1966, he successfully recruited NBA Hall of Famer Calvin Murphy to Niagara and served as Murphy's coach on the freshman team. Donohue would remain at Niagara until taking over as the new head coach at King's prior to the 1968-69 season.

Everybody at Kings knew about Calvin Murphy and we were tickled pink to have Ed Donahue at our school. When we christened our new Scanlon Gymnasium in 1969, Ed Donahue had arranged for Adrian Dantley and the Fighting Irish to play basketball in Wilkes-Barre, Pa. As a letterman, I had the pleasure of being an usher at the game and it was even more than amazing. Kings played so tough, it had a chance of victory but in the battle between energy and desire v raw phenomenal talent, as long as the clock continues to tick, and the game goes on, the human body can take only so much and thus talent has the edge. I won't tell you the final score as that is not the whole game. Both halves were much different. We were very proud of our fellow Kingsmen.

At Kings, Donahue was well respected, and he really made a difference in basketball for a too-short fifteen great years. Meanwhile in 1968 Kings also won the National Club Football Championship. Now, I wish I played Club Football, but I did play football as I loved the game. Like many, I played just in the sandlots and loved every minute.

After the conclusion of his coaching career, the verified rumor is that Ed Donohue returned to one of his true passions - sports art. He is a longtime sketch artist, and now has his own company, Pro Art, where he designs awards for a number of high schools and colleges. Ed is one of the best in whatever he does. He has also done work for the NCAA and the National Association of Basketball Coaches. He retired full-time in 1993 and he moved to his current home of Newport Richey, Fla. in 1997. I want to live there too!

I have a great friend in New Port Richey, Mark George, who is also an American hero, but well save Marks story for another book. Mark has a great spare bedroom and some great dogs. Next time I visit, we'll have to call on Ed to mix the martinis.

If I had a Gonzaga football story, I'd probably try to sneak it in as I add my human-interest stories to complement the great facts in a book such as this. For my money, I wish Niagara and Gonzaga were playing football today and I wish that Syracuse was playing at a level that the immortals would appreciate and be proud. Quite frankly even in his eighties, I am still convinced that a guy with the moxie of Ed Donahue, who chose Kings instead of Syracuse could lead the Orangemen on the path to continual victory once again. If you have the time, Syracuse fans, give Ed a call.

We have to find people with the guts to win. I have yet to meat Dino Babers and he has run the team for the last two years well enough to get another shot at delivering the Syracuse Dream. Good Luck

Dino! We always must remember that SU is Division I, and nothing less than Division I caliber football can be acceptable.

Continuing the 1948 Season

On Oct 2, at Holy Cross, SU lost again to the Big Green L (7-33). On Oct 8, on a Friday at home, SU lost to Penn State at Archbold, L (14-34) Then, on Saturday Oct 16, at home v Cornell, ranked # 13 at the time, the Orangemen could not bring in the win and in fact, were dominated by Cornell L (7-34).

On Oct 23, at #10 ranked Northwestern, SU lost in a blowout-shutout L (0-48). Next was a game at Boston University, who stood their ground and defeated the Orangemen l (7-12)

On Nov 6, at Temple, the Owls got the chance to scob Syracuse of whatever dignity was remaining as this dismal season was coming to a close. Temple got its due L (0-20). All the fresh air was gone from the prior Colgate match as the Orangemen went down again at the hands of Colgate, Nov 13 in a close loss against their favorite nemesis L (13-20) Then, as normal SU seasons went, it was off to Columbia for the annual encounter. SU was defeated on Nov 20 in a very close game but again, no cigar L (28-34)

Pre Schwartzwalder post script

This wraps up the pre-Ben Schwartzwalder portion of the book in which, despite some recent (in this book) poor years such as 1944 to 1948, the team record from day one was still a very impressive 305-194-41. This early record is actually better than the later record from 1949 on of 458-379-8. You see what I see.

The old-time Orangemen have a much better record than the new Orange. Just saying! Before SU can line up the best coaches, the administration must be committed, and the alumni cannot just expect wins—it must squeeze the administration for all it has to produce a great football team. Settle for good but, always plan and commit for greatness and excellence. Otherwise, as has happened in a number of SY years with the wrong coaches, especially in more modern times, complacency sets in and "medsa-medsa" is all that can be achieved when the goals of the Administration are no higher than medsa-medsa.

Sometimes a lot of grit on the part of the students and the teams and the twenty-year old coaches is all you need for success, even without a dedicated university. We saw that from 1899 to 1948. But, eventually that gets old. Especially when equipment and facilities are concerned.

Startup teams are thrilled to have train fare paid by the university to play away games, but student players on established teams have a right to expect the support of the university in all ways. Football is a big deal or SU would not insist on being in Division I. Players in the early years of football are documented to have lost their lives on the gridiron or be maimed when playing their roughest and toughest for the honor of the school.

It stands to reason that once a school chooses to get out of cheap sandlot-style football to play Division I, if the university does not do what it must to support the efforts of all parts of the team, it's time to move to Club Football is saving money is the primary objective instead of school honor. Other teams have dropped football when it was time.

For example, basketball powerhouse Gonzaga dropped football after World War II just like Niagara. Both concentrated on basketball and gave that sport its support. Like in A Christmas Carol, what seems to be happening at Syracuse are not things that must be but are things that will be if nothing changes.

Dear Administration of Syracuse University. Just like Academics. Either you do your absolute best, or you must get out of the game. Support the players and the students and the alumni and the school or admit that you can't and stop the mediocrity. Football, just like the study of the world, is not for the faint of heart. Maybe as administrators, if you cannot bring success to Syracuse University's football program, somebody else can. So, another solution would be for you, the Administration responsible for the mediocrity, all the way to the board of Directors, resign post haste and pass the torch. ... I bet I am right.

Pardon my abruptness.

When Rockne was at Notre Dame for example, the university somehow believed that wins just came because they were Notre Dame—no other reason necessary. Then the losses came—one after another—after Rockne's untimely death. Only when Notre Dame realized coaching and consistency win football games, not prior legacies, did the Irish turn things around but there were a number of weak years for football before the turnaround. Great coaches such as Frank Leahy, Dan Devine, Ara Parseghian, and Lou Holtz, broke the institution's own rules to assure that Notre Dame was a championship contender for all of the institution's constituencies, whether the institutions liked it or not.

Think of the time before Ben Schwartzwalder. The longest continuous period for any coach at Syracuse was Ossie Solem's tenure of eight seasons. Somebody should have bit the bullet and had a heart to heart with Ossie Solem, while he was at Syracuse. His story and Vic Hanson's story demonstrate the administration's lack of support for such a great program that almost ran on its own.

Solem held the coaching position for nine years though the team did not compete in 1943 due to the war. Just as it did with many college football teams, the war really played havoc with SU college football. Solem was such a great coach he thought it was his fault and thinking he was doing the honorable thing, he stepped down.

Yes, Buck O'Neill put in eight years also, but his years were spilt in three distinct tenures of two years, then three years and then three years again. Syracuse football spent its first fifty-nine years as a stepchild wearing the institution's hand-me downs. Yet it still attained a phenomenal record for a startup 305-194-41. I bet the current teams would love the program to be riding at such an impressive clip.

Every now and then a ray of hope for the SU football program would appear such as Ben Schwartzwalder. The guy with the long name was just what the many doctors who graduated from Syracuse University had ordered but they had been ignored and ignored again and again. As a writer, I now look forward to moving to a different era for Syracuse University football. Let's enjoy it together.

Chapter 12 Coach Ben Schwartzwalder From 1949 to 1973

Ben Schwartzwalder, Coach # 22

Year	Coach	Record	Conf
1949	Ben Schwartzwalder	4-5-0	Ind
1950	Ben Schwartzwalder	5-5-0	Ind
1951	Ben Schwartzwalder	5-4-0	Ind
1952	Ben Schwartzwalder	7-3-0	Ind
1953	Ben Schwartzwalder	5-3-1	Ind
1954	Ben Schwartzwalder	4-4-0	Ind
1955	Ben Schwartzwalder	5-3-0	Ind
1956	Ben Schwartzwalder	7-2-0	Ind
1957	Ben Schwartzwalder	5-3-1	Ind
1958	Ben Schwartzwalder	8-2-0	Ind
1959	Ben Schwartzwalder	11-0-0	Ind
1960	Ben Schwartzwalder	7-2-0	Ind
1961	Ben Schwartzwalder	8-3-0	Ind
1962	Ben Schwartzwalder	5-5-0	Ind
1963	Ben Schwartzwalder	8-2-0	Ind
1964	Ben Schwartzwalder	7-4-0	Ind
1965	Ben Schwartzwalder	7-3-0	Ind
1966	Ben Schwartzwalder	8-3-0	Ind
1967	Ben Schwartzwalder	8-2-0	Ind
1968	Ben Schwartzwalder	6-4-0	Ind
1969	Ben Schwartzwalder	5-5-0	Ind
1970	Ben Schwartzwalder	6-4-0	Ind
1971	Ben Schwartzwalder	5-5-1	Ind
1972	Ben Schwartzwalder	5-6-0	Ind
1973	Ben Schwartzwalder	2-9-0	Ind

Ben Schwartzwalder was carried off the field by SU players following the team's 48-21 thrashing of Penn State in the Carrier Dome on Oct. 17, 1987. Schwartzwalder was the last SU coach to beat the Nittany Lions before the undefeated 1987 Orangemen pulled off the feat.

It gives me great pleasure that in the next half of this book, before we jump and leap and sometimes limp to 2018, that we cover the twenty-five years of Ben Schwartzwalder in this one big chapter. Without having written one word of the big stories in this chapter yet, I anticipate that it will be one of the longest chapters in this book. Otherwise I may have to come up with a lengthy lecture as a summation. God bless Ben Schwartzwalder and the Syracuse Orangemen.

1949 Ben Schwartzwalder Coach # 22

For those football aficionados who just are not sure who Ben Schwartzwalder is, you are about to find out. Suffice it to say that he is one of the football immortals, a legend in the game of football. Knute Rockne became the first big time legend after coaching just 13 seasons with Notre Dame. Ben Schwartzwalder gained his immortality after a brilliant 25-year tenure with the Syracuse Orangemen. Ben made a big difference.

I was one-year old when Schwartzwalder took the reins at Syracuse and until I was twenty-six years old, in my fifth year at IBM, the name Schwartzwalder was forever ingrained in my mind as one of the greatest coaches ever. During these first five years of my 23 ½ years with IBM, I spent the first two years in Utica, NY just 46 miles from Syracuse. Syracuse was our Regional Office, so I spent a lot of time in classes as well as at the big IBM data center. When I asked people in Utica, as a 21-year old Assistant Systems Engineer, where to go for fun, the did not hesitate to tell me that Syracuse was only 46 miles away. Great down and I was back many times for football games. Everybody in Syracuse and even in my home town in Northeastern, PA knew Ben Schwartzwalder. He was a living immortal.

Ben Schwartzwalder was a "little guy" but only in stature. He was tough as nails. Schwartzwalder played center at West Virginia University, despite weighing only 146 pounds. He was also an all-campus wrestler in 1930 in the 155-pound weight class. He was captain of the WV football team in 1933. He loved Syracuse and he loved WV, engaging the Mountaineers in an annual rivalry game from when he took over the SU program in 1949.

Chapter 12 Coach Ben Schwartzwalder From 1949-1953

Floyd Burdette "Ben" Schwartzwalder was head football coach at Syracuse University from 1949 to 1973, leading the SU team to an impressive record of 153 wins, 91 losses, and 3 ties.

At Syracuse, this immortal coach trained future National Football League stars such as Jim Brown, Larry Csonka, Floyd Little and Ernie Davis, the first African American to win the Heisman Trophy. Ben (Ben was a childhood nickname) Schwartzwalder was born in Point Pleasant, West Virginia, on June 2, 1909. He attended West Virginia University, where he received a bachelor's degree in physical education in 1933 and a master's degree in education in 1935. Schwartzwalder then coached high school football in West Virginia and Ohio until 1941.

During World War II, Schwartzwalder enlisted and served as a paratrooper in the United States Army. As a member of the famed 82nd Airborne, he parachuted onto Normandy Beach on D-Day in 1944. He rose to the rank of major and was awarded a Silver Star, a Bronze Star, a Purple Heart, four battle stars, and a Presidential Unit citation. He retired as a lieutenant colonel.

After the war Schwartzwalder became head football coach at Muhlenberg College in Allentown, Pennsylvania, and compiled a 25-5 record between 1946 and 1948.

Schwartzwalder became head football coach at Syracuse University in 1949. He led the football team to a 1959 National Championship, four Lambert Trophies, and 7 bowl games. He recruited such notable players as Jim Brown, Ernie Davis, Jim Nance, Floyd Little, and Larry Csonka. Schwartzwalder retired after the 1973 season.

In 1959 Schwartzwalder was voted Coach of the Year, and in 1967 he was elected President of the National Football Coaches Association. Inducted into the College Football Hall of Fame in 1982, he is also in the Huntington High School Hall of Fame and West Virginia University Hall of Fame. Schwartzwalder also has a trophy named after him that goes to the winner of the annual Syracuse University-West Virginia University football game.

Schwartzwalder and his wife, Ruth ("Reggie") had two daughters, SU san and Mary.

He died on April 28, 1993, in St. Petersburg, Florida. He was one of a kind. I think you are going to enjoy our recounting of the 25 great Schwartzwalder years.

The 1949 Season

The 1949 Syracuse Orangemen football team competed in their sixtieth season of intercollegiate football. They were led by the soon-to-be immortal, Ben Schwartzwalder in his first of twenty-five seasons as head coach of the Syracuse Orangemen. This SU squad finished this year with a much better record (4-5-0) than the last several years. The team, the fans, and the alumni were expecting big things from their new coach and for the most part they would not be disappointed. The team captain was James Fiaccio

The Orangemen played their season opener on Sept 23, 1949 at Archbold Stadium on the campus of Syracuse University, and the Orangemen lost to Boston University W (21-33). On Oct 1 at home, SU defeated Lafayette in a tough match, W (20-13) before 22,000 fans. On Oct 7 at home Temple beat Syracuse L (14-7). Then, on Oct 15, at Archbold Stadium, SU beat Rutgers W (21-9). On Oct 22, at Fordham in a game played at the Polo Grounds in NYC, Syracuse lost L (21-47).

On Oct 29, at New Beaver Field in University Park, PA, SU was beaten by Penn State L (21-33) before 18,600 fans.
Next at #7 ranked Cornell, on Nov 5, the Orangemen lost at Schoellkopf Field in Ithaca, NY L (7–33) before 33,000 fans. On Nov 12 at home, SU defeated Holy Cross W (47–13). The real test for Ben Schwartzwalder was "could he beat Colgate? On Nov 15, like always at Archbold Stadium in Syracuse, NY, this game however, had an atypical outcome as Syracuse mopped up Colgate W (35–7) before a packed house at 36,232.

1950 Ben Schwartzwalder Coach # 22

The 1950 Syracuse Orangemen football team competed in their sixty-first season of intercollegiate football. They were led by Ben Schwartzwalder in his second of twenty-five seasons as head coach of the Syracuse Orangemen. This SU squad finished this year with an even 500 record at (5-5-0). The lose all the time years were done. years. The team, the fans, and the alumni were tuning in to the big things that would come from their new coach. The captains this year were elected for each game and they were known as game captains.

The Orangemen played their season opener on Sept 23, 1950 at Archbold Stadium on the campus of Syracuse University, and the Orangemen defeated Rutgers University, W (42-12). On Sept 29, at home, SU lost to Temple at Temple Stadium in Philadelphia, PA by an extra point L (6–7). On Oct 7 at home, Cornell put a mini-licking on the Orangemen L (7-26). Then, on Oct 14, at Archbold Stadium, SU beat Penn State W (27-7). On Oct 21, at Holy Cross Fitton Field in Worcester, Mass, SU prevailed W (34-27).

On Oct 28, at Boston, University, in a game played at Fenway Park, Boston, MA., the Orangemen walked away with the win W (13-7). On Nov 4, at Lafayette's Fisher Field in Easton, PA SU claimed the win W (34-9) before 9,000 fans.

On Nov 10, at John Carroll in Cleveland Stadium in Cleveland, OH the Orangemen took one in the teeth L (16–21) before 16,724 fans. Then on Nov 18, a repeat victory over Colgate would not occur at Archbold Stadium Syracuse, NY in the traditional at-home every year rivalry. Colgate charmed the Orangemen again into losing a tough game L (14–19) before a packed house of 38,000. Instead of Columbia, in the season finale this year it was a tough Fordham team fighting at the Polo Grounds in New York, NY. SU sustained a close loss L (6–13), before 13,832 fans.

1951 Ben Schwartzwalder Coach # 22

The 1951 Syracuse Orangemen football team competed in their sixty-second season of intercollegiate football. They were led by Ben

Schwartzwalder in his third of twenty-five seasons as head coach of the Syracuse Orangemen. This SU squad finished this year with the first positive record in seven years (5-4-0). The team, the fans, and the alumni were becoming more and more pleased. The captains this year were Ed Dobrowolski & John Donat.

The Orangemen played their season opener on Sept 23, 1951 at Archbold Stadium on the campus of Syracuse University, and the Orangemen defeated Temple University in a shutout, W (19-0). On Sept 29, at home, SU lost to #20 Cornell at Schoellkopf Field in Ithaca, NY L (14–21) before 25,000. On Oct 6, Lafayette met a brick wall at Archbold Stadium in Syracuse, NY as the Orangemen pitched a blowout shutout W (46–0) before 13,000 fans. On Oct 13 # 7 Illinois entered Archbold Stadium Syracuse, NY to get a piece of the rebounding Orangemen and they got more than their due share L (20–41) before 27,000.

On Oct 20 at Dartmouth Memorial Field in Hanover, NH. The Orangemen were shut out L 0–14by the Big Green. Before 11,000. On Oct 27 Fordham arrived in Archbold Stadium in Syracuse, NY expecting to beat the Orangemen again but they did not as SU got the big W, W (33–20) before 5,000. On Nov 10 at Penn State's New Beaver Field in University Park, PA in the annual rivalry game, PSU had their way and defeated SU L (13–32) before 15,000.

Colgate always played its home games v Syracuse at Archbold Stadium because it was not far from Hamilton, NY. For years, Colgate provided big lickings to the Syracuse team. At one point, SU had not won a game for thirteen seasons with two-ties mixed in. On this particular Nov 17, with Ben Schwartzwalder at the helm at Archbold Stadium in Syracuse, NY, in this well-publicized rivalry game, Syracuse defeated Colgate against W (9–0) before a packed house of 34,000 excited fans.

On Nov 24, at Boston University in a game played at Fenway Park in Boston, MA, Syracuse got the big win W (26–19) before 10,148 in the Red Sox baseball park

1952 Ben Schwartzwalder Coach # 22

The 1952 Syracuse Orangemen football team competed in their sixty-third season of intercollegiate football. They were led by Ben Schwartzwalder in his fourth of twenty-five seasons as head coach of the Syracuse Orangemen. This SU squad finished this year with a very respectable record of (7-3-0). The team, the fans, and the alumni were very pleased. The captains this year were Richard Beyer & Joe Szombathy

All American Robert R. Fleck

R. R. Fleck was the beloved husband of Mary Krawchuk Fleck with whom he shared 63 years of marriage. He was the son of the late John and Esther Briggs Fleck.

He was a life-long resident of Coatesville, graduating from St. Horace Scott High School in 1949, where he was a two-sport athlete.

Bob attended Manlius Prep before entering Syracuse University, where he was selected as an All-American in 1952 and 1953 for Football. He was selected as a member of their All-Century Team in 2000. Bob served in the U.S. Army from 1954 to 1962. He was employed at Lukens Steel Company until his retirement in 1992.

In 1952, Syracuse had jumped the line again from mediocrity to greatness because the team was getting support from the administration and they had a great coach. This was a historically successful season for the Orangemen, which included victories over rivals Penn State and Colgate. Syracuse lost only twice in the regular season: their season opener against the former college all-stars of the Bolling Air Force Base, and to eventual national champions Michigan State.

The Orangemen were quite pleased with themselves and their coach as they finished the regular season with a record of 7–2 and were ranked 14th in the final AP Poll. This was their first ranked finish in school history. The team was awarded its first Lambert Trophy, which signified them as champions of the East.

The Orangemen were invited to the 1953 Orange Bowl, the school's first ever bowl game, where they lost to Alabama The best that I can say about the Alabama game is that at the end of the first quarter, the score was 6-7 in favor of Alabama. This was such a great breakaway year for Ben Schwartzwalder and Syracuse coming from the pits of the 1940's that you'll have to look someplace else than in this positive season summary to find the specifics of the Orange Bowl v Alabama. There would be many more fine seasons for the Orangemen.

The Orangemen played their season opener on Sept 20, 1952 against a military all-star team from Bolling Field at Archbold Stadium in Syracuse, NY before 18,000 fans and could not survive the tough play of the all-stars. L (12–13). On Sept 27, at home, SU defeated Boston University W (34–21). On Oct 3 at Temple at Temple Stadium in Philadelphia, PA , SU beat the Owls W (27–0). On Oct 11, at home v Cornell, the Orangemen defeated the Red Raiders W 26–6 before 23,000 fans. On Oct 18 at #1 ranked Michigan State at Macklin Stadium in East Lansing, MI, despite working hard, SU could not overcome the talent of the Spartans and were defeated L (7-48) before 32,254.

On Oct 25 at home v Holy Cross, SU prevailed W (20–19) before 18,000. On Nov 8 # 15 Penn State arrived to claim a victory v the Orangemen but the strong SU team sent them home with a defeat W

(25–7) before 15,000. Then, on Nov 15, an always tough Colgate team now faced a #13 ranked SU team at Archbold Stadium in Syracuse, NY and Colgate went home weeping after the Orangemen got the victory W (20–14) before a packed stadium of 32,000.

On Nov 22 #15 SU played Fordham at Triborough Stadium in New York, NY and came home with the win W (26–13) before 10,000 fans. SU was then ranked #14 and got to play Alabama in the Orange Bowl.

On January 1, 1953, #14 SU paired off against # 9 Alabama at Burdine Stadium in Miami, FL in the Orange Bowl. After the first quarter which was very tight, SU lost its edge and succumbed to an embarrassing Orange Bowl defeat of L (6–61) before 66,280.

1953 Ben Schwartzwalder Coach # 22

The 1953 Syracuse Orangemen football team competed in their sixty-fourth season of intercollegiate football. They were led by Ben Schwartzwalder in his fifth of twenty-five seasons as head coach of the Syracuse Orangemen. This SU squad finished the year with a very respectable record of (5-3-1). The captains were assigned by game and known as game captains.

The Orangemen played their season opener on Sept 26, 1953 against Temple at Archbold Stadium in Syracuse, NY before 18,000 fans and defeated the Owls in a major shutout W (42-0). On Oct 2 at home v Boston University at home, the teams played to a tie T (14014). On Oct 10 at home. SU defeated Fordham W (20–13) before 20,000. On Oct at Penn State's New Beaver Field in University Park, PA, the Orangemen did not survive the Nittany Lions L (14–20) before 21,500 fans. On Oct 24 at # 7 Illinois's Memorial Stadium in Champaign, IL, the Orangemen almost achieved victory but lost despite a fine effort, L (13–20) before 30,076

On October 31 at Holy Cross on Fitton Field in Worcester, MA, SU won the game W (21–0) before 15,000. Then, on Nov 7 at Cornell's Schoellkopf Field in Ithaca, NY, the Orangemen dominated W (26–

0). Always worried about Colgate, on Nov 14, at Archbold Stadium in Syracuse, NY, SU prevailed W (34–18) before a packed house of 37,000. In the season finale, on Nov 21, at Villanova in Franklin Field, Philadelphia, PA SU dropped a close on L (13–14). It was a great season and with a little extra luck, it would have been better.

1954 Ben Schwartzwalder Coach # 22

The 1954 Syracuse Orangemen football team competed in their sixty-fifth season of intercollegiate football. They were led by Ben Schwartzwalder in his sixth of twenty-five seasons as head coach of the Syracuse Orangemen. This SU squad finished this year with a medsa record of (4-4-1). The captains this year were assigned by game and known as game captains.

Jim Brown, # 44 All American

All American Jim Brown
#44 — JIM BROWN, RB, SYRACUSE (1954-56)
It is a number owned by Syracuse, and here is the man who started the legend. Brown was the perfect blend of power and speed. He set an NCAA record in 1943 by scoring 43 points against Colgate — six

touchdowns and seven PATs — and was a unanimous All-America selection as a senior in 1956. — Runner-up: Ernie Davis, RB, Syracuse (1959-61)

The Orangemen played their season opener on Sept 25, 1954 against Villanova at Archbold Stadium in Syracuse, NY before 25,000 fans and defeated the Wildcats W (28-6). On Oct 2, SU lost to #10Penn State at home (0-13) before18,000. On Oct 16 at Boston University Field, in Boston, MA the Eagles beat the Orangemen L (19–41). On Oct 23 at Illinois Memorial Stadium in Champaign, IL, the Schwartzwalder squad dropped another L (6–34) before 41,820 fans.

Then, on Oct SU defeated Holy Cross at Archbold Stadium W (25-20 before 20,000. On Nov 6, at Cornell's Schoellkopf Field in Ithaca, NY, the Orangemen were defeated by the Big Red, L (6–14). In the big rivalry game on Nov 13 v Colgate at Archbold Stadium, SU defeated the Red Raiders W (31–12) before 37,000 fans. Notice as the years go by, as we move from the fifties to the sixties to 2018, and beyond, bigger stadiums were built. Interest in college football increased and attendance would eventually reach and surpass 100,000 fans per game in the nation's largest stadiums. On Nov 20 at Fordham in a game played at the Polo Grounds in New York, NY, the Orangemen gained a win in their season finale W (20–7) before 10,423

1955 Ben Schwartzwalder Coach # 22

The 1955 Syracuse Orangemen football team competed in their sixty-sixth season of intercollegiate football. They were led by Ben Schwartzwalder in his seventh of twenty-five seasons as head coach of the Syracuse Orangemen. This SU squad finished this year with a winning record of (5-3-0). The captains this year were assigned by game and known as game captains.

The Orangemen played their season opener on Sept 24, 1955 against Pittsburgh's Panthers at Archbold Stadium in Syracuse, NY before 16,000 fans and were defeated by the Panthers L (12-22). On Oct 8 SU beat Boston University at home W (27–12) Then, for the first time in many years, on Oct 15, SU defeated # 18 Army at Michie Stadium in West Point, NY W (13–0) before 12,500. On October 22 SU lost to #2 Maryland at Archbold Stadium in Syracuse, NY L (13–34) before a packed house of 32,500. On Oct 29 at #13 Holy Cross in Fitton Field, Worcester, MA, SU prevailed in a blowout win W (49–9).

SU was then ranked at #18 after the Holy Cross win. The following week, on Nov 5 at Penn State. The always tough Nittany Lions beat Syracuse by one point at New Beaver Field in University Park, PA L (20–21) before 30,434. On Nov12, in the traditional rivalry v Colgate at Archbold Stadium, SU kept the streak going with a nice win W (W 26–19) before a packed house of 39,500. On Nov 19, SU p picked up its fifth win in the season finale against #13 West Virginia at Mountaineer Field in Morgantown, WV. W (20-13) Because Ben Schwartzwalder was a WVA graduate, this became a new SU rivalry and was played every year in the Schwartzwalder years.

The Ben Schwartzwalder Trophy is the trophy that was presented annually to the winner of the game. It was introduced in 1993 and is named after former WVU football player and Syracuse head coach Ben Schwartzwalder, who died in April of that year. It was sculpted by Syracuse player Jim Ridlon.

1956 Ben Schwartzwalder Coach # 22

The 1956 Syracuse Orangemen football team competed in their sixty-seventh season of intercollegiate football. They were led by Ben Schwartzwalder in his eighth of twenty-five seasons as head coach of the Syracuse Orangemen. This SU squad finished this year with a fine record of (7-2-0) which included the Bowl game. The captains this year were assigned by game and known as game captains.

Syracuse finished its regular season with a record of 7–1 and were ranked 8th nationally in both final polls. They were awarded the Lambert Trophy, which signified them as champions of the East. Syracuse was invited to the 1957 Cotton Bowl, where the team was defeated by TCU.

This 1956 team was led by unanimous All-American halfback Jim Brown. Brown set school records in average yards-per-carry (6.2), single-season rushing yards (986), single-game rushing touchdowns (6, vs. Colgate), and most points scored in a game (43, vs. Colgate).He was drafted sixth overall in the 1957 NFL Draft and went on to become one of the most celebrated professional athletes of all time.

I remember when my dad bought us our first TV for the family. It was a B/W 1957 Admiral. It had many tubes and a 21-inch picture tube. My dad often told me about Jim Brown as he played for the Cleveland Browns when Paul Brown was the coach in those days. He also said that to maintain his speed, Jim Brown did not wear hip pads. I learned recently that he taped foam rubber inside his football pants to help cushion the blows – a little trivia.

The Orangemen played their season opener on Sept 22, 1956 against Maryland's Byrd Stadium in College Park, MD. Syracuse defeated the Terrapins W (26–12) before 27,000. On September 29 at #10 Pittsburgh #7 Syracuse lost to Pitt in Pitt Stadium, Pittsburgh, PA L (7–14) before 49,287 fans.

Two weeks later, on Oct 13 #20 West Virginia lost to Syracuse at Archbold Stadium on the campus of Syracuse University in Syracuse, NY in the newly christened rivalry game W (27–20) before

25,000. On Oct 20 #13 Syracuse defeated Army at home in Syracuse, NY W (7–0) before a top crowd of 40,053. On Oct 27, #14 ranked SU defeated Boston University in Nickerson Field in Boston, MA W (21–7).

Highlights Syracuse V Penn State

On Nov 3, #17 ranked Syracuse defeated #12 ranked Penn State at home W (13-9) before 35,475 fans in Archbold Stadium.

On Nov. 3, 1956, Syracuse got to celebrate five Eastern Football Championships and one game this season, when the Orange finished with a 7-2 record. Syracuse finished the regular-season on a six-game winning streak. The highlight of that winning streak was this 13-9 win over No. 12 Penn State. Syracuse came into the game ranked No. 17. The Orange were led this season by Jim Brown, considered by many to be the greatest running back ever to play the game.

On Nov 10 #9 Syracuse beat Holy Cross at home W (41–20). Then in one of the worst beatings ever delivered by SU over Colgate, on Nov 17, the Orangemen walloped the Red Raiders W (61-7) at Archbold field before 39, 701. SU finished at 7-1 and then headed off to the Cotton Bowl on November 1 ranked # 8 in the country.

Let's talk about Jim Brown's last regular season game in this great recap by Lincoln Werden of the New York Times

Jim Brown's Farewell: 6 Touchdowns
By LINCOLN A. WERDEN   November 17, 1956

SYRACUSE   far as the Colgate football team was concerned, there was just too much Jimmy Brown in the game today. The crushing Syracuse left halfback from Manhasset, L.I., in an individual performance of all-America proportions, led his team to a 61,7 triumph before a sellout crowd of 39,701.

In his final game for the Orange, Brown accounted for 43 points, scoring six touchdowns and kicking 7 extra-point placements. No other team in this fifty-seven-year-old series had tallied as many points as the Syracuse aggregation did in Archbold Stadium this cold gray afternoon. The highest total credited to any previous Syracuse squad came in 1944. That was 43 points, the total that Brown amassed by the time he made his final exit early in the fourth period. In 1898, Colgate defeated Syracuse, 58 to 0, and that was the scoring mark shattered by Brown and this alert, fast-moving squad that rolled on to accumulate 511 yards by rushing.

Brown's share of this figure was 197 yards on twenty-two carries. As a result, the senior left-half sent his season's ground-gaining yardage to 986 yards. This erased the previous best by any Syracuse player, which was the 805 yards compiled by George Davis in 1949.

With Governor Harriman among the spectators, the Syracuse fans enjoyed this concluding game of one of the Orange's successful football seasons. There are rumors on the campus that their team may be selected for a post-season bowl game. Colgate, victor over Yale earlier in the season, had been beaten thrice before this contest. Syracuse was the pre-game favorite, having lost only once, by 14,7, to Pitt. But no one anticipated the stunning show Brown was about to put on.

This victory put Syracuse's string at six over the Red Raiders, a record. At halftime, the press box announcer jocularly said: "The score is now Brown 27, Colgate 7." Brown was responsible for scoring all of his team's points in the first half. His longest score of the day was on a pitch-out from quarterback Chuck Zimmerman midway in the first period with Syracuse ahead by 14,0. Brown raced down his right sideline 50 yards for the touchdown. It was 20,7 and Brown's try for the extra point was wide.

Jim Brown's 43 points stood as the National Collegiate Athletic Association's single-game record until Howard Griffith scored 48 points on eight touchdowns for the University of Illinois in 1990.

The Cotton Bowl.

On January 1, 1957 #8 SU faced off against #14 TCU in the Cotton Bowl Classic. The game was played in the Cotton Bowl Stadium in Dallas Texas. The Horned Frogs beat the Orangemen in a very exciting game L (27-28) before 68,000 fans.

Syracuse had just one loss. It was to Pittsburgh, who enjoyed a great season but ended up losing in the Gator Bowl). SU was 8th ranked, led by Jim Brown, who would play his last game before becoming an NFL player. Texas Christian had finished 2nd in the Southwest Conference, but was invited to play in the Cotton Bowl due to first place Texas A&M being under NCAA sanctions. This was TCU's fifth Cotton Bowl appearance, having lost their previous four (and not winning since 1937). This was Syracuse's first appearance, along with their first bowl game since the 1953 Orange Bowl, which was not a good story.

Game summary

TCU had two 14-point leads, both near the end of the halves. John Nikkel started the scoring for TCU with a touchdown catch from Chuck Curtis, and in the second quarter, Jim Shofner caught a TD pass to make it 14-0. But Jim Brown got it going and ran for two touchdowns in a span of 6:52 to tie the game at halftime.

Late in the third quarter after Brown fumbled the ball back to TCU, Curtis scored on a touchdown run to give TCU the lead back. After another Brown fumble in the fourth quarter, Jim Swink ran in for a touchdown to give TCU a 28-14 lead with 11:44 to go. But Brown would not be stopped as Syracuse went 49 yards in 13 plays and scored on a Brown run. Brown went up for his third PAT attempt of the day to try and narrow the lead to 7.

But Chico Mendoza blocked the extra point, keeping the score 28-20. But Syracuse had one last drive in them, going 43 yards in 3 plays and with 1:17 left, Jim Ridlon caught a pass from Charles Zimmerman to narrow the lead to 28-27. Syracuse kicked it deep but TCU held on and did not let Syracuse get the ball back, in what would turn out to be TCU's last bowl win until 1998. Jim Brown and Norman Hamilton were named Outstanding Players of the game. What a game. Football is a game of inches and luck for sure.

Syracuse University's Jim Brown runs for some of the 132 yards he gained during the 1957 Cotton Bowl against Texas Christian University in Dallas.

1957 Ben Schwartzwalder Coach # 22

The 1957 Syracuse Orangemen football team competed in their sixty-eighth season of intercollegiate football. They were led by Ben Schwartzwalder in his ninth of twenty-five seasons as head coach of the Syracuse Orangemen. This SU squad finished this year with a winning record of (5-3-1). The captains this year were assigned by game and known as game captains.

The Orangemen played their season and home opener on Sept 28, 1957 against Iowa State at Archbold Stadium on the campus of Syracuse University in Syracuse, NY. The game ended in a tie (7-7). On Oct 5 Boston University at Archbold Stadium, SU got the win W (27–20). On Oct 12 at Cornell's Schoellkopf Field in Ithaca, NY,

SU won again, W (34–0) before 25,000 fans. Then on Oct 19 at Nebraska Memorial Stadium in Lincoln, NE. the Orangemen defeated the Cornhuskers W (26–9) before 37,582. On Oct 26 at home in Archbold Stadium, PSU beat the SU L (12–20) before 35,000.

On Nov 2 at Pittsburgh's Pitt Stadium in Pittsburgh, PA, SU got the win against the Panthers, W (24–21) before 35,430. Then on Nov 9 SU lost by one point against Holy Cross at Archbold Stadium L (19-20). On Nov 16, Syracuse beat Colgate again in Archbold Stadium in Syracuse, NY 34–6 before 38,500 fans. On Nov 23 in the new rivalry for the Ben Schwartzwalder Trophy (before the Trophy was given) at West Virginia Mountaineer Field, Morgantown, WV, Syracuse was barely beaten by the Mountaineers.

1958 Ben Schwartzwalder Coach # 22

The 1958 Syracuse Orangemen football team competed in their sixty-ninth season of intercollegiate football. They were led by Ben Schwartzwalder in his tenth of twenty-five seasons as head coach of the Syracuse Orangemen. This SU squad finished this year with a great record of (8-1-0). SU was ranked #9 in the AP and got to play Oklahoma in the Orange Bowl where they were defeated. The captains this year were assigned by game and known as game captains.

All American Ronald Luciano

Luciano was born in Endicott, in southern upstate New York, 150 miles (240 km) southwest of Albany, near the Pennsylvania border, and lived his entire life there. The 6-foot-4, 260-pound Luciano was a standout offensive and defensive tackle at Syracuse University, where he majored in mathematics. He played in the 1957 Cotton Bowl and was named to the 1958 College Football All-America Team.

In 1959, he played on the Orangemen's national championship squad with future Heisman Trophy winner Ernie Davis.

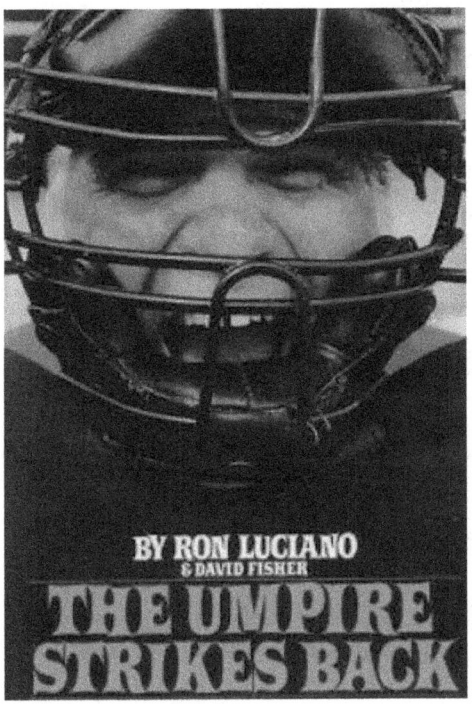

The Baltimore Colts selected him as an offensive tackle in the third round of the 1959 NFL Draft, and immediately traded him to the Detroit Lions; but he suffered a serious shoulder injury in the College All-Star Game, and never played for the Lions. He was traded in 1960 to the Minnesota Vikings, who released him at the end of the season. The AFL Buffalo Bills picked him up in 1961, but a knee injury forced his retirement after only two games. He was a famous major league umpire.

Games of the 1958 season

The Orangemen played their season and home opener on Sept 27, 1958 against Boston College at Archbold Stadium on the campus of Syracuse University in Syracuse, NY. SU defeated the Eagles W (24–14) before 15,000. Holy Cross was a major contender in college football in the 1950's and gave SU a run for its money. In a season spoiler on Oct 4 at Holy Cross' Fitton Field in Worcester, MA, Syracuse did not have enough to take this game and lost by just one point L (13–14) before. This would be the only loss of the regular season for Ben Schwartzwalder's Orangemen.

On Oct 11 SU beat Cornell at Archbold Stadium in a shutout / blowout W (55–0). Then, on Oct 18 SU beat Nebraska at home in a shutout W (38-0). On Oct 25 at Penn State's New Beaver Field in University Park, PA in a tough match, the Orangemen defeated the Nittany Lions W (14–6) before 27,000.

Highlight Match SU v Rival Pittsburgh

On Nov 1, SU beat # 12/10 Pittsburgh at home in a very tight match W (16–13) before 38,000. It was a great game.

It was November 1, 1958 and the season was coming to a close. The Orangemen ended the regular-season on a seven-game winning streak, highlighted by this 16-13 victory over No. 12 Pittsburgh. The Orange was unranked entering the game but jumped up to No. 12 afterward. The Orange climbed as high as No. 9, losing to Oklahoma in the Orange Bowl (game highlights at end of this section). Syracuse's success this season was a springboard to its national title run the following year.

On Nov 7, now ranked #12, in a game played at Boston University's Nickerson Field in Boston, MA, the Orangemen shut out the Terriers W (42–0). Then, on Nov 15 at home, SU shut out Colgate W (47-0). In the season finale on Nov 22 at West Virginia, now ranked #10/11, in a game played at Mountaineer Field Morgantown, WV, the Orangemen defeated the Mountaineers W 15–12 giving them a berth in the 1959 Orange Bowl. So far SU had bad luck in Bowl Games.

The Orange Bowl

On January 1, 1959, playing # 5 Oklahoma, the #9/10 Syracuse Orangemen were defeated in the Orange Bowl in Miami, FL playing in the Orange Bowl game L (6–21) before 75,281

This year, Oklahoma's made its fourth Orange Bowl appearance in six seasons while Syracuse was playing in its second Orange Bowl in six seasons. Oklahoma was a very well-known and powerful team and had won its thirteenth straight Big-Seven title and Syracuse was an independent and thus had no conference affiliation and title to chase. The first of the day's four major bowl games this year had its kickoff at 1 p.m. EST. It was shown on CBS TV, and Oklahoma was everybody's thirteen-point favorite.

Game Summary

Oklahoma wasted no time scoring early with Prentice Gautt's torrid rushing attack and touchdown just three minutes into the game. With the first quarter running down, Syracuse was driving and in the red zone but fumbled the ball back to the Sooners. The Sooners had avoided a red-zone showdown. With 2:56 left this quarter, Oklahoma's Brewster Hobby caught a lateral and then passed the ball to Ross Coyle, who took off unimpeded for 79 yards. He got the TD and the Sooners had a 14-0 lead.

The teams were now settled in and it was one punt after another back and forth and there was no scoring in the second quarter. There were a lot of punts. Oklahoma made the most of a third quarter punt when Hobby sealed the game for Oklahoma by returning an Orangeman punt 40 yards for a third touchdown to make the score 21–0 after three quarters. SU could not get its offensive engine going.

Mark Weber finally gave the Orangemen their only points on his touchdown run after a 69-yard drive in the fourth quarter but a try for a two-point conversion failed as the pass went incomplete. That was it for the scoring in this game that was hard fought but otherwise dull. Despite Syracuse's run attack, poor fundamentals doomed the Orangemen as they committed two fumbles by the backs and two passes were intercepted. They had missed a number of chances but overall were not playing well. Oklahoma won its fourth Orange Bowl in six seasons. Those reading ahead know that in the following season, the Orangemen were undefeated and won the national title.

1959 Ben Schwartzwalder Coach # 22

The 1959 Syracuse Orangemen football team competed in their seventieth season of intercollegiate football. They were led by Ben Schwartzwalder in his eleventh of twenty-five seasons as head coach of the Syracuse Orangemen. This SU squad finished this year with a great record of (11-0-0). SU was ranked #1 in both polls and won the national championship. It was not mythical. It was real. They beat

Texas in the Cotton Bowl Classic. Gerhard Schwedes was the team captain for the 1959 championship team.

All American Guard Roger Wilfred Davis

He was born June 23, 1938. Davis is an all-American lineman for Syracuse University who played on the 1959 championship team at outside linebacker. He is a former professional American football player who played offensive lineman for seven seasons for the Chicago Bears, the Los Angeles Rams, and the New York Giants. He was drafted by the Bears in the first round (7th overall) of the 1960 NFL Draft, and is one of only two guards drafted in the first round by the team (Kyle Long being the other).

All American End Frederick J. "Fred" Mautino

He was born November 7, 1936 and was an all American on the 1959 SU National Championship team. He was an American football player. A native of Reading, Pennsylvania, Mautino attended Reading High School and Staunton Military Academy. He then played college football at the end position for Syracuse. He helped lead the 1959 Syracuse Orangemen football team to the school's only national championship. Prior to the 1960 Cotton Bowl, Mautino proclaimed the 1959 Orangemen "the greatest college team of all time."

He was selected by the Associated Press as a first-team player on its 1959 College Football All-America Team. He was also selected at the 1959 athlete of the year for Berks County, Pennsylvania. As a senior in 1960, he was selected as a third-team All-American by the American Football Coaches Association and the United Press International.

All American OL Robert E. Yates

Yates was born November 20, 1938 and passed away on April 16, 2013. He was an American football offensive lineman who played college football for Syracuse and professionally in the American Football League (AFL) for the Boston Patriots. Born in Montpelier, Vermont, Yates was a standout student-athlete at Montpelier High School.

At Syracuse, Yates was a member of the undefeated Orange national championship team in 1959. He was named first-team All-American and was later honored as one of the "Forty-Four Players of the Century" at Syracuse.

After graduation, Yates was an original member of the AFL's Boston Patriots, playing from 1960 to 1965 as an offensive lineman and kicker.

Yates coached and taught for 34 years at colleges and high schools in Massachusetts and Vermont, including Burlington High School. Steven Yates, one of three sons, played for him at BHS, which saw a football rebirth during Yates' era from 1979–1987.

Yates is the only Vermont native to have played major-league American professional football, and in 2012 was inducted into the inaugural class of the Vermont Sports Hall of Fame.

Games of the 1959 championship season

The Orangemen played their season and home opener on Sept 26, 1959 against Kansas at Archbold Stadium on the campus of Syracuse University in Syracuse, NY. SU defeated the Jayhawks, W (35-21) before 25,000. Big things were coming this year and there was a feeling in the air. Opening day had the most fans in many years. On Oct 3 Maryland was shut out by #20 ranked Syracuse at Archbold Stadium W (29–0). On Oct 10 at Navy at Foreman Field Norfolk, VA in the Oyster Bowl field, SU won W (32–6). Then, on Oct 17 at home SU defeated Holy Cross in a big win W (42–6). Now, undefeated at 4-0, on Oct 24 at home, #6 SU shut out West Virginia W (44–0) before 35,000

On Oct 31 at Pittsburgh, at Pitt Stadium in Pittsburgh, PA SU shut out the Panthers W (35–0) before 25,761 fans. Then, on Nov 7 at #7

Penn State, at New Beaver Field in University Park, PA, #4 Syracuse beat the Nittany Lions W (20–18) in a nail biter before 32,800 fans—closest game of the year.

Best SU game of the year 1959

They called it The Game of the Year of the Day, 1959. The final score was Syracuse 20, Penn State 18. For Ben Schwartzwalder's Syracuse Orangemen, it was one of the 50 best games of all time in all of football. The date was November 7, 1959. The matchup was great as SU was heading for its first National Championship ever. Thus, it was #4 Syracuse at-6-0) at #7 Penn State at 7-0. It was a great matchup, but the teams still had to play to see who at the end of the game, would go home with the victory. Victory was what it was all about on this game day.

Though there was no BCS or FBS back then, the stakes were still high. Two undefeated teams each looking good and the battle was for the mythical national title even though it was a giant mess with few teams playing outside of their respective region. Nonetheless, this game was so big, the winner would become the East's representative in the title race.

This was Schwartzwalder's eleventh season at Syracuse. His slow building process was beginning to bear major fruit at Syracuse. After just one ranked finish in his first seven years, the Orange(men) finished eighth in 1956 and ninth in 1958, and with sophomore Ernie Davis emerging as the perfect complement to Ger Schwedes, Ben had exactly the pieces for the "run, and then run some more" offense.

After dealing with an unexpectedly tough game in the season opener, a 35-21 win over Kansas, SU had caught fire, outscoring Maryland, Navy, Holy Cross, and WVU by a combined 147-12. Whew! Meanwhile, Rip Engle's Nittany Lions were on their way to their best season in five years. The Nittany Lions had already won at Missouri and Army and had handled No. 13 Illinois, 20-9, in Cleveland (of all places). They would go on to take down #4 Alabama in the Liberty Bowl as well. But to earn a possible claim of a national title, they would need to beat the best Syracuse team of all time. Thanks to their spiffy special teams, they nearly did.

This great game story comes from *"50 Best."*:

On Nov 7, 1959, both the #1 and the #2 teams in the country would lose. This meant that the Syracuse / PSU winner would have a sudden claim to the top spot in the polls. The moment was not lost on the crowd of 32,800, the largest to fill Beaver Stadium to date; as many as 10,000 more fans trying to get tickets were turned down. (Penn State was in the process of expanding its stadium. It didn't expand it soon enough.

A year earlier, college football had adopted a two-point conversion option: After scoring a touchdown, you could choose to either attempt a one-point kick or line up with your offense and try to score a two-pointer from the 3. As Syracuse took a commanding 20-6 lead early in the fourth quarter, nobody was thinking about that rule change much. But they would soon enough.

On the ensuing kickoff after Davis' touchdown gave the Orangemen a 20-6 lead, Roger Kochman fielded the ball near the right sideline, weaved toward the middle of the field to meet up with his blockers, cut back to the right at the 30, then outran everyone else to the end zone. PSU missed an attempted two-point conversion, but it was a game again, 20-12.

Moments later, PSU's Andy Stynchula burst through the Syracuse line and blocked Bob Yates' attempted punt. The Nittany Lions recovered at the 1, and Sam Sohczak scored with 4:15 left. Penn State suddenly needed only a two-point conversion to tie the game. PSU faked an option left, and quarterback Richie Lucas handed the ball to Kochman on a counter. He was stuffed on the 1. Syracuse got the ball back and completely took special teams out of the equation by rushing for enough first downs to kill the clock and escape with a 20-18 win.

The box score:

Statistics

	Syracuse	Penn State
First Downs	19	8
Rushing Yardage	287	111
Passing Yardage	61	24
Passes	5-13	3-6
Passes intercepted by	1	0
Punts	4-35	7-13
Fumles lost	1	0
Yards penalized	45	15

Think about how many times a special teams play has triggered an upset? It almost derailed Syracuse's amazing season here. (A kickoff return touchdown is also what allowed Kansas to stick around for a bit.) The 'Cuse and PSU split the turnover battle, and the Orangemen won the yardage battle, 348-135. But the double dose of Kochman's return and the blocked punt nearly spoiled everything. It didn't, though. And from this moment forward, Syracuse resumed playing like a title-worthy team. The Orange beat Colgate and Boston U. by a combined 117-0, went out west and destroyed UCLA, 36-8, then took on former # 1 Texas in the Cotton Bowl and survived a bitter slugfest, 23-14.

After 1959, Ben Schwartzwalder put together another couple of nice seasons with Ernie Davis, and Davis would famously win the Heisman in 1961 and become the No. 1 pick in the 1962 NFL draft before succumbing to leukemia in 1963.
Penn State, meanwhile, would finished ranked each year from 1959-62 before trailing off a bit in Engle's last few seasons. Assistant Joe Paterno took over in 1966 and the rest is history.

Rest of the 1959 Games before the Cotton Bowl

O Nov 14, SU was #1 and they played Colgate at home in Archbold Stadium and shellacked the Red Raiders in a blowout W (71-0)

On Nov 21at Boston University, still #1 Syracuse played at Nickerson Field in Boston, MA and shut out the Terriors W 46–0 before 22,000. Just one more game for an undefeated regular season. It came on Dec 5at #17 UCLA played at the Los Angeles Memorial Coliseum in Los Angeles, CA. #1 Syracuse beat the Bruins, handily, W 36–8 before 46,436 fans. SU won a berth to the Cotton Bowl.

On Jan 1, 1960 #1 Syracuse paired off against #4 Texas in the Cotton Bowl Classic held at the Cotton Bowl in Dallas, TX. SU was not about to go home disappointed and won the game by nine points W (23–14) before 75,504 fans.

Bowl Game Highlights by Life Magazine

In January 1960, an undefeated Syracuse team whipped Texas, 23-14, in the Cotton Bowl. But it wasn't especially pretty, as LIFE magazine reported in its Jan. 11, 1960, issue:

> As the game moved back and forth and the normal tensions of the players were increased by the body-crunching fury of the play, an ugly undercurrent of racial bitterness began to spread — with shocking results.
>
> At first in the game, the Syracuse players outdid themselves in showing what good sports they were, helping blocked Texans off the ground and slapping their rumps for friendly good measure. But this was short-lived. "Texas was really dirty," said one Syracuse player afterward. "We've never met a bunch like that before."
>
> What enraged them most was that much of Texas' dirty play seemed to be directed toward Syracuse's Negro players. Once when he was plowing through the line, said Negro fullback Art Baker, "one of them spit right in my face."
>
> John Brown, a Negro lineman, played nose to nose against 235-pound Texas tackle Larry Stephens. To goad him off balance, Brown claimed, Stephens kept calling him "a big black dirty

nigger." Finally, Brown warned him not to call him that again. When Stephens did, Brown swung.

Afterward Stephens apologized to Brown. But Brown had already forgiven him. "That Texas boy was just excited," he said. "Let's forget it."

Much of this on-field race-baiting was dramatized in The Express, the lukewarmly received 2008 film about Syracuse running back Ernie Davis' life. (Davis was the first black Heisman winner and the 1960 Cotton Bowl MVP who died of acute monocytic leukemia in 1963, at just 23 years old). Former Texas players have stated in the years since that no racial animus at all was on display in that Cotton Bowl, and that the Davis film itself was something of a factually challenged abomination; a number of Syracuse players, meanwhile, respectfully disagree with that neat, clean version of the game's history and have confirmed that, yeah, some decidedly ugly stuff went down on the field.

What's pretty clear from LIFE's reporting, though, even if it is a necessarily imperfect "first draft of history," is that something set those players off all those years ago — and we feel pretty confident that snide remarks about, say, the cultural shortfalls of upstate Onondaga County, New York, versus the glories of eastern Texas probably played very little if any role in the ruckus.

Ben Cosgrove is the editor of LIFE.com. Picture This is his weekly, and occasionally more frequent, feature for The Stacks and Deadspin.

Photo Credit: Robert W. Kelley—Time & Life Pics/Getty Images

The Action of the 1960 Cotton Bowl Game

The Orangemen had just completed a perfect season for the first time in their history and as such were declared national champions. But they were looking to win their first Cotton Bowl Classic, having lost previously in 1957 and having had tough luck in two Orange

Bowls. The Longhorns were co-champions of the Southwest Conference after losing to TCU late in the season, dropping from #2 to #4. This was the first Cotton Bowl Classic appearance for Coach Royal and the first for the Longhorns since 1953.

Photo Courtesy of the Cotton Bowl

The longest TD pass in Cotton Bowl Classic history happened in this game as Gerhard Schwedes, QB and team captain, threw an 87-yard pass to Ernie Davis early in the first quarter to give the Orangemen an early lead 1:13 into the game. Davis added another TD run midway through the second quarter to give the Orangemen a 15–0 lead at halftime.

Jack Collins caught a 69-yard pass from Bobby Lackey to narrow the lead 1:46 into the third quarter, but the conversion failed, making it only 15–6. While driving to try to narrow the lead, Davis intercepted a Lackey pass at the Texas 24. Three plays later Schwedes ran in for a 3-yard touchdown run to make it 23–6 after another conversion success. Lackey narrowed it to 23–14 on a touchdown run in the fourth quarter, but only 7:21 was left on the clock by then. From that point on, the two teams did not seriously threaten to score again as the game ended with a great Syracuse win, capping its finest season in history.

1960 Ben Schwartzwalder Coach # 22

The 1960 Syracuse Orangemen football team competed in their seventy-first season of intercollegiate football. They were led by Ben Schwartzwalder in his twelfth of twenty-five seasons as head coach of the Syracuse Orangemen. This SU squad finished this year with a great record of (7-2-0) after the prior year's national championship of 11-0-0. Al Bemiller, Fred Mautino, & Richard Reimer were the team captains for the 1960 team. SU finished 19th in the nation this year and were not invited to a bowl game. Junior halfback Ernie Davis continued to gain national attention, earning consensus All-American honors while rushing for 877 yards and 8 touchdown

All American HB Ernie Davis

Ernie Davis became the first African-American to win the Heisman Trophy before his life was tragically cut short by leukemia at the age of 23.

He was a three-time All-American halfback and 1961 Heisman Trophy winner, Ernie Davis led Syracuse University to the national championship as a sophomore and was inducted into the College Football Hall of Fame in 1979. He was the first African-American man to win the Heisman Trophy and to be picked first overall in the NFL draft, but he never played a pro game and died at 23 after contracting leukemia.

Games of the 1960 season

The Orangemen played their season and home opener on Sept 24, 1960 against Boston University at Archbold Stadium on the campus of Syracuse University in Syracuse, NY. SU defeated the Terriers, W (35-7) before 30,000.

Highlight SU v Kansas to stay unbeaten

On Oct 1 at # 5 Kansas, #2 SU defeated the Jayhawks at Memorial Stadium in Lawrence, KS W (14–7) before 40,000 fans.

Yes, this date was Oct. 1, 1960. Syracuse was fresh off the only national championship in school history. The team was still ranked No. 1 and the Orangemen went on the road to face No. 5 Kansas in the second week of the season. The Orange earned a tough 14-7 win, starting off the year with five consecutive wins.

On Oct 8 at Holy Cross, in the #1 position of rankings and undefeated at this point, SU defeated the Crusaders at Fitton Field in Worcester, MA W (15–6). Because of the closeness of the game, SU dropped to fourth place. Then, on Oct 15 No. 20 Penn State played # 4 Syracuse at Archbold Stadium and the Orangemen won the close game W (21–15). On Oct 22 at West Virginia, the #3 ranked Orangemen played at Mountaineer Field in Morgantown, WV and shut out the Mountaineers W (45–0.

So far undefeated but when Pitt came by on Oct 29 to play ball at Archbold Stadium v #3 Syracuse, the party unbeaten party was over. SU lost its first game in two years and it would not be the last this year as Pitt got the best of the Orangemen, L (0-10) before 41,872. A tough Army team just happened to be next on the 1960 schedule in a game played on Nov 5 at Yankee Stadium in the Bronx. Then #9 ranked SU lost by a squeaker to the Cadets L (6-9). Undefeated then seemed *a-long-ways- away*. Colgate was having its own troubles and could no longer compete against Syracuse under Ben Schwartzwalder.

On Nov 12, Colgate was shellacked again by #17 Syracuse at Archbold Stadium Syracuse, NY (Rivalry) W 46–6 23,000. Wrapping up the season, thinking there was a chance for a bowl game, on Nov 18, Syracuse defeated # 14 Miami at the Miami Orange Bowl in Miami, Florida in a tight game W (21-14). Syracuse, finishing for some reason at #19, was not offered a bowl game.

1961 Ben Schwartzwalder Coach # 22

The 1961 Syracuse Orangemen football team competed in their seventy-second season of intercollegiate football. They were led by Ben Schwartzwalder in his thirteenth of twenty-five seasons as head coach of the Syracuse Orangemen. This SU squad finished this year with a great record of (8-3-0). Dick Easterly was the team captain for the 1961 team. SU finished 16/14 in the two national polls this year and were invited to the Liberty Bowl in Philadelphia. Running back Ernie Davis became the first African-American football player to win the Heisman Trophy.

The #10 ranked Orangemen played their season opener on Sept 23, 1961 against Oregon State at Multnomah Stadium, Portland, OR, and SU claimed victory W 19–8 before 35,729. Then on Sept 30, at home, SU, ranked #5 in the nation beat West Virginia W (29-14) in the home opener at Archbold Stadium on the campus of Syracuse University in Syracuse, NY before 25,000 fans.

On Oct 7, #7 SU traveled to Maryland's Byrd Stadium in College Park, MD and lost a nail-biter, L 21–22 before 35,000 against the tough Terrapins. On eth mend from the close defeat at Maryland, on Oct 14 at Nebraska Memorial Stadium in Lincoln, NE, the Orangemen came back W (28–6) before 35,387 fans. Penn State was getting sick of losing to Syracuse and so on Oct 21 at Penn State's brand new Beaver Stadium at University Park, PA, the Nittany Lions shut out Syracuse L (0–14) before 44,390.

On Oct 28 SU beat Holy Cross at home in Archbold Stadium W (34–6) before 31,000 fans. Then, making up for last year's defeat at Pitt. On Nov 4, the Orangemen beat Pitt's Panthers W (28-9) at home before a packed Archbold house of 40,152. On Nov 11, SU p ripped Colgate apart at Archbold Stadium W (51-8) before 25,000. As Colgate was losing its zip as a Division I team, Archbold attendance went down. On Nov 18 at Notre Dame, #10 Syracuse faced off with the Fighting Irish at Notre Dame Stadium in South Bend, IN and lost the close game L (15–17) before 49,246 in the house that Rock Built. On Nov 25 at Boston College's Alumni Stadium in Chestnut Hill, MA, SU beat the Eagles W 28–13 before 17,600

Liberty Bowl

In a minor bowl game, the Liberty Bowl played early on December 16 vs. Miami (FL) at Philadelphia Municipal Stadium, Syracuse beat Miami in a nail-biter W (15-14) in Philadelphia, PA.

1962 Ben Schwartzwalder Coach # 22

The 1962 Syracuse Orangemen football team competed in their seventy-third season of intercollegiate football. They were led by Ben Schwartzwalder in his fourteenth of twenty-five seasons as head coach of the Syracuse Orangemen. The leftovers of the championship squad were gone, and SU faced a comeuppance year with a break-even record of (5-5-0). The best of times had come to a quick halt for one year. Next year there would be a great rebound.

The offense scored 159 points while the defense allowed 110 points. Leon Cholakis was the team captain for the 1962 team. SU finished 16/14 in the two national polls this year and were invited to the Liberty Bowl in Philadelphia. Running back Ernie Davis became the first African-American football player to win the Heisman Trophy.

The Orangemen played their season opener on Sept 22, 1962 against Oklahoma at Oklahoma Memorial Stadium in Norman, OK and lost L (3–7) before 54,000. Then on Sept 29, at Army in the Polo Grounds of New York, NY, the Orangemen were beaten by the Cadets L (2–9) before 29,500 fans. On Oct 13 SU beat Boston College at home in Archbold Stadium, W (12-0). Penn State had climbed onto the better side of lady luck in playing Syracuse as on Oct 20 at Penn State's first Beaver Stadium (not Beaver Field) at University Park, PA, the Nittany Lions just beat the Orangemen in a tough batch L (19–20) before 46,920.

Then, on Oct 27 at Holy Cross Fitton Field in Worcester, MA, SU defeated a resistant Crusaders team W (30–20) before 20,000 fans. Then on Nov 3, at Pittsburgh's Pitt Stadium in Pittsburgh, PA, the Panthers got the best of the Orangemen L (6–24) before 23,473. On Nov 10, Syracuse beat Navy at home in Archbold Stadium W (34-6) before 40,500. The Service academies drew the biggest home crowds at Syracuse.

On Nov 17, SU beat George Washington at home in Archbold Stadium , W (35–0) before a discriminating crowd of 18,000. On Nov 24 West Virginia beat the Orangemen at Archbold Stadium L (6–17) before 13,000. After a lot of rest, and a lot of lectures by Ben Schwartzwalder, Ben led his team cross country expecting nothing less than a win, which he got on Dec 8 at UCLA in the Los Angeles Memorial Coliseum, Los Angeles, CA W (12–7) before 14,485. There were no excuses for Ben Schwartzwalder. This was a bad year with a lot of almost's but few cigars. He would bring the team back in 1963.

1963 Ben Schwartzwalder Coach # 22

The 1963 Syracuse Orangemen football team competed in their seventy-fourth season of intercollegiate football. They were led by

Ben Schwartzwalder in his fifteenth of twenty-five seasons as head coach of the Syracuse Orangemen. SU overcame its straggler year and roared back onto the field with a great team with a great 8-2-0 record.

The offense scored 255 points while the defense allowed 101 points Richard Bowman & James Mazurek were the captains for 1963. SU finished #12 in the two national polls this year and despite their great season, they were not among the media favorites invited to bowl games this year.

The Orangemen played their season and home opener on Sept 21, 1963 against Boston College at home in Archbold Stadium on the Syracuse University Campus in Syracuse NY. SU won the game W (32-21) before 30,000. On Sept 28 at Kansas Memorial Stadium in Lawrence, KS, SU was shut out in a close match L (0–10). On Oct 5 at home, SU shut out Holy Cross in a blowout W (48-0). Then on Oct 11, the Orangemen raveled to UCLA at Los Angeles Memorial Coliseum in Los Angeles and got the win W (29–7) before 22,949. On Oct, at home SU shut out Penn State in a close match W (9-0) before 39,600 fans.

On Oct at home, SU beat Oregon State W (31–8). On Nov 2 at No. 10 Pittsburgh at Pitt Stadium in Pittsburgh, PA, the Orangemen lost in a close one (L 27-35) before 44,090 fans. Then, on Nov 9, at home SU squeaked by West Virginia W (15-13. On Nov 16 at home the #18 Orangemen defeated Richmond in a blowout W (50–0). On Nov 28, at Yankee Stadium in New York, NY Syracuse defeated Notre Dame W (14–7) before a nice crowd of 56,972

All American Jim Nance 1963 & 1965

Jim Nance started for three years at Syracuse University, Nance tied the school record for career touchdowns (13) and led the Orangemen in rushing in 1964, scoring in ten straight games. In 1963 and 1965 Jim Nance was the NCAA heavyweight wrestling champion and received All-America honors.

He went in the 19th round of the AFL draft by the Boston Patriots in the as well as the 4th round by the Chicago Bears. He signed with the. He began unimpressive, but he led the AFL in rushing the next two seasons after his rookie year. He was a powerful fullback who carried 299 times in 1966, for 17 touchdowns and 1,458 yards. He retired as the Patriots' all-time leading rusher with 46 career touchdowns, a record he still holds.

1964 Ben Schwartzwalder Coach # 22

The 1964 Syracuse Orangemen football team competed in their seventy-fifth season of intercollegiate football. They were led by Ben Schwartzwalder in his sixteenth of twenty-five seasons as head coach of the Syracuse Orangemen. SU had a winning season record of 7-4-0.

The offense scored 264 points while the defense allowed 157 points Billy Hunter & Richard King were the captains for 1964. SU finished # 38 of 120 teams and they were invited to the Sugar Bowl this year.

All American Center Pat Killoran

> My name is Jessie Killorin Keating, I'm the daughter of Patrick Killorin (SU '66, two-time All American Center, 3rd round Pittsburgh Steelers draft pick, humanitarian, business mogul, amazing dad.) Football raised me, the men who taught me honor, discipline, family, and love for the game were all the guys who played with my dad and continued to play for SU as he grew older and supported the club in every way he knew how.7

Chapter 12 Coach Ben Schwartzwalder From 1949-1953

Pat Killorin, Syracuse's two-time All-American center, is a Semi-Pro Football Hall-of-Famer

When Dad won the 2014 Zunic Award from the University, I spoke to this group of men on behalf of my father and felt as if they were all my Dads! They've been there for my family in great times and in the worst of times, and every one of them will tell you that my Dad has been there for them too.

I'm writing to you for help. This is my dad's final year of eligibility to be inducted into the NFF College Football Hall of Fame. This week, we were notified that Dad will be inducted into the Semi Pro Football Hall of Fame in Canton, OH on June 27 for his incredible record as a coach and player for the Watertown Red & Black. We are thrilled with this honor! But it's been a tragic oversight by the University that they have not advocated for Patrick Killorin to be inducted into the College Football HOF.

He was a TWO TIME All American – once is fantastic, but twice?? He was drafted into the Pros and played until he destroyed both knees! Not uncommon. But football remained his passion, and he went directly to Semi Pro, bringing the Watertown Red & Black to an undefeated season in 1971 and 1974. I was 1 and 4 at the time J. Since then, he has been an undying supporter of the Syracuse University football team, while starting two multimillion dollar companies in Syracuse, selling them both for millions, and continuing to give back to the Syracuse community as a Hospice volunteer who literally helps people DIE, and a philanthropist who would lay down his life for Syracuse football.

In order to get a College Football Hall of Fame nomination, strong advocacy must come from the Syracuse University Athletic Director Daryl Gross, who has so far not stepped up to the plate. My dad is an incredible man in so many ways, but as an SU Football player blocking for Floyd Little and the 1965 Bill Horr Award as the team's MVP, he deserves this honor. Floyd has been an incredible advocate!! But the hard press needs to come from Daryl Gross.

In a million years my dad would not advocate for himself, and any guy who knows him, knows that awards and recognition for his many talents, skills and good work don't matter to him. Only his GOD matters to him. But it matters to me, and it matters to my family. If this is not in the cards for my Dad, so be it. But he, and all the other football stars he played with, raised me to never quit, and I will go the mat making every effort possible to see my father get his due and be inducted into the CFHOF. All of us desperately want to see this happen while my dad is alive.

My ask to you is simple – would you be willing to step up with the rest of the Syracuse community and push Dr. Gross to do the right thing? So far, hundreds have stepped up to help with a letter writing campaign to Dr. Gross and the Chancellor Syverud. My favorite letter came from Rockette Pirro, SU Offensive Line Coach Rock Pirro's daughter. Her wonderful dad has passed, but her words say it all. Please, help us see this through? It's the right thing, and the general feeling is that Dr. Gross's neglect of the older generation of SU players is a gross oversight:

"Dear Dr. Gross and Chancellor Syverud,

Please accept this email in support of Patrick Killorin's nomination into the National Football Foundation and College Hall of Fame.

I know you have been hearing from so many who love and support Pat, but I speak from a little different perspective - I speak as the daughter of someone who coached Pat at Syracuse University and knew firsthand of his accomplishments, dedication, and true love of SU football. My dad, Offensive Line Coach

Rock Pirro, is not here today to speak to Pat's virtues, but I can tell you that he would be the first to ask that you seriously consider endorsing Pat for an honor that is long overdue. In fact, it is truly amazing that this man has not been recognized for his numerous accomplishments by now - we cannot let this oversight go on any longer.

My dad loved Pat Killorin - he loved him as a player and loved him as a great man - because, not only did Pat excel on the SU gridiron, he has excelled in life! Syracuse University should be proud to call Pat Killorin one of its own, and I sincerely ask that you wholeheartedly (with the heart of the Orange) to endorse Patrick Killorin to be nominated to the College Hall of Fame. He brings honor to all of us who bleed Orange.
Many thanks for your consideration."

All American RB Floyd Little

Floyd Little is the only three-time All-American running back to compete for the Syracuse University Orangemen. He finished 5th in Heisman Trophy voting in both 1965 and 1966. Here are some stats:

- 1964: 157 carries for 874 yards and 9 TD. 17 catches for 257 yards and 1 TD.[3]
- 1965: 193 carries for 1065 yards and 14 TD. 21 catches for 248 yards and 1 TD.
- 1966: 162 carries for 811 yards and 12 TD. 13 catches for 86 yards and 2 TD.

In 1975, Little retired as the NFL's 7th all-time leading rusher with 6,323 yards rushing and 54 total touchdowns (rushing, receiving and returns). He also threw a TD pass to receiver Jerry Simmons in a 1972 upset over the Oakland Raiders. During his rookie year, Little led the NFL in punt returns with a 16.9-yard average. He led the NFL in combined yards in 1967 and 1968. Little was Denver Broncos team captain all 9 seasons, including his rookie season.

Little was a charter member of the Broncos Ring of Fame in 1984, which included Rich Jackson, Lionel Taylor and Goose Gonsoulin. He was the first Bronco to win a rushing title, leading the AFC in rushing in 1970 with 901 yards and the following year he became the first Bronco to eclipse 1,000 yards, gaining 1,133 to lead the NFL. Little was the first player to lead his conference in rushing for a last place team [5] and the 13th player ever in professional football to rush for at least 1,000 yards in one season.[6]

He was an American Football League All-Star in 1968. In a week 12 win over Buffalo, he caught 4 passes out of the backfield for 165 yards, including a 66-yard touchdown, setting a franchise record of 41.25 yards per reception that still stands.[7] He was named first-team "All-AFL" in 1969, and made the AFC-NFC Pro Bowl in 1970, 1971 and 1973. At 5'10" and 195 pounds, Little was the smallest back to lead the league in rushing since World War II. He led the league in combined yards in 1967 and 1968 and was the only player to return punts for TDs in both seasons. During a 6-year period, 1968–1973, Little rushed for more yards and more yards from scrimmage (rushing and receiving) than any RB in the NFL.[8] In 2009 Little was a finalist for induction into the Hall of Fame.[9] He was voted in on February 6, 2010, his induction took place in Canton, OH on August 7, 2010.

Some nice information about Floyd Little

Little finished 40th in his class of 140 at the University of Denver law school, from which he received his master's in legal administration degree in 1975. Little owned automobile dealerships in Denver, the Seattle area and Santa Barbara. On May 15, 2016, Little received his honorary doctorate from Syracuse University in Humane Letters.

The #9 ranked Orangemen played their season opener on Sept 19, 1964 at Boston College's Alumni Stadium in Chestnut Hill, MA and were beaten by the Eagles L (14–21). On Sept 26 SU defeated Kansas in the home opener in Archbold Stadium on the Syracuse University Campus in Syracuse NY. SU won the game W (38-6) before 28,000. On Oct 3 at Holy Cross in Fitton Field, Worcester, MA, SU defeated the Crusaders W 34–8 before 14,000. Then, back at home on Oct 10, SU defeated UCLA W (39–0) before 35,000.

Then on Oct 17 SU beat the Nittany Lions at Penn State's Beaver Stadium in University Park, PA W (21–14) before 46,900. On Oct 24 at Oregon State's Multnomah Stadium in Portland, OR , #8 SU lost L (13–3) before 24,326. Then on Oct 31 at home SU defeated Pittsburgh W (21–6) before 35,000. On Nov 7 at Army, played in Yankee Stadium New York, NY, the Orangemen beat the Cadets W (27–15) before 37,552. SU won again at home on Nov 14 against Virginia Tech W (20–15) before 24,000. Then on Nov 21, it was off to West Virginia in Morgantown, WV. SU lost by one-point L (27–28) before s sparse crowd of 14,000
Sugar Bowl

Sugar Bowl January 1, 1965

In the Sugar Bowl on January 1, 1965 vs. #7 LSU in Tulane Stadium, New Orleans, LA, the Orangemen could not hold on and lost the game L (10–13) before 65,000. The 1965 Sugar Bowl featured the seven-ranked LSU Tigers, and the unranked Syracuse Orangemen.

Syracuse jumped on top at the beginning of the game following a 23-yard Smith field goal, taking a 3–0 lead. When Syracuse got the ball next, LSU's defense forced a safety, making it 3–2. Syracuse's Clarke then returned a blocked punt 28 yards for a touchdown, as Syracuse led 10–2. In the third quarter, LSU quarterback Ezell threw a 57-yard touchdown pass to Doug Moreau, with a two-point conversion tying the game at 10. In the fourth quarter, Moreau kicked the winning 28-yard field goal, as LSU won 13–10. Moreau was named Sugar Bowl MVP. SU could not hold on to the lead and eventually lost the game.

1965 Ben Schwartzwalder Coach # 22

The 1965 Syracuse Orangemen football team competed in their seventy-sixth season of intercollegiate football. They were led by Ben Schwartzwalder in his seventeenth of twenty-five seasons as head coach of the Syracuse Orangemen. SU had a winning season record of 7-3-0.

The offense scored 237 points while the defense allowed 146 points Harris Elliott was the captains for 1965. SU finished # 25 of 120 teams. Their record was better than last year's, yet they were not among the media favorites invited to bowl games this year.

The Orangemen played their season opener on Sept 18, 1965 at Navy at the Navy–Marine Corps Memorial Stadium in Annapolis, MD. SU beat Navy W (14–6) before 20,367. On Sept 25 SU lost to Miami (FL) in the home opener in Archbold Stadium on the Syracuse University Campus in Syracuse NY. SU lost this game in a shutout L (0–24) before 32,000. On Oct 2 at Maryland's Byrd Stadium in College Park, MD, SU beat the Terrapins W 24–7 before 35,000. On Oct 9 at UCLA in Los Angeles Memorial Coliseum in

Los Angeles, CA, Syracuse could not take out the Bruins L (14–24) before 27,729.

On Oct 16 at home SU beat the Nittany Lions of Penn State in a close match W (28–21) before 39,000. On Oct 23 at home, SU beat Holy Cross W (32–6) before 15,000. Then on Oct 30, it was off to another big stadium for a game against Pitt. The venue was She Stadium in New York, NY. SU won big W (51–13) before 24,590. On Nov 6 at home v Oregon State, SU lost by just one point to the Beavers L (12–13) before 33,000.

Then on Nov 13, it was off to West Virginia's Mountaineer Field in Morgantown, WV, where Syracuse defeated the Mountaineers W (41–19) before 33,500. The last game of the season was at home and it pitted the Orangemen against a scrappy Boston College. SU took the close game by W (21-13) before 20,000.

All American Charles E "Charlie" Brown 1965

Charles Edward Brown was born September 13, 1942). He is a former American football defensive back in the National Football League(NFL) for the Chicago Bears. He played college football at Syracuse University and was first team All-American. and in 1968, he played in the American Football League(AFL) for the Buffalo Bills.[1] He finished his career in the Canadian Football League in 1969 with the Hamilton Tiger-Cats, where he returned an interception for 115 yards and a touchdown, at the time the second longest, and now the fifth longest return in league history.

1966 Ben Schwartzwalder Coach # 22

The 1966 Syracuse Orangemen football team competed in their seventy-seventh season of intercollegiate football. They were led by Ben Schwartzwalder in his eighteenth of twenty-five seasons as head coach of the Syracuse Orangemen. SU had a winning season record of 8-3-0.

The offense scored 266 points while the defense allowed 156 points Floyd Little & Herb Stecker were the captains for 1966. SU finished # 16th in the polls this year. After losing their first two games of the season, Syracuse won the next eight games, finishing the regular season with a record of 8–2 The Orangemen were invited to the Gator Bowl, where they lost to Tennessee.

All American Gary A. Bugenhagen 1966

Bugenhagen earned 1966 All-American honors as a tackle at Syracuse University SU. Bugenhagen aided fellow All-American Larry Csonka in rushing for 1,012 yards in 1966. He was part of a team that holds the seventh-best rushing record in SU history (431 yards vs. West Virginia). He was named to Syracuse University's All-Century team in November 1999.

AFL
Bugenhagen played in the AFL with the Buffalo Bills and Boston Patriots.

All American Larry Csonka 1966-1067

Larry Csonka was born on Christmas Day, 1946.

At nine pounds and 13 ounces, word is that he was a lot to handle right from the start. He grew into a 6'3", 237 lb. All-American fullback for the Syracuse Orangemen with all American honors in both 1966 and 1967.

The Miami Dolphins selected him in the first round of the 1968 NFL Entry draft with the eighth overall pick.

<<Picture on the left is from 1972

As a pro rookie, Csonka started each of the 11 games in which he appeared. He scored a team high (and an AFL fourth best) six rushing touchdowns for the 5-8-1 Dolphins, finishing second to fellow rookie Jim Kiick with 138 rushes for 540 yards. He also caught 11 passes for 118 yards and another score.

In 1969, Csonka again started 11 games for Miami, as the team finished at the bottom of the AFL with a 3-10-1 record. He again ranked second on the team with 131 carries for 566 yards and two scores. He also caught a career high 21 passes for 183 yards and another touchdown. In a week nine 17-16 victory over the Boston Patriots, he rushed 16 times for 121 yards and a touchdown, his first 100+ yard effort. He kept getting better.

Csonka was inducted to both the College Football Hall of Fame (1989) and Pro Football Hall of Fame (1987). With the Miami Dolphins, he was a member of their perfect season in 1972 and won SU per Bowl championships in 1972 and 1973.

Games of the 1966 season

The Orangemen lost their season opener on Sept 10, 1966 at Baylor in Floyd Casey Stadium, Waco, TX L (12–35) before 31,000. . On Sept 24 SU lost to UCLA in the home opener in Archbold Stadium on the Syracuse University Campus in Syracuse NY. SU lost this game by the score of L (12-31) before 35,000. On Oct 1 at home against Maryland, SU beat the Terrapins W (28–7) before 25,000. On Oct 8 at home against Navy, Syracuse beat a tough group of Midshipmen W (28-14) On Oct 15 at Boston College in Alumni Stadium in Chestnut Hill, MA, SU shut out the Eagles W (30–0 before 24,500

On Oct 22 at Holy Cross's Fitton Field, Worcester, MA SU beat the Crusaders W (28–6). On Oct 29 Syracuse beat Pittsburgh at home in Archbold Stadium W (33–7) before 30,000. On Nov 5 at Penn State's Beaver Stadium in University Park, PA, the Orangemen prevailed over the Nittany Lions in a close match W (12–10) before 46,314. On Nov 12 at home, Syracuse beat Florida State W (37–21) before 35,405. Wrapping up the regular season at West Virginia Mountaineer Field, Morgantown, WV, on Nov 19, SU beat the Mountaineers W (34–7) before 19,000.

The Gator Bowl December 31, 1966

On December 31, 1966, New Year's Eve, Syracuse squared off in the Gator Bowl against Tennessee at Gator Bowl Stadium in Jacksonville, FL and in another close bowl game, lost by a touchdown, L (12–18) before 60,213

The Vols had finished 5th in the Southeastern Conference, with an 11–10 loss to #3 Alabama being especially damaging. Nevertheless, they were invited to their 2nd straight bowl appearance, the first time they had made consecutive bowl seasons since 1956–57. As for the Orangemen, this was their fourth bowl appearance in the decade. This was the first Gator Bowl for either team.

On Dec. 31, 1966) the Tennessee Volunteers won their second consecutive bowl game under Coach Doug Dickey by defeating

Syracuse 18-12 in a game in which each team dominated for one half. The team that dominated the first half won the game.

Despite an early fumble that gave Syracuse favorable field position, the Vols got field goals from Gary Wright in the first and second quarters to lead 6-0. Another field goal appeared to be in the offing in the second period at the Syracuse 24, but the Vols caught Syracuse by surprise and quarterback Dewey Warren hit tight end Austin Denney instead for the touchdown and a 12-0 lead.

Bill Young's interception led to the third Vol score, which came on a 2-yard strike from Warren to flanker Richmond Flowers.

Syracuse, in the second half was led by the running of future pro stars Floyd Little and Larry Csonka, scored on their first possession of the second half. They lost the ball on downs at the Vol 3 later in the period. So, with the score 18–0 at halftime. SU knew it had to catch up quickly. As noted, on the first drive of the second half, Larry Csonka scored on a 8-yard touchdown plunge to make it 18–6 (after a failed conversion play). The game moped on and then with only 46 seconds left in the game, Floyd Little made it 18–12 on a 3-yard touchdown plunge (with another failed conversion play), but it wasn't enough. Little (216 on 29 carries) and Csonka (114 on 18 carries) combined for 330 yards rushing in a losing effort. It should have been enough to win.

1967 Ben Schwartzwalder Coach # 22

The 1967 Syracuse Orangemen football team competed in their seventy-eighth season of intercollegiate football. They were led by Ben Schwartzwalder in his nineteenth of twenty-five seasons as head coach of the Syracuse Orangemen. SU had a winning season record of 8-2-0. It would be Ben Schwartzwalder's last eight-win season.

The offense scored 210 points while the defense allowed 127 points James Cheyunski & Larry Csonka were the captains for 1967. SU finished # 12th in the polls this year. Losing just two games this season, Syracuse won eight, finishing the regular season with a record of 8–2-0. With such a great record, the Orangemen were passed over and did not receive an invitation to any post-season bowl.

Some highlights: In 1967, Tom Coughlin, who later was the long-time NY Giants Coach, set the school's single-season pass receiving record. Larry Csonka was in his senior season and was named an All-American. He broke many of the school's rushing records, including some previously held by Ernie Davis, Jim Nance, Floyd Little, and Jim Brown.

In his three seasons at Syracuse, Csonka rushed for a school record 2,934 yards, rushed for 100 yards in 14 different games, and averaged 4.9 yards per carry. From 1965 to 1967, he ranked 19th, 9th and 5th in the nation in rushing. He was the Most Valuable Player in the East–West Shrine Game, the Hula Bowl, and the College All-Star Game. He went on to play for Miami in the NFL.

On Sept 23 SU defeated Baylor in the home and season opener in Archbold Stadium on the Syracuse University Campus in Syracuse NY. SU won this game by the score of W (7-0) before 31,000.

On Sept 30, at home, SU beat West Virginia W (23–6) before 28,435. Then, on Oct 7 at Maryland at Byrd Stadium in College Park, MD, SU defeated the Terrapins W (7–3). SU was rolling along with a great team and along comes Navy, a tough competitor every year. In a game played on Oct 14 at Navy–Marine Corps Memorial Stadium in Annapolis, MD, Syracuse could not hold on L (14–27). Then, at home on October 21 SU beat California by one touchdown, W (20-14) in a close match. The next week at home again, Penn State beat Syracuse L (20–29) before 41,750.

On Nov 4th at Pittsburgh's Pitt Stadium in Pittsburgh, PA, Syracuse squeaked out another close win W (14–7). On Nov11, in the annual Holy Cross Game, again SU had its way with the crusaders in a nice victory W (41–7) before 32,000. On Nov 8 at Boston College's Alumni Stadium in Chestnut Hill, the Orangemen got the win W (32–20) before 16,200. In the final 1967 game,
November 25 at consensus #4 UCLA in a game played at the Los Angeles Memorial Coliseum in Los Angeles, CA, SU played a great game and won W (32–14). Despite a great season and a great finish, there was no bowl game for the Orangemen.

1968 Ben Schwartzwalder Coach # 22

The 1968 Syracuse Orangemen football team competed in their seventy-ninth season of intercollegiate football. They were led by Ben Schwartzwalder in his twentieth of twenty-five seasons as head coach of the Syracuse Orangemen. SU had a winning season record of 6-4-0.

The offense scored 252 points while the defense allowed 154 points Anthony Kyasky was the team captains for 1968. SU finished # 47 of 119. Syracuse finished the regular season with a record of 6-4-0. The Orangemen did not receive an invitation to any post-season bowl games in 1968.

All American Anthony J. Kyasky 1968

Anthony "Tony Kyasky" received first team All-American honors as a safety at Syracuse University in 1968. He was selected by AP, NEA, UPI, WC, and Time. Tony played WR and safety on the team.

Games of the 1958 Season

The season opener was on Sept 21 at Michigan State's Spartan Stadium in East Lansing, MI. The Spartans defeated the Orangemen L (10–14) before 63,488. On Sept 28 SU defeated Maryland in the home opener in Archbold Stadium on the Syracuse University Campus in Syracuse NY. SU won this game by the score of W (32–14) before 31,000. On Oct 5, at home, SU defeated UCLA W (20–7) before 37,367. On Oct 12 at home, Syracuse beat Pittsburgh at home W (50–17). On Oct 26 at #11 California at California Memorial Stadium in Berkeley, CA the Orangemen were shutout L (0–43) before 52,172

On Nov 2 at Holy Cross's Fitton Field in Worcester, MA, SU dominated the game W (47–0). On Nov 9 SU shut out William & Mary at home W (31–0) before 22,889. On Nov 16, at home, SU defeated Navy W (44–6) before 33,785. On Nov 23 at West Virginia's Mountaineer Field in Morgantown, WV SU lost the game L (6–23). On Dec 7 at #3 Penn State in Beaver Stadium, University Park, PA, in the traditional rivalry, the Nittany Lions defeated the Orangemen L (12–30) before 38,000

1969 Ben Schwartzwalder Coach # 22

The 1969 Syracuse Orangemen football team competed in their eightieth season of intercollegiate football. They were led by Ben Schwartzwalder in his twenty-first of twenty-five seasons as head coach of the Syracuse Orangemen. SU had a break-even season record of 5-5-0.

The offense scored 169 points while the defense allowed 126 points SU had no one captain but instead used game captains for 1969. SU finished # 55 of 122. The Orangemen did not receive an invitation to any post-season bowl games in 1969.

On Sept 20 SU defeated Iowa State in the home opener in Archbold Stadium on the Syracuse University Campus in Syracuse NY. SU won this game by the score of W (14-13) before 30,491. On Sept 27 at Kansas Memorial Stadium in Lawrence, KS, SU was shut out L (0–13) before 44,500 fans. On Oct 4, my wedding anniversary to-be, at Wisconsin's Camp Randall Stadium in Madison, WI, Syracuse got the win W (43–7) before 45,540. On Oct 11 at Maryland's Byrd Stadium in College Park, MD, the Orangemen won their second in a row W (20–9). Then on October 18 at home, #5 Penn State got the win by one-point L (14–15) before 42,491

On Nov 1at Pittsburgh's Pitt Stadium in Pittsburgh, PA, SU lost again by just one point L (20–21). The next week, on Nov 8. SU shut-out Arizona W (23-0). On Nov 15, at Navy in a game played in the Navy–Marine Corps Memorial Stadium, Annapolis, MD, the Orangemen beat the Cadets W (15–0). On Nov 22 #18 West Virginia came to Archbold Stadium for a win and they got it in another close match for the Orangemen L (10–13). To finish the season, an always tough Boston College team played at Archbold Stadium and they beat the disheartened Syracuse Orangemen L (10–35).

They say when the going gets tough, the tough get going. Well, 1969 was a tough year for SU with so many close games and they could not keep it going even when they had a shot at breaking away. They lost to Pitt and Penn State by one point and later to West Virginia by just three points. It was the difference between a nice 8-2 year and their record of 5-5 for 1969.

1970 Ben Schwartzwalder Coach # 22

The 1970 Syracuse Orangemen football team competed in their eighty-first season of intercollegiate football. They were led by Ben Schwartzwalder in his twenty-second of twenty-five seasons as head coach of the Syracuse Orangemen. SU had a winning season record of 6-4-0.

The offense scored 248 points while the defense allowed 208 points Paul Paolisso, Raymond White & Randolph Zur were the co-captains for 1969. SU finished # 41 of 123. The Orangemen did not receive an invitation to any post-season bowl games in 1970.

After a disappointing year in 1969, Syracuse could not get it going in 1970 and lost its first three games. It was like they could not shake the bad cloud from the prior year. Nonetheless, Ben Schwartzwalder never lost faith. He kept drilling them to become excellent and finally their season turned around.

All American Joseph C. Ehrmann 1970

Joseph Charles "Joe" Ehrmann was born March 29, 1949. He is a former National Football League (NFL) defensive lineman, originally drafted as the 10th pick in the first round of the 1973 NFL Draft out of Syracuse University to the Baltimore Colts. Ehrmann is currently a minister and motivational speaker. Ehrmann played with Baltimore for eight years and was selected to the Pro Bowl in 1978. He finished his NFL career with the Detroit Lions as part of their vaunted defensive line in the early 1980s. He was an NFL defensive tackle from 1973 through 1982. He then played in the USFL for the Chicago Blitz, Arizona Wranglers and Orlando Renegades.

Ehrmann attended Syracuse University, where he was a three-year football letterman in 1969, 1970 and 1972. Primarily, he played at defensive tackle. Ehrman was an All-American selection in 1970. He was named to the university's football All-Century Team on October 28, 1999. He was also the recipient of the George Arents Pioneers Medal, the university's highest alumni honor, in 2004.

Games of the 1970 Season

On Sept 19 SU was defeated by # 15 Houston in the season opener at the famed Astrodome in Houston, TX. SU was lackluster in this game and lost decidedly L (15–42) before 40,439. On Sept 26, in the home opener in Archbold Stadium on the Syracuse University Campus in Syracuse NY. SU lost another game. This was against Kansas by a score of W (14-31) On Oct 3, at Illinois Memorial Stadium in Champaign, IL, Syracuse lost its third without a win—this time by a shutout L (0–27). It was time for Ben to come up with his best pep talks and some better plays and he did.

On Oct 10, SU picked up a nice win at home—its first win of the year—against Maryland in Archbold Stadium. The Orangemen beat the Terrapins W (23–7). Feeling like a Ben Schwartzwalder team, on Oct 17, the Orangemen traveled to Penn State's Beaver Stadium in University Park, PA and pulled off their second straight win W (24–7) before 50,540.

Riding the win high, on Oct 24 SU beat Navy at home W (23-8). Next was Pittsburgh, always a tough competitor. In a home game, at Archbold Stadium, Syracuse got its fourth win in a row W (43–13). On Nov 7, at Army playing at Michie Stadium in West Point, NY against an always-tough Cadets, team, SU pulled off another victory W (31–29) before a packed Army house of 41,062. On Nov 14 at West Virginia's Mountaineer Field, Morgantown, WV, the Ben rivalry favored WV L (19–28). Ready again to play at the top of its game, the Orangemen walloped Miami of Florida at home in Archbold Stadium W (56–16) for a great finish to a turnaround season.

1971 Ben Schwartzwalder Coach # 22

The 1971 Syracuse Orangemen football team competed in their eighty-second season of intercollegiate football. They were led by Ben Schwartzwalder in his twenty-third of twenty-five seasons as head coach of the Syracuse Orangemen. SU had a breakeven season record of 5-5-1. Joe Ehrmann & Dan Yochum were team captains for 1971. The Orangemen again did not receive an invitation to any post-season bowl games in 1971.

All American Thomas P. Myers 1971

Tom Myers, pictured when he played for New Orleans, was born on October 24, 1950). He is a former American football safety (DB) in the National Football League. He was drafted by the New Orleans Saints in the third round of 1972 NFL Draft. He played college football at Syracuse where he was an all-American. He was quite a player.

Myers played for the New Orleans Saints his entire post-Syracuse career from 1972-1981 as the team's starting free safety for each of those seasons. In 1978, Myers recorded a 97-yard interception return for touchdown against the Minnesota Vikings, a Saints record. His best season was in 1979 when he was selected to the Pro Bowl and was named on the All-Pro team. As of the 2016 NFL season, Myers is still #2 on the All-Time New Orleans Saints Career Interceptions List. He later played two seasons for the Houston Gamblers of the United States Football League

1971 games of the season

On Sept 18 SU tied Wisconsin T (20-20) in the home opener in Archbold Stadium on the Syracuse University Campus in Syracuse NY. On Sept 25 at Northwestern in Dyche Stadium, Evanston, IL. the Orangemen could not get enough points on the board and lost the game L (6–12) before 27,529. On the road on Oct 2 to Indiana Memorial Stadium in Bloomington, IN, Syracuse picked up a tight shutout win against the Hoosiers W (7–0). On Oct 9 at Maryland's Byrd Stadium, College Park, MD, SU got the victory W (21–13) before 20,100. Then, on Oct 16, when #9 Penn State came to SU's home field of Archbold Stadium in Syracuse, NY for the annual rivalry game the surprise was the Syracuse would be shut-out L (0–31) before 41,382, almost all of whom were rooting for Syracuse.

On October 23, SU blew out Holy Cross at home W (63–21) before a small crowd of 18,308. Then, away on October 30 at Pittsburgh's Pitt Stadium in Pittsburgh, PA, in a rivalry match, the Panthers clawed their way to victory and Syracuse notched in another loss L (21–31). On Nov SU lost to BC (Boston College) at home -- Archbold Stadium, in a tough close match L (3–10). Then, on Nov 13 at Navy in Navy–Marine Corps Memorial Stadium, Annapolis, MD, Syracuse lost to the Midshipmen, L (14–17) in a very close game. On Nov 20, at home, SU defeated West Virginia W (28-24). In the season finale, SU traveled to Miami FL in the Miami Orange Bowl to beat the Hurricanes W (14–0) in the SU season closer before 17,224 fans.

1972 Ben Schwartzwalder Coach # 22

The 1972 Syracuse Orangemen football team competed in their eighty-third season of intercollegiate football. They were led by Ben Schwartzwalder in his twenty-fourth of twenty-five seasons as head coach of the Syracuse Orangemen. SU had a losing season record of 5-6-0. In 1972, SU went back to game captains v individual season captain. The Orangemen again did not receive an invitation to any post-season bowl games in 1972.

On Sept 9 SU beat Temple W (17-10) in the home opener in Archbold Stadium on the Syracuse University Campus in Syracuse NY. On Sept 16 at NC State Parker Stadium in Raleigh, NC Syracuse lost to the Wolfpack L (20–43) before 27,100.

On the road on Sept 23 at Wisconsin Camp Randall Stadium in Madison, WI, Syracuse lost its second game of the season L (7–31) before 67,234. On Sept 30, at home, SU defeated the Maryland Terrapins in a close match, W (16-12)

On Oct 9 at Maryland's Byrd Stadium, College Park, MD, SU got the victory W (21–13) before 20,100. Then, on Oct 16, when #9 Penn State came to SU's home field of Archbold Stadium in Syracuse, NY for the annual rivalry game the surprise was the Syracuse would be shut-out L (0–31) before 41,382, almost all of whom were rooting for Syracuse. On Oct 7 at home Syracuse lost its third game of the season to Indiana L (2–10) 18,444. As the Orangemen kept struggling, attendance was dropping.

On Oct 14, at home, Syracuse beat Navy W (30-14) before 22,187. On Oct 21 at #12 ranked Penn State in a game played at Beaver Stadium in University Park, PA(Rivalry), the Orangemen were shut out by the Nittany Lions L (0–17) before 60,465. On Oct 28 at home, SU defeated Pitt W (10-6).

On Nov 4, at Boston College's Alumni Stadium in Chestnut Hill, MA, BC shut out SUL (0–37) in a runaway. before 21,216. On Nov 11 at home, SU defeated Army W (27-6) before 19,525. On Nov 18 in the season close at West Virginia's Mountaineer Field in Morgantown, WV, the Mountaineers laid a big defeat on the Orangemen in the rivalry game L (12–43) before 31,500

1973 Ben Schwartzwalder Coach # 22

The 1973 Syracuse Orangemen football team competed in their eighty-fourth season of intercollegiate football. They were led by Ben Schwartzwalder in his twenty-fifth and last of twenty-five seasons as head coach of the Syracuse Orangemen. SU had its worst season ever under Coach Ben – 2-9-0. Again, SU did not nominate season captains but instead used game captains. The Orangemen again did not receive an invitation to any post-season bowl games in 1973.

On Sept 15 SU lost to Bowling Green L (14-41 in the home opener in Archbold Stadium on the Syracuse University Campus in

Syracuse NY. On Sept 22, at home SU lost to Michigan State L (8-14). On Sept 29, 6 at Washington Husky Stadium, Seattle, WA, Syracuse lost its third game of the season L (7–21) before 54,800

On the road on Oct 6 at Maryland's Byrd Stadium College Park, MD. SU lost its fourth in a row, L (0–38) before 32,800. On Oct 13, at Navy Navy–Marine Corps Memorial Stadium Annapolis, MD SU lost # 5 in a row, L (14–23) before 20,591.

On Oct 20 SU lost #6 in a row at home to #5 Penn State in a blowout L (6-49) before 27,595. On Oct 27 at home SU lost #7 in a row, to Miami (of FL) L (23–34) before 19,369. Then, on November 3 at Pittsburgh Pitt Stadium in Pittsburgh, PA, Syracuse lost its eight in a row L (14–28) 24,932.

On Nov 10 at Holy Cross Fitton Field in Worcester, MA SU picked up its first of just two wins this season with baseball-like score W (5–3) before 16,404. On Nov 17 at home, Syracuse won its second and last win of the season against Boston College W (24-13) before an empty stadium of 11,199. On Nov 24 at home West Virginia spoiled the season finale of a dismal season by beating the Orangemen L (14–24) before 12,917 disappointed fans.

Ben Schwartzwalder leaves Syracuse Football

Please enjoy this submission from:
http://cuse.com/sports/2011/9/28/Schwartzwalder.aspx
It is titled simply, BEN SCHWARTZWALDER (1909-93)

> The game ended, and Ben Schwartzwalder walked to the middle of the field, shook hands, exchanged a few words with his opposing coach, then turned and headed toward the dressing room. It was a scene he had repeated several hundred times but on this particular day, November 24, 1973, it was different. It marked the end of the brilliant coaching career of Floyd (Ben) Schwartzwalder, head man of the Syracuse Orange for the past 25 years. He had retired, after a quarter of a century as the head coach at one school.

Less than a dozen men rank in this category. And less than a handful of men who have entered the coaching profession since Princeton and Rutgers started the madness back in 1869 have recorded as many victories as did this crew-cut, bespectacled quiet little giant out of the hills of West Virginia.

His report card shows 178 wins, 96 losses and three ties during his 28-year tenure as a head coach (three years at Muhlenberg, 25 at Syracuse).

How does one describe Ben Schwartzwalder? What made him tick and what made him one of the giants of the game?

A good starting place is his home state of West Virginia. It is where the seeds of the fierce competitor were nurtured and matured. He didn't starve as a boy growing up, but he knew what it was to want. By the time he was in college, it was apparent that he wasn't going to weigh much more than 150 and grow taller than 5-9. But none of these shortcomings stopped Ben Schwartzwalder from plunging head first into the field of battle. This is where that appetite of desire was whetted and the burning determination to succeed was honed.

Ben enrolled at West Virginia University and went out for football. He was the starting center at 152 pounds for the Mountaineers of coach Greasey Neale. He also wrestled and dodged a young coed who was just as fierce a competitor as he when it came to getting her man. And thus, Ruth Simpson became Mrs. Floyd Schwartzwalder.

Both taught and Ben began coaching in his home state. By 1941, he had earned a name for himself and was offered the head coaching job at Canton McKinley High School in Ohio, one of the top jobs in the Midwest. Ben was clearly on his way to the top. But there was to be a delay.

Shortly after Dec. 7, 1941, Canton McKinley lost a coach and the U.S. Army gained a soldier.

Although in his thirties, Ben decided he was going to be a paratrooper. He served with the 82nd Airborne and was in the first wave of troops that jumped on D-Day in 1944. Dropped far behind enemy lines and miles off target, Ben organized his command immediately and a week later brought a bunch of prisoners to the Allied lines.

He rose to the rank of major and in the process picked up the Silver Star, Bronze Star and Purple Heart, four battle stars and a Presidential Unit Citation. He was personally decorated by Matthew Ridgeway who recalled Ben well. "I never expected to see you here to receive this award," said the commander of the 82nd.

Adversity and Ben were old combatants and Ben usually won.

The war ended, and football again became his life. In 1946, Ben came east and guided Muhlenberg to a 25-5 slate in three years. Meanwhile, up in central New York, Syracuse was struggling for survival. The Orangemen had won but nine games in four years and everyone was unhappy. A call for help went out and, in the end, it was that man who was to win more games than Knute Rockne, Frank Leahy, Bud Wilkinson or Earl Blaik that answered.

The rest is now history. Ben gave Syracuse its finest hours in football. He produced 22 straight years of non-losing football, took the Orange to seven bowls, and won the national championship in 1959. He developed some of the most impressive running backs the game has ever seen - Jim Brown, Ernie Davis, Jim Nance, Floyd Little and Larry Csonka. Orange teams outrushed opponents by more than 22,000 yards under Ben.

The public Ben Schwartzwalder often appeared to be a cross between a wounded bear and a crossed bull. He was basically a shy, quiet individual who never got very close to the press or general public. The private Ben was a very devoted family man who loved to putter around in his garden or who always had time to stop and give a stray dog a reassuring pat on the head or say hello to a youngster. And enthusiasm!! He had the same burning drive in 1973 as he did as a rookie coach back in West Virginia in 1933.

"Sometimes outstanding individuals are never appreciated until they are gone," said Beano Cooke, a former sports information director and now with ABC-TV. "I have a strange feeling that in the years to come, officials, alumni and fans might finally realize what a tremendous asset Ben was. The funny part is that so many people have known this for years, including myself."

Ben always refused to pick a favorite team or make comparisons. The team he was coaching at the time was his favorite simply because of his great love of coaching.

"We football coaches are most fortunate," Ben said as he left office as the president of the American Football Coaches Association. "By doing the best we can do with the job we have, wherever it is, we can serve our nation in its greatest task."

The winner of the annual Syracuse-West Virginia football game receives the Ben Schwartzwalder Trophy. Schwartzwalder coached Syracuse and was a graduate of West Virginia.

Syracuse was never so luck as to have Ben Schwartzwalder for so long at the helm. The school became accustomed to winning.

Please read his obituary which I have provided below. It offers even additional insights into this great man.

Ben Schwartzwalder Dies at 83; Revitalized Football at Syracuse
By ROBERT McG. THOMAS Jr.
Published: April 29, 1993
Correction Appended

Ben Schwartzwalder, who recruited a series of acclaimed running backs as he restored Syracuse to football glory during 25 sparkling seasons that included an undefeated campaign in

1959, died yesterday at Northside Hospital in St. Petersburg, Fla. He was 83.

Mr. Schwartzwalder, a resident of Syracuse who maintained a winter home in St. Petersburg, died of a heart attack, his wife said.

When Floyd Burdette Schwartzwalder (Ben was a childhood nickname bestowed by a brother) arrived at Syracuse at the age of 41 in 1949, he was not at all what the alumni had hoped for to revive their football program.

Syracuse, once a national powerhouse, had won all of nine games over the previous four seasons, and Schwartzwalder, a former high school coach whose collegiate career consisted of three seasons at tiny Muhlenberg College in Allentown, Pa., seemed hardly the man to turn things around.

As Schwartzwalder later put it, "The alumni wanted a big-name coach. They got a long-name coach."

Most Victorious Coach

But Schwartzwalder, a decorated World War II paratrooper, simply went to work developing a program that made him the most victorious coach in Syracuse history, with a record of 153-91-3.

Although he later became famous for his recruitment of a long line of talented running backs -- including Jim Brown, Ernie Davis, Jim Nance, Floyd Little and Larry Csonka -- Schwartzwalder's success was founded on an earlier triumph, persuading the Syracuse chancellor, William Pearson Tolley, to increase the number of football scholarships from 12 a year to eventually 25 a year.

As the number of scholarships increased, Schwartzwalder, an honors student during his years playing football and wrestling at the University of West Virginia, did not chafe under the directive that he recruit only academically qualified players. He said good students generally made better athletes, anyway. So did a good coach.

His running offenses, based on an unorthodox unbalanced line, were impenetrable to rival coaches, and his practices, generally conducted at full tilt, were all but unbearable to his players. A Legend in Pajamas

Schwartzwalder became a campus legend for his absent-mindedness (he once wore his pajama bottoms to a morning practice), but it was a foible with an advantage. As his wife once explained, "He simply refuses to clutter up his mind with anything but football."

The concentration paid off. In 1959, the year the Orangemen were voted the nation's top team after capping an 11-0 season with a 23-14 victory over Texas in the Cotton Bowl, Schwartzwalder was named coach of the year.

The offense led the nation, averaging 313.6 rushing yards, 451.5 total yards and 39 points a game, and the defense led the nation in holding opponents to just 96.2 yards a game and only 19.3 rushing yards.

Mr. Schwartzwalder, who retired after the 1973 season, is survived by his wife, Ruth, known as Reggie; two daughters, Mary Scofield of Winesburg, Ohio, and SU san Walker of South Salem. N.Y., and five grandchildren.

Correction: April 30, 1993, Friday an obituary yesterday about Ben Schwartzwalder, the former football coach at Syracuse, misstated his age in some editions. He was 83.

There is a lesson in every life and in every death. I find it very revealing that in 1993, just twenty years after Schwartzwalder and twenty-five years ago, that the Times wrote this about the football program. It is not a tribute to SU officials.

"Syracuse, **once a national powerhouse***, had won all of nine games over the previous four seasons, and Schwartzwalder, a former high school coach whose collegiate career consisted of three seasons at tiny Muhlenberg College in Allentown, Pa., seemed hardly the man to turn things around. As Schwartzwalder later put it, "The alumni wanted a big-name coach. They got a long-name coach."*

I would ask Syracuse officials to ask themselves if they really want to be known as "once a national powerhouse." Do they want the Orange legacy to be "once a national powerhouse?" See Chapter 20 for details. Only the administrative officials and the Board at Syracuse can make that decision folks; but Syracuse fans and alumni should pay attention to what they do.

Now, before we move on to the next chapter with Coach Frank Maloney, let's look at my favorite blogger pundit who has been annotating coach's seasons since we began this book back in 1899. Here is what he has to say about Ben Schwartzwalder, and then, quite reluctantly, we will move the cursor to the Frank Maloney Era.

Here is another look at Ben S. from Part II of the included Part II of the SWC75 blogger's essay:

Famous Coaches (From the Past) by SWC75.

Ben Schwartzwalder was born in West Virginia and played football for the Mountaineers under Coach Greasy Neale in the early 30's as a 146-pound center, (he was also a wrestler in the 155-pound class). By the time he was a senior he'd built himself up - to 152 pounds-

and was team captain. He was also one of the best wrestlers they'd ever had at the school. He became a high school coach at a place called Sisterville, where his team had a roster of 13 guys. When two of them got hurt he had to send the team's 112-pound manager in. He then moved on to Parkersburg and then to McKinley High in Canton, Ohio, winning a couple of state championships.

When the war came, he was commissioned in the US Army and became a paratrooper and a company commander in the 82nd airborne. He trained his men like a football team, which they then became during the D-Day preparations in England and they had a 10-0 record, not even being scored upon. But war was the primary occupation and he half-joked about his paratroopers: "When I say Jump! they jump!" They jumped over Normandy.

Ben landed in a river and nearly lost his left hand when a wound became infected. His unit started out with 170 men and 13 officers and after 38 days of fighting they had 43 men left and one officer- Ben Schwartzwalder. Ben later fought in the Battle of the Bulge and was awarded the Silver Star, the Bronze Star, the Purple Heart, four Battle Stars and Presidential Unit Citation and a promotion to Major. When General Mathew Ridgeway pinned his medals on him, he remarked "Ben, I never expected to see you here to receive this award."

Back in the states, he looked for another coaching job and was recommended for Muhlenberg, which today is a Division II school but at that time was more like a 1AA school. There he went 25-5 in three years, winning something called the Tobacco Bowl over St. Bonaventure, another basketball school that used to play football back in the day.

The president of the college called Schwartzwalder into his office and Ben assumed there would be congratulations and a possible raise. Instead he was told "Ben, we've had an understanding with the Mid-Atlantic Conference folks that we can win in basketball and track, but you're messing up the agreement on the football field. You can't win over half your games." The non-plussed Schwartzwalder immediately started to search for another job. [It was a time when men were men.]

When Schwartzwalder started he was only allowed to give out 12 scholarships per year, less than half the number big time schools were giving out. "I was hopeful of doing some business with Colgate, maybe to catch Cornell. We had no further horizons at the moment. I complained, and the chancellor bawled me out for it. But they were doing so little for football that Old Ben was desperate. Finally, in 1952, Chancellor Tolley allowed him to issue 16 scholarships. As his teams got better, that was expanded to 22 and then to 25, (this is from Ken Rappoport's book: he does not specify when the latter two changes occurred).

Ben had an early "false positive" with the 1952 Lambert Trophy winners. Army, which had been the big power in the East, had suffered its cribbing scandal and the other schools in the East were in decline or rebuilding. We found ourselves in the Orange Bowl against perennial national power Alabama and got humiliated 6-61 on national television. It took four years to fully recover from that.

In Jim Brown's senior year, we went 7-1 and won another Lambert and this time went to the Cotton Bowl where TCU, then as now a respected power, barely beat us on a blocked extra point, 27-28. Two years later, we were in the Orange Bowl again, this time taking on the King Kong of 50's football, Wilkinson's Oklahoma team, and losing 6-21 despite out-gaining the Sooners. The next year we were all-conquering with one of the greatest teams ever and won our only national championship. Schwartzwalder was a miracle worker!

There were no more miracles after that but there were some good teams and great players Like Ernie Davis, John Mackey, Jim Nance, Floyd Little and Larry Csonka. But eventually events caught up with Bantam Ben.

Archbold Stadium should have been replaced after the national championship. Instead Manley Field House was built as an indoor practice facility until the school realized they could make more money by promoting the basketball team. Then, in 1964, the NCAA gave up its attempt to use rules to enforce one platoon football. This required schools to recruit many more players: not only were there separate teams playing offense and defense, but players could now specialize in various functions.

Top schools could no longer be satisfied to recruit players from their own area where players grew up being aware of the program. They had to pull in recruits from all over the country. For that they needed a lot of money for facilities and recruiting. Typically, the Syracuse administration thought that since we were doing well, nothing more needed to be done. Schools like Penn State, which expanded its stadium from 30,000 at the beginning of the decade, eventually to over 100,000, were prepared to win those recruiting wars. Syracuse was not.

[Syracuse, it's time, must either blank or get off the pot with regard to football, its highest grossing and netting sport. One must invest in order to collect on investments. He without a lottery ticket has no chance of winning the lottery.]

Dave Meggsey decided he didn't like being a football player anymore and wrote a book trashing everyone he had ever dealt with in the game, including Ben, whom he claimed had "dehumanized" him. It was a condemnation of football in general, but many took it as a condemnation of football at Syracuse.

[Like Joe Paterno, Ben Schwartzwalder did not have a racist bone in his body but that would not stop him from being a victim of reverse racism, or so some say.]

Then came the black boycott of 1970, (simultaneously with several similar actions across the country) and a demand that a black assistant coach be hired. Since Ben had no more money for assistant coaches, he would have had to fire one of his long-time assistants.

[A wise man once said that poor planning on your part does not necessarily constitute an emergency on my part. From the black side or the white side surprise demands were never appreciated my management.]

There had also been a fight between a white player and a black player and an incident at a basketball game where some black players refused to stand for the national anthem, which angered Ben. Schwartzwalder was then derided as a "super patriot". Ben promised an "interim" black coach for spring practice. That turned out to be

Floyd Little, who criticized the players for their attitude. [The team's black players were not impressed with Floyd Little. They felt he was just a "mouthpiece" for Schwartzwalder.]

[They were ready, and they chose to walk out. Eventually a black coach was hired, Carlmon Jones. It was not enough as demands that are met are often changed.]

[The boycotters added to the issue.] They claimed they got inferior medical attention and academic support and weren't getting secret payments from the alumni as they claimed the white players were. These allegations were unprovable. Jim Brown then entered the fray, announcing an intention to sue the NCAA for racial discrimination.

Suddenly Ben [otherwise a great coach] had a segregated team. They lost the first three games of the year, then rallied to win 6 of 7, including a shocking 24-7 win at Penn State and a season ending demolition of Miami in Archbold, 56-16, (a game that greatly resembled the 1998 victory over the same school). But the damage had been done. The black boycott got national publicity and branded Schwartzwalder and the school as racist.

Then came a movement within the institution to re-examine the financial aspect of the football program. This committee determined that it was a waste of money and recommended putting an end to it. Meanwhile, Archbold Stadium had reached a crisis point. The fire department wanted to condemn it. They were persuaded to do it a section at a time.

When I was a student there in the early 70's the stadium had a listed capacity of 41,000 but an actually capacity of 19,000 due to the roped off sections. Then came a decade long debate over whether to build a new stadium, where to put it and how to finance it. We had no formal weight room until a guy's office was cleared out and some barbells put in it. It wasn't solved in Schwartzwalder's time. People who think we have a crisis in facilities now have no idea what a real crisis is.

Ben finally had a losing record in his second to last year, his first since his initial year of 1949. Then the program finally collapsed like a dying elephant in 1973, getting blown out by Bowling Green in their first game and losing 8 in row. I recall the guy who did the "bottom ten" column in the national newspapers each week said we were the worst team in America, (Army, UTEP and, believe it or not, Florida State went winless that year), "because of all the money they spend on football up there".

In fact, that was the problem- we weren't spending anywhere near enough. Fans insisted, as they often do, that "the game had passed him [Ben] by". I remember my barber telling me that the players just didn't have the "spirit" they had in the old days.

Still, the Orange rallied with a win over Holy Cross and a big upset of Boston College. They final game was played against his old school, West Virginia, in a downpour. It looked for a while like we might pull off another upset, but the Mountaineers clinched it with a late score, 14-24.

I still remember Ben Schwartzwalder, the man who had been SU's coach for my entire lifetime, walking slowly across the field in the rain to shake hands with the West Virginia coach, (Bobby Bowden), then walking off the field to the locker room with his head down and his thoughts to himself.

There were stories at the time that Don Nehlen, the Bowling Green coach who had embarrassed Ben's last team, or Tubby Raymond, the coach at Delaware who had won a couple of small college championships there, wanted to come to Syracuse. Considering the circumstances, it's hard to see why. What we wound up with was Michigan's linebacker coach, Frank Maloney. There were a few bright spots on Maloney's record but not enough to please the fan base.

1974	Frank Maloney	2	9	0
1975	Frank Maloney	6	5	0
1976	Frank Maloney	3	8	0
1977	Frank Maloney	6	5	0
1978	Frank Maloney	3	8	0
1979	Frank Maloney	7	5	0
1980	Frank Maloney	5	6	0

After Ben Schwartzwalder, winning coaches were hard to find.

Chapter 13 Coach Frank Maloney From 1974 to 1980

Coach Frank Maloney #23

Year	Coach	Record	Conf
1974	Frank Maloney	2-9-0	Ind
1975	Frank Maloney	6-5-0	Ind
1976	Frank Maloney	3-8-0	Ind
1977	Frank Maloney	6-5-0	Ind
1978	Frank Maloney	3-8-0	Ind
1979	Frank Maloney	7-5-0	Ind
1980	Frank Maloney	5-6-0	Ind

Coach Frank Maloney in 1980

Famous Coaches (From the Past) by SWC75.

Maloney had his limitations, (especially in-game adjustments: we had a lot of games where we looked great in the first quarter and went downhill from there). But Frank has never received the credit he deserved for keeping the football program alive while the politicians bickered about building a new stadium and the school slowly awoke to the need to get modern facilities such as a genuine weight room. He somehow managed to recruit some fine players such as Bill Hurley, Art Monk, Joe Morris, Craig Wolfley and Jimmy Collins whose ability in key positions allowed the team to remain competitive and interesting. He produced three winning seasons and actually won a bowl game, albeit a very minor one, (the Independence Bowl over McNeese State).

But there were also seasons of 2-9, 3-8, 3-8 and 5-6 and when the promising 1979 team went into a slump the members of the 1959 team signed a petition asking for Frank to be fired. Also, Jake Crouthamel had become athletic director and new AD's like to bring in their own people. Officially, Frank resigned to spend more time with his family. There was talk he might get the Northwestern job, being from Chicago, (the Wildcats had started on their record winning streak), but it didn't happen. Frank wound up with a long-term job running the ticket office for the Chicago Cubs.

1974 Frank Maloney Coach # 23

The 1974 Syracuse Orangemen football team competed in their eighty-fifth season of intercollegiate football. They were led by Frank Maloney in his first of seven seasons as head coach of the Syracuse Orangemen. SU got back on a winning track this year with a record of 6-5-0. Maloney picked Bob Petchel & John Rafferty as team captains for 1974. The Orangemen again did not receive an invitation to any post-season bowl games in 1974.

On Sept 7 SU beat Oregon State W (23-23) in the home opener in Archbold Stadium on the Syracuse University Campus in Syracuse NY. Frank Maloney's squad won their first game played for the new coach. On Sept 14, at home SU lost to Kent State L (14-20). On Sept 21, at Michigan State Spartan Stadium, East Lansing, MI SU lost to the Spartans L (0–19)before 66,847. On Sept 28, #13 NC State defeated the Orangemen L (22-28*. On Oct 5 at home, Maryland shut out the Orangemen L (0-31). In the second and last win of the season, on Oct 12 at home, Syracuse defeated Navy W (17-9)

On Oct 19 at #11 Penn State at Beaver Stadium in University Park, PA, SU lost to the Nittany Lions L (14–30) before 59,100. On Nov

2, at home, SU lost to Pittsburgh L (13–21) before 25,177 fans. On Nov 9, at West Virginia's Mountaineer Field in Morgantown, WV, Syracuse took a shellacking L (11-39). Then, on the road on Nov 16 at Boston College's Alumni Stadium in Chestnut Hill, MA, the Eagles shut out the Orangemen L0–35) before 18,651. On the road again on Nov 22 at Miami (FL) in the Orange Bowl, Miami, FL, Syracuse was beaten in a close game by the Hurricanes. L (7–14) before 12,208.

1975 Frank Maloney Coach # 23

The 1975 Syracuse Orangemen football team competed in their eighty-sixth season of intercollegiate football. They were led by Frank Maloney in his second of seven seasons as head coach of the Syracuse Orangemen. SU got back on a winning track this year with a record of 6-5-0. Maloney picked Raymond Preston as team captain for 1975. The Orangemen again did not receive an invitation to any post-season bowl games in 1975.

All American Raymond N. Preston 1975

Raymond Preston was born on January 25, 1954 in Lawrence, Massachusetts) is a former American football linebacker who played nine years from 1976 to 1984with the San Diego Chargers of the National Football League.

 Preston played his college football at Syracuse University, where he earned All-America honors in 1975 and was a team captain. He was drafted in the eleventh round of the 1976 NFL Draft by the Chargers. His son Duke Preston is currently an offensive lineman for the Dallas Cowboys.

Games of the 1975 Season

On Sept 13 SU beat Villanova W (24-17) in the home opener in Archbold Stadium on the Syracuse University Campus in Syracuse NY before 22,867 fans. On Sept 20, at home SU defeated Iowa W (10-7) On Sept 27, at Tulane in the Louisiana Superdome New Orleans, LA the Orangemen won W (31–13) before 33,200. On Oct 4, at Maryland's Byrd Stadium in College Park, MD, the Terrapins beat the Orangemen L (7–24) before 43,863. Then on Oct11 at Navy, Annapolis, MD, the Midshipmen prevailed L (6–10).

On Oct 18, #9 Penn State beat Syracuse at home L (7–19) before 28,153. On Oct 25 at home, Syracuse defeated Boston College W (22–14). On Nov 1 at home, SU were shut out by Pitt L (0-38). On Nov 15 at Virginia Scott Stadium, Charlottesville, VA Syracuse beat the Wahoo's W (37–0). Then on Nov 22, at home, SU defeated West Virginia by one point W (20–19) before 15,336. Then in the season finale against Rutgers at Rutgers Stadium in Piscataway, NJ, the Orangemen were defeated L (10–21) before 22,000 fans.

1976 Frank Maloney Coach # 23

The 1976 Syracuse Orangemen football team competed in their eighty-seventh season of intercollegiate football. They were led by Frank Maloney in his third of seven seasons as head coach of the Syracuse Orangemen. SU got off track again this year with a losing record of 3-8-0. Maloney picked William Zanovich as team captain for 1976. The Orangemen again did not receive an invitation to any post-season bowl games in 1976.

On Sept 11 SU lost to Bowling Green in the home opener in Archbold Stadium on the Syracuse University Campus in Syracuse NY L (7-22) before 23,859 fans. On Sept 18, while on the road at Kinnick Stadium in Iowa City, IA, SU lost big to Iowa, L (3–41) before 54,129

On Sept 25, at home, Syracuse lost to the Terrapins of Maryland L (28-42) before 21,109, On Oct 2 at home SU defeated Oregon State W (21–3) before 18,591. Then at home on Oct 9, SU defeated Tulane in a nail-biter W (3–0) before 11,223 fans. On Oct 16 at Penn

State's Beaver Stadium, University Park, PA, PSU won a nice victory L (3–27) before 61,474.

On Oct 23 at home, SU defeated Temple W (24-16). Then, on Oct 30 at #2 Pittsburgh's Pitt Stadium in Pittsburgh, PA, Syracuse lost L (13–23) before 50,390. On Nov 6 at home SU lost to Navy L (10-27). Then on Nov 13 at Boston College's Alumni Stadium, Chestnut Hill, MA, Syracuse was defeated L (14–28) before 25,433. In the Season Finale, Syracuse lost on Nov 20 at West Virginia's Mountaineer Field in Morgantown, WV L (28–34) before 27,848

1977 Frank Maloney Coach # 23

The 1977 Syracuse Orangemen football team competed in their eighty-eighth season of intercollegiate football. They were led by Frank Maloney in his fourth of seven seasons as head coach of the Syracuse Orangemen. SU got back on track this year with a winning record of 6-5-0. Rather than picking a team captain for the season, Maloney decided to use game captains. for 1977. The Orangemen again did not receive an invitation to any post-season bowl games in 1977.

On Sept 10 SU lost at Oregon State at Parker Stadium Corvallis, OR L 12–24, before 20,540. On Sept 17, Syracuse lost in a shutout to NC State to in the home opener in Archbold Stadium on the Syracuse University Campus in Syracuse NY before 20,696 fans. On Sept 24, at home SU defeated Washington in a tight match, W (22-0) On Oct 1 at Illinois Memorial Stadium, Champaign, IL, Syracuse defeated the Fighting Illini W (30–20) before 52,015. Then on Oct 8 at Maryland's Byrd Stadium in College Park, MD, the Orangemen were defeated by the Terrapins L (10–24) before 39,100.

Then, on Oct 15 at home against #10 Penn State, the Orangemen were defeated by the Nittany Lions L (24–31) before 27,029. On Oct 22 at #14 Pittsburgh in a rivalry game played at Pitt Stadium, Pittsburgh, PA the Orangemen were defeated by the Panthers L (21–28) before 43,551. On Oct 29 at home, SU barely beat the Wahoos, W (6–3) before 20,859.

On Nov 5 at Navy's Navy–Marine Corps Memorial Stadium in Annapolis, MD, the Orangemen defeated the Midshipmen W (45–34) before 16,709. On Nov 12, at home, SU defeated Boston College W (20-3) before16,409. In the season finale on Nov 19, at home, Syracuse defeated West Virginia W (28-9) before another small crowd of 16,118.

1978 Frank Maloney Coach # 23

The 1978 Syracuse Orangemen football team competed in their eighty-ninth season of intercollegiate football. They were led by Frank Maloney in his fifth of seven seasons as head coach of the Syracuse Orangemen. SU slipped off track again this year with a losing record of 3-8-0. Rather than picking a team captain for the season, Maloney again decided to use game captains. for 1978. The Orangemen again did not receive an invitation to any post-season bowl games in 1978.

On Sept 9, Syracuse lost in a shutout to Bobby Bowden's Florida State Seminoles in the home opener in Archbold Stadium on the Syracuse University Campus in Syracuse NY L (0-28) before 24,272 fans. On Sept 16, at NC State in a game played at Carter Stadium, Raleigh, NC, the Orangemen lost to the Tar Heels L (19–27). Then, on Sept 23 at Michigan State's Spartan Stadium in East Lansing, MI, the Orangemen lost L (21–49) before 74,571 fans.

On Sept 30 at home, SU lost to Illinois L (14-28) before 20,101. On Oct 7 at West Virginia's Mountaineer Field in Morgantown, WV, Syracuse got its first of three wins for the season W (31–15) before 32,491 fans. On Oct 14 at home SU lost to #10 Maryland L (9-24) before a small crowd of 15,079. On Oct 21 in a rivalry game at #2 ranked Penn State at Beaver Stadium in University Park, PA, SU lost big L (15–45) before 77,827. PSU's Beaver Stadium kept growing.

On Nov 4, at home, another PA team beat the Orangemen in this dismal year. #19 Pittsburgh barely got by the Orangemen L (17-18) before 26,037. On Nov 11 at home against Navy, the Orangemen defeated the Midshipmen W (20-17). This would be the last game the Orangemen played at Archbold Field. In the next game, on Nov

18, SU got a win at Boston College's Alumni Stadium in Chestnut Hill, MA W (37–23) before 15,855. Syracuse lost its final game on Nov 25 at Miami (FL) in the Miami Orange Bowl venue in Miami, FL L (9–21) before 15,739.

1979 Frank Maloney Coach # 23

The 1979 Syracuse Orangemen football team competed in their nineteenth season of intercollegiate football. They were led by Frank Maloney in his sixth of seven seasons as head coach of the Syracuse Orangemen. SU had its best year under Maloney this year with a winning record of 7-5-0. Maloney picked Jim Collins, Bill Hurley & Craig Wolfley to be team captains for 1979. The Orangemen were invited to the 1979 Independence Bowl, where they defeated McNeese State, 31–7.

Due to the ongoing construction of Syracuse's new stadium, the "indoor" Carrier Dome, SU home games in 1979 were played in various locations in New York and New Jersey. SO, SU games were played at Giants Stadium, (Capacity: 80,242); Rich Stadium, (Capacity: 80,020); and Schoellkopf Field, (Capacity: 25,597)

Since the Carrier Dome was built in the exact location of Archbold Stadium, this magnificent concrete structure was torn down before the 1979 season to permit the Carrier Dome's construction.

Art Monk All American 1979

Art Monk is principal of Art Monk Companies, located in Northern Virginia. An outstanding football letter winner and All-American at Syracuse, Monk joined the Washington Redskins in 1980. In 1997, he was the Redskins' all-time leading receiver, with 888 receptions and 12,026 receiving yards. In 1994, he joined the New York Jets and, a year later, the Philadelphia Eagles.

Monk has earned significant records and accolades as a business professional and football player, including being named All-American in 1979, and, upon his graduation from Syracuse in 1980, he was listed as the all-time leading receiver. Monk was inducted into the Pro Football Hall of Fame in 2008.

However, Monk prefers to be known for his engagement with Every Child Fed, a vision of two fellow business partners that was founded in 2000. The foundation's mission is to harness their collective passion, energy, gifts, talents, resources and determination to deploy self-sustaining manufacturing facilities of Ready-to-Use Therapeutic-Food and mobilize feeding clinics to distribute life-saving Ready-to-Use Therapeutic Food to severely malnourished children in SU b-Saharan Africa.

For Syracuse University, Monk is a member of the Executive Committee and the Academic Affairs and Facilities committees. He received the Arents Award, the University's highest alumni honor, in 2012. He and his wife, Desiree '81, are the parents of Danielle, James, and Monica '09.

Games of the 1979 season

In the season opener on Sept 8 against Earle Bruce's Ohio State team in Ohio Stadium, Columbus, OH, SU lost L (8–31) before 86.205. This was the first year Ohio State played after Woody Hayes. On Sept 15, Syracuse beat West Virginia W (24-14) as an SU home game played at Giants Stadium, East Rutherford, NJ before 10,375. On Sept 22 at Northwestern's Dyche Stadium in Evanston, IL, SU got a nice win W (54–21) before 20,121. On Sept 29, in a home game against Washington State, played in Rich Stadium, Orchard Park, NY, SU defeated the Cougars W (52–25) before 10,004.

On Oct 6 at Kansas Memorial Stadium in Lawrence, KS, SU got the win, W (45–27) before 36,720. On Oct 13 at Temple in Veterans Stadium, Philadelphia, PA, the Orangemen lost to the Owls in a blowout L (17–49) before 18,504. On Oct 20, at home played at Giants Stadium in East Rutherford, NJ, the Orangemen lost to the Nittany Lions of Penn State L (7–35) before 53,789. On Oct 27, at home played at Rich Stadium in Orchard Park, NY, SU defeated Miami W (25–15) before 7,729.

Then, on Nov 3 at #12 Pittsburgh's Pitt Stadium, Pittsburgh, PA, the Orangemen were defeated by the Panthers L (21–28) before 43,005 fans. Then, on Nov 10 at Navy in a game played in the Navy–Marine Corps Memorial Stadium, Annapolis, MD, the Orangemen defeated the Midshipmen W (30–14) before 20,385, In the final regular season home game on Nov 17, Boston College beat Syracuse at Schoellkopf Field in Ithaca, NY L (10–27) before 20,245

Independence Bowl Game Dec 15, 1979

On Dec 15, 1979. McNeese State and Syracuse tangled in the 1979 Independence Bowl at State Fair Stadium, Shreveport, LA W (31–7) before 27,234 fans. This was McNeese State's 2nd Southland Conference title in three years. This was Syracuse's first bowl game since 1966.

The Game

With his 40-yard field goal. Gary Anderson gave the Orangemen a 3-0 lead in the second quarter. SU went into halftime leading 3-0. Ken Mandeville made it 10-0 by way of a 1-yard run. McNeese State got its TD when Chad Millet ran for a score make it 10-7 going into the fourth quarter.

Syracuse then unleashed a 15 play, 73-yard drive culminating with an Art Monk touchdown catch from Bill Hurley. Hurley late got another TD to make the score 24-7. Tom Matichak made it 31-7 on a touchdown run of his own to end the scoring and give the Orangemen their first bowl win since the 1961 Liberty Bowl. Joe Morris ran for 155 yards on 33 carries for Syracuse in a fine showing.

McNeese made one more bowl appearance in 1980, in the Independence Bowl. Syracuse made four more bowl appearances in the decade. They have not returned to the Independence Bowl since this game.

1980 Frank Maloney Coach # 23

The 1980 Syracuse Orangemen football team competed in their ninety-First season of intercollegiate football. They were led by Frank Maloney in his seventh and last of seven seasons as head coach of the Syracuse Orangemen. SU had a losing season under Maloney this year of 5-6-0 in the team's first season in the Carrier Dome. Maloney picked Jim Collins, Joe Morris & Dave Warner to be team captains for 1980. At the conclusion of the season, head coach Frank Maloney resigned, with a record of 32–46 after seven seasons.

In the season opener on Sept 13 at Earle Bruce's Ohio State team in Ohio Stadium, Columbus, OH, SU lost L (12-31) before 86.205. On Sept 20, at home, Syracuse beat Miami (OH) at the Carrier Dome, on the campus of Syracuse University in Syracuse, NY W (36-24). On Sept 27 at home SU defeated Northwestern W (42–21) before 34,739. On Oct 4, at home on my wedding anniversary, SU defeated Kansas L (8–23) before 43,126 in the new dome. On Oct 11 at home, SU beat Temple W (31–7) before 36,485.

On Oct 18 at #12 Penn State's Beaver Stadium in University Park, PA PSU defeated SU L (7–24) before 84,790. On Oct 25 at home, Syracuse defeated Rutgers W (17–9) before 39,937 fans. On Nov1 at home, SU was defeated by #11 Pitt in a rout L (6–43) before 50,243 fans.

On Nov 8 at home SU was defeated by Navy in a nail-biter L (3–6) before 50,350 fans. On Nov 15, at Boston College's Alumni Stadium, Chestnut Hill, MA the Eagles defeated the Orangemen L (16–27) before 22,000. In the final game of the season on Nov 22, SU finished off well with a win W (20-7) at West Virginia's Mountaineer Field in Morgantown, WV before 34,441 fans.

Chapter 14 Coach Dick Macpherson From 1981 to 1990

Coach Dick MacPherson #24

Year	Coach	Record	Conf
1981	Dick MacPherson	4-6-1	Ind
1982	Dick MacPherson	2-9-0	Ind
1983	Dick MacPherson	6-5-0	Ind
1984	Dick MacPherson	6-5-0	Ind
1985	Dick MacPherson	7-5-0	Ind
1986	Dick MacPherson	5-6-0	Ind
1987	Dick MacPherson	11-0-1	Ind
1988	Dick MacPherson	10-2-0	Ind
1989	Dick MacPherson	8-4-0	Ind
1990	Dick MacPherson	7-4-2	Ind

Famous Coaches (From the Past) by SWC75.

AD Crouthamel remembered **Dick MacPherson** who had beaten his Dartmouth teams twice when coaching at Massachusetts. That was before Division 1AA and Dartmouth was considered a major college team while UMASS was a small college team. Before that, he'd been Maryland's defensive backfield coach back in 1966 when SU's Jim Del Gaizo threw a record-tying four TD passes in a 28-7 win. MacPherson also had pro experience as an assistant coach for the

Denver Broncos and Cleveland Browns. In fact, he was the Brown's linebacker coach when Jake hired him to be the new Syracuse coach.

I [SWC75] remember being at work when the announcement came. A co-worker said they'd hired someone named MacPherson. Who? But he was coming from the pros and people figured he was hired to put the program's coaching on a more professional level, now that we were in the Dome and were going to be a big-time program. Maloney's last team had not been that bad. They would have had a winning season if Joe Morris hadn't been injured and had to miss several games. Joe was back and healthy, so Dick had plenty to work with.

That made it all the more dismaying to see the team start out the 1981 season with three straight losses, the first two to Rutgers and Temple, both of whom Maloney had beaten the year before. It was also disappointing to see MacPherson's slovenly, disheveled appearance during games, with his shirttail pulled out. He didn't look professional at all. And the team seemed disorganized with a chaotic sideline and nobody very sure of themselves on the field either.

The toughest part of the schedule was in the middle with Maryland, Penn State and Pittsburgh in a row. We somehow managed to beat Indiana and tie the Terps but were 1-5-1 heading into a stretch run. Fortunately, Crouthamel had scheduled the first Colgate game in 20 years and we won it 47-24. Then, after a loss on the road to Navy we came home to upset Boston College and West Virginia to finish 4-6-1 with Joe Morris playing all season and setting records along the way. The next year the team totally collapsed to 2-9, the same record that ended Ben Schwartzwalder's career and started Frank Maloney's. We had thought such disasters were in the past. This was supposed to be the great new Carrier Dome Era.

Coach Mac's third year didn't look any better when it opened with a third straight loss to Temple in Philadelphia, a game where top recruit Don McPherson injured his knee and was out for the year, (which is why he was still around for the 1987 season). Mac's record at this point was 6 wins, 16 losses and a tie, (G-Rob was 5-18 in his first 23 games). Fortunately, our next opponent was Kent State, who had the country's longest losing streak.

I [SWC75] was one of an official 24,605 fans in the Dome that day, (I remember it as a lot less than that). Syracuse fumbled the first three times we got the ball. As I recall it was twice on kick-off and once on the first play from scrimmage. The Golden Flashes got a field goal and then a touchdown out of it and then got the ball back a third time. A woman next to me said in my ear "This is actually funny." Then something happened. The four defensive linemen, Tim Green, Blaise Winter, Bill Pendock and Jamie Kimmel started motioning to the crowd to make some noise: "get behind us!".

The fans started cheering them on- why not? They stuffed that third possession and SU slowly took over the game. That line, which came to know as "Four Wheel Drive" kept forcing punts and turnovers and Don McCauley kept kicking field goals for the Orange. We got it to 9-10 by halftime, then took the lead at 12-10 and 15-10 and final punched over a touchdown to win 22-10. The crowd got louder and louder as the game went on and made as much noise as I've heard from any capacity crowd. In the subsequent years of great success, I was very proud to say that I was one of the fans who had been there at the Kent State game.

Syracuse went on to win three in a row and suddenly we were 3-1. Then we went out to play one of Nebraska's greatest teams and got crushed like a soda can, 7-63, the first of four straight losses. But the team rallied to win its last three and finish 6-5 against a schedule that included 6 bowl teams when there were less than half as many bowls as we have now.

The next year was just as tough, with 5 bowl teams and a 9-1-1 Florida team on probation. This was the year of the great win over Nebraska, followed by three straight road losses at Florida, West Virginia and Penn State. Then we rallied for three wins before losing to Heisman Trophy winner Doug Flutie's Boston College team, 16-24, for another 6-5 record. Both those teams would have gone to bowls today. The following year we did go to a bowl, losing the Cherry Bowl in Michigan to Maryland. But that gave us "bowl credibility" and allowed Mac to recruit a class full of big offensive linemen.

Hopes were high the next year but there was too much rebuilding to do. We opened the season with four straight losses- all close- and a group called the "Sack Mac Pack" started up. But we rallied to a 5-2 finish and then all those big guys moved into the O-line to clear the way for Donnie McPherson, Moose Johnson, Robert Drummond and Michael Owens and we went on an 11-0 tear. Mrs. MacPherson even convinced the coach to start wearing a blue blazer with an orange tie. He looked like the CEO of a successful corporation. It was the beginning of a 15-year run of winning seasons, something only Michigan, Nebraska and Florida State accomplished in those same years.

1981 Dick MacPherson Coach # 24

Dick MacPherson, resurrected the declining football program at Syracuse University—the decade you just read about from the Maloney years—and after the "Great Coaches" primer above, you are about to read about how Big Mac returned Syracuse Football to national prominence. MacPherson was head coach of the Syracuse Orangemen between 1981 and 1990. He posted a record of 66-46-4. After the team finished 5-6 in 1986, MacPherson took Syracuse on a magical run in which the Orangemen were 36-10 including an 11-0-1 mark in 1987 that included a berth in the Sugar Bowl and a fling with the national championship.

The 1981 Syracuse Orangemen football team competed in their ninety-second season of intercollegiate football. They were led by Frank Maloney in his first of ten seasons as head coach of the Syracuse Orangemen. SU had a losing season under MacPherson this year of 4-6-1 in the team's second season in the Carrier Dome. Syracuse had developed a culture of losing and it took a few years for MacPherson to turn it around. MacPherson picked Ike Bogosian & Joe Morris to be team captains for 1981.

All American Gary Anderson 1981

Gary Anderson was an All American for Syracuse University in 1981. His NFL career has included tenures with the Steelers, Eagles, 49ers, Vikings, and Titans. He holds the SU record for season field

goals made (18) and highest season percentage of field goals made (94.7%), both in 1981.

<< **Anderson** took part in SU's NCAA record setting consecutive PAT streak that lasted from 1978-1989. He won the 1998 Gold Toe Award in the NFL. He was named to Syracuse University's All-Century team in November 1999.

On Sept 5, in the home and season opener Rutgers defeated Syracuse in a nail-biter L (27-29) at the Carrier Dome, on the campus of Syracuse University in Syracuse, NY before 38,715. On Sept 12 at Temple in Veterans Stadium, Philadelphia, PA SU lost another L (19–31) before 15,091. Then, on Sept 19 at Illinois Memorial Stadium in Champaign, IL, SU suffered their third loss in a row, L (14–17) before 57,579. Back at the Carrier Dome on Sept 26, SU picked up win # 1 v Indiana before 32,060.

Then it was off on Oct 3 to Maryland's Byrd Stadium, College Park, MD, as the Terrapins and Orangemen played to a tie T (17-17) before 32,000. On Oct 17, at home, Syracuse lost to #2 ranked Penn State L (16-41). The following week on Oct 24, SU played # 2 Pitt at Pitt Stadium in Pittsburgh, PA and were beaten by the Panthers L (10–23) before 50,330. On Oct 31, SU began playing Colgate again and defeated the Red Raiders at home in the Carrier Dome W (47–24) before 40,309

On Nov 7 at Navy in Navy–Marine Corps Memorial Stadium, in Annapolis, MD, the Midshipmen had their way L (23–35) before 23,355. On Nov 14 at home in the Carrier Dome, Syracuse defeated Boston College W (27-24) before 35,623. In the last game of the season on Nov 21, Syracuse pulled off a close win at home against West Virginia in the Carrier Dome W (27–24) before 33,117

1982 Dick MacPherson Coach # 24

The 1982 Syracuse Orangemen football team competed in their ninety-third season of intercollegiate football. They were led by Dick MacPherson in his second of ten seasons as head coach of the Syracuse Orangemen. SU had a losing season of three under MacPherson this year -- 2-9-0 in the team's third season in the Carrier Dome. Syracuse had developed a culture of losing and would break away from this affliction in the next year. MacPherson would turn it around. MacPherson picked Gerry Feehery to be team captain for 1982.

All American Mike Charles 1982

Michael William Charles, who also is known as "The Beast From the East" was born September 23, 1962 in Newark. He received all American status in 1982 as a Nose Tackle from Syracuse University. Charles played nine seasons in the National Football League. He was picked in the second round of the draft and had a great pro career playing for the Miami Dolphins (1983–1986), San Diego Chargers, (1987–1989), Los Angeles Raiders, (1990), and Los Angeles Rams (1991)g

Games of the 1982 Season

On Sept 4, in the season opener at Rutgers in Giants Stadium, East Rutherford, NJ, SU won W (31-8) before 20,890. Then, on Sept 11, SU lost to Temple in a close match L (18-23) in the home opener at the Carrier Dome, on the campus of Syracuse University in Syracuse, NY before 29, 574. On Sept 18 at home, SU was defeated by Illinois in a blowout L (10-47). Then, on Sept 25 at Indiana Memorial Stadium in Bloomington, IN, SU lost a close on L (10–17) before 42,020

On Oct 2 at home Syracuse was beaten by the Maryland Terrapins at the Carrier Dome L (3–26) before 30,214. Then, on Oct 16 at #8

Penn State's Beaver Stadium in University Park, PA, the Nittany Lions bested the Orangemen L (7–28) before 84,762. The next loss came in an outing on Oct 23 at home against #2 ranked Pittsburgh. The Panthers won the game in a low-scoring shutout L (0–14) before 42,321 at the Carrier Dome. On Oct 30 in another Carrier Dome experience, SU grabbed win # 2 against the Colgate Red Raiders W (49-15)

On Nov 6 at home, SU lost a close match to Navy at the Carrier Dome L (18–20) before 43,443. The following week on Nov 13 at Boston College's Alumni Stadium in Chestnut Hill, MA, Syracuse lost another close game L (13–20). Still in its losing way as the MacPherson injection had not yet taken hold yet, on Nov 20 at #16 West Virginia Mountaineer Field Morgantown, WV SU lost its last game of its worst season under Dick MacPherson L (0–26) before 48,456.

1983 Dick MacPherson Coach # 24

The 1983 Syracuse Orangemen football team competed in their ninety-fourth season of intercollegiate football. They were led by Dick MacPherson in his third of ten seasons as head coach of the Syracuse Orangemen. SU had its first winning season under its newest coach, MacPherson this year–6-5-0 in the team's fourth season in the Carrier Dome.

Before Coach MacPherson, SU had unfortunately gotten accustomed to losing year-in and year-out and this year, after two dismal seasons, the new coach would break them away from this pattern this year. He was the new ingredient that SU needed, and he turned the program and the attitudes around. Nothing in life worth doing is easy and it was not easy, but the positive signs were beginning to show. MacPherson picked Blaise Winter & Brent Ziegler, standout team players to be team captains for 1983.

On Sept 2, in the season opener at Temple, in a game played at Franklin Field in Philadelphia, Syracuse lost L (6–17) before 11,549 fans. Then, on Sept 10, SU beat Kent State W (22-10) in the home opener at the Carrier Dome, on the campus of Syracuse University in Syracuse, NY before 24, 605. On Sept 17 at home, SU beat Northwestern in a shutout W (35-0). On Sept 24, at home, Syracuse defeated Rutgers at the Carrier Dome W (17–13), Moving to October, on the first day of the new month, before 76,382 fans at #1 ranked Nebraska's Memorial Stadium in Lincoln, NE, Syracuse took a shellacking from the Cornhuskers L (7–63).

On Oct 8 at #16 ranked Maryland's Byrd Stadium in College Park, MD, the Terrapins got the best of the Orangemen L (13–34) before 43,700. Then, on Oct 15 at home, Penn State beat Syracuse in the Carrier Dome L (6–17) before a packed crowd of 50,010. On Oct 29, at Pittsburgh's Pitt Stadium in Pittsburgh, PA, in a close rivalry match, the Panthers won against the Orangemen L (10–13) before 52,374.

On Nov 5 at Navy, in the Navy–Marine Corps Memorial Stadium, Annapolis, MD, Syracuse nudged Navy W (14–7) before 22,009. On Nov 12, #13 at home, Syracuse engaged Boston College in the Carrier Dome and defeated the Eagles W (21–10) before 41,225. Finishing up the season with a nice win against rival West Virginia at home in the Carrier Dome, Syracuse took the win W (27–16) before 36,661

1984 Dick MacPherson Coach # 24

The 1984 Syracuse Orangemen football team competed in their ninety-fifth season of intercollegiate football. They were led by Dick MacPherson in his fourth of ten seasons as head coach of the Syracuse Orangemen. SU had its second winning season under its newest coach, MacPherson this year–6-5-0 in the team's fifth season in the Carrier Dome. MacPherson picked Marty Chalk, Jaime Covington, Jim Gorzalski & Jamie Kimmel to be the team captains for 1984.

All American Timothy Green 1984, 1985

Timothy Green Was the 1985 National Scholar-Athlete Awards presented by Fidelity Investments recipient. Tim Green excelled on the field and in the classroom. He was a 3-time All-East selection and in 1985 unanimous All-America. He received a National Football Foundation Scholarship for academic excellence.

As a defensive tackle, he sacked quarterbacks and stopped runners. He set three Syracuse records for most sacks: 45.5 career, 15 one year, 4 one game. He had 341 tackles in his career. In 1985 he was Syracuse co-captain and was named Co-player of the Year in the Eastern Collegiate Athletic Conference (ECAC). He graduated in 1986 with a major in English.

Green played for the Atlanta Falcons 1986-93. He obtained a law degree in 1994 and practiced as an attorney, then added a career as a football broadcaster. Green has also excelled as an author and public speaker. In 2001, he was inducted into the College Football Hall of Fame.

Games of the 1984 season

On Sept 8, in the season opener at Maryland's Byrd Stadium in College Park, MD Syracuse got the win over the Terrapins W (23–7) before 38,850. On Sept 15 at Northwestern's Dyche Stadium in Evanston, IL, Syracuse pulled out a close victory W (13–12) before 23,199Then, on Sept 22, SU lost to Rutgers L (0-19), the State University of New Jersey, in the home opener at the Carrier Dome, on the campus of Syracuse University in Syracuse, NY before 41,810.

Highlight Syracuse Knocks off #1 Nebraska

On Sept 29 at home, Syracuse knocked off then ranked #1 Nebraska at the Carrier Dome W (17–9) before 47,280.

Yes, Dick Macpherson could show great emotion at the right times

It was September 29, 1984, when a tough Syracuse squad knocked off #1 Nebraska 17-9 in Dick MacPherson's fourth year. The performance helped quell any concerns about MacPherson's job security and catapulted the Orange forward to bigger things ahead under the legendary coach.

It also remarkably reversed a 63-7 result from the season before. The winning score was ultimately a 40-yard touchdown pass from Todd Norley to Mike Siano. Many of the players from that team point to the opening kickoff as the key, when SU linebacker Derek Ward decked Nebraska fullback Tom Rathman and knocked him out of the game. Those were the days, my friend.

There was little reason to believe that the SU football team stood a chance on that September Saturday in the Carrier Dome. Nebraska was the No. 1-ranked team in the country, favored by 25 points, and had defeated SU the year before 63-7. But this game turned out to be the biggest shocker in Orange football history.

Nebraska scored twice: a touchdown in the first quarter and a safety in the final seconds of the game. In between, Orange quarterback Todd Norley threw a spectacular 40-yard pass to Mike Siano, who out-jumped two Huskers at the goal line for a touchdown. Later, with just 1:29 left at the Nebraska 1-yard line, SU fullback Harold Gayden got the ball and carried it straight into the end zone. The game ended with SU's 17-9 victory over Nebraska; its first win against a top-ranked team in the history of its program.

After the momentous upset, fans swarmed onto the field and celebrated for more than an hour, with SU players coming back out for a curtain call. Yes, those were the days, my friend.

Continuing the 1984 Season Games

On Oct 6 at Florida at Florida Field in Gainesville, FL, SU lost to the Gators L (0–16) before 70,189. On Oct 13 at West Virginia's Mountaineer Field in Morgantown, WV, SU lost in this annual rivalry game L (10–20) before 57,741. On Oct 20 at #19 Penn State at Beaver Stadium in University Park, PA, the Orangemen took a defeat L (3–21) before 85,860 fans. On Oct 27 at home v Army at the Carrier Dome, Syracuse defeated the Cadets in a tough match W (27–16) before 41,438

On Nov 3 at home, Syracuse beat Pittsburgh in the Carrier Dome W (13–7) before 46,489. On Nov 10, at home, Syracuse beat Navy at the Carrier Dome in a nice shutout W (29-0) before 44,000. Then in the season close this year on Nov 17, the #13 Boston College Eagles got the best of the Syracuse Orangemen at Sullivan Stadium in Foxborough, MA L (16–24) before 60,890.

1985 Dick MacPherson Coach # 24

The 1985 Syracuse Orangemen football team competed in their ninety-sixth season of intercollegiate football. They were led by Dick MacPherson in his fifth of ten seasons as head coach of the Syracuse Orangemen. SU had its second winning season under its newest coach, MacPherson this year–7-5-0 in the team's sixth season in the Carrier Dome. MacPherson picked Tim Green & Rudy Reed to be the team captains for 1985. Syracuse finished with a 7–4 regular season record and played in the 1985 Cherry Bowl against Maryland, where they lost, 18–35. Throughout their history, SU has had a problem winning bowl games.

Notable players on this year's team included captain Tim Green, who earned unanimous All-American honors at defensive tackle and was a finalist for the Lombardi Award. Green was drafted 17th overall in the 1986 NFL Draft, ending his career at Syracuse as the school's all-time leader in sacks with 45.5, a record that he still owns.

On Sept 14, in the season opener at Mississippi State's Scott Field in Starkville, MS SU lost L (3–30) On Sept 21 in the home opener at the Carrier Dome, on the campus of Syracuse University in Syracuse, NY before 29,822, SU shut out Kent State W (34-0) before 29,822. On Sept 28 at Virginia Tech at Lane Stadium in Blacksburg, VA, SU lost to the Hokies L (14–24) before 33,400 fans. Then, on Oct 5 at home against Louisville in the Carrier Dome, SU blanked the Cardinals W (48–0) before 26,922

On Oct 19 at home, #6 Penn State barely got by the Orangemen L (20–24) before a packed Dome of 50,021. On Oct 26 at home, Syracuse defeated Temple at the Carrier Dome W (29–14) before 45,391. On Nov 2 at Pittsburgh's Pitt Stadium in Pittsburgh, PA, Syracuse beat the panthers in a close match W (12–0) before 25,500

Then, on Nov 9 at Navy in the Navy–Marine Corps Memorial Stadium, Annapolis, MD, Syracuse beat the Midshipmen W (24–20) before 25,049.

On Nov 16 at home, Syracuse beat the Eagles of Boston College in the Carrier Dome W (21–21) before 45,790. Then, on Nov 23 at Rutgers in Rutgers Stadium, Piscataway, NJ, the Orangemen defeated the Scarlet Knights W (31–14) before 19,685 fans. Then, in the final game of the 1985 season on Nov 30 at home in the Carrier Dome, SU lost to West Virginia in a close match in the annual rivalry, L (10–13) before 33,431.

Cherry Bowl 1985

1985 Cherry Bowl #20 Maryland vs Syracuse

This was the first seven-game win season since before Frank Maloney and it earned the Orangemen a berth in the Pontiac, MI(Cherry Bowl) held on December 21 in the Pontiac Silverdome vs. the #20 Maryland Terrapins, a team no stranger to the Syracuse

Orangemen. This game, the Terrapins had the oomph to finish off the Orangemen L (18–35).

The 1985 Cherry Bowl was once a postseason college football bowl game. It featured Maryland's Terrapins, of the Atlantic Coast Conference and Syracuse of the Big East Conference.

The game was not very spectacular, but SU could have grabbed all the marbles if it had hung in there. After having a nice early lead of 10–6 lead, The Orangemen stopped playing top-notch ball and gave up 22 second-quarter points. At this point, a comeback was too far out of reach for the Orangemen and the Terrapins won by a final score of 35–18.

This was just the second Cherry Bowl ever, but it would be the last. After this game, the bowl committee and the whole deal had folded because the officials found themselves $2,000,000 in debt with no apparent escape. It was not until 1997 that another try at such a bowl was attempted. At that time the reincarnation was the Motor City Bowl, which was launched and the MAC Championship Game was first played on a neutral site.

1986 Dick MacPherson Coach # 24

The 1986 Syracuse Orangemen football team competed in their ninety-seventh season of intercollegiate football. They were led by Dick MacPherson in his sixth of ten seasons as head coach of the Syracuse Orangemen. SU had its third losing season under McPherson this year–5-6-0 in the team's seventh season in the Carrier Dome. MacPherson picked Pete Ewald, Jim Leible & Tim Pidgeon to be the team captains for 1986. Syracuse finished with an OK record, but it was not good enough for a bowl invitation.

On Sept 6, in the season and home opener at the Carrier Dome, on the campus of Syracuse University in Syracuse, NY before 34,212, SU lost by a TD to Mississippi State L (17-24). On Sept 13 at Army's Michie Stadium in West Point, NY, the Cadets beat the Orangemen L (28–33) before a packed house of 38,822 On Sept 20 at home, SU was defeated by Virginia Tech at the Carrier Dome Syracuse, NY L

(17–26) before 33,400. On Sept 27 at home, Syracuse was beaten by Rutgers at the Carrier Dome L (10–16).

On Oct 4, my wedding anniversary, at home, Syracuse defeated Missouri in a nice match W (41–9) before 41,035. On Oct 18 at #6 Penn State in the rivalry game at Beaver Stadium in University Park, PA, the Nittany Lions defeated Syracuse in a rout L (3–42) before 85,512. On Oct 25 at Temple in a tight game played at Veterans Stadium in Philadelphia, PA, SU barely beat the Owls, W (27–24) 19,422

Nov 1 at home Syracuse defeated Pittsburgh at the Carrier Dome before 34, 114 W (24–20). Again at home at the Carrier Dome the following week on Nov 8 SU squeaked out a nice win against Navy W (31–22) before 36,796 fans. On Nov 15 at Boston College's Alumni Stadium in the rivalry played this year in Chestnut Hill, MA, the Eagles got the best of the Orangemen L (9–27) before 32,000. In the last game of the season SU traveled to West Virginia to take on the Mountaineers in the rivalry game held at Mountaineer Field in Morgantown, WV(Rivalry). SU came home with the win W 34–23 before 40,106 fans.

Despite a tough record this season, Dick MacPherson had found his niche at Syracuse and the word on the street and beyond is that if he wanted more than the four years he put in, ending in 1990, he could have had that and more. Next year is the kind of up and down year SU fans have become accustomed to but regardless of the emotional roller coaster at the end of the season. 1987 would be one of the best in SU history. I can't wait to tell you about it.

1987 Dick MacPherson Coach # 24

The 1987 Syracuse Orangemen football team competed in their ninety-eighth season of intercollegiate football. They were led by Dick MacPherson in his seventh of ten seasons as head coach of the Syracuse Orangemen. SU had its best season under McPherson this year–11-0-1 in the team's eighth season in the Carrier Dome. MacPherson picked Paul Frase, Ted Gregory & QB Don McPherson to be the team captains for 1987. What a year! Syracuse finished with a great record, and got a great bowl invitation but, suffered a season destroying tie against Auburn in the Sugar Bowl in what otherwise was a great game.

On the positive side in such a positive year, the 11 wins by the Orangemen matched the school record set by the national champion 1959 team, and their 4th-ranked finish in the AP Poll was the first ranked finish since 1961. When great things happen, there should be no misgivings but then again there are guys like me and many others who wonder whether SU could have found just one more point somehow in that game.

All American Theodore Gregory 1987

As a nose guard, Ted Gregory was an All American for Syracuse in 1987,

He ranks eighth on Syracuse's career sacks list. He led a team that recorded 21 sacks in 1985, an SU record. In 1987, he was a finalist for the Vince Lombardi Award which recognizes the most outstanding lineman or linebacker. Gregory went on to play one NFL season with the New Orleans Saints in 1988. He was named to Syracuse University's All-Century team in November 1999.

<< Theodore Gregory

At Syracuse, Gregory quickly became the cog of a very good defense, which included six future pros on the Sugar Bowl team. Without Gregory in 1986-- he missed nine games with a broken leg--Syracuse's run defense was ranked 105th (dead last) in the country. The following year, it soared to No. 1 before slipping to 16th after Gregory injured his knee in the seventh game. "In my 10 years at Syracuse," former coach Dick MacPherson said, "we had four impact players, people who affected the whole program Tim Green, Don McPherson, Rob Moore and Ted Gregory. When they stepped on the field, they made a difference.

All American Don McPherson 1987

The 1987 football campaign at Syracuse was McPherson's finest. He was The Maxwell Award winner as the college football player of the year and the Heisman Trophy runner-up, McPherson led the nation in passing efficiency with a Syracuse-record 164.3 rating.

He set 22 Syracuse records, including the single-season marks for passing yards per game (212.8), touchdown passes (22), and most consecutive games with a touchdown pass (10). He won the Maxwell Award (most outstanding player), Davey O'Brien Award (most outstanding quarterback) and Johnny Unitas Golden Arm Award (most outstanding senior quarterback).

McPherson finished his Syracuse playing career in 1987 with the program's all-time passing yards, completions and pass attempts records. After graduating, McPherson continued his football career with the NFL's Philadelphia Eagles and Houston Oilers. McPherson was inducted into the College Football Hall of Fame in 2008. In 2013, Syracuse University honored McPherson by retiring his No. 9 jersey.

Upon retiring from pro football in 1994, McPherson joined Northeastern University's Center for the Study of Sport in Society as director of Athletes in Service to America. During this time, McPherson turned his focus to the issue of "men's violence against women," as director of Sport in Society's Mentors in Violence Prevention Program. In 2002, McPherson founded the Sports Leadership Institute at Adelphi University and served as its executive director. He was also an independent consultant and vice president of The Hopewell Group, Inc., a philanthropic advising and consulting company located in New York City.

It's been 26 years now since Syracuse University's Don McPherson finished second to Notre Dame's Tim Brown in the Heisman Trophy balloting. As McPherson was the toast of Eastern football and the quarterback of an Orange team that went 11-0-1 and finished fourth in the nation, it was (and remains) a sporting injustice. (Mike Greenlar | mgreenlar@syracuse.com)

Throughout his professional life, McPherson has used the power and appeal of sport to address complex social issues. Since 1995, McPherson has served as a national leader and advocate for the prevention of sexual and domestic violence. He has conducted workshops and lectures for more than 200 college campuses, community organizations and national sports and violence prevention organizations, and was a facilitator at the first NCAA Student-Athlete Leadership Conference in 1997. His programs and lectures have reached more than one million people.

McPherson has worked as a college football analyst for ESPN, BET and NBC and currently provides regular expert analysis on XM Satellite Radio. In 2000, while a board member of the Nassau County Sports Commission, McPherson created the John Mackey

Award, which recognizes college football's most outstanding tight end.

He has served in a consulting and advisory capacity for several national organizations and currently sits on the board of directors of the Family and Children's Association, Stop It Now! and the Ms. Foundation for Women.

Games of the 1987 Season

On Sept 5, in the season and home opener at the Carrier Dome, on the campus of Syracuse University in Syracuse, NY before 35,234, SU defeated Maryland in a great opening match W (35-11). The Orangemen were off. On Sept 12 at Rutgers in Rutgers Stadium, Piscataway, New Jersey, SU fought hard for the win against a fine team W (20–3) On Sept 19at home against Miami (OH) in the Carrier Dome, the Orangemen were undaunting in pursuing victory this game and this whole year W (24–10) before 33,838. On Sept 26, SU traveled to play Virginia Tech at Lane Stadium in Blacksburg, VA and the Orangemen came home with a fine win W (35–21) against the Hokies finest before 33,300.On Oct 3 at Missouri Memorial Stadium in Columbia, Missouri, the Orangemen got the best of the Tigers W (24–13) before 36,773.

Highlight: PSU v Syracuse – A game for the ages

In a number of the prior years in the PSU v SU rivalry, always top-ranked under Joe Paterno, Penn State had been having its way with the Orange prior to 1987. This year would call a pause to the Nittany Lions onslaught over the years on the Orangemen. On Oct 17, another high ranked Penn State team (#10) came into the Carrier Dome ready to rip apart an always struggling but this year a ranked #13 Syracuse squad. Penn State did its best as always but there was so much might on the SU side that it was impossible for the Nittany Lions to not give up 48 points against the Orangemen. The game ended W (48–21) before a max sellout crowd at the Carrier Dome 50,011 fans. It was a great standing room only game

It happened on Oct. 17, 1987

Syracuse's 48-21 home destruction of No. 10 Penn State, the defending national champions, highlighted Syracuse's unbeaten season in 1987. The Orange came in ranked No. 13 and would climb as high as No. 4 before tying Auburn in the Sugar Bowl and finishing without a loss. Syracuse had lost 42-3 at Penn State the previous year. Don McPherson completed 15 of 20 passes for a school-record (at the time) 336 yards. He opened the game with an 80-yard touchdown pass to Rob Moore. It is one of just two unbeaten seasons in school history.

On Oct 24 Colgate played #9 SU at home in the Carrier Dome and were beaten in a blowout W (52-6) before 48,097. Then, on Oct 31 at Pittsburgh, #8 SU defeated the Panthers at Pitt Stadium, Pittsburgh PA W (24–10) before 52,714. An always tough Navy squad pulled out all the stops but could not stop the onslaught of the 1987 #8 Syracuse Orangemen on Nov 7 at Navy at the Navy–Marine Corps Memorial Stadium in Annapolis, Maryland W (34–10).

On Nov 14 Boston College faced # 6 nationally ranked SU at home in the Carrier Dome and were defeated W (45–17) before 49,866. On

Highlight A perfect regular season for Syracuse

Nov 21 #6 SU defeated West Virginia in the Carrier Dome W in the closest game of the regular season W (32–31) before 49,866

This highlight game, one of the best in SU history occurred on Nov. 21, 1987. This is the only Syracuse win over an unranked opponent that is in our highlight games. This was a critical game in Syracuse history, as well as a 32-31 thriller over West Virginia.

The victory clinched a perfect 1987 regular season and sent the Orange off to face Auburn in the Sugar Bowl. Syracuse trailed by a touchdown with less than two minutes left but got a touchdown connection from Don McPherson to Pat Kelly, then a two-point conversion option run from Michael Owens to win the game. Sadly,

Pat Dye wouldn't make the same choice in New Orleans, settling for a tie.

The 1988 Sugar Bowl

On January, 1988, #4 ranked Syracuse took on # 6 ranked Auburn at the Louisiana Superdome in New Orleans, Louisiana in this year's Sugar Bowl. The team's played tough to a tie T (16–16) before 75,495. In eight more years, the rules would change. The rules were changed to their current format in 1996. Instead of ties, on the average, about 32 college games go into overtime every year.

How Syracuse and Auburn Met in the 1988 Sugar Bowl

Dick MacPherson would not let go of the trophy.

He went from interview to interview clutching the 35-pound, ornate, silver vessel, the symbol of Sugar Bowl supremacy.

"It's getting heavy," the Syracuse coach said an hour after the final whistle of a 16-16 New Year's Day deadlock with Auburn, "but they'll have to fight me to take it away."

From the All State Sugar Bowl Archives:

The source of MacPherson's ire was the decision by Tiger coach Pat Dye to send place-kicker Win Lyle onto the field for a 30-yard field goal attempt with four seconds remaining. Dye, whose 9-1-1 team had no chance at a national championship or any other postgame laurels, was willing to settle for the tie.

54th Annual Sugar Bowl Classic ~ January 1, 1988
Score 16 for #4 Syracuse (Final record: 11-0-1, #4)
Score 16 for #6 Auburn (Final record: 9-1-3, #7)

Lyle's own frustrated teammates tried to wave him off the field before he made the tying kick, which produced boos from both sides, the only tie in the long annals of the Sugar Bowl (just the seventh in major bowl history, and the first since 1959), the only blot on Syracuse's record (11-0-1), and a fire in MacPherson's belly.

When Lyle's third field goal of the night sailed through the yellow uprights, MacPherson vented his anger by throwing his game plan – three sheets of rolled-up paper – to the Superdome turf. He had to walk onto the playing surface to retrieve it.

"I was mad at myself," MacPherson said.
Minutes before, when his team had to decide whether to go for it on fourth-and-inches at the Auburn 22, MacPherson's choice had been to kick for a 16-3 lead, feeling a team with no shot at No. 1 would have to go for the winning touchdown against an unbeaten, untied opponent in a bowl game.

"I told my guys a field goal was like a touchdown," MacPherson said. "I told them if we made it, Auburn would have to go for the touchdown. If I had thought in my wildest imagination he'd go for a field goal, we would have gone for a first down."

At that point, all the Syracuse coach could do was smolder.

Dye said his Tigers – two and a half point favorites – simply played with "too much character and class" to risk going for a 13-yard touchdown in the fading seconds against the fourth-ranked Orangemen. "You win some, lose some and some end in ties," Dye said.

"I made up my mind early on (in Auburn's last drive) what I was going to do. I wasn't going to let my team get beat. If they (Syracuse) wanted to win, they should have blocked the field goal."

The Tiger athletes, on the other hand, vividly remembered the Tennessee game. "I remember how happy Tennessee was with the tie and how disgusted I felt at the time." Auburn offensive guard Stacy Searles reflected in the Sugar Bowl aftermath.

The disappointment, and the sniping and roaring between the Sugar Bowl foes on the first night of 1988, put a forlorn face on to the Sugar Bowl, a sharp contrast to the euphoria of a month earlier when the match was made.

This was the scenario: With just over two minutes remaining, with a fourth-and-inches at the Auburn 22, Tom Vesling booted the go-ahead field goal.

MacPherson would second-guess himself later, but upon reflection said, "I think that was the right call." Dye agreed. "It put his team ahead (16-13)."

Auburn was 75 yards from their 10th victory of the season, and in that time-span made up 62 of those yards.

At that point Dye sent in Lyle, to the accompaniment of boos from all ends of the Superdome. MacPherson made note of the fact that Auburn didn't throw into the end zone once on the last drive. "They were just fooling around with other things," he said, his anger showing through. "What the hell was (Dye) thinking? What the hell did they come here for in the first place?"

A Syracuse radio station, incensed by Dye's strategy, made a call for Orangemen fans to send Dye ties, the ugliest they could find. An estimated 2,000 ties flooded the Tiger athletic department in the days following the Sugar Bowl.

Dye, however, found a "moral victory" in the intended insult. He autographed each one, and included the score of the game, and had the athletic department sell them to fans for $100 apiece, with the proceeds donated to Auburn's general fund.

Sales totaled $25,000.

A Montgomery radio station, WHHY, felt a response was in order, however. Disc jockey Blake Scott said sour grapes were exactly what Syracuse fans deserved. He asked Auburn fans to donate sour grapes to Dick MacPherson.

"We're looking for a warm warehouse to store them," Scott said, "then for the slowest transportation available."

1988 Dick MacPherson Coach # 24

The 1988 Syracuse Orangemen football team competed in their ninety-ninth season of intercollegiate football. They were led by Dick MacPherson in his eighth of ten seasons as head coach of the Syracuse Orangemen. SU had its second-best season under McPherson this year–10-2-0 in the team's ninth regular season in the Carrier Dome. MacPherson picked Daryl Johnston & Markus Paul to be the team captains for 1988. Another fine year! Syracuse finish with a great record. They got another great bowl invitation to the 1989 Hall of Fame bowl where they defeated LSU.

On Sept 3, in the season and home opener at the Carrier Dome, on the campus of Syracuse University in Syracuse, NY before 35,234, SU defeated Temple in a great opening match W (31-21). The Orangemen were off again. Unfortunately, the joy would ring out only until the following week on September 10 at Ohio State's huge Ohio Stadium in Columbus, OH as the Buckeyes defeated the Orangemen L (9–26) before 89,768. With an extra week to sweat out the loss to OSU, on Sept 24 at home, the Orangemen got their game together well enough to shut out the Hokies of Virginia Tech at the Carrier Dome W (35–0) before 41,118. Then, on Oct 1, at home, SU defeated Maryland W (20-9).

All American Markus Paul 1988

Markus Paul holds the Syracuse football records for game (three) and career (19) interceptions. In 1987 and 1988, Paul was named a finalist for the Jim Thorpe Award which recognizes the nation's top defensive back. In 1988, he earned All-American honors. Paul was a member of the Chicago Bears and the Tampa Bay Buccaneers in the NFL. He was named to Syracuse University's All-Century team in November 1999.

Remaining Games of the 1988 Season

On Oct 8 at home, SU defeated Rutgers W (34-20) before 48, 798. Then on Oct 15 at Penn State's Beaver Stadium in University Park, PA, SU beat the Nittany Lions W (24–10) before 85,916. On Oct 22 #19 SU defeated East Carolina at Ficklen Memorial Stadium, Greenville, NC W (38–14) before 16,450. Then, at home on Nov 5, the Orangemen beat Navy W (49-21). On Nov 12, #15 SU defeated Boston College at Alumni Stadium in Chestnut Hill, MA W (45–20) before 32,000.

Then, on Nov 19 at # 4 West Virginia, the #14 Orangemen were defeated by the Mountaineers L (9-31) before 65,127. Then, in the season closer at home in the carrier Dome, on Dev 3, Syracuse defeated Pittsburgh W (24-0) before49,860

Hall of Fame Bowl

On January 2 #17 Syracuse tangled with #16 LSU inside Tampa Stadium in Tampa, FL in the Hall of Fame Bowl. The Orangemen beat the Tigers W (23–10) before 49,860. The Orangemen finished #12 for the season.

Syracuse 23, Louisiana State 10
January 2, 1989
Tampa, Florida

Dick MacPherson had the Syracuse program screaming. So, it was natural that for the second straight season the Orangemen reached double figures in wins, culminated by dumping Southeastern Conference co-champion Louisiana State 23-10 in the third Hall of Fame Bowl at Tampa.

The Orange took the opening kickoff and went 80 yards, capped off by Robert Drummond's two-yard touchdown. Drummond ended his SU career in style, winning MVP honors with 122 yards and two touchdowns on 23 carries. David Holmes was the defensive star for the Orange, intercepting two passes, breaking up two more and coming up with six solo tackles. Daryl Johnston added 74 yards and Todd Philcox completed 16 of 23 passes for 130 yards and a TD. Rob Moore had six catches for 56 yards. It was a great day for Syracuse. The SU defense was led by Terry Wooden and Rob Burnett, allowed the Tigers just 76 yards rushing. Dan Bucey had a game-high 10 tackles.

1989 Dick MacPherson Coach # 24

The 1989 Syracuse Orangemen football team competed in their one hundredth season of intercollegiate football. They were led by Dick MacPherson in his ninth of ten seasons as head coach of the Syracuse Orangemen. SU had its second-best season under McPherson this year–8-4-2 in the team's tenth regular season in the Carrier Dome. MacPherson picked Blake Bednarz, Dan Bucey, Rob Burnett, Michael Owens & Terry Wooden to be the team captains for 1989.

It was another fine year of football for Syracuse. As noted, the team finished with an 8–4-0 record and played in the 1989 Peach Bowl, where they beat Georgia, 19–18. They also played a regular season game in Tokyo, Japan, in the Coca-Cola Classic against Louisville.

On Sept 9, in the season opener at Temple, #14 ranked Syracuse defeated the Owls at Veterans Stadium in Philadelphia, PA in a blowout W 43–3 before 20,150. On Sept 16, in the home opener at the Carrier Dome, on the campus of Syracuse University in Syracuse, NY before 48,331, Syracuse barely got by a tough Army squad, W (10-3) On Sept 23 at #13, the #10 ranked Orangemen lost to Pittsburgh at Pitt Stadium in Pittsburgh, PA L (23–30) before 45,762. On Oct 7 at home in the Carrier Dome, #17 Syracuse was beaten by #22 Florida State in a close match L (10–41) before 49,832. On Oct 14, at home, unranked Syracuse lost to #23 Penn State at the Carrier Dome L (12–34) before a packed house of 49,876

On Oct 21, at Rutgers, in Rutgers Stadium, Piscataway, NJ, Syracuse defeated the Scarlet Knights W (49–28) before 29,276. On Oct 28, at home in the Carrier Dome, Syracuse defeated East Carolina in a very tight match W (18–16) before 48,731. Again, at the Carrier Dome for a home game on Nov, Syracuse defeated the Eagles of Boston College W (23–11). Then, on Nov 11 at Navy at the Navy–Marine Corps Memorial Stadium in Annapolis, MD, the Orangemen defeated the Midshipmen W (38–17).

On Nov 23, SU lost another home game at the Carrier Dome—this one against #17 West Virginia L (17–24). In a special tribute game overseas, the Coca Cola Classic, SU defeated Louisville in the Tokyo, Tokyo, Japan W (24–13) before 50,000. SU finished the regular season 7-4-0.

The Peach Bowl

On December 30, one day before New Year's Eve, unranked Syracuse defeated unranked Georgia in the Peach Bowl in Atlanta, GA in a one point match W (19–18) before 44,911 stadium fans giving the Orangemen full record of 8-7 for 1989.

**Syracuse 19, Georgia 18
December 30, 1989
Atlanta, Georgia**

The newly Macpherson-invigorated Syracuse Orangemen found themselves in their third consecutive bowl season and they produced a spectacular come-from-behind, 19-18 victory over Georgia. John Biskup finished off a wild SU rally with a 26-yard field goal with just 25 seconds remaining. The Orange defense held Georgia to four first downs and 84 total yards in the second half.

SU trailed 18-7 before quarterback Mark McDonald came off the bench to replace Bill Scharr. McDonald guided SU to a 32-yard Biskup field goal to close the third quarter. Clutch running by game MVP Michael Owens (116 yards) and crisp passing by McDonald brought the Orange within striking distance. A 19-yard pass to Rob Moore cut the Bulldogs' lead to 18-16 with just a bit more than 10 minutes remaining. A potential game-tying conversion attempt fell incomplete.

SU began its final drive from its own 27 with 3:37 left. After moving to its own 43-yard line, the Orange faced a fourth and five. McDonald then hit Owens down the sideline for 29 yards and a crucial first down to set up Biskup's game-winning field goal. It was a great victory for the Orangemen.

1990 Dick MacPherson Coach # 24

The 1990 Syracuse Orangemen football team competed in their one hundred-first season of intercollegiate football. They were led by Dick MacPherson in his tenth and last of ten seasons as head coach of the Syracuse Orangemen. SU had its third best season under McPherson this year–7-4-2. MacPherson picked John Flannery, Duane Kinnon, Gary McCummings & Rob Thomson to be the team captains for 1990. It was another fine year of football for Syracuse. With their season record of 6-4-2, the team was invited and played in the 1990 Aloha Bowl and shut out Arizona W (28-0)

This season marked the end of two eras for Syracuse football. First, it was Dick MacPherson's final year as head coach. He would leave to coach the 1991 New England Patriots. Second, it was the final season for Syracuse football as an independent. Starting with the 1991 season, the Big East Conference, of which Syracuse was a founding member, began sponsoring football competition.

In the first ever August football game in Syracuse football history, on Aug 31, in the season opener against USC at Giants Stadium in East Rutherford, New Jersey for the Raycom Kickoff Classic # VIII, Syracuse could not find what it needed and the Orangemen were defeated by the Trojans L (16–34) before 57,293. On Sept 8, in the home opener at the Carrier Dome, on the campus of Syracuse University in Syracuse, NY before 38,925, Syracuse had a difficult time in beating a tough Temple squad W (19-9). On Sept 15 in a rare night game at home, SU tied #19 Michigan State in the Carrier Dome T (23–23) before 49,822.

All American John Flannery 1989, 1990

John Flannery was a Syracuse University All-American in 1989 and 1990. As center, he helped anchor an offensive line that went 3-0-1 in four bowl games during his tenure with the Orange

<< John Flannery.

Flannery was drafted in the second round by the Houston Oilers, where he made the NFL All-Rookie Team in 1991. He later enjoyed stops with the Dallas Cowboys and St. Louis Rams. He was named to Syracuse University's All-Century team in November 1999.

More games from 1990

On Sept 22 at home, Syracuse tied #25 Pittsburgh at the Carrier dome before 47, 996 T (20–20). Then on Oct 6 at Vanderbilt in Vanderbilt Stadium, Nashville, Tennessee, the Orangemen defeated the Commodores, W 49–14 before 30,037. On Oct 13 at Penn State's Beaver Stadium, University Park, Pennsylvania, the Orangemen lost to the Nittany Lions in a close match L (21–27) before 86,002. On Oct 20 12:00 at home, the Orangemen shut-out the Scarlet Knights of Rutgers at the Carrier Dome Syracuse, New York, W (42–0) before 49,521. Then on Oct 27 at Army's Michie Stadium in West Point, New York, Syracuse beat the Cadets W (26–14) before a packed house of 41,153.

On Nov 3 at Boston College's Alumni Stadium in Chestnut Hill, Massachusetts, the Orangemen whipped the Eagles, W (35–6) before 32,213. Then, on Nov10, at home, The Green Wave of Tulane defeated the Orangemen in a very close match at the Carrier Dome L (24-26). On Nov 17 at West Virginia's Mountaineer Field in Morgantown, West Virginia, Syracuse prevailed W (31–7) before 44,669 fans. On Saturday, Nov 24 during Thanksgiving weekend, SU lost a big game against #2 Miami (FL) at the Miami Orange Bowl in Miami L (7–33) before 66,196.

The Aloha Bowl

On Christmas Day, December 25, 1990 at 3:30 PM, Syracuse squared off against Arizona in Aloha Stadium, Honolulu, Hawaii in the Aloha Bowl.). The Orangemen shut out the Wildcats W (28-0) before 32,217 while basking in the glow and the physical warmth of our nation's 50th state.

Lots more than the game was going on in Hawaii on Dec. 25, 1990. Syracuse snapped the Arizona Wildcats' 214-game scoring streak, the second-longest in NCAA history, with a 28-0 victory. Arizona hadn't been shut out since a 31-0 loss to Arizona State in 1971.

SU Quarterback Marvin Graves was voted Syracuse's most valuable player after running for two scores and throwing for two more TDs. Cornerback Todd Burden, with two interceptions and a forced fumble, was chosen the player of the game for Arizona (7-5).

Dick MacPherson moves on

The 1990 season at Syracuse was the last for Dick Macpherson. He could have coached as long as he wanted but he was ready to try his hand at professional football.

Those who have been reading this book like a book rather than using it as a reference know that the Syracuse University football team enjoyed few winning seasons during the 1970s. Then came Dick MacPherson followed immediately by Paul Pasqualoni and after twenty-dive years of these two coaches, Syracuse was a national power again.

In that 1970's decade, mostly post Schwartzwalder, the Orange made it to one postseason game. Syracuse defeated McNeese State 31-7 in the Independence Bowl on Dec. 15, 1979.

That was the only bowl game in which a Syracuse team led by head coach Frank Maloney ever played. Mr. Maloney compiled a record of 32-46-3 with the Orange. Syracuse football had definitely fallen on hard times.

And then came Dick MacPherson. He helped the football program regain its prestige, earning a record of 66-46-4 as its head coach for 10 seasons.

Richard F. MacPherson had a wonderful life. died Tuesday at Crouse Hospital in Syracuse at the age of 86. It was less than a year ago from when I began to put this book together--August 8, 2017. Here are some parts of his obituary as they tell nice story about the life of this great man and great coach:

He is survived by his wife, Sandra; his daughters Maureen and Janet; four grandchildren; and many friends and admirers.

He held various coaching positions at several other schools (Illinois, UMass, Cincinnati and Maryland) before arriving at Syracuse. He also served as an assistant coach for the Denver Broncos from 1967 to 1970 and the Cleveland Browns from 1978 to 1980.

Despite the potential, Mr. MacPherson didn't look like he would fare much better when he took over as Syracuse's head coach in 1981 than did his predecessor. His team went 4-6-1 in his first season and a dismal 2-9 in his second season at the helm. Syracuse was a in serious doldrums, and it was not until year three that Macpherson was able to begin the big turnaround. SU went 7-5 in 1985 and lost to Maryland in the Cherry Bowl 35-18.

Many fans turned on Mr. MacPherson in 1986 when, after some big successes, the Orange had a losing season at 5-6. Some of them formed the Sack Mac Pack, creating signs and bumper stickers urging the school to dump the head coach.

But athletic director Jake Crouthamel stuck by his longtime friend. Mr. MacPherson repaid this loyalty by leading the Orange to an undefeated season in 1987 and a No. 4 ranking.

On Jan. 1, 1988, Syracuse tied Auburn 16-16 in the Sugar Bowl. While the score kept the Orange from being beaten that season, the result irked the coach and the school's many fans.

"Of all the games MacPherson coached, the Sugar Bowl tie with Auburn, spoiling an undefeated season, may have rankled him the most. The game ended when coach Pat Dye of Auburn decided to attempt a 30-yard field goal with four seconds left rather than try to win the game with a touchdown," according to an Associated Press story published Wednesday in the New York Times. "The kick was successful, tying the score at 16-16. MacPherson was bitter about the rival coach's call. 'What did they come here for in the first place?' he said. He added, 'I gotta believe his menu was to stop us from being 12-0.'"

Mr. MacPherson left Syracuse after the 1990 season to serve as head coach of the New England Patriots for two years. Paul Pasqualoni succeeded him as the Orange's skipper and continued building the football program's winning tradition. Over 14 seasons, Mr. Pasqualoni compiled a record of 101-59-1 and led the team to nine bowl appearances.

In 2009, Mr. MacPherson was inducted into the College Football Hall of Fame. After retiring from coaching, he became a color commentator for Syracuse football on radio and television. His grandsons Cameron and Mackey both played for the Orange; Mackey is a graduate assistant coach with the team.

Those who knew Mr. MacPherson have lauded his passion for football and his rapport with players. He was an exceptional mentor to many people.

A native of Maine, he returned to Syracuse in retirement to continue his association with the school. He often spent his time in the Thousand Islands area. Dick MacPherson leaves a remarkable legacy, one that still enriches our region.

A full obit below:

> Richard "Dick" F. MacPherson, age 86, passed away on August 8, 2017. He died peacefully in Syracuse, New York surrounded by family.
>
> Coach Mac was born in Old Town, Maine on November 4, 1930, to Hugh and Ludovic (Moreau) MacPherson. He was the eleventh of twelve children. He attended Old Town High School, graduating in 1948. After serving in the United States Air Force, Mac graduated from Springfield College, where he played on the football team as a center and linebacker. At Springfield, he met the love of his life, Sandra. They were married in 1958, beginning Mac's 58 years as a loving, devoted husband.
>
> Mac was the head coach of the UMass Minutemen from 1971 to 1977, during which time the team went from a struggling program to winners of the Boardwalk Bowl. He won four Yankee Conference championships and twice earned New England Coach of the Year honors. He then went to the

Cleveland Browns, leaving there in 1981 when he accepted the favorite job of his life, head coach of the Syracuse Orangemen.

At Syracuse, Coach Mac's tenure included the 1987 undefeated season, five bowl appearances (four of which he won), and every single Coach of the Year honor given in 1987. Mac was then named head coach of the New England Patriots in 1991. He retired with 111 wins as a college head coach and was inducted into the College Football Hall of Fame in 2009.

To Coach Mac, the most important pillars of life were faith and family. A lifelong Catholic, Mac was known for his rosary beads, daily missals, and warm greetings. He loved golf, bridge, Time magazine, and watching his grandchildren play football, row crew, and cheerlead. More than anything, he loved caring for people and sharing his joyful love with those around him, family and stranger alike.

A proud Mainer with an accent to prove it, Coach Mac came to happily call Syracuse his home. He enthusiastically supported the Salvation Army, the Joslin Diabetes Center, and numerous other community charities. He was thrilled to lead Syracuse's St. Patrick's Day Parade as Grand Marshall in 2010.

Chapter 15 Coach Paul Pasqualoni From 1991 to 2004

Coach Paul Pasqualoni #25

Year	Coach	Record	Conf
1991	Paul Pasqualoni	10-2-0	Big East (5-0 #1)
1992	Paul Pasqualoni	10-2-0	Big East (6-1)
1993	Paul Pasqualoni	6-4-1	Big East (3-4)
1994	Paul Pasqualoni	7-4-0	Big East (4-3)
1995	Paul Pasqualoni	9-3-0	Big East (5-2)
1996	Paul Pasqualoni	9-3-0	Big East (6-1)
1997	Paul Pasqualoni	9-4-0	Big East (6-1 #1)
1998	Paul Pasqualoni	8-4-0	Big East (6-1 #1)
1999	Paul Pasqualoni	7-5-0	Big East (3-4)
2000	Paul Pasqualoni	6-5-0	Big East (4-3)
2001	Paul Pasqualoni	10-3-0	Big East (6-1)
2002	Paul Pasqualoni	4-8-0	Big East (2-5)
2003	Paul Pasqualoni	6-6-0	Big East (2-5)
2004	Paul Pasqualoni	6-6-0	Big East (4-2)

Coach Pasqualoni -- A little required fun after a win

Famous Coaches (From the Past) by SWC75.

Ben Schwartzwalder had been offered the job of being the first ever coach of the New England Patriots after the national championship season. When Coach Mac, a New Englander, got the same offer after the 1990 season, he took it. Since we were now a successful program, Jake Crouthamel decided to promote from within and we got our third straight linebacker coach elevated to the status of a head coach, Paul Pasqualoni.

Before coming to Syracuse he'd been a Penn State linebacker, (a Nittany Lion coaching the Orange!), and head coach at Western Connecticut State, a Division III team. He'd inherited a 1-8 squad from 1982 and took them to 9-1 by 1984. In 1985 they went 10-1 and made the DIII playoffs. Mac hired him in 1987. His youth and comparatively brief tenure with the program made him a surprise choice but that put him in a category with Coach Mac and Ben Schwartzwalder. Paul went on to become the 2nd winningest coach in Syracuse history, going 107-59-1.

He got off to a great start, going 10-2 in his first two years, crushing Steve Spurrier's Florida team in 1991 and coming up just short of upsetting #1 Miami in 1992. The 1993 team strangely fell apart, losing consecutive games to Miami and West Virginia by a combined 0-92. That team and the next broke the string of bowl teams at 6 in a row, (none of which we lost) but extended the string of winning seasons. Then came the Donovan McNabb Era where we were very good but could never quite break through to greatness. We had a 41-0 Gator Bowl blow-out of Clemson, a 34-0 kick-off Classic rout of Wisconsin, ran Michigan out of the Big House, 38-28, (it was 38-7 at one point), and beat Miami back to back by 96-26. Who could imagine that we'd ever do such things?

But it created an intolerance for upset losses and uncompetitive performances, such as the two losses each to East Carolina, North Carolina State and later Rutgers and Temple when they were the dregs of the conference, as well as 0-62 and 7-51 losses at Virginia Tech, 13-45, 0-59 and 7-49 losses to Miami, and in his final season 0-51 to Purdue to open the season and 14-51 to Georgia Tech to close it. Eventually the talent and patience level declined and a new

Athletic Director, Dr. Daryl Gross, fired him and brought in his own man, leaving us to argue about what really went wrong ever since.

1991 Paul Pasqualoni Coach # 25

The 1991 Syracuse Orangemen football team competed in their one hundred-second season of intercollegiate football. They were led by Paul Pasqualoni in his first of fourteen seasons as head coach of the Syracuse Orangemen. Coach Mac had left a fine nucleus for Coach Pasqualoni to work with. SU had its best season under its new coach this year and would have a similar 10-2-0 season next year and they were 5-0 in their first year in the Big East. This season matched Coach Mac's second-best season when Syracuse was independent.

Pasqualoni picked Andrew Dees, Mark McDonald, Tim Sandquist & Greg Walker to be the team captains for 1991. It was another fine year of football for Syracuse. With their season record of 10-2-0, the team was invited and played in the Hall of Fame Bowl v Ohio State on January 1.

Two new eras began for Syracuse football in 1991. It was the first season as head coach for Paul Pasqualoni, who was promoted from assistant after Dick MacPherson, who had led the Orangemen for the previous 10 seasons, left to take the head coaching job at the New England Patriots. More important in the long term, this was the first season in which the Big East Conference sponsored football—although the conference would not establish a full round-robin schedule in the sport until the 1993 season. Syracuse as noted was 5-0 v Big East Teams this year. Miami, the #1 team in the nation was 2-0 in the Big East in 1991. SU and Miami did not play in 1991. Syracuse U was very fortunate after such a great coach as Dick Mac, to find another great one, Paul Pasqualoni. Picking an existing coach does not always work…but it sure worked with P.P.

On Sept 7, in the home opener at the Carrier Dome, on the campus of Syracuse University in Syracuse, NY before 35,541, Syracuse soundly beat a tough Vanderbilt squad W (37-10). On Sept 14 at Maryland, the #22 ranked Orangemen beat the Terrapins at Byrd Stadium in College Park, MD W (31–17) before 41,310.

All American Qadry Ismail 1991

Qadry Ismail, aka, the Missile, is the bother of Raghib, aka the Rocket from Notre Dame. Both came from Meyers HS in Wilkes-Barre PA. Qadry did some time in HS at QB because his brother got the ball all the time. In college, he played wide receiver and kick returner like his brother Raghib. Both Ismail boys were as quick as lightening.

When Coach Mickey Gorham's undefeated Meyers Mohawks team was heading to Dallas HS to play Coach Ted Jackson's Mountaineers, it is strongly rumored that to keep the fleet footed Ismail's from destroying Dallas with their speed, Jackson, a smart HS coach, whose teams have won PA state championships, ordered the grass not be cut in anticipation. The grass sure was long when Meyers got off the bus and began to warm up for the game.

Here's the story

Coach Ted Jackson, coach of Dallas, knew the speed of the Ismail brothers, Raghib (Rocket) and Qadry (Missile)—Qadry went to Syracuse and Raghib went to ND. Jackson knew they would rip his team apart with their blinding speed.

Both were great high school football players and phenomenally fast track stars. To negate the speed of the Ismail's, the rumor mill says Jackson had a trick that in 1987 was perfectly legal.

Some say Coach Ted Jackson refused to permit the grass to be cut at Dallas, PA Stadium before the Meyers game. Consequently, the Ismail's' were in essence "caged in" by the high grass and were easy pickings for Dallas Defenders. The folklore says the grass was knee high. "Maintenance made a mistake," joked Dallas head coach Ted

Jackson. "They cut the grass. Fire that guy." Jackson was a win at all costs kind of coach and very clever.

Qadry surely remembers that game. At Syracuse, as a receiver Qadry Ismail compiled 5,137 yards and reached the end zone 33 times in the pros. He was an All-BIG EAST First Team wide receiver and conference second-team kick returner at Syracuse. He was drafted by the Minnesota Vikings in the second round of the 1993 NFL Draft. He was a 1991College All-American.

In the NFL, he was a Receiver/Kick returner in 1993-96, with the Minnesota Vikings; then 1997 with Green Bay's Packers and Miami Dolphins; In 1998, New Orleans Saints; and in 1999-01 with the Baltimore Ravens. He wrapped up his football career with the Indianapolis Colts.

Out with the old and in with the new

Enjoy this introductory article to Paul Pasqualoni that was published after his second game leading Syracuse in 1991. The season games continue right afterwards.

FOOTBALL; Syracuse's Pasqualoni Makes Himself Known
By WILLIAM N. WALLACE
Published: September 19, 1991

> So far, so good for Syracuse. The Orange is unbeaten after easy victories over Vanderbilt and Maryland in its first season under a new coach named Paul Pasqualoni who is as understated as his predecessor, Dick MacPherson, was flamboyant.
>
> While Mac from Maine, now the head coach of the New England Patriots, had a long agenda, Pasqualoni just wants to coach football, according to Larry Kimball, the Syracuse sports information director.
>
> Pasqualoni's first major coaching challenge comes up Saturday when Florida, also undefeated and ranked among the nation's

top 10 teams, arrives for a match in the Carrier Dome starting at noon. "We'll have our hands full," said Pasqualoni.

MacPherson's assistants took such a distant back seat that when Pasqualoni was promoted last Jan. 9, not many Syracuse followers knew who he was although he had been an Orange assistant for four years. A Surprise for many

"I was a surprise to a lot of people," he said in a recent interview.

In the ensuing months this quiet 42-year-old bachelor moved around to introduce himself, especially to members of the Orange Pack, the support organization for Syracuse sports.

Paul Pasqualoni, Raw deal in the end at Syracuse?

"I didn't feel I had to go on a campaign to identify who I am," he said, and he deplored his photo poster distributed by Kimball's sports information department. "I'm coaching the team in my style, not trying to follow Coach Mac. I need to be myself."

The style is different. When MacPherson entered a room, or paced a sideline, everyone was aware of his presence. But Pasqualoni melts into an audience.

The players have noticed. 'He's All Business'

"Coach Mac was always joking around," said Tim Sandquist, the defensive back and one of the four co-captains. "Coach P., he's all business. I guess he'll loosen up after he gets used to being the head man."

The major question is how much effect the coaching change has had on the football team and the deduction is not much.

In 10 seasons, MacPherson, with the considerable aid of Athletic Director Jake Crouthamel, brought the football program to unprecedented heights. The last four Orange teams have played in bowl games, Sugar, Hall of Fame, Peach and Aloha, winning three and tying one.

The material residual is a new $1 million addition to the field house called the Manley Football Wing whose feature is a two-story atrium enclosing a football hall-of-fame gallery. Its intended purpose? To impress 18-year-old high school athletes on recruiting visits.

Pasqualoni survived his first recruiting challenge last winter. Because MacPherson left precipitately for New England and Pasqualoni was such an unknown, there had been concern that Syracuse would lose many of the recruits who had made verbal commitments to enroll.

But the new coach and four scrambling assistants managed to cling to all 18 recruits from seven states who make up one of

Syracuse's most impressive group of freshmen. Luck? Maybe.

Right Place, Right Time

When he cites his football past, Pasqualoni mentions "lucky," as to being in the right place at the right time.

As a player he claims to have been, on the 1971 team that had an 11-1 record, "the worst linebacker Penn State has ever had."

Following graduation, he went home to Cheshire, Conn., where he was an assistant coach at his old high school for five seasons while obtaining a master's degree at Southern Connecticut in New Haven.

He was an assistant there for six years before becoming head coach, athletic director and associate professor of physical education at Western Connecticut in Danbury in 1982.

This small state university had no athletic tradition and Pasqualoni achieved miracles as his teams won two-thirds of their games and, in 1985, the New England Conference Championship, plus selection for the Division III playoffs.

'Chance to Move Up'

In 1987 he accepted an offer to come to Syracuse from MacPherson. "It was a chance to move up," said Pasqualoni. "Another good break along the way."

Four years later Crouthamel, a former player and coach of distinction at Dartmouth, waited only four days before selecting MacPherson's successor without interviewing any outside candidates.

Pasqualoni acknowledges he inherited a lot of good football players. Among them are Marvin Graves, the exciting quarterback; Andrew Dees and Terrence Wisdom, offensive linemen; Chris Gedney, the tight end; Shelby Hill, the wide receiver; Kevin Mitchell and George Rooks on the defensive line and linebacker Dan Conley, who tore up a knee against Maryland and is out for the season.

Another top-10 opponent will be Florida State on Oct. 5. The last five foes are conference ones from the Big East: Pitt, Rutgers, Temple, Boston College and West Virginia. If Syracuse can win five or six of these contests, then Paul Pasqualoni no longer will be the coach no one knows.

Photo: Syracuse's Paul Pasqualoni: "I'm coaching the team in my style, not trying to follow Coach Mac." (Associated Press)

More games from 1991 season

Highlight game from a great season

On Sept 21, at home, #5 Florida engaged # 17 Syracuse in the Carrier Dome and they were defeated in a nice match W (38–21) before a packed house of 49,823.

It was Sept 21, 1991, that SU's Kirby Dar Dar took a handoff on the opening kickoff and reversed the field for a 95-yard touchdown, setting the stage for Syracuse's 38-21 beatdown of Florida. This was the third game in a four-game unbeaten streak to open the year for the Orange. Syracuse was ranked # 18 and climbed into the Top 10 after the win, while Florida came in at #5, Syracuse went on to finish 10-2 and win the Hall of Fame Bowl over Ohio State.

On Sept 28 in a night game at Tulane's Louisiana Superdome in New Orleans, LA, the Orangemen shut out the Green Wave W (24–0) before 19,729.

On Oct 5, #10 SU got to play the #1 ranked team in the nation, Florida State at Doak Campbell Stadium in Tallahassee, FL. The Seminoles were ready for the Orangemen and put them down handily L (14–46) before a nice crowd of 61,231. On Oct 12 at home, #15 ranked SU had not yet shaken in off the big loss and they lost again, this time to unranked East Carolina in a close Carrier Dome match L (20–23) before 37,767. Then, on Oct at #20 Pittsburgh in Pitt Stadium, Pittsburgh, PA, #24 Syracuse got the big win by a small shoe-nail, W (31–27) before 42,707. Then, on Oct 26 at Rutgers in Rutgers Stadium, Piscataway, NJ, #21 Syracuse won another W (21–7) before 30,162.

On Nov 2 at home, Temple came to beat #18th ranked SU at the Carrier Dome but fell to the Orangemen W (27–6) before 46,819. Then, on Nov 16 at home, at noon, Boston College faced off against #17 Syracuse at the Carrier Dome. The Orangemen got the best of the Eagles W (38–16) before 45,453. Then, on Nov 23 at home in the Carrier Dome. Unranked West Virginia got the loss against #16 Syracuse W (16-10). This brought the regular season record to 9-2-0 and SU earned a match in the Hall of Fame Bowl v Ohio State.

1991 Hall of Fame Bowl

On January 1, 1992 at 1:00 PM #16 Syracuse squared off vs. unranked Ohio State at Tampa Stadium in Tampa, FL for the Hall of Fame Bowl game. SU defeated the Buckeyes W (24–17) before 57,789 fans.

Syracuse 24, Ohio State 17
January 1, 1992
Tampa, Florida

Celebrated QB Marvin Graves of Syracuse won bowl MVP honors for the second straight year, leading the Orangemen in its win against Ohio State at the sixth Hall of Fame Bowl in Tampa. Graves, the 1990 Aloha Bowl MVP, completed 18 of 31 passes for a career-high 309 yards. His touchdown passes of 50 yards to Shelby Hill and the 60-yard game-winner to Antonio Johnson, were the two longest pass plays in Hall of Fame Bowl history.

The Orangemen led 14-3 at the half, with Graves accounting for the scoring on a pass to Hill and a three-yard run. SU opened the second half with a 32-yard John Biskup field goal, but the Buckeyes came right back with a touchdown by Carlos Snow to cut the lead to 17-10. Nothing was guaranteed without hard play.

Punter Pat O'Neill had a big day for SU (46.8-yard average), but had a punt blocked with eight minutes to play. This resulted in the ball being recovered by the opposition in the end zone, thus tying the game. It took just two minutes for the Syracuse offense to come up with the big play it needed. Johnson broke free on a play-action pass and Graves hit him for the deciding touchdown. It was a great game indeed. The D put in a great game also.

John Lusardi tallied 11 tackles and George Rooks had seven to lead the SU defense. The Orange sacked Ohio State quarterback Kirk Herbstreit four times.

1992 Paul Pasqualoni Coach # 25

The 1992 Syracuse Orangemen football team competed in their one hundred-third season of intercollegiate football. They were led by Paul Pasqualoni in his second of fourteen seasons as head coach of the Syracuse Orangemen. SU equaled its best season under new coach Pasqualoni this year after a similar 10-2-0 season in 1991. They were 6-1 in their second year in the Big East after a close loss to undefeated Miami.

Pasqualoni picked David Qalker and Geln Young to be the team captains for 1992. It was another fine year of football for Syracuse. With their season record of 10-2-0, the team was invited and played in the Fiesta Bowl v Colorado on January 1.

All American Christopher J. Gedney 1992

Christopher Joseph Gedney was born on August 9, 1970 in Liverpool NY and he played football graduated from Liverpool HS there. He played tight end in the National Football League(NFL) for six seasons. He played college football for Syracuse University, and earned All-American honors. He played professionally for the Chicago Bears and Arizona Cardinals of the NFL. He is currently the assistant athletics director for major gifts at Syracuse University.

While playing for the Syracuse Orangemen football team from 1989 to 1992, he was a standout, achieving first-team consensus All-American status as a senior in 1992.

The Chicago Bears selected Gedney in the third round (61st overall pick) in the 1993 NFL Draft, and he played for the Bears from 1993 to 1995. He later played for the Arizona Cardinals from 1997 to 2000. His most productive season came in 1997, where he caught 23 passes for 261 yards and 4 touchdowns.

Chris currently lives in Syracuse, New York. He previously worked as the development liaison for the SU's Football Lettermen's Club and an analyst for the Syracuse Sports Network. On April 29, 2010, Gedney was promoted to senior associate athletic director for major gifts at Syracuse University.

Games of the 1992 season

On Sept 5 at East Carolina's Ficklen Memorial Stadium in Greenville, North Carolina, the Orangemen defeated the Pirates W (42–21) On Sept 12, in the home opener at the Carrier Dome, on the campus of Syracuse University in Syracuse, NY before 49,238, #9 Syracuse beat a tough Texas team W (31-21). On Sept 19, Ohio State defeated #8 Syracuse at the Carrier Dome L (12–35) before 49,629. On Oct 3, at Louisville's Cardinal Stadium in Louisville, Kentucky, the #17 ranked Orangemen defeated the Cardinals W (15–9) before 37,323.

Then, on Oct 10 at home, #15 Syracuse defeated Rutgers in a high scoring match W (50-28). On October 17 at #24 West Virginia, at Mountaineer Field in Morgantown, West Virginia, for the (Ben Schwartzwalder Trophy), Syracuse beat the Mountaineers W (20-17) On Oct 24 at Temple in a game played at Veterans Stadium in Philadelphia, SU won the day W (38–7) before 11,221. On Oct 31 at home SU beat Pittsburgh at the Carrier Dome W (41–10) before

48,837 On Nov 7, #10 Syracuse beat the Hokies of Virginia Tech at the Carrier Dome W (28–9) in a packed house.

Highlights SU v BC

On Nov 14, before 33,298, at #17 Boston College, at Alumni Stadium, Chestnut Hill, Massachusetts #10 SU beat BC in the rivalry match W (27-10).

On November 14, 1992, Syracuse managed a fine 27-10 win on the road against Boston College. With this win, a Top 10 battle against Miami in the final week of the season was set up. The Orange had earned a #10 ranking heading into the game, while the Eagles sat at #17. Syracuse went on to lose to the Hurricanes in a 16-10 battle but still finished 10-2, with a visit to the Fiesta Bowl—shown below. Marvin Graves threw two touchdowns in this game and ran for another.

On Nov 21, in its final game the #8 Syracuse Orangemen took their second loss of the season against the #1 ranked Miami Hurricanes at the Carrier Dome in a very tight game L (10–16) before 49,857

1993 Fiesta Bowl

On January 1, 1993, #6 Syracuse teed off against #10 Colorado in SU n Devil Stadium, Tempe, Arizona in the Fiesta Bowl. Syracuse was becoming a regular bowl game winner and got the win in this game W (26–22) before 70,224.

Syracuse 26, Colorado 22
January 1, 1993
Tempe, Arizona

Marvin Graves was named the Offensive Player of the Game and Kevin Mitchell earned defensive honors as No. 6 Syracuse defeated No. 10 Colorado. Graves, who earned his third straight bowl MVP award, scored on a 28-yard run and led an SU attack that rushed for 201 yards. David Walker led the way with 80 yards on 16 carries and Terry Richardson added 63 yards on seven carries.

On defense, Mitchell wreaked havoc on the Colorado attack. The nose guard had eight tackles, two sacks and two tackles for loss. Glen Young and Dan Conley combined for 23 tackles and Dwayne Joseph, Bob Grosvenor and Tony Jones each picked off a pass from Kordell Stewart, the nation's fifth-rated passer. Colorado pulled to within 19-16, but Kirby Dar Dar ran the ensuing kickoff 100 yards for what proved to be the winning TD, closing out a 20-point third quarter for Syracuse.

Despite dreadful field conditions, John Biskup was perfect on the day, hitting field goals of 46 and 34 yards and both of his PAT attempts. Colorado's Mitch Berger did not fare as well, missing a field goal and two PATs, which as hindsight shows us, was the game margin.

1993 Paul Pasqualoni Coach # 25

The 1993 Syracuse Orangemen football team competed in their one hundred-fourth season of intercollegiate football. They were led by Paul Pasqualoni in his third of fourteen seasons as head coach of the Syracuse Orangemen. SU had a winning season 6-4-1 but not at the level of the last several. They were 3-4- in their third year in the Big East. Pasqualoni picked Marvin Graves, Dwayne Joseph, and John Reagan to be the team captains for 1993. Syracuse did not play in a bowl game this year.

On Sept 4, in the home opener at the Carrier Dome, on the campus of Syracuse University in Syracuse, NY before 45,090, #6 ranked Syracuse beat a tough Ball State Team W (35-12). On Sept 9, at East Carolina's Dowdy–Ficklen Stadium in Greenville, NC, the #6 Orangemen defeated the Pirates W (41–22) before 33,055. Then, on Sept 18 at Texas's Texas Memorial Stadium in Austin, TX, SU tied the Longhorns T (21–21) before 65,897. On Sept 25 in a night game at the Carrier Dome, the #12 Orangemen squeaked out a win against Cincinnati W (24–21) before 48,312. Then, in another home match, on Oct 2, #13 Syracuse lost to Boston College L (29-33)

SU no longer had a rivalry with Penn State as Joe Paterno's Nittany Lions gave up independent status and began to play ball this year in the Big 10.

On Oct 16 at Pittsburgh's Pitt Stadium, Pittsburgh, PA #24 SU defeated Pitt W (24–21) before 34,268. On Oct 23 in a blowout, #23 Syracuse was pushed around by #6 Miami at the Miami Orange Bowl in Miami, FL L (0–49) before 63,194. On Oct 30, at home, SU was beaten again in a big shutout—this time by #13 West Virginia in the Ben Schwartzwalder Trophy game L (0–43) before 49,268. On Nov 6. At home SU defeated Temple in a blowout W (52-3).

On Nov 13 Syracuse lost to Virginia Tech at Lane Stadium in Blacksburg, VA L (24–45) before 44,722 fans. On Nov 26 at Rutgers in Giants Stadium, East Rutherford, NJ, the Orangemen beat the Scarlet Knights W (31–8) before 26,101.

1994 Paul Pasqualoni Coach # 25

The 1994 Syracuse Orangemen football team competed in their one hundred-fifth season of intercollegiate football. They were led by Paul Pasqualoni in his fourth of fourteen seasons as head coach of the Syracuse Orangemen. SU had picked up the pace winning one more game than last year -- 7-4-0. They were 4-3- in their fourth year in the Big East. Pasqualoni picked Wilky Bazile, Eric Chenoweth, Dan Conley, and Tony Jones to be the team captains for 1994. Syracuse was not selected for a bowl game this year.

On Sept 3, in the home opener at the Carrier Dome, on the campus of Syracuse University in Syracuse, NY before 45,090, unranked Syracuse was beaten in a one-point nail-biter against #16 ranked Oklahoma L 29-30). On Sept 10 at Cincinnati's Nippert Stadium in Cincinnati SU won W (34–19) before 21,735. On Sept 17 at home in the Carrier Dome, SU won a one-point battle against Rutgers W (37–36) before 44,925. On Sept 24 at East Carolina's Ficklen Memorial Stadium, Greenville, North Carolina, SU beat the Pirates W (21–18). On October 1 SU beat #14 Virginia Tech W (28-20).

On Oct 8 at home in the Dome, #21 SU beat the Pittsburgh Panthers W (31–7). On Oct 22 at Temple in a game played at Veterans Stadium, SU defeated the Owls W (49–42) before a small crowd of 12,241. On Nov 5 at home, #10 ranked SU lost to #5 ranked Miami at the Carrier Dome L (6–27) before 49,565.

On Nov 12 at #25 Boston College at Alumni Stadium in Chestnut Hill, Massachusetts in the annual rivalry, the Eagles dominated and shutout the Orangemen L (0–31) before 44,500. On Nov 19, at home #24 SU defeated Maryland W (21-16). Then, in the season closer on Nov 24, Thanksgiving day at West Virginia's Mountaineer Field Morgantown, West Virginia, the Mountaineers captured the Ben Schwartzwalder Trophy L (0–13) before 40,369

1995 Paul Pasqualoni Coach # 25

The 1995 Syracuse Orangemen football team competed in their one hundred-sixth season of intercollegiate football. They were led by Paul Pasqualoni in his fifth of fourteen seasons as head coach of the

Syracuse Orangemen. SU had picked up the pace again, winning nine games this year 9-3-0. They were 5-2- in their fifth year in the Big East. Pasqualoni picked Cy Ellsworth, Marvin Harrison, and Darrell Parker to be the team captains for 1995. Syracuse was selected for the Gator Bowl this year and they beat Clemson in a blowout shutout.

All American Marvin D. Harrison 1995

Marvin Daniel Harrison was born August 25, 1972. He played wide receiver in the National Football League (NFL). Before his NFL career, he played wide receiver for Syracuse University. Harrison was an All-American in 1995.

He was drafted by the Indianapolis Colts in the first round of the 1996 NFL Draft. He spent all 13 of his NFL seasons with the Colts, most of them with quarterback Peyton Manning, and is widely considered as one of the greatest and most productive wide receivers in NFL history.

He earned a SU per Bowl ring with the team in SU per Bowl XLI over the Chicago Bears. Harrison was a Pro Football Hall of Fame finalist for the Classes of 2014 and 2015 before being elected in 2016, the same year his former coach Tony Dungy was voted into the Hall.

Games of the 1995 season

On Sept 2 at #20 North Carolina's Kenan Memorial Stadium in Chapel Hill, North Carolina, Syracuse won W (20–9) before 52,400. On Sept 9, in the home opener at the Carrier Dome, on the campus of Syracuse University in Syracuse, NY before 39,547, #22 ranked Syracuse was beaten by a flied goal against unranked East Carolina L 24-27). On Sept 23 at home, Syracuse defeated Minnesota at the Carrier Dome W (27–17) before 42,780. On Sept 30 at Rutgers Stadium in Piscataway, NJ, SU won W (27–17). On Oct 7, at home, Syracuse defeated Temple W (31–14) before 40,646.

On Oct 14 at home, Syracuse put away Eastern Michigan at the Dome in a high scoring match W (52–24) before 38,902. Then, on Oct 21 at home against West Virginia Syracuse won the Ben Schwartzwalder Trophy W (30–7) before 48,880. On Nov 4 at Virginia Tech in Lane Stadium, Blacksburg, VA, SU lost to the Hokies L (7–31) before 51,239.

On Nov 11 at Pittsburgh's Pitt Stadium in Pittsburgh PA, SU got the win W (42–10) before 20,279. On Nov 18 at home v Boston College, #23 SU beat BC W (58–29) before 49,384. On Nov 25 in a tight match, #22 SU lost to #25 Miami at the Miami Orange Bowl venue in Miami FL L (24–35) before 47,544.

The 1996 Gator Bowl

On January 1, 1996, New Year's Day the Gator Bowl pitted then unranked Syracuse v #23 Clemson in the Gator Bowl game hosted in Jacksonville Municipal Stadium, Jacksonville, Florida. The Orangemen blew out the Tigers in a one-way game W (41-0) before 45,202

Game highlights

Syracuse 41, Clemson 0
January 1, 1996
Jacksonville, Florida

Syracuse fans loved this season finish as it was done in grand style. The Orangemen got credit for the most-lopsided victory of all of the 51 Gator Bowls. SU defeated Clemson, 41-0, in rain-soaked Jacksonville. SU scored early and more often than expected against a typically tough Clemson Tigers team. SU had a 20-0 lead after the first quarter. For Clemson, there was not much to write home about.

Bowl MVP Donovan McNabb was on the mark as he threw for three TDs and ran for one more. McNabb was a real scrambler on the field and this always helped the team. Marvin Harrison, who suffered a broken thumb in the game continued playing and he continued to excel. He had seven receptions for 173 yards and two TDs to close out his stellar career.

Several Florida-born players had outstanding performances, led by Jacksonville-native Malcolm Thomas, who ran for two TDs. Tampa's Kevin Abrams returned from an elbow injury suffered against Boston College, and had two interceptions and Donovin Darius led SU with 10 tackles.

Sean Reali set an SU record with a 73-yard punt. Every eligible player entered the game. The scoring started with a Thomas TD run, followed by McNabb's TD run. The first quarter ended with a 38-yard TD pass from McNabb to Harrison. SU put the game out of reach with a pair of third quarter TDs, Thomas' second run and a 56-yard pass from McNabb to Harrison. A 15-yard TD pass from McNabb to Kaseem Sinceno capped the scoring for SU. It was games like this that helped Donavan McNabb become a great Philly QB, though Philadelphia did not let him be the great scrambler he was with the Orangemen

With this bowl victory, Paul Pasqualoni tied Dick MacPherson in SU bowl victories, moving his bowl record to 3-0. The win was SU's sixth straight bowl victory and ninth overall. Before Macpherson and Pasqualoni, bowl wins were few and far between, even with Ben Schwartzwalder. Besides Ben Schwartzwalder, Macpherson and Pasqualoni were top flight. IMHO, SU would have rebuilt and been a contender again if the cries to fire Pasqualoni as we close in on year 14 were put to bed. Pasqualoni is a great coach. These wins did not come by accident.

For Syracuse fans, who are still Paul Pasqualoni fans, you will feel vindicated as you check out the post SU Pasqualoni career. He is well known for his defensive acumen. On February 7, 2018, just a few weeks ago about when I began writing this book, Pasqualoni was named defensive coordinator of the Detroit Lions. He is a pro.

I will root for Detroit when they are not playing my other favorite teams for sure. As a lifetime Pennsylvanian, I live just one hundred miles north of Philadelphia, home of the 2018 SU per Bowl Champs. Go Eagles! Sorry…could not help it after so many dry years.

1996 Paul Pasqualoni Coach # 25

The 1996 Syracuse Orangemen football team competed in their one hundred-seventh season of intercollegiate football. They were led by Paul Pasqualoni in his sixth of fourteen seasons as head coach of the Syracuse Orangemen. SU had picked up the pace again, winning nine games again this year 9-3-0. They were 6-1 in their sixth year in the Big East. Pasqualoni picked Kevin Abrams, Harvey Pennypacker, and Malcolm Thomas to be the team captains for 1996. Syracuse was selected for the Liberty Bowl this year and they defeated Houston in a nice game. This was four bowl game wins of four played for Pasqualoni.

All American Kevin R. Abrams 1995, 1996

Kevin Abrams signed his letter of intent to play college football at Syracuse University in 1992, the same year as fellow defensive back Tyvan Sunday.

Abrams was born on February 28, 1974. He played professional NFL football as a cornerback. He was drafted by the Detroit Lions in the second round of the 1997 NFL Draft. He played four years with the Lions before he ended his career.

All American Donovin L Darius 1997

Darius played free Safety for Syracuse and was selected as an All American in 1997. He was the BIG EAST Defensive Player of the Year in 1997 and an All-BIG EAST selection in 1996 and 1997. Darius intercepted 12 passes and had 379 tackles in his career. He was a defensive mainstay for the NFL's Jacksonville Jaguars. He led SU in tackles in the 1996 Gator Bowl and the 1996 Liberty Bowl wins. He was named to Syracuse University's All-Century team in November 1999.

Games of the 1996 season

On Sept 7 in the season and home opener at the Carrier Dome, on the campus of Syracuse University in Syracuse, NY before 48,097, unranked Syracuse was out-muscled by #24 North Carolina's Tar heels L (10-27). On September 21 at Minnesota's Hubert H. Humphrey Metrodome in Minneapolis, MN, the Orangemen lost their second game by two points L (33–35) before 45,756 On Sept 28, back at the Carrier Dome, before 49,069, unranked Syracuse got the win against the Virginia Tech Hokies W (52-21). On Oct 5 at home, SU shut-out Rutgers in the Carrier Dome W (42–0) before 48,112. Then, on Oct 12 at home, SU beat Pitt in a big blowout W (55-7). Syracuse was on a roll.

On Oct 26, continuing the rivalry with Boston College at Alumni Stadium in Chestnut Hill, MA(Rivalry), SU lined up all the chips its way and took the game W (45–17) before 44,500. On Nov 2, at #18 West Virginia's Mountaineer Field in Morgantown, WV for the Ben Schwartzwalder Trophy, Syracuse got the prize W (30–7) before 56,312.

On Nov 9 at Tulane in the Louisiana Superdome, New Orleans, LA the Orangemen defeated the Green Wave W (31–7) before a sparse crowd of 13,537. On Nov 16, at home, a #19 ranked SU team played a reinvigorated #22 Cadets team at the Carrier Dome and defeated Army W (42–17) before 49,257. On Nov 23 at Temple, #16 Syracuse defeated the Owls at Veterans Stadium in Philadelphia, PA W (36015). Always having a tough time with Miami, this year on Nov 30, was no different as the Big East-powered-Hurricanes put out all the stops and in what for them was an away game at the dome. They barely got out with their skins in a close SU loss L (31-38). It could have been different. 49, 426 others thought it should have ended differently.

1996 Liberty Bowl

On December 27 at 3:00 PM, #23 Syracuse engaged Houston in the Liberty Bowl Game in Memphis, TN. Syracuse's eight game streak was preserved in this great win W (30–17) before 49,163

Syracuse 30, Houston 17
December 27, 1996
Memphis, Tennessee

The pundits have written that Syracuse put aside its usual balanced offense and rode its powerful running game to a 30-17 victory in the 1996 St. Jude Liberty Bowl in Memphis. For SU fans, it was as always, the past few years, a thing of beauty.

Malcolm Thomas won the Most Outstanding Offensive Player Award with a 201-yard rushing performance, scoring one touchdown. SU rushed for 396 yards and four TDs in the game. Quarterback Donovan McNabb rushed for 49 yards and a pair of touchdowns but as a great rushing quarterback, he made it easier for all the backs and all the receivers to have the day they needed to get a big win.

Entering the fourth quarter, SU led by two, 16-14, before McNabb and Thomas took control. Both scored a TD in the final period, giving SU its margin of victory. It looked easier than it actually was.

McNabb completed only four of 10 passes for 76 yards, but the Orange running game, powered by the offensive line, was too much for the Cougars, the first-ever Conference USA champions. SU finished 9-3 overall and won the school's seventh straight bowl game. SU fans and alums love to win, especially against the toughest teams in the bowl games.

Rod Gadson won the Most Outstanding Defensive Player Award, after intercepting a Cougar pass in the end zone. Donovin Darius had 12 tackles and Phil Nash made a touchdown-saving tackle on the second half-opening kickoff. It was a great performance overall. This was an all-Pasqualoni team.

1997 Paul Pasqualoni Coach # 25

The 1997 Syracuse Orangemen football team competed in their one hundred-eighth season of intercollegiate football. They were led by Paul Pasqualoni in his seventh of fourteen seasons as head coach of the Syracuse Orangemen. SU had a great pace going winning nine games again this year for the third time in a row 9-4-0. They were 6-1 in their seventh year in the Big East. Pasqualoni picked Keith Downing, Donovin Darius, Rod Gadson, and Brad Patkochis to be the team captains for 1997. Syracuse was selected for the Fiesta Bowl and they were defeated by Kansas State in a nice game. This was the first bowl game loss for Pasqualoni out of five tries.

On Aug 24 in the season opener against #24 ranked Wisconsin in Giants Stadium, East Rutherford, New Jersey in the Kickoff Classic, Syracuse shutout the Badgers W (34–0) before 51,185. On Aug 30, in the home opener at the Carrier Dome, on the campus of Syracuse University in Syracuse, NY before 42, 742, #13 Syracuse was slightly out-muscled by North Carolina's Tar Heels by one-point L (31-32). On Sept 6 at Oklahoma's Oklahoma Memorial Stadium in Norman, Oklahoma, SU lost its second of its first three games L (34–36) before 68,342. On Sept 13 at #22 Virginia Tech in Lane Stadium, Blacksburg, Virginia ESPN the Orangemen record went to 1-3 with the loss L (3–31) to the Hokies before 50,137.

Then, on Sept 20 at home, SU defeated Tulane in the Carrier Dome W (30–19_. On Oct 4, my wedding anniversary, before 44054, the Orangemen pummeled East Carolina W 56-0. Then, on Oct 9 at Rutgers in Rutgers Stadium, Piscataway, New Jersey, the Orangemen racked up another big win W (50–3) before 19,044 subdued fans. Then, on Oct 18 at home against Temple in the Carrier Dome, Syracuse delivered a walloping W (60–7) to the too-complacent Owls.

Highlight SU v West Virginia

On Nov 1, #17 West Virginia played SU at the Carrier Dome and were whooped by Syracuse W (40–10) before 49,273.

On Nov. 1, 1997, in the middle of an eight-game winning streak after starting the year 1-3, Syracuse beat down No. 17 West Virginia by a score of 40-10. The impressive margin helped boost Syracuse into the Fiesta Bowl, where the Orange lost to Kansas State (discussed below). Kyle McIntosh led the Orange, rushing for 145 yards. Syracuse also got 188 yards passing from Donovan McNabb.

On Nov 8, at home #22 Syracuse defeated a stubborn Boston College team W (20-13) before a packed house of 49,153. On Nov 15 at Pittsburgh un-ranked Pitt were beaten by #19 Syracuse at Pitt

Stadium in Pittsburgh, Pennsylvania in the annual rivalry game W 32–27) before 46,102. Then, on Nov 29 playing unranked Miami, the #16 Orangemen got a long-awaited win in Miami, FL at the Orange Bowl from the Hurricanes W 33–13 before 25,147

1997 Fiesta Bowl

On New Year's Eve, December 31, 1997 at 6:00 PM, a ready and able # 14 Syracuse Orangemen Squad faced off against the #10 national squad of Kansas State at SU n Devil Stadium in Tempe, Arizona in the annual Fiesta Bowl game. After winning seven games in a row, Syracuse dropped this game L (18–35) before 69,367.

The Orangemen jumped out to a 3-0 lead on the first of Nate Trout's three field goals.. In Q2, Kansas State quarterback Michael Bishop took the Wildcats to three-consecutive touchdowns in the second quarter.

Following a failed fake field goal attempt by Syracuse, Bishop completed a 19-yard pass to Darnell McDonald. Bishop then followed with a 12-yard TD rush on their next possession, with a 28-yard completion to Justin Swift on a tight end screen. Syracuse came back to score 12 points in the final 2:18 to cut the lead to 21-15 at the half.

There was no scoring by either team in the third quarter. But, in the fourth Q, McDonald caught a 77-yard TD pass, and then KS followed with a 41-yard reception with 3:17 remaining to seal the game away.

Summarizing the game, Bishop threw for four touchdown passes, completing a career-high 14 passes for a career-best 317 yards. He was the offensive hero, finishing the game with 390 yards in total offense including 317 yards passing and 73 yards rushing. McDonald caught seven of Bishop's passes for a school-record of 206 yards and three touchdowns. His 77-yard reception in the fourth quarter was the longest in Fiesta Bowl history. Swift caught a career-high five passes for a career-high 98 yards and one touchdown.

Bishop earned the Offensive Player of the Game award, while KSU linebacker Travis Ochs, was named Defensive Player of the Game after he had an interception and fumble recovery.

QB McNabb was not at his best though he performed well, passing for 271 yards and running for 81 yards. Hiss accuracy was off as he completed just 16 of 39 passes and the rushing attack was not there to bail the QB out of jams. Syracuse's seven-game bowl game win streak had ended.

1998 Paul Pasqualoni Coach # 25

The 1998 Syracuse Orangemen football team competed in their one hundred-ninth season of intercollegiate football. They were led by Paul Pasqualoni in his eighth of fourteen seasons as head coach of the Syracuse Orangemen. SU had a fine season winning eight games against four losses. 8-4-0. They were 6-1 again in their eight year in the Big East. Pasqualoni picked Scott Kiernan, Rob Konrad, Donovan McNabb, and Jason Poles to be the team captains for 1998. Syracuse was selected for the Orange Bowl Fiesta Bowl and they were defeated by Florida in a nice game

All American Kevin L Johnson 1998

Kevin L. Johnson Jr was born in July 1999 in Trenton, N.J. He is the son of Kevin Johnson Sr. and Shoniece Johnson. His dad, Kevin Sr., played for the Orangemen from 1995-98 and holds the Syracuse record for most kickoffs returned for a touchdown

In High School, Kevin played wide receiver for head coach Kevin Wright at IMG Academy in Florida. He had previously attended The Hun School in New Jersey.

As a senior at IMG, he played special teams and helped the Ascenders to an 8-0 record and the #2 final ranking in the USA Today Top 25 poll. He earned All-MAPL First Team honors from the Mid-Atlantic Prep League coaches after catching 32 passes for 795 yards and seven touchdowns as a junior at Hun.

<<Kevin L. Johnson

As a senior kick returner at Syracuse, he was named the 1998 BIG EAST Special Teams Player of the Year and an AFCA First Team All-American ...

Johnson Sr. was selected by the Cleveland Browns in the second round of 1999 NFL Draft and played seven seasons in the league for the Browns (1999-2003), Jacksonville Jaguars (2003), Baltimore Ravens (2004) and Detroit Lions (2005) He has one brother, one sister and was a Communications and rhetorical studies major at SU.

Games of the 1998 Season

On Sept 5 in the season and home opener against #10 ranked Tennessee at the Carrier Dome, on the campus of Syracuse University in Syracuse, NY before 49,550, #17 Syracuse lost by one point in a nail-biter L (33-34).

Highlight #13 Michigan v unranked Syracuse

On Sept 12 at #13 Michigan at Michigan Stadium (The Big House) in Ann Arbor, MI, Syracuse beat the Wolverines W (38–28) before the largest crowd to ever attend an SU game--111,012.

This game on Sept. 12, 1998 found Syracuse beginning its run to the 1998 Orange Bowl in just the second game of the season, upsetting No. 13 Michigan at The Big House. The game came on the heels of a heartbreaking loss to #10 Tennessee to open the year. Led by senior Donovan McNabb, the Orange went on to play Florida in the Orange Bowl. McNabb threw for 233 years and three touchdowns. Michigan's Tom Brady threw for 104 yards and split time with Drew Henson. Yes, it was the same Donavan McNabb from the Eagles and yes, Tom Brady did not get to play the whole game.

On Sept 19 at home Syracuse shellacked Rutgers in a blowout at the Carrier Dome W (70-14). On Oct 1 at NC State's Carter–Finley Stadium in Raleigh, NC. #11 Syracuse could not keep up with the Tar Heels and lost L (17–38) before

On Oct 10 at home, Syracuse beat Cincinnati in a blowout W (63-21) before 47,251. On Oct 17 in a major rivalry game at Boston College's Alumni Stadium in Chestnut Hill, MA, SU defeated the Eagles W (42–25) before 43,413. On Oct 31 at home, #17 Syracuse defeated Pittsburgh's Panthers W (45–28) before 49,012. On Nov 7 at West Virginia's Mountaineer Field in Morgantown, WV, Syracuse lost by a TD L (28–35) before 54,655

On Nov 14 at home, SU defeated Virginia Tech's Hokies in the Carrier Dome in a close match W (28–26) before 49,336. Then, on Nov 21 at Temple in a game played at Veterans Stadium,

Philadelphia, PA, the Orangemen beat the Owls W (38–7) before 12,483.

Game highlights SU V Miami

On Nov 28, at home, #21 SU pummeled #19 Miami (FL) W (66-13).

This November 28, 1998 game was a meeting of Top 20 teams, Syracuse clinched its second consecutive Big East championship with a 66-13 thrashing of No. 19 Miami. The Orange entered the game ranked No. 21 in the country. In his final game in the Carrier Dome, Donovan McNabb rushed for three touchdowns and passed for two more. The Orange went on to play in the Orange Bowl.

1999 Orange Bowl

On January 2, 1999, in the Orange Bowl game, Paul Pasqualoni's #18 ranked Syracuse Orangemen squared off against Steve Spurrier's # 7 Florida Gators at the Miami Orange Bowl field in Miami, FL. The Gators defeated the Orangemen L (10–31) 67,919

Florida 31, Syracuse 10
January 2, 1999
Miami, Florida

This was one of those games where as you replay it, should have gone the Orangemen's way. Donavan McNabb was either hot or not. This day, McNabb was not bad; but he was not hot.

Syracuse's 31-10 loss to the University of Florida in the 1999 FedEx Orange Bowl at Orange Bowl Stadium in Miami was the final game for a bunch of Orangemen—14 in total. The list includes captains Donovan McNabb, Rob Konrad, Scott Kiernan and Jason Poles. This game marked the 19th bowl appearance and the third Orange Bowl appearance for SU.

Despite Syracuse's edge in time of possession in the first quarter (10:46 to 4:14), the Gators jumped out to an early 14-0 lead on two touchdowns by Travis Taylor. Florida used just three plays on each drive and scored the two TDs less than three minutes apart. After a 36-yard field goal by Nate Trout opened up the second quarter to get SU on the board, Florida extended its lead to 31-3 on one passing touchdown, one rushing touchdown and one field goal. McNabb connected with sophomore Maurice Jackson for a 62-yard touchdown play with just more than three minutes remaining for the 31-10 final.

McNabb threw for 192 yards on 14-of-30 passing. He also led the Orange in rushing with 72 yards on 20 attempts. Jackson's TD catch made him Syracuse's leading receiver. Senior Kevin Johnson caught four passes for 49 yards. On the defensive end, Quentin Harris led SU with a career-high 17 tackles, nine unassisted, and Keith Bulluck recorded 12. In more ways than one, it was an off-day for the Orangemen, though Steve Spurrier's teams were never easy to beat.

1999 Paul Pasqualoni Coach # 25

The 1999 Syracuse Orangemen football team competed in their one hundred-tenth season of intercollegiate football. They were led by Paul Pasqualoni in his ninth of fourteen seasons as head coach of the Syracuse Orangemen. SU had a winning season again 7-5-0. They were 3-4 in their ninth year in the Big East. Pasqualoni picked Mark Baniewicz, Keith Bulluck, Donald Dinkins, Quinton Spotwood, and Nate Trout to be the team captains for 1999. Syracuse was selected for the Music City Bowl and they defeated Kentucky in a nice game.

On Sept 2 at Toledo in the season opener in the Glass Bowl—a stadium in Toledo, Ohio that was renamed after WWII, (The stadium has many glass components and may very well be a reflection of the Owens Illinois company that was headquartered in Toledo for many, many years.) Syracuse brought home the victory W (35–12) before 27,900. On Sept 11 in the home opener against Central Michigan at the Carrier Dome, on the campus of Syracuse University in Syracuse, NY before 45,563, Syracuse won in a blowout W (47-7).

On Sept 18 at home, SU was beaten by the Michigan Wolverines in a lose match L (13-18). On Sept 25 at home, for the Ben Schwartzwalder Trophy, Syracuse defeated West Virginia, W (30–7) before 44,890. On Oct 2 at home SU defeated the Tulane Green Wave by the score of W (47–17) before 48,286. On Oct 7 in the traditional rivalry game at Pittsburgh's Pitt Stadium in Pittsburgh, SU grabbed a tough victory W (24–17) before 45,455. Then, on Oct 16 at #4 Virginia Tech's Lane Stadium in Blacksburg, Virginia, SU was simply shellacked by the Hokies L (0–62) before 53,130.

Still not recovered from the trouncing from the prior week, at home on Oct 30 Syracuse gave up another loss to Boston College L (23-24) in hard fought close match before 48, 487. On Nov 6 at home SU beat Temple W (27-10). Then on Nov 13 at Rutgers in Rutgers Stadium, Piscataway, New Jersey, the Orangemen lost to the Scarlet Knights L (21–24) before 17,919. On the road on Nov 27 at Miami (FL)'s Miami Orange Bowl, the Hurricanes got the best of the Orangemen L (13–45) before 35,208

1999 Music City Bowl

On December 29, 1999 at 4:00 PM, Syracuse took on Kentucky at the Adelphia Coliseum in Nashville, Tennessee in the Music City Bowl and the Orangemen defeated the Wildcats W 20–13 before 59,221 stadium fans.

December 29, 1999 - Adelphia Coliseum
Syracuse 20, Kentucky 13
Attendance: 59,221

Syracuse had failed in its last three bowl games after winning seven in a row. This day, the Orangemen were ready to begin a new winning streak, but they scared a lot of fans in pulling it off.

Nonetheless, in the nick of time, Syracuse remembered how to win. The win would mark their first victory in the 1999 season since November 6. Syracuse ended the regular season by losing its last two games and four of its last five. Syracuse secured the win by outscoring Kentucky 13-3 in the 4th quarter.

"All in all, we just persevered, and we just needed a win," Syracuse defensive star Keith Bulluck said after recording a team-high 15 tackles in the game. "The thrill of victory – we haven't had it in such a long time." Bulluck played his final collegiate game on the same field in which he would eventually shine for the Tennessee Titans.

Game MVP James Mungro rushed for 162 yards and two long touchdowns in the game, both in the 4th quarter, capping the Syracuse comeback. The game MVP was James Mungro, RB, Syracuse

2000 Paul Pasqualoni Coach # 25

The 2000 Syracuse Orangemen football team competed in their one hundred-eleventh season of intercollegiate football. They were led by Paul Pasqualoni in his tenth of fourteen seasons as head coach of the Syracuse Orangemen. SU had a winning season again 6-5-0. They were 4-3 in their tenth year in the Big East. Pasqualoni picked, Morlon Greenwood, Kyle Johnson, and Pat Woodcock, to be the team captains for 1999. Syracuse was not selected for a bowl game this year.

On Sept 2 in the home opener against Buffalo in the Carrier Dome, on the campus of Syracuse University in Syracuse, NY before 40,634, Syracuse won in a blowout W (63-7) On Sept 9 at Cincinnati's Nippert Stadium in Cincinnati, OH SU lost to the Bearcats L (10–12) before 17,717. SU lost two in a row on Sept 23 at East Carolina's Dowdy–Ficklen Stadium in Greenville, NC L (17-34) 33,026, On Sept 30 at home, SU defeated BYU at the Dome W (42–14) before 43,090. Then, in the rivalry against Pittsburgh at the Carrier Dome, SU triumphed W (24-17) before 40,699.

On Oct 14 at Boston College's Alumni Stadium in Chestnut Hill, MA SU lost to BC L (13–20) before 44,500. Then, on Oct 21, at home, #2 Virginia Tech beat Syracuse L (14–22) before 49,033. On Nov 4 at West Virginia's Mountaineer Field in Morgantown, WV, for the Ben Schwartzwalder Trophy), Syracuse played well and defeated the Mountaineers W (31–27) in a tough match before 51,422

On Nov 11, at Temple, in Veterans Stadium, Philadelphia, PA, the Orangemen defeated the Owls W (31–12) before 16,132. Then on Nov 18 at home, #2 Miami of Florida beat the Orangemen in a shutout L (0-26). In the season closer, at home, SU had its moxie all back and the Orangemen whipped Rutgers W (49-21) before 35, 589. There was no bowl game in 2000.

2001 Paul Pasqualoni Coach # 25

The 2001 Syracuse Orangemen football team competed in their one hundred-twelfth season of intercollegiate football. They were led by Paul Pasqualoni in his eleventh of fourteen seasons as head coach of the Syracuse Orangemen. SU had a fine winning season 10-3-0, which would be their last winning season under Coach Pasqualoni. They were 6-1 in their eleventh year in the Big East. Pasqualoni picked, P. J. Alexander, Dwight Freeney, Quentin Harris, Kyle Johnson, and Graham Manley to be the team captains for 2001. Syracuse played and won the Insight Bowl in 2001.

All American Dwight Freeney 2001

Freeney was born in Hartford, Connecticut where he later attended Bloomfield High School in Bloomfield, Connecticut. Freeney was a four-sport letterman, earning four letters in baseball; four in basketball; three in football, in which he played both ways; and one in soccer, in which he played goalie in his freshman year before switching over to football.

Freeney holds the record for sacks at his high school and used to hold the record for most sacks in a high school career in the Connecticut record book. Bloomfield High retired his No. 44 football jersey.

Freeney came to Syracuse on an athletic scholarship, where he played for the Syracuse Orangemen football team from 1998 to 2001. A two-year starter for the Orangemen, he set a school record with 17.5 sacks in his senior season and his 34 career sacks rank second in school history to Tim Green (45.5). He was SU's premier pass rusher, and once had a string of 17 consecutive games with at least one sack. Against Virginia Tech, Freeney sacked elusive Hokies quarterback Michael Vick 4.5 times in one game.

Dwight Freeney

Freeney finished his college career with 104 tackles (68 unassisted), 34 quarterback sacks, 51 tackles for a loss, and 43 quarterback pressures.[6] He was a first-team All-Big East Conference selection in 2000 and 2001, and was recognized as a unanimous first-team All-American following his senior season in 2001.

He was selected by the Indianapolis Colts with the 11th selection in the 2002 NFL Draft.[10] He set an NFL rookie record in 2002 with 9 forced fumbles, three of which occurred in a single game against former Syracuse football player, Donovan McNabb. Freeney was the runner up for the NFL Defensive Rookie of the Year award.

Dwight Freeney was very fast. When drafted by Indianapolis at 270 lbs., Freeney was clocked at 4.48 seconds in the 40-yard dash and the same 40 inch vertical jump. I'd love to see his current clockings.

In 2004, Freeney's third season, he led the NFL with 16 sacks. At the end of his third season, Freeney's season marked him as the 3rd fastest player to achieve 40 sacks. He developed a spin move which became his trademark pass rush move. In 2006, Freeney helped the Colts defeat the Chicago Bears in SU per Bowl XLI to become NFL Champions.

On February 15, 2013, Freeney was told he would not be re-signed by the Colts.[21][22] Freeney left as the all-time franchise leader in sacks with 107.5, eventually being surpassed by former teammate Robert Mathis the next season.

On May 18, 2013, Freeney signed a two-year deal with the San Diego Chargers. On October 12, 2015, Freeney signed a one-year, $870,000 deal with the Arizona Cardinals,

On August 2, 2016, Freeney signed a one-year deal with the Atlanta Falcons. He played in 15 games, totaling three sacks. The Falcons won the NFC Championship to advance to SU per Bowl LI, bringing Freeney to his third career SU per Bowl. Freeney had one sack in the big game,[36] although the Falcons lost to the Patriots by a score of 34–28.

On October 24, 2017, Freeney signed a one-year deal with the Seattle Seahawks.[38] After playing in four games recording three sacks, Freeney was released by the Seahawks on November 21, 2017.

On November 22, 2017, Freeney was claimed off waivers by the Detroit Lions. That is a long NFL career. Dwight Freeney is the Energizer Bunny

Games of the 2001 season

On Aug 26 v #10 Georgia Tech at Giants Stadium in East Rutherford, New Jersey in the 2001 College Kickoff Classic), Syracuse lost L (7–13) before 41,517. Then a week later on September 1, v #8 Tennessee at Neyland Stadium in Knoxville, Tennessee, SU went down L (9–33) before a huge crowd of 107,725. In week 3 of the 2001 season, on Sept 8 in the home opener against UCF in the Carrier Dome, on the campus of Syracuse University in Syracuse, NY before 35938, Syracuse won the game W

(21-10) for the Orangemen's first win of the year. Then, on Sept 22 at home, SU defeated Auburn at the Carrier Dome W (31–14) before 43,403.

Then on Sept 29 at home against East Carolina, the Orangemen defeated the Pirates W (44–30) before 36,347. Then, on Oct 6 at Rutgers in Rutgers Stadium, Piscataway, New Jersey, SU beat the Scarlet Knights W (24–17) before 17,511, Moving on to Pittsburgh, PA on Oct 13 at the new Heinz Field, the Orangemen grabbed another win W (42–10) before 52,367. Then on Oct 20 at home, SU defeated Temple† at the Carrier Dome W (45–3).

On Oct 27 at #5 Virginia Tech at Lane Stadium in Blacksburg, Virginia, the Orangemen prevailed against the Hokies W (22–14) before 53,662. Two weeks later on Nov 10, at home in the Carrier Dome, # 18 SU defeated West Virginia W (24–13) before 43,753. Then, on Nov 17, SU played as #14 against #1 ranked Miami in the Miami Orange Bowl stadium, the Orangemen could not find a breath against the National Championship Hurricanes and went down in a shutout blowout L (0–59) before 52,896. The season was not over until all the games were played and so on Nov 24, at home SU defeated BC, #25 Boston College in the Carrier Dome, for another SU win in the rivalry W (39–28) before 45,063.

2001 Insight Bowl

On December 29, 2001. At 5:30 PM, #18 Syracuse took on Kansas State, playing at Bank One Ballpark, Phoenix, Arizona in the Insight.com Bowl. The Orangemen prevailed W (26–3) before 40,028 intrigued fans.

Game highlights

Syracuse 26, Kansas State 3
December 29, 2001
Phoenix, Arizona

When the # 17 Syracuse Orangemen played the Kansas State Wildcats, and beat them 26-3, to become the 2001 Insight.com Bowl Champions before 40,028 at Bank One Ballpark., it was a glorious day for Syracuse University. The Orange were powered by three James Mungro touchdowns and a phenomenally stifling defense spearheaded by junior linebacker Clifton Smith. And, so, the Orangemen won their 12th bowl game in SU school history.

The School football team finished the season with a 10-3 record. The 2001 Orangemen were only the fifth Syracuse squad to accumulate 10 or more wins in one season. Three of SU's 10-win seasons came during Paul Pasqualoni's head coaching tenure. He was one of the greatest SU coaches of all time under anybody's calculations. Tis game was another ripper for Syracuse.

SU opened the scoring on a 65-yard touchdown run by Mungro. The senior took a pitch from quarterback R.J. Anderson and busted the run to the outside, tight-roping the sideline on the way to the endzone.

With 12:12 to play in the second quarter junior receiver David Tyree tackled Mike Ronsick, the Kansas State punter who had bobbled the snap. Tyree forced Ronsick to fumble and junior running back Barry Baker made the recovery at the Wildcats' four-yard line. Two plays later Mungro punched in his second score on a one-yard run. After a blocked point after attempt, SU led 13-3.

Cornerback Willie Ford had one of his two interceptions on Kansas State's next drive. Mungro added his third touchdown, just 52 seconds after his second trip to the endzone. Mungro, playing in his final collegiate game, rushed for 112 yards on 20 carries. Mungro was an SU phenomenon.

With 3:22 to play in the fourth quarter Anderson and Johnnie Morant connected for a 52-yard touchdown, making the score 26-3. The Orangemen defense held Kansas State to 32 yards rushing and forced four turnovers. The Wildcats converted just four of 18 third down attempts. The SU defense limited Kansas State quarterbacks to completing 35 percent of their passes (14-of-40). Smith led the

Syracuse defense with 12 tackles and one sack. When you are good, you are good!

2002 Paul Pasqualoni Coach # 25

The 2002 Syracuse Orangemen football team competed in their one hundred-thirteenth season of intercollegiate football. They were led by Paul Pasqualoni in his twelfth of fourteen seasons as head coach of the Syracuse Orangemen. This was the worst year of Pasqualoni's coaching tenure and his first losing season 4-8-0. They were 2-5 in their twelfth year in the Big East. Pasqualoni picked Clifton Smith, Chris Davis, Will Hunter, Troy Nunes, and David Tyree, to be the team captains for 2001. Syracuse was not selected for a bowl game in 2002.

On Aug 29 at BYU's LaVell Edwards Stadium in Provo, the Cougars defeated the Orangemen L 21–42 before 65,612. In week 2 of the 2002season, on Sept 7 in the home opener against North Carolina in the Carrier Dome, on the campus of Syracuse University in Syracuse, NY before 39444 fans, Syracuse lost the game L (22-30 for the Orangemen's second loss of the year. Then, on Sept 14 at home, for their first win of the season, SU defeated Rhode Island at the Carrier Dome in a blow-out W (63-17) before 43,408. Then, on Sept 28 at 9:00 PM at #25 Auburn's Jordan–Hare Stadium in Auburn, AL, the Orangemen went down in a well-fought, very close match L (34–37) before 83,667

SU had beaten Pittsburgh 11 straight times until Oct 5 at home when SU lost big to Pittsburgh L (24-48) Then, on Oct 12 12:00 at Temple in Veterans Stadium, Philadelphia, PA, the Owls beat the Orangemen in a close game, L (16-17) before 17,220. Then for the fourth loss in a row, on Oct 18, the Orangemen traveled to the West Virginia Mountaineer Field, Morgantown, WV and were defeated L (7–34) before 45,088. Next up on Oct 25 at home was Rutgers. The Orangemen found their bearings and defeated the Scarlet Knights W (45–14) before 37,158.

On Nov 2 v UCF in a game played in the Citrus Bowl, Orlando, FL, the Orangemen grabbed the victory W 38–35 before 24,043.

Highlight SU v #8 Virginia Tech

Then, on Nov 9, at home, the Orangemen won their first OT game against #8 Virginia Tech W (50–42) before 48,239.

Looking back from November 9. 2002, the last time Syracuse beat a team ranked inside the AP Top 10 before this particular Friday came on this night in triple-overtime against No. 8 Virginia Tech. Syracuse won 50-42 in triple overtime, getting a Damien Rhodes touchdown and an interception from Maurice McClain in the final period to end the game. Unfortunately for the Orange it was part of a 4-8 season, but the drama of the game makes it one to remember.

On Nov 16, at rival Boston College's Alumni Stadium in Chestnut Hill, MA, the Orangemen took their seventh loss of the season L (20–41) before 36,221. Miami was in its prime, sitting in the #1 position when they came to the Carrier Dome on Nov 30 and beat the Orangemen at 1:00 PM by a big score L (7-49) before 45,679.

2003 Paul Pasqualoni Coach # 25

The 2003 Syracuse Orangemen football team competed in their one hundred-fourteenth season of intercollegiate football. They were led by Paul Pasqualoni in his thirteenth of fourteen seasons as head coach of the Syracuse Orangemen. This was a comeback year after the worst year of Pasqualoni's coaching tenure. The Orangemen had an even record of 6-6-0. It was two more wins than the prior season. They were 2-5 in their thirteenth year in the Big East. Pasqualoni picked R.J. Anderson, Keith Belton, and Rich Scanlon, to be the team captains for 2003. Syracuse was not selected for a bowl game in 2003.

This was the last season in which Syracuse used the "Orangemen" nickname. Beginning with the 2004–05 school year, the school adopted its current nickname of "Orange." Some pundits and alums persist in calling the new Orange, the Orangemen and that is OK—it's just not official.

On Sept 6 at North Carolina's Kenan Memorial Stadium in Chapel Hill, North Carolina, in triple overtime, SU got the victory W (49–47) before 47,000. In week 2 of the 2003 season, on Sept 13 in the home opener against Louisville in the Carrier Dome, on the campus of Syracuse University in Syracuse, NY before 38,550 fans, the Orangemen lost the game to the Cardinals L (20-30 for the team's first loss of the year. On Sept 20 at home, for their second win of the season, SU defeated UCF at the Carrier Dome W (38-14) before 35,103. On Sept 27 at home SU defeated Toledo at the Dome W (34–7) before 36,083

On Oct 11, at #4 Virginia Tech's Lane Stadium in Blacksburg, Virginia, the Hokeys beat the Orangemen in a blowout L (7–51) before 65,115. On Oct 18 at home, SU defeated Boston College in the annual rivalry W (39–14) before 45,313. In the Pittsburgh rivalry, Pitt won its second in a row against Syracuse on Oct 25 at Pittsburgh's Heinz Field in Pittsburgh, PA L (14–34) before 61,421. Then on Nov 8 at home, SU defeated Temple at the Carrier Dome W (41-17) before 43,149 fans.

On Nov 15, Syracuse traveled south to play #14 ranked Miami (FL) in the Miami Orange Facility in Miami but were beaten by the Hurricanes in a close match L (1017) before 48,130. On Nov22 at home, Syracuse lost another close match to #25 West Virginia and the Mountaineers went home with the Ben Schwartzwalder Trophy L (2334). On Nov 29, a tougher than usual Rutgers team would not give up an inch to the Orangemen as SU went down by three scores L (7-24). This game was played at Rutgers Stadium in Piscataway, New Jersey before 18,563.

After years of a breakeven bus trip from Scranton, PA to the Carrier Dome for an always-great SU game, a 2001 trip left me with enough unsold tickets that my loss was in four digits. My wife stepped in and said, "no more." I wanted to come back again and this particular year, I did, to see one of my favorite teams in all Sports, Notre Dame play the Orangemen in the Dome.

My best friends Dennis Grimes and Gerry Rodski accompanied me to a hotel that was once a Holiday Inn, just a few blocks from the Dome but in the snow, the walk took forever. At the time, we were all rooting for Notre Dame, but ND was having a lot of trouble winning that year as did Syracuse. Both were 5-6 going into this contest.

The game was on Dec 6 at 1:00 PM in the Carrier Dome and the Orangemen won big. It was as if Notre Dame was not even there. W (38-12). Syracuse gave ND a licking even worse than the score SU was great on both sides of the ball. Notre Dame stunk the house out.

My aging brain still remembers James Mungro being the star of the game. But, every time I look it up, I find that it was Walter Reyes and not James Mungro. Mungro was a great back who joined the NFL after the SU 2001 season. He toted a 6 yds per carry average. Reyes broke a lot of Mungro's records at Syracuse.

Walter Reyes was a one-man wrecking crew in the ND game. Tyrone Willingham was in his second season as Irish coach. After a 10-3 2002 season the year before, Irish fans were looking for good stuff from Willingham.

With SU 5-6 and ND 5-6, ND fans thought it would be a 6-6 season for the Irish. Irish fans had never seen Walter Reyes with no holds barred. The post-game write ups of the game were highly complementary to Syracuse and they reported exactly what Gerry, Dennis, and I saw from our comfortable seats in the dome.

In what seemed to be a blink of an eye, it was one, two, three, four, and then five touchdowns by Reyes and in between he got a lot of yardage. ND did not know what hit them. It was the best game I had ever seen SU play and I saw quite a few.

Check out this write-up which places the 2003 SU-ND game #3 in the top 5 all-time SU games:

> "You could say Syracuse beat Notre Dame on Dec. 6, 2003 at the Carrier Dome, but it would be more accurate to say running back Walter Reyes beat Notre Dame that day.
>
> Reyes had one of the most productive days ever by an SU player. In addition to his five touchdowns, he ran for 189 yards on 19 carries. Reyes tied Floyd Little (vs. Kansas, 1964) for

second place on the SU single-game rushing touchdown and points scored lists. His touchdown total and 30 points were both Carrier Dome records.

Reyes became Syracuse's single-season and career leader in rushing touchdowns, both records he still owns to this day."

2004 Paul Pasqualoni Coach # 25

The 2004 Syracuse Orangemen football team competed in their one hundred-fifteenth season of intercollegiate football. They were led by Paul Pasqualoni, a fine coach, and one of the best ever at SU, in his fourteenth and last season as head coach of the Syracuse Orange. This year was almost an exact duplicate of the prior year's record, 6-6-0. They were 4-2 in the Big East. Pasqualoni picked Julian Pollard, Walter Reyes, Matt Tarullo, to be the team captains for 2004. Syracuse was not selected for a bowl game in 2004.

It was expected there would be controversy after this season if the plusses were not more than the minuses. There were many SU fans and alumni headhunters looking for Pasqualoni's scalp on a platter after three non-winning seasons in a row. The Orange had an even record of 6-6-0 again this year but it was not enough and there would be no fourth chance to make amends.

Dick Macpherson and Paul Pasqualoni were such great coaches they had given SU fans a taste of what it was to win consistently. It felt good. Just like when Ben Schwartzwalder had a few bad years at the end, there was little patience. When Pasqualoni had a few non-winning years, SU seemed to think that that could go "poof" and hire anybody off the street to take this great coach's place. Let's see how that works out as, after this season, for this book, we have just thirteen more seasons to go for this version of this book.

I regret to tell you fine readers that this is not the worst news for the year. This was the first season in which Syracuse used the nickname of Orange. For some this is moot but for others, Orangemen was not something to be given up because Nike thought it was a good idea.

As most know, previously, Syracuse had respectively used "Orangemen" for men's sports, including football, and "Orangewomen" for women's sports. The equality movement in men and women's sports is intense, and it was determined by the "experts that a name without the sex of the participant in the name would be a better name than one with about a hundred-year tradition. To each his or her own. I express no opinion on that matter.

I do however have a spur on my spine for the NCAA, a group of better than thou-ers who come in post facto and ruin football seasons for clean living university teams such a Syracuse.

The rich beyond all expectations NCAA hounds universities for years to admit wrongdoings so they can be punished and can lose wins to the NCAA. These are wins that no team could take from them on the field.

To me the NCAA is disgusting and as Jesus once said, "Let he without sin throw the first stone." There is no alternate universe NCAA to check on whether this world's NCAA itself is clean or dirty. It is just we mere mortals who know that they are as clean as dirt.

There are many honest pundits who believe the NCAA should be casting no first stones. SU losing games is bull. You and I both know it. I would like to see officials from universities across the country man-up and figure out another way—with or without the blowhards from the NCAA. This is the seventh "Great Moments" book that I have written to highlight great football universities. The NCAA is a poor player in each of these books because they hurt players, universities and fans and they are cocky, conceited, and they walk like they own the world.

From my experience in writing about twenty-four books about football programs in seven universities, they are not worthy of support from anybody, especially, John Q. Public. I will not print their vacated stats in my books from this moment on. Moreover, I will go back to see if I have done so in the past and in due time, I will fix those books. Then, you can look here instead of the NCAA to get the real unabated records of great university teams.

Regardless of what the people think, in 2015, Syracuse vacated the six wins from this season among others from the 2005 and 2006 seasons following an eight-year NCAA investigation, as the NCAA found that some football players who committed academic fraud participated in the wins.

The irony of the NCAA "vacating" the four Big East and Six in total wins for the year, they did not vacate the losses. This demonstrates the absurdity. In their investigations, the NCAA did not check to see if the bad students were sick or on the bench in any of those losses or wins. Perhaps it was their poor play that caused the loss. In a full investigation, if a bad grade student screwed up a game, and should not have been playing, why should a win not be recorded or whatever the opposite of vacate means.

The games from Paul Pasqualoni's last season

On Sept 5 at # 25 Purdue's Ross–Ade Stadium in West Lafayette, IN, Syracuse took a KO to the chin in a huge shutout L (0–51) before 56,827. On Sept 11, at Buffalo in UB Stadium, Amherst, NY, SU beat the Bengals W (37–17) before 29,013. In week 3 of the 2004 season, on Sept 18 in the home opener against Cincinnati in the Carrier Dome, on the campus of Syracuse University in Syracuse, NY before 32, 893 fans, the Orangemen beat the Bearcats W (19-7) for the team's second win loss of the year. On Sept 25 at No. 12 Virginia's Scott Stadium in Charlottesville, VA, Syracuse lost to the Wahoos L (0–31) before 59,699. Then to begin October, on Oct 2, at home, SU defeated Rutgers W (41–31)

On Oct 9 at home, in a close match against # 8 Florida State, the Seminoles defeated the Orange L (13–17) before 40,359. On Oct 21 at # 15 West Virginia Mountaineer Field in Morgantown, WV, SU lost to the Mountaineers L (6–27) before 52,909. On October 30 at home, Syracuse defeated Connecticut W (42–30) before 34,545. On Nov 6 at home for the Pittsburgh rivalry game, Syracuse beat the Panthers W (38–31) before 37,211.

On Nov 13 at Temple in a game played at the new Lincoln Financial Field in Philadelphia, Syracuse did not have enough to beat the supercharged Owls L (24–34) before 15,564. On Nov 27, SU beat #17 Boston College at Alumni Stadium in Chestnut Hill, MA W (43–17) before 44,500.

2004 Champs Sports Bowl

On December 21, 2004, with a 6-6-0 record SU qualified minimally for a bowl bid and agreed to play a tough Georgia tech team in the Champs Sports Bowl. The venue was the Citrus Bowl Stadium in Orlando, FL. The Champs Sports Bowl found Georgia Tech dominating Syracuse L (14–51) before 28,237.

Georgia Tech 51, Syracuse 14
December 21, 2004
Orlando, Florida

All Syracuse fans wanted a win. They were very pleased that a 6-5 record got the team to display its real prowess in a national bowl game Pasqualoni got them to the game, but everybody wanted a win or a good showing to feel good about the great coach and some vindication for the season. It was not coming in this game.

The Syracuse football team lost, 51-14, to Georgia Tech on Tuesday, December 21, in the Champs Sports Bowl at Florida Citrus Bowl Stadium in Orlando, Fla. Jared Jones finishes his career with 102 receptions and 1,189 yards, becoming the seventh SU receiver to tally over 100 receptions and 1000 yards.

Jones' 102 receptions ties him with Art Monk for sixth all-time at SU. Sophomore quarterback Perry Patterson threw for 219 yards on 21-of-34 passing with one touchdown and one interception.

Patterson also rushed for a score. Standout Senior tailback Walter Reyes left the game in the first half after aggravating a shoulder injury.

Georgia Tech quarterback Reggie Ball finished the game 12-of-19 for 207 yards, two touchdowns and one interception. Ball also ran for 38 yards and a touchdown. Running back P.J. Daniels finished with

119 yards on 17 carries and two touchdowns. Wide receiver Calvin Johnson had two catches for 61 yards and a touchdown and rushed twice for 12 yards and one touchdown. The stats all favored the Yellow Jackets.

The Yellow Jackets scored four unanswered touchdowns in the first half, including three in a span of 3:09. The Orange went three and out on its ensuing possession. Georgia Tech tacked on two touchdowns in the second half on runs by Ball and Daniels, to give the Yellow Jackets an insurmountable 49-6 lead. In this game the Orange were outmatched.

Patterson hooked up with Gregory at the 11:22 mark of the fourth quarter for a 25-yard touchdown. SU converted the two-point attempt on a pass from Rhodes to tight end Brandon Darlington, his first career reception. Georgia Tech recorded a safety late in the fourth quarter to make the final score 51-14. It was a less than proud moment in Syracuse football but not one that Pasqualoni should have been fired for—just my opinion.

Seattle Times on Pasqualoni Firing

Notebook: Syracuse fires coach Pasqualoni
Originally published December 30, 2004 at 12:00 am Updated December 29, 2004 at 8:52 pm
By The Associated Press

> SYRACUSE, N.Y. — Syracuse fired football coach Paul Pasqualoni yesterday, eight days after a 37-point loss in a bowl game — and less than a month after giving him a vote of confidence.
>
> "Sometimes you just know you need to make a change," athletic director Daryl Gross said. "He's had a long tenure here. He served the student-athletes well. He is a tremendous man. The things he's done here, you can marvel at.
>
> "I just think it's time to go in a different direction. We're going into the heart of the recruiting season right now. We needed to act one way or another."

Pasqualoni, who was unavailable for comment, departs after 14 years with a 107-59-1 record and a 6-3 mark in bowl games. He is the second-winningest coach in school history, behind Ben Schwartzwalder, who had 153 victories.

But the Orange struggled to break even after going 10-3 and finishing ranked No. 14 in 2001. They were 4-8 in 2002, Pasqualoni's only losing season, and 6-6 the last two years.

Gross, a former assistant at USC who was hired two weeks ago to replace the retiring Jake Crouthamel, said a search for Pasqualoni's replacement will begin immediately.

Pasqualoni, who had one year left on his contract, becomes the 11th Division I coach to be fired this year. His firing came after chancellor Nancy Cantor announced Dec. 6 that he would return for his 15th season. But Gross was hired 11 days later, and the Orange's 51-14 loss to Georgia Tech in the Champs Sports Bowl helped seal Pasqualoni's fate.

Greg Robinson Replaces Pasqualoni at Syracuse
By the Daily Orange, Student Newspaper

Just weeks after coming to Syracuse University, new Director of Athletics Daryl Gross decided it was time for a 'different direction' for the SU football program – one without head coach Paul Pasqualoni. [IMHO—as a long-time SU fan, who saw SU recover over the years, this was a big mistake]

And 13 days after Pasqualoni's Dec. 29 dismissal, Gross introduced his replacement: Greg Robinson, the former co-defensive coordinator of the Texas Longhorns. Despite Coach P's many contributions throughout the years, [according to the AD and the students] it was a necessary move for the new AD.

Pasqualoni stands out as one of the best coaches in SU football history. In 14 years as head coach, he boasts 11 straight winning seasons, nine bowl games and four Big East conference titles.

That being said, recent history proved Pasqualoni was not the best person to be leading the program.

SU had not had a winning football season since 2002 and only appeared in one bowl game, which the Orange lost to Georgia Tech, 51-14, on Dec. 21. In the last few years, Pasqualoni also lost control of some of the recruiting elements necessary to build a winning team. While the blame doesn't lie solely on Pasqualoni, one of the realities of college sports is that if you can't produce the goods, you may be replaced. The change to Robinson may be just what the football program needs to get out of its slump.

With a tight search schedule and the coaching options rapidly evaporating, Gross came up with a great candidate to take over the program. Robinson is an experienced coach who has proven himself at both the collegiate and professional level. He coached in the NFL for 14 years and earned two SU per Bowl rings as the Denver Broncos' defensive coordinator. He's starting off with a clean slate and has the potential to do some great things with the football program.

While it may be difficult for Robinson to come in and immediately produce a winning team, it is important for him to strive to meet former AD Jake Crouthamel's criteria for success.

'The university's expectations of its football program are at a minimum: 1) finishing in the top three of the Big East; 2) finishing among the Top 25 annually; 3) frequent bowl participation; and 4) a high graduation rate,' Crouthamel said October 2002.

It is unfortunate that Pasqualoni is leaving the university at a low point in his career instead of a high one. He had to be replaced, though, and Greg Robinson should prove to be an excellent fit.

After we review the Robinson years, I will make some additional comments in Chapter 20.

General George S. Patton once said that "when everybody is thinking the same thing, somebody is not thinking. Paul Pasqualoni still has not been replaced at Syracuse, regardless of the consensus thinking that suggested he be fired.

Chapter 16 Coach Greg Robinson From 2005 to 2008

Coach Greg Robinson #26

Year	Coach	Record	Conf
2005	Greg Robinson	1-10-0	Big East (0-7)
2006	Greg Robinson	4-8-0	Big East (1-5)
2007	Greg Robinson	2-10-0	Big East (1-6)
2008	Greg Robinson	3-9-0	Big East (1-6)

Coach Robinson with Team

Famous Coaches (From the Past) by SWC75.

AD Gross had come from USC and his new man, on advice of Pete Carroll, was Greg Robinson, a handsome, silver-haired man with a ready smile and a confident gaze. He'd had a thirty-year career with several top college programs and NFL teams, including two Super Bowl rings earned as defensive coordinator of the Denver Broncos. His most recent job was with the Texas Longhorns who had re-emerged as a national power and would win the national championship with players Robinson coached during Greg's first year in Syracuse. The A-Team had arrived?

Except it turned out to be the " " team as we found out why Robinson had been an assistant for 30 years. His teams were out of shape. The game plans didn't seem to make much sense. New to the East, he didn't seem to know where to recruit. His first team went from 6-6 the previous year to 1-10, our worst record since 1892. His four-year record of 10-37 was the worst such stretch in SU history. That was it for "G-Rob". At least he lowered the bar for his successors. If Coach P had come after G-Rob, he'd be everyone's hero now. Maybe he still should be?

2005 Greg Robinson Coach # 26
*NCAA sanctions vacated SU's one season win

The 2005 Syracuse Orange football team competed in their one hundred-sixteenth season of intercollegiate football. They were led by Greg Robinson in his first of four seasons as head coach of the Syracuse Orange. After giving up on Coach Pasqualoni, the new consensus pick coach produced the worst football record in Syracuse history--1-10; 0-7 in the Big East. Syracuse was not selected for a bowl game in 2005.

In week 1 of the 2005 season, on Sept 4 in the home opener against West Virginia in the Carrier Dome, on the campus of Syracuse University in Syracuse, NY before 45,418 fans, the Orangemen lost in a close match to the eventual Big East Champion, Mountaineers L (7-15). On September 10 at home SU won its only game of the season against Buffalo W (31–0) before. The rest of the season, shown below in tabular form, were all losses

Date	Vs. /venue	Score	Attendance
Sept 17	home, #25 Virginia,	L (24-27,	40,027
Oct 1	away #6 Florida State	L (14–38)	83,717
Oct 7	away Connecticut	L (7–26)	40,000
Oct 15	home Rutgers	L (9-31)	39,022
Oct 22	away Pittsburgh	L (17–34)	33,059
Oct 29	home Cincinnati	L (16–22)	42,457
Nov 12	home South Florida	L (0–27)	40,144
Nov 19	away #6 Notre Dame	L (10–34)	80,795
Nov 26	away #17 Louisville	L (7–4)	37,896

2006 Greg Robinson Coach # 26
*NCAA sanctions vacated SU's four season wins

The 2006 Syracuse Orange football team competed in their one hundred-seventeenth season of intercollegiate football. They were led by Greg Robinson in his second of four seasons as head coach of the Syracuse Orange. This would be Coach Robinson's best record year at Syracuse (4-8), 1-5 in the Big East. Syracuse was not selected for a bowl game in 2006.

In week 1 of the 2005 season, on Sept 2 at Wake Forest's Groves Stadium, Winston-Salem, North Carolina the Orange lost to the Demon Deacons L (10–20) before 34,121. On Sept 9 in the home opener against Iowa in the Carrier Dome, on the campus of Syracuse University in Syracuse, NY before 37,199 fans, the Orange lost in a close match to the Hawkeyes L (13-20).

On Sept 16 at Illinois Memorial Stadium in Champaign, Illinois, the Orange beat the Fighting Illini W (31–21) before 40,657. Then, on Sept 23 at home against Miami (OH), SU won W (34–14) before 35,274. On Sept 30 at home, in the Carrier Dome, the Orange defeated the Cowboys W 40–34 in double OT.

On Oct 7, at home v Pittsburgh, SU lost to the Panthers L (11-21) before 41,870. Then, on Oct at #5 West Virginia's Mountaineer Field in Morgantown, West Virginia, the Mountaineers beat the Orange, L (17–41) before 60,051. On Oct 21 at home, #6 Louisville beat the Orange L (13–28) before 35,708. At Cincinnati's Nippert Stadium in Cincinnati. OH. On Oct 28, the Bearcats outscored the Orange L (3–17) before 20,146. Then, on November 11 at South Florida's Raymond James Stadium in Tampa, Florida, SU lost another L (10–27) before 43,413.

On Nov 18 at home, Syracuse defeated Connecticut in the Carrier Dome W (20-14) before 35,079. In the season closer, SU lost to #15 Rutgers, on Nov 25, at Rutgers Stadium in Piscataway, New Jersey L (7–38) before 43,791.

2007 Greg Robinson Coach # 26
*No NCAA sanctions or vacated wins this year

The 2007 Syracuse Orange football team competed in their one hundred-eighteenth season of intercollegiate football. They were led by Greg Robinson in his third of four seasons as head coach of the Syracuse Orange. This Orange record this year was 2-10. 1-6 in the Big East. Syracuse was not selected for a bowl game in 2007.

On Aug 31 in the home and season opener against Washington, at home in the Carrier Dome, on the campus of Syracuse University in Syracuse, NY before 40,329 fans, the Orange were overpowered the Huskies, L (42-12) On Sept 8 t Iowa's Kinnick Stadium in Iowa City, Iowa , the Orange were beaten by the Hawkeyes in a shutout L (0-35) before 70,585. On Sept 15 at home against Illinois in the Carrier Dome Syracuse lost their third in a row, L (20-41) before 34,188. At Louisville's Papa John's Cardinal Stadium in Louisville, Kentucky, on Sept 22, the Orange defeated the Cardinals by three points for their first win of the year before 40,922.

Paring against Miami (OH)* on Sept 29, at Yager Stadium in Oxford, Ohio, the Orange were defeated by the RedHawks L (17–14) before 16,800 in a very close game. On Oct 6, at home, #13 West Virginia came to the Carrier Dome meaning business and they won the game in a blowout L (55–14) against the Orange before 35,345. On Oct 13, and increasingly powerful Rutgers squad defeated the Orange at home at the Dome L (38-14) before 36,226. In another Carrier Dome matchup, Syracuse beat Buffalo on Oct 20 W (20–12) before 30,897. It was the last SU win of 2007.

On Nov 3 at Pittsburgh Heinz Field in Pittsburgh, Pennsylvania, the Panthers gained a close win from the Orange L (17-20) before 31,374. On Nov 10 at home the Orange lost to the Bulls of South Florida L (41–10) before 38,039. At #25 Connecticut, a week later on Nov 17, in a game played at Connecticut Rentschler Field in East Hartford, the Huskies defeated the Orange L (30–7) before 40,000. In the season finale on Nov 24, #24 Cincinnati overpowered the Orange L (52-31) before 30,040

You had to go way back past Paul Pasqualoni and Dick MacPherson to find opponents kicking around the Orangemen as they did in the Robinson years. Pasqualoni got three years with less than normal but not dismal records after proving himself while Robinson got a fourth season without showing any promise. What happened to the AD who forced Pasqualoni out? I bet I know!

In 2015, his proper fate caught up to Daryl Gross whose first move was to fire Paul Pasqualoni. Gross was fired but should have been ousted long before 2015. As you recall my comments about the firing of 14-year head coach Paul Pasqualoni, when Gross, the know-it-all exchanged a great grizzled veteran for flashy Greg Robinson, who arrived with a West Coast offense and a Southern California pedigree. Widely applauded at the time, the switch turned out to be a flop, with the football program bottoming out under Robinson and continuing to push toward average.

Folks, I do not know Greg Robinson. He may be an OK coach, who just has not shown it yet, though he had 30 years' experience when he arrived at Syracuse. We have one more year of Robinson before we move on to the next SU coach who was somewhat better. But, when I asked the question about Greg Gross and what happened to him. I could not help sharing his fate with SU fans though his comeuppance did not come for another seven or so years. Meanwhile almost everybody in football has been willing to get Pasqualoni on their coaching staff.

2008 Greg Robinson Coach # 26
*No NCAA sanctions or vacated wins this year

The 2008 Syracuse Orange football team competed in their one hundred-nineteenth season of intercollegiate football. They were led by Greg Robinson in his third of four seasons as head coach of the Syracuse Orange. This Orange record this year was 3-9. 1-6 in the Big East. Syracuse was not selected for a bowl game in 2008.

It was August 30 at Northwestern's Ryan Field in Evanston, IL that the Orange played its season opener and defeated the Wildcats L (10-30) before 20,015. Then the next week on Sept 6 in the home opener against Akron in the Carrier Dome, on the campus of Syracuse University in Syracuse, NY before 31,808, the Orange were beaten by the Zips L (28-42). On Sept 13, after a long hiatus,

#17 Penn State, still led by Joe Paterno came into the Carrier Dome and were relentless in defeating the Orange L (13-55) before 45,745. On Sept 20 at home, SU got a close win against Northeastern W (30-21) before 34,694

On Sept 27, SU lost to long-time rival Pittsburgh at home L (24-34) before 27,549. On Oct 11, at West Virginia Mountaineer Field in Morgantown, WV in the Battle for the Schwartzwalder Trophy, SU left the trophy behind L (6-17) before 58,133. On Oct 18 at #19 South Florida at Raymond James Stadium in Tampa, FL, the Orange went town easy L (13-45) before 51,384

Back at home on Nov 1 in the Carrier Dome, the Orange managed to win a nice game against Louisville W (28-21) before 32,917. Rutgers still was not taking "no" for an answer as they again defeated the Orange, this time it was on Nov 8 at Rutgers Stadium in Piscataway, NJ L (17-35) before 42,172.

On Nov 15 at home against Connecticut, the Orange lost the game against the RedHawks, L (14-39) before 28,081. Somehow SU had ND's number and the scored a big win against the Charlie Weis version of The Fighting Irish on Nov 22 at Notre Dame Stadium, South Bend, IN W (24-23) before 80,795. Stranger things have happened but the same team that beat Notre Dame in an away game could not do the same against the team coached by Brian Kelly at Cincinnati on Nov 29 at # 16 Cincinnati's Nippert Stadium in Cincinnati, OH. The Orange lost to the next ND Coach's team, the Bearcats, L (10-30) before 34,603

Coach Greg Out at Syracuse

Football coaches are a dime a dozen but if you pay a dime, chances are you get no takers and if you get a taker for the dime a dozen price, you get no real results. Syracuse University's embattled AD, who I have not liked from the moment he fired Paul Pasqualoni bowed to pressure and fired a coach whose full win production in four years as head coach of just ten games would not be enough in some years to finish in the top ten rankings of national teams. Considering that Robinson had years of 1, 4, 2, and 3 wins, his record warranted the axe after year one.

Syracuse University head football coach Greg Robinson was fired on a Sunday in November 2008, by director of athletics Daryl Gross, with two weeks left in the season. This seemed to end a turbulent era that began with great optimism only to deteriorate into misery, hopelessness and the worst four-year run in the program's 119 years of competition. Just like it is not good to fool Mother Nature, it is not good to mess with a team already mentored by a great coach, aka- Paul Pasqualoni.

Some say Robinson's record at Syracuse is 9-36 overall and 3-24 in the Big East, but I have found he achieved ten wins as described above. The Orange at this point in time in 2008 when this article was put together were 2-8 and 1-5 after losing to Connecticut 39-14 on Saturday night at the Carrier Dome.

At the time, the Orange had remaining games against Notre Dame on Saturday, which they won, and Cincinnati on November 29, which they lost. I think I could have coached better than Robinson simply by bringing Coach Paul back. Robinson, who had a year remaining on his contract earned $1.1 million per season. At a $100K per game, he was expected to coach the Orange for the last two games, and he did.

Chapter 17 Coach Doug Marrone From 2009 to 2012

Coach Doug Marrone # 27

Year	Coach	Record	Conf
2009	Doug Marrone	4-8	Big East (1-6)
2010	Doug Marrone	8-5	Big East (4-3)
2011	Doug Marrone	5-7	Big East (1-6)
2012	Doug Marrone	8-5	Big East (5-2)

Coach Doug Marrone Happy about the prospects of playing in the ACC

Famous Coaches (From the Past) by SWC75.

Doug Marrone came after G-Rob, another career assistant but one who had played here and had notebooks full of his plans for bringing the program back from the abyss. He immediately made it more competitive, even if he won only one more game than G-Rob's last year. The next year he won four league road games, thanks to Scott Shafer's excellent defense. Then came a mysterious collapse after a 5-2 start in 2011, followed by a second bowl win in three years, followed by a mysterious, (to us, anyway), exit to be replaced by Shafer.

Our thank you's to ESPN for permission to reprint their take on Doug Marrone's coming to Syracuse when Greg Robinson was fired.

Syracuse hires Doug Marrone as football coach
Updated: December 12, 2008, 6:01 PM ET
Associated Press

SYRACUSE, N.Y. -- Greg Robinson learned to bleed Orange. New Syracuse coach Doug Marrone already has that part down "When I went into coaching, I always prepared myself for this," the Bronx-born Marrone said Friday after being hired to replace Robinson as football coach. "This has been the job I have always wanted."

The offensive coordinator for the New Orleans Saints since 2006, Marrone is returning to the school where he played to try to resurrect a program that hasn't had a winning season since 2001. Robinson was fired in November after going 10-37 in four seasons.

"Not a lot of times in your life can you actually accomplish your dream," said Marrone, a three-year letterman at Syracuse under former coach Dick MacPherson in the mid-1980s. "Today is the greatest day of my life. This is my school and these are my people. You're going to be proud, and we're going to win football games."

Terms of Marrone's contract were not revealed. Robinson had one year left on a deal that paid $1.1 million per season.

Money wasn't on Marrone's mind as he contemplated working two jobs for a while.

"We need everyone to believe," he said. "We need the alumni, we need the fans. I love the people here."

The 44-year-old Marrone was selected by a football search committee that included former Syracuse players Tim Green, Art Monk, Don McPherson and Floyd Little, as well as MacPherson.

Athletic director Daryl Gross interviewed East Carolina coach Skip Holtz earlier in the week, but Holtz issued a statement through his athletic department on Thursday that he had withdrawn his name from consideration.

"We feel at the end of the day we got the best guy," Gross said. "He brings hope to our football program, brings hope to our student-athletes. He's got a group of kids that are just so hungry to win. It's time to rally around. He's going to be here a long time."

Like Robinson, this will be Marrone's first stint as a head coach. It doesn't figure to be a cakewalk. Robinson's tenure featured the only two 10-loss seasons in school history, too many of them by lopsided scores.

The team's poor performance under Robinson, who had three offensive coordinators in his four seasons, hurt the school financially. In 21 homes games over his first three seasons, more than 260,000 seats were not sold, average attendance fell to a 21-year low in 2007, and attendance numbers again were abysmal in 2008.

"For me to sit here and say that Doug Marrone is the right guy is what I would love to say, but I can't say that because I don't know at this point if Doug is the right guy for Syracuse football," said Green, a close friend of Marrone's in college. "

This is a daunting task that he's going to face. It's one of the most difficult things in the world of sports, to take a college football program that's down and resurrect it."

Marrone joins basketball coach Jim Boeheim and lacrosse coach John Desko as Syracuse alumni who returned to work at their alma mater. Of course, Boeheim and Desko have won national championships.

"We are not in a rebuilding process. We are in the process of rejuvenating this program," Marrone said as several players listened intently. "I don't have any options. I cannot fail. I cannot fail. My option is only to win, and that's what I'm going to do."

Marrone began his coaching career as an assistant at Cortland State, just south of Syracuse, and coached at Coast Guard, Northeastern, Georgia Tech, Georgia and Tennessee. He was a New York Jets assistant for three years before joining the Saints.

Marrone played for the Miami Dolphins in 1987 and the Saints in 1989, and was with the London Monarchs of the World league in 1991.

Under Marrone's guidance, the Saints have become one of the NFL's most explosive and consistent offenses. New Orleans set an NFL record with 440 completions in 2007 and also set team highs for passing first downs (222), attempts (652), touchdown passes (28) and completion percentage (67.5), also allowing the fewest sacks in the league with 16.

That Marrone has been out of the college ranks for several years doesn't figure to inhibit him at Syracuse.

"I knew someone would say, 'He doesn't have the recruiting ties.' Well, I kept those recruiting ties," said Marrone, whose interview presentation included three binders that he assembled and tailored specifically for the Syracuse job. "I know what we need to win. I've been setting this plan for a long time."

Marrone said he would evaluate the current coaching staff before naming his assistants. Dan Conley, a star at Syracuse for Paul Pasqualoni in the 1990s, just completed his first season as linebacker's coach and would appear to be a perfect fit for the new regime.

Copyright 2008 by The Associated Press. This story is from ESPN.com's automated news wire. Wire index

This piece was written so succinctly, and it said all I wanted to say that I decided to use this piece and thank ESPN for their kindness, rather than taking the raw facts from other pieces on the Internet and cobbling my own story about Marrone. So, far, from what I have read, I like Marrone. How about you?

2009 Doug Marrone Coach # 27

The 2009 Syracuse Orange football team competed in their one hundred-twentieth season of intercollegiate football. They were led by Doug Marrone in his first of four seasons as head coach of the Syracuse Orange. The Orange record this year was 4-8, And 1-6 in the Big East. Syracuse was not selected for a bowl game in 2009.

On Sept 5 SU played its home and season opener against Minnesota in the Carrier Dome, on the campus of Syracuse University in Syracuse, NY before 48,617. The Orange were beaten by the Golden Gophers in OT L (20-23) on Sept 12 at #5 Penn State's Beaver Stadium in State College, PA, the Orange lost in a tough battle L (7–28) before a huge crowd of 106,387.

On Sept 19 at home, SU defeated a tough Northwestern squad at the Carrier Dome W (37-34) before 40,251. Then, on Sept 26, at home the Orange defeated Maine at the Carrier Dome by the score of W (41–24) before 35,632

On Oct 3 at home, South Florida was the visiting team and they played well enough to beat the home team SU Orange L (20-34) before 40,147. On Oct 10 at home SU lost again to West Virginia at the Carrier Dome L (13–34) before 40,144. Akron came into the Dome on Oct 24 and they were ready for a win but SU held them back and got one for the Orange W (28–14) before 36,991. On Oct 31, at home a tough #7 Cincinnati team, coached by ND's Brian Kelly beat the Orange in a fair fight L (7-28).

On Nov 7, SU played rival #14 Pittsburgh M at Heinz Field in Pittsburgh, PA and the Orange was beaten by the Panthers L (10–37). At Louisville's Papa John's Cardinal Stadium in Louisville, KY on Nov 14, the Cardinals won again against the Orange L (9–10) before 33,223. Then on Nov 21 at home against Rutgers in the Carrier Dome, Syracuse defeated the Scarlet Knights W (31–13) before 36,759. In the last game of the year, on Nov 28 against

Connecticut at its Rentschler Field in East Hartford, CONN, the Orange lost its eighth game of the season. L (31–56) before 40,000.

2010 Doug Marrone Coach # 27

The 2010 Syracuse Orange football team competed in their one hundred-twenty-first season of intercollegiate football. They were led by Doug Marrone in his second of four seasons as head coach of the Syracuse Orange. The Orange record this year was 8-5, their best in ten years. The team was 4-3 in the Big East. Syracuse was also selected for a bowl game in 2010. For the first time since Paul Pasqualoni was fired following the 2004 season, the Orange won enough games to become bowl eligible. Syracuse played Kansas State in the Inaugural Pinstripe Bowl at Yankee Stadium where they won 36–34 to finish the season 8–5, 4–3 in Big East. There was reason for hope at the Big Orange.

On Sept 4 at Akron in the InfoCision Stadium, Akron, Ohio, Syracuse came home with the win W (29–3) before 15,969. On Sept 11 at Washington Husky Stadium Seattle, WA, SU lost to the Huskies L (20–41) before 62,418. On Sept 18 SU played its home opener against Maine in the Carrier Dome, on the campus of Syracuse University in Syracuse, NY before 37,758. The Orange beaten by the Black Bears W (38-14). On Sept 25 at home, SU defeated Colgate W (42-7) Then, on Oct 9 at South Florida's Raymond James Stadium in Tampa, the Orange defeated the Bulls W (13–9) before 41,917.

In the yearly rivalry, on Oct 16 at home, the Orange lost to the Panthers of Pittsburgh[†] in the Carrier Dome before 40,168. On Oct 23, at #19 West Virginia at Mountaineer Field in Morgantown, WV, for the Ben Schwartzwalder Trophy, the Orange prevailed W (19–14) before 58,122. On Oct 30 at Cincinnati's Nippert Stadium, Cincinnati, OH, the Orange triumphed W (31–7) before 32,072. Then, in a tough game against Louisville at the carrier Dome, the Orange were barely defeated by the Cardinals L (20–28) before 40,735.

On Nov 13 at Rutgers in Rutgers Stadium, Piscataway, New Jersey the Orange tot by the Scarlet Knights in a close match W (13–10) before 49,911. On Nov 20, at home, Syracuse lost to Connecticut, L (6–23) before 41,635. In the final matchup of the season at home, it was rival Boston College defeating the Orange in the Carrier Dome L (7–16) before 42,191.

The Inaugural Pinstripe Bowl

On Dec 30, one day before New Year's Eve, Syracuse was matched with Kansas State for the Pinstripe Bowl at Yankee Stadium in The Bronx, New York. Syracuse won this close game W (36–34) before a cold crowd of 38,274 in 32-degree weather.

A view of play between the Kansas State Wildcats and the Syracuse Orange during the Pinstripe Bowl at Yankee Stadium. (Dec. 30, 2010) Photo Credit: Getty Images

Text taken from The San Diego Union-Tribune

> The first Pinstripe Bowl was a shootout for sure. Delone Carter ran for 198 yards and two touchdowns, Marcus Sales caught three long TD passes and Syracuse gained some yardage from a celebration penalty on Kansas State to beat the Wildcats 36-34 on Dec 30, 2010, at Yankee Stadium.
>
> Adrian Hilburn escaped a tackle and raced to a 30-yard touchdown catch with 1:13 remaining to pull Kansas State

within two. Hilburn saluted the crowd behind the visitor's dugout and was flagged 15 yards for unsportsmanlike conduct, which pushed the 2-point conversion attempt back to the 17-yard line. Big penalty.

Carson Coffman overthrew Aubrey Quarles in the end zone, and when Kansas State (7-6) couldn't come up with the onside kick, Syracuse (8-5) only had to take a knee to win a bowl game for the first time since 2001.

Daniel Thomas ran for three touchdowns for Kansas State, which was making its first bowl appearance since 2006.

KS's Coffman finished 17 for 23 for 228 yards and two touchdowns. Thomas was held to 90 yards on 22 carries by a defense that was geared to stopping him.

SU's Ryan Nassib passed for 239 yards and hooked up with Sales on touchdowns of 52, 36 and 44 yards.

It was Big East against the Big 12 in the first bowl game in New York since the Gotham Bowl matched Nebraska and Miami at the original Yankee Stadium in 1962. The weather was pretty much as expected: cold. But temperatures in the low 30s were more than tolerable for the crowd of 38,274.

2011 Doug Marrone Coach # 27

The 2011 Syracuse Orange football team competed in their one hundred-twenty-second season of intercollegiate football. They were led by Doug Marrone in his third of four seasons as head coach of the Syracuse Orange. The Orange had a losing record this year at 5-7, their best in ten years. The team was 1-6 in Big East play to finish in a tie for seventh place. Syracuse was not selected for a bowl game in 2011.

On Sept 1 at home, Syracuse defeated Wake Forest W (36-29) in OT in its home and season opener in the Carrier Dome, on the campus of Syracuse University in Syracuse, NY before 40,833. On Sept 10 at home, Syracuse defeated Rhode Island W (21-14). On Sept 17 at

USC in a game played at the Los Angeles Memorial Coliseum in Los Angeles, the Trojans defeated the Orange L (17–38) before 65,873. Then, on Sept 24 at home, Syracuse beat Toledo in OT W (33-30) before 39,116. On Oct 1, at home, in double overtime, Syracuse was defeated by Rutgers L (16-19) before 42,152

In a game against Tulane on Oct 8 in the Louisiana Superdome in New Orleans, Syracuse beat the Green Wave in a close match W (W 37–34) before 39,116. Two weeks later on Oct 21, at home Syracuse defeated #11 West Virginia in the Carrier Dome for the Ben Schwartzwalder Trophy W (49–23) before 45,265. Then, on Oct 29 at Louisville's Papa John's Cardinal Stadium in Louisville, the Orange lost to the Cardinals L (10–27) before 44,817

On Nov 5 at Connecticut's Rentschler Field in East Hartford, CT, the Huskies defeated the Orange by a TD L (21–28) before 38,769. At home against South Florida on Nov 11, Syracuse was beaten L (17-37 before 41,582. Then, on Nov 26 at home against Cincinnati, the Bearcats defeated the Orange L (13-30) before 38,159. In the final game of the season against rival Pittsburgh on Dec 3 at 12:00 PM at Heinz Field in Pittsburgh, the Panthers defeated the Orange L (20–33) before 40,058

2012 Doug Marrone Coach # 27

The 2012 Syracuse Orange football team competed in their one hundred-twenty-third season of intercollegiate football. They were led by Doug Marrone in his fourth and last season as head coach of the Syracuse Orange. The Orange had a winning record this year at 8-5, tied for their best in twelve years. The team was 5-2 in Big East play and finished with a share of the Big East Conference championship that was split four ways. They were invited to the Pinstripe Bowl where they defeated long-time rival West Virginia, whom they did not play in the regular season due to the Mountaineers' move to the Big 12 Conference.

The 2012 season also proved to be the final one for Marrone as the Orange head coach. After the conclusion of the season, head coach Doug Marrone was mentioned by several sportswriters as a possible candidate for a head coaching job in the National Football League. On January 6, 2013, Marrone was introduced as the head coach of the Buffalo Bills. Offensive coordinator Nathaniel Hackett departed for Buffalo as well, leaving a number of coaching positions open. On January 9, Syracuse announced the promotion of defensive coordinator Scott Shafer to head coach. Shortly thereafter, George McDonald was announced as the new offensive coordinator, and Chuck Bullough was announced as the new defensive coordinator.

I had a great feeling about Doug Marrone. I don't know why I just did. He moved on to Buffalo though he loved Syracuse. At Buffalo, after two years and bringing the team to 9-7, the owner died and Marrone had a chance to exercise a major contract opt-out if he did not want to stay with the new owners. He took a job as offensive coordinator with Jacksonville, had a great relationship with his head coach and then one day, the Jags fired that coach and promoted Marrone to be the head coach.

In his first year at the helm, Marrone's Jags posted a 10-6 record and were on top of the AFC South. In the Playoffs, they beat Buffalo W (10-3), and Pittsburgh W (45-42), and then lost in the AFC Championship to the Patriots L (20-24). Doug Marrone is destined to be a Parcells, or a Belichick and there will be other great coaches wanting to be a Marrone. That's about it. Too bad Syracuse could not hold onto him.

On offense for 2012, the Orange are returning senior quarterback Ryan Nassib, starting for his third consecutive season. Key offensive players such as Alec Lemon, Marcus Sales, Jerome Smith, and Prince-Tyson Gulley are also returning. On defense, key players returning include Shamarko Thomas, Marquis Spruill, and Deon Goggins.

In 2011, the program lost a number of significant contributors in the 2011 campaign, including tight end Nick Provo and defensive end Chandler Jones, and such losses left a number of questions regarding how a relatively young defense would be able to mature without many experienced players.

In its preseason rankings, College Football News ranked the Orange 57th in the country, and projected that they would go 6-6 in 2012.

Their 2012 schedule is the 42nd-toughest in the nation, according to rankings compiled by statistician Jeff Sagarin. Marrone's last SU record of 8-5 fooled them all. Good for Marrone. Good for SU

2012 Season's games

On Sept 1 at home, Syracuse just barely lost to Northwestern in a shootout L (41-42) in its home and season opener in the Carrier Dome, on the campus of Syracuse University in Syracuse, NY before 37,830 A week later, on Sept 8, expecting a big crowd, SU lost another home game against #2 USC at MetLife Stadium (former Giants Stadium) in East Rutherford, NJ L (28–42) before a Carrier Dome size crowd of 39,507. On Sept 15 at home, SU beat #17 FCS team Stony Brook W (28-17) before 34,512. Then, on Sept 22 at Minnesota's TCF Bank Stadium in Minneapolis, MN, the Orange lost their third game of the year, L (10–17) before 50,805.

On October 5 at home in a game against rival Pittsburgh, SU grabbed the victory in a one-point match W (14-13) before 40,394 Rutgers got its Rutgers Stadium a nice remodeling and a nice sponsor and a new name --High Point Solutions Stadium. The old Rutgers place had significant reconstruction from 2008 to 2009 to increase its capacity to 52,454.

And so, Syracuse got to test drive these new digs on October 12, when they were beaten by #19 Rutgers at High Point Solutions Stadium in Piscataway, NJ L (15–23) before a nice crowd of 48,011. On Oct 19 at home, SU defeated Connecticut W (40-10) before 36,715. Then on Oct 27 at South Florida's Raymond James Stadium in Tampa, SU won another W (37-36) before 38,562.

On Nov 3 at Cincinnati's Nippert Stadium in Cincinnati, OH, the Bearcats beat the Orange L (24–35). At home the next week on Nov 10, SU beat the Louisville Cardinals W (45–26) before 40,312. Then on Nov 17 at Missouri's Faurot Field in Columbia, MO. The Orange won again W (31–27) before 63,045. On Nov 23, SU defeated Temple at Lincoln Financial Field in Philadelphia, PA W (38–20) before 22,317

The 2012 Pinstripe Bowl

On December 29 at 3:15 PM, the Syracuse Orange defeated the West Virginia Mountaineers at Yankee Stadium in the Bronx, NY in the third Pinstripe Bowl W (38–14) before 39,098

After a slow start in snowy Yankee Stadium on Saturday afternoon in the New Era Pinstripe Bowl, Syracuse eventually began to pull away from the West Virginia Mountaineers in the second half as they found their way to a 38-14 lopsided Orange victory. The Orange has now won two of the three Pinstripe Bowls played, earning the Orange the George M. Steinbrenner Trophy on both occasions. In both outings, coach Doug Marrone led the Orange to the victory.

Early-season Heisman candidate Geno Smith had a tough day for the Mountaineers in his college swan song college finale, as he gave up two safeties in the game and threw for just 187 yards. This was the 60th meeting between the former Big East rivals. The Orange extended their slim lead in the series to 33-27 and have won the last three matchups between the two teams.

In the first half, playing defense was a bit tricky in the snow. Syracuse quarterback Ryan Nassib took a hard shot courtesy of Terence Garvin, with Geno Smith of the Mountaineers being clobbered just a few minutes later. Smith's takedown resulted in the first of two safeties on the day for the Orange defense.

Syracuse led just 12-7 at halftime, but when the Orange offense exploded in the second half, it was all over but the counting. They clocked up 23 points in the third quarter, thanks to Nassib and running back Prince-Tyson Gulley. Nassib finished the game a pedestrian 12 of 24 passing for 127 yards and two touchdowns, with one interception. Gulley dominated the West Virginia defense, running for 215 yards on 26 carries, and also catching five balls for 50 yards.

By Bud Poliquin | bpoliquin@syracuse.com
on January 06, 2013 at 8:19 PM, updated January 07, 2013 at 6:46 AM

Syracuse, N.Y. -- If it's true what that anonymous sage once declared -- that even when opportunity knocks, a fella has to be smart enough to get up off his duff and answer the door -- then Doug Marrone is to be commended for having rousted himself over the weekend.

The man is a football coach, and a team in the greatest professional league ever assembled in any sport offered him the chance to sign on at a substantial raise in pay. And so, even if that outfit was the Buffalo Bills and it plays in a city that shivers along the shore of Lake Erie, Marrone wisely chose to accept the promotion.

There are decisions, and then there are easy decisions. And this one made by Marrone -- who once claimed that ramrodding the football program of his alma mater, Syracuse University, was his "dream job" (now, an unfortunate choice of words) -- was a decision that could have been made while sitting in a bubble bath.

On the one hand, there is the NFL with its grand stage, filled with spectacular athletes and decorated coaches, that always has been the brighter football beacon to Marrone. And on the other is the Orange operation that is about to lose so much of the offensive personnel that had made SU so effective -- and, thus, Marrone so attractive -- this past season.

Indeed, with Ryan Nassib, Justin Pugh, Alec Lemon and Marcus Sales departing, and with the heightened challenges of the ACC looming, the timing was right for Marrone to skedaddle along with his stars. As hot a commodity as he could ever hope to be, Doug simply took advantage of his happy situation and has left us while the leaving was good.

There will be, of course, some hard feelings in all of this. And considering the nature of the proceedings that were equal parts clumsy and clandestine, that should not be unexpected. Because both Marrone, who supposedly did not communicate with his Orange assistants, and his boss, Syracuse athletic director Daryl Gross, burrowed deeply into their undergrounds while the rumors spread in the aftermath of the Pinstripe Bowl, neither will be entirely spared of wrath.

That, however, is the way of these matters.
Nobody can logically deny that Marrone, who lasted through four campaigns in our town before finding something more appealing, effected a minor miracle while walking the Syracuse bridge. He did, after all, exhume the Orange program from the dead by transforming a 26-57 graveyard into a 25-25 resurrection that included four wins over Top 25 clubs and two bowl victories.

And people should applaud Gross, who was reluctant to hire Marrone back in late 2009 (preferring, to Doug's simmering dismay, the likes of Skip Holtz and Turner Gill and others), but thereafter pretty much provided Marrone with everything that was within his power to provide.

But for some, no soap. Marrone will be viewed here and there as a thin-skinned turncoat who spent too much time worrying about Carrier Dome attendance, Central New York's timid response to his players' success and a perceived lack of commitment by the university; Gross, meanwhile, will be scorned in certain pockets as the guy who should have put less effort into the branding of his product and more into the appeasing of his head football coach to thus numb his NFL aspirations (assuming, that is, such a task could ever be accomplished).

The better choice, though, may be for everybody to understand that (a) Marrone looked out for No. 1, which is what most folks inevitably do; and (b) that Daryl was in no position to seriously compete with the NFL, which happens to most little fish when big fish swim by.

Simply, we should do that and move on.
The future? Well, since most NFL coaches fail, Doug may find a few miles of hard road over there in Buffalo, where the Bills -- whose choice of Marrone, a Sean Payton disciple, is nothing if not imaginative -- haven't qualified for the playoffs since Doug Flutie got benched against Tennessee 13 years ago.

As for the Orange, because the word out of Buffalo is that Doug will not be raiding the SU staff of more than a body (or two or three), it may have the chance to both maintain some continuity and rescue a recruiting class if Gross opts to shove, oh, Scott Shafer or Nathaniel Hackett into the big chair.

All of which suggests that the words offered on Sunday by the last guy to depart Syracuse for a head-coaching gig in the NFL, make more than just a bit of sense.

"I don't want to call this a blessing for anybody," declared Dick MacPherson, who left us in 1991 for the New England Patriots . . . and, therefore, has walked along this uncertain path, "and I don't want to call it a curse, either."

No, what it is, was a knock at the door. And Doug Marrone answered it. Wise, on his part . . . unsettling on ours.

(Bud Poliquin's columns, "To the Point" observations and "Morning Orange" reports appear virtually every day on syracuse.com. His work can also be regularly found on the pages of The Post-Standard newspaper. Additionally, Poliquin can be heard weekday mornings between 10 a.m.-12 noon on the sports-talk radio show, "Bud & The Manchild," on The Score 1260-AM. Poliquin can be reached at bpoliquin@syracuse.com.)

The legacy of Doug Marrone
By Tyler Greenawalt
January 8, 2013

Although he coached at Syracuse for only four seasons, former head football coach Doug Marrone helped revitalize a fading program.

It was only a matter of time before another team decided it needed Doug Marrone's help. Eight days after leading the

Syracuse football team to its second bowl victory in three years, Marrone accepted the head coaching position at the Buffalo Bills.

"I had said that the Syracuse job was my dream job, and I meant what I said, and having had the opportunity to restore the great tradition of Syracuse football a reality," Marrone said at a Bills press conference Monday. "Today, I'm experiencing another dream come true."

"Doug has restored Syracuse football to its rightful place and we are appreciative of the foundation he has laid on and off the field for the future success of the program." -Syracuse Director of Athletics Dr. Daryl Gross

Regardless of what people think of Marrone's decision to leave the Orange, his four years of service have left a lasting impression on a program seemingly fading out of the spotlight. After a dismal three years of Greg Robinson that ended with a 10-37 record, Marrone was hired to rejuvenate the program.

Before coming to Syracuse on Dec. 8, 2008, Marrone coached on offensive side of the ball for the New York Jets from 2002-2005 and then for the New Orleans Saints from 2006-2008. As the Saints offensive coordinator, Marrone helped create the NFL's number one offense.

But it wasn't just his offensive-style that brought Marrone and Syracuse together; it was Marrone's collegiate connection. A three-year starter on the offensive line for the Orange from 1983-1985, Marrone was already knowledgeable about the SU football program.

"We've hired a guy that is a Syracuse graduate, who bleeds orange, who brings in tremendous, tremendous knowledge of football from his college and especially his pro experience," said SU athletic director Dr. Daryl Gross back in 2008. "He's someone that we can look forward to exciting offenses, seeing a lot of snaps per game. Better than that, he's somebody that brings leadership, who comes from the Bronx. When you talk about New York's College team, he fits the profile perfectly. He will be a tremendous recruiter in the Northeast, who knows the coaches. He's somebody that we believe will win at Syracuse."

Luckily for Syracuse, Marrone did just that in his four seasons. Picking up the pieces from Greg Robinson, Marrone and the Orange had a sub-par 2009 campaign. His 4-8 season was not the kind of start SU fans were hoping for, but Marrone did give them something to cheer about. Many statistical rankings increased significantly- all on the defensive side- most likely due to the hiring of defensive coordinator Scott Shafer in 2009. Shafer, who will reportedly replace Marrone in 2013, instilled a defense that consistently tried to put pressure on the quarterback.

It was not until Marrone's second season that Syracuse saw the switch from a BCS bottom-feeder to a bowl-contender, as the Orange finished with a 7-5 record. Syracuse also played in its first bowl game since 2004 against Kansas State in the New Era Pinstripe Bowl. SU won the game by a score of 36-24, its first bowl victory since 2001.

Two seasons in, and Marrone had already constructed a winning program. 2011 looked just as promising, with Syracuse winning five of its first seven games, including a 49-23 upset of No. 15 West Virginia. However, complacency seemed to set in, as the Orange finished Marrone's third season with a six-game losing streak, finishing with a 5-8 record.

2012 was the complete opposite of 2011 for Marrone and the Orange. Syracuse began the season with a 2-4 record but ended with a 7-5 record and another New Era Pinstripe Bowl berth, this time against former Big East rival West Virginia. Syracuse defeated the Mountaineers 38-14 for Marrone's second bowl victory in three years.

Unfortunately, that's where the story ends for Marrone with the Orange. The Buffalo Bills interviewed Marrone on Jan. 4 and he was hired the next day and signed a contract on Jan. 7.

"Doug has restored Syracuse football to its rightful place and we are appreciative of the foundation he has laid on and off the field for the future success of the program," Gross said in a statement released by university on Monday. "We wish him the absolute best in his opportunity in the NFL."

Syracuse University Chairman of the Board of Trustees Richard Thompson and Chancellor and President Nancy Cantor also released a statement, congratulating Marrone and praising his work over the past four years.

"We congratulate Coach Marrone on having this opportunity to become a head coach at the highest level. Under his leadership, we have restored the rich, winning football tradition at Syracuse, and we wish him continued success as he moves to the National Football League."

Marrone did exactly what he was brought in to do: build a program that could compete at a high level. He has multiple victories over top-25 teams, a couple of bowl wins, and changed the landscape of Syracuse football by instilling an idea of winning. He's coached players who moved on to the NFL level, including Mike Williams, Delone Carter and Chandler Jones, and it appears quarterback Ryan Nassib and offensive lineman Justin Pugh may also be heading to some NFL team as well.

Moving forward, it appears that Scott Shafer-hired by Marrone in 2009- will replace his former boss for the 2013 season, although no statements by the university have been made yet.

Chapter 18 Coach Scott Shafer From 2013 to 2015

Coach Scott Shafer # 28

Year	Coach	Record	Conf
2013	Scott Shafer	7-6	ACC (4-4)
2014	Scott Shafer	3-9	ACC (1-7)
2015	Scott Shafer	4-8	ACC (2-6)

Coach Shafer ready to take team onto the field

Famous Coaches (From the Past) by SWC75.

Scott's first year has been a roller-coaster ride, and nobody knows if he will be successful here, but we are hopeful because, launching ourselves into a new conference, we need him to be a success. If he isn't, we'll have to start all over again with someone else.

[At the time SWC75 wrote this piece on SU coaches, Shafer was in his first year of coaching. It would not work out and that is why Dino Babers is now the coach.] This is the third straight coach we've had who had never been a head coach before. We've never hired a coach in the post- World War II Era who had ever previously coached a major college football team. In our entire history we've hired two coaches who already had some measure of prominence as head coaches: Bill Hollenbeck, who filled in for Buck O'Neill when he was tending to his law practice in 1916 and Ossie Solem, who had had a losing record at Iowa.

2013 Scott Shafer Coach # 28

The 2013 Syracuse Orange football team competed in their one hundred-twenty-fourth season of intercollegiate football. They were led by Scott Shafer in his first of three season as head coach of the Syracuse Orange. The Orange had a winning record this year at 7-6. -5. The team was 4-4 in the ACC. They tied for third in the Atlantic Division of the ACC. They were invited to the Texas Bowl after the season where they defeated Minnesota.

On Aug 31, Syracuse played well but lost a close game to Penn State L (17-23) in its home and season opener played in MetLife Stadium, East Rutherford, NJ before 61,202 . Typically, SU home games are played at the Carrier Dome, on the campus of Syracuse University in Syracuse, NY. On Sept 7, #20 Northwestern beat Syracuse at Ryan Field in Evanston IL, L (27–48) before 38,033. On the home field for the first time in 2013, on Sept 14, at the Carrier Dome, SU shut out Wagner W (54-0) before 33,299.

Tulane came into the Carrier Dome hoping to extend their 2-1 record, but the Green Wave was beaten by the Orange in a shootout W (52-17) before 36,128. On Oct 5, Clemson defeated Syracuse in a blowout L (14-49).

The Orange traveled on Oct 12 to NC State's Carter–Finley Stadium in Raleigh, NC and played fine game beating the Tar Heels W (24-10) before 56,639. On Oct 19 against Georgia Tech in Bobby Dodd Stadium, Atlanta, GA, the Yellow Jackets whipped Syracuse in a blowout-shutout L (0–56) before 45,704. Then, on Nov 2 at home, Syracuse shut out Wake Forest at the Carrier Dome W (13-0).

On Nov 9, at Maryland's Byrd Stadium in College Park, MD, the Orange defeated the Terrapins W (20–3) before 37,213. In another blowout, Syracuse got walloped by #2 Florida State at Doak Campbell Stadium in Tallahassee, FL L (3–59) before 74,491. The next game was the annual rivalry at home on Nov 23 against Pittsburgh at the Dome in a one-point loss L (16–17) before 35,317. In another rivalry in the last game of the season, SU got it together on Nv 30 at home to defeat Boston College's Eagles, in a close match W (34-31) before 37,406

The 2013 Texas Bowl

At 6-6, the Orange wee bowl eligible and they were invited to the Texas Bowl to play for a 5:00 PM December 27 6outing to play Minnesota at Reliant Stadium in Houston, TX, where they defeated the Cougars W (21–17) before a crowd of 32,327.

This was the eighth edition of the Texas Bowl. It featured the Minnesota Golden Gophers of the Big Ten Conference against the Syracuse Orange of the Atlantic Coast Conference. Syracuse quarterback Terrel Hunt, completed 19 of 29 passes for 188 yards and he rushed for 2 touchdowns. For this effort, he was awarded the game's most valuable player.

In conference play, SU had lost their first game to Clemson, who at the time was ranked number four in the country, and then they split their next two games before beginning a two-game winning streak, during which they defeated Wake Forest and Maryland. After that, they lost two of their final three games, including a loss to #2 Florida State, who ultimately ended up in the 2014 BCS National Championship Game.

After receiving the opening kickoff, Minnesota's opening drive stalled, forcing the Golden Gophers to punt. After Syracuse and Minnesota lost fumbles on back-to-back drives, Syracuse was able to drive deep inside Minnesota territory. With a 4th down and 7 to go, on Minnesota's 24-yard line, Syracuse attempted a fake field goal play, but did not get the TD. At the end of 1Q, the game was scoreless. In Q2, SU got the lead on a 1-yard touchdown run by

Jerome Smith. After a punt exchange, Minnesota got a field goal as time expired in the first half.

Syracuse punted after the second half kickoff, and the Golden Gophers were also forced to punt in their first 2nd half possession. From the 14, Syracuse went 86-yards on plays and capped it off with a 5-yard TD run from Terrel Hunt, making it 14-3 with 2:57 remaining in the third quarter.

Starting the fourth quarter, Minnesota got a 20-yard touchdown pass from Mitch Leidner to Maxx Williams making the score 14-9. The 2-pt conversion attempt failed. After SU was forced to punt, the Golden Gophers grabbed the lead with a 55-yard TD toss from Mitch Leidner to Drew Wolitarsky. And the 2-pt. conversion was good making the lead three points.

After SU punted from Minnesota's 39-yard line and then forced a 3 and out. Syracuse drove into Minnesota territory but missed a 45-yard field goal with 3:31 left in the game. On the ensuing drive, Minnesota was able to a get a first down on a 15-yard rush by David Cobb. However, the Golden Gophers were unable to get another first down to close out the game and were forced to punt with 2:03 remaining in the game.

This was very fortunate for SU as Brisly Estime returned the punt 70 yards to Minnesota's 14-yard line. The Orange then took a 21-17 lead after Terrel Hunt scrambled 12-yards for a touchdown with 1:14 remaining in the game. Syracuse then fought off two Hail Mary attempts by Minnesota and the Orange sealed the victory.

2014 Scott Shafer Coach # 28

The 2014 Syracuse Orange football team competed in their one hundred-twenty-fifth season of intercollegiate football. They were led by Scott Shafer in his second of three season as head coach of the Syracuse Orange. The Orange had a losing record this year at 3-9. The team was 1-7 in the ACC. They were not selected to play in a bowl game in 2014.

On Aug 29, SU played its season opener and home opener against #12 ranked (in FCS) Villanova, at the Carrier Dome, on the campus of Syracuse University in Syracuse, NY. SU won by one point (W (27-26) after a missed Villanova PAT in the 2nd OT. On Sept 13 at Central Michigan in Kelly/Shorts Stadium, Mount Pleasant, MI SU won the game W (40–3) before 25,531. On Sept 20 at home. The Maryland Terrapins defeated the Orange L (20–34) before 40,511. On Sept 27 8:00 PM SU was beaten by #8 Notre Dame at MetLife Stadium in East Rutherford, NJ L (15–31) before 76,802.

On Oct 3 at home, Louisville defeated Syracuse at the Carrier Dome L (6–28) before 37,569. On Oct 11 12:at home, #1 Florida State defeated Syracuse L (20–38) before 43,295. On Oct 18 at Wake Forest's BB&T Field in Winston-Salem, NC, the Orange prevailed W (30–7) before 25,107. Then on October 25 at #20 Clemson in a game played at Memorial Stadium in Clemson, SC. The Tigers defeated the Orange L (6–16) before 80,031

On Nov 1 at home, SU lost to NC State at the Carrier Dome L (17–24) before 40,787. Then, on Nov 8 at home SU lost to #22 Duke at the Carrier Dome L (10–27) before 39,331. In the rivalry with Pittsburgh, this year the game was played on Nov 22 at Heinz Field in Pittsburgh, PA, with the Panthers scoring the win L (7–30) before 32,549 In another major rivalry, on Nov 29, SU lost to Boston College at Alumni Stadium in Chestnut Hill, MA L (7-28) before 30,267 fans.

2015 Scott Shafer Coach # 28

The 2015 Syracuse Orange football team competed in their one hundred-twenty-sixth season of intercollegiate football. They were led by Scott Shafer in his third and last season as head coach of the Syracuse Orange. The Orange had a losing record this year at 4-8. The team was 2-6 in the ACC. They were not selected to play in a bowl game in 2015. On November 23, head coach Scott Shafer was fired. He stayed on to coach their final game on November 28. Shafer finished at Syracuse with a three-year record of 14–23.

Games of the 2015 Season

On Sept 4, SU played its season opener and home opener against Rhode Island at the Carrier Dome, on the campus of Syracuse University in Syracuse, NY. SU won in a blowout (W 47-0). On Sept 12 at home, SU beat Wake Forest in the Carrier Dome W (30–17) before 26,670. In the Carrier Dome again on Sept 19 against Central Michigan, the Orange put the game in gear and prevailed W (30–27) in one OT, before 27,949. Then, on Sept 26, at home the Orange fell to # 8 LSU at the Carrier Dome L (24–34) before 43,101. Then, on 10 at 3:30 PM at South Florida in Raymond James Stadium, Tampa, FL, SU went down again L (24–45) before 27,235.

On Oct 17 at Virginia, in Scott Stadium, Charlottesville, VA, the Orange could not match the score L (38–44) with 3OT's to win but no cigar. Before 39,223. On Oct 24 at home in a major rivalry game v #25 Pittsburgh, the Orange could not pull it off and lost to the Panthers L (20–230 before 29,832. On Oct 31 SU travelled a thousand miles to fight #17 Florida State at Doak Campbell Stadium in Tallahassee, FL. The Seminoles had it all their way in a runaway game L (21–45) before 67,630.

On Nov 7 in an away game at Louisville's Papa John's Cardinal Stadium in Louisville, KY, the Orange took it on the chin again against the Cardinals L (17–41) before 46,158. Clemson was inching its way to the National Championship in one fine season after another. In this game on Nov 14 at home in the Carrier Dome against #1 Clemson, Syracuse lost a close one to the Tigers L (27–37) before 36,736. On Nov 21 at NC State's Carter–Finley Stadium in Raleigh, SU was stung by the Wolfpack L (29–42) before 55,260.

Then against an eternal rival in the last regular game of the year, on Nov 28, at home, the Orange got up the muster to defeat Boston College in the Carrier Dome in a close game W (20–17) before 30,317. No bowl games are offered for 4-8 teams.

Scott Shafer Out at Syracuse

By Stephen Bailey sbailey@syracuse.com on November 23, 2015 at 9:48 AM, updated November 23, 2015 at 11:35 PM

SCOTT SHAFER FIRED

Syracuse, N.Y. — Scott Shafer has been fired as Syracuse's head football coach, the school announced on Monday.

Shafer, who was promoted from defensive coordinator after Doug Marrone's departure in January 2013, is 13-23 in three seasons. The Orange is currently 3-8 this year heading into its season finale against Boston College. Shafer will coach in the final game.

Syracuse athletic director Mark Coyle expressed appreciation toward Shafer, who is in his third year at the helm, but said in a statement that a "change in leadership" was required.

"I want to thank Scott, his wife Missy, and their family for their seven years of dedication and service to SU Athletics and Syracuse University," Coyle said. "Scott has worked tirelessly to educate our students on and off the field and to build our program. However, I feel a change in leadership is needed at this time.

A national search will begin immediately." After coaching SU to a 7-6 record and Texas Bowl win in his first season, Shafer struggled through a 3-9 campaign mired in injury and lowlighted by the demotion of offensive coordinator George McDonald.

Facing one of the largest defensive rebuilds in college football history, Syracuse opened 2015 with its first 3-0 start since 1991 before losing its next eight contests — the longest in-season skid since 2005. An embattled fan base became more disgruntled as upset scares of No. 1 Clemson and then-No. 2 LSU weighed against a host of questionable in-game decisions.

Coyle, who started in July, has not spoken publicly since issuing a wait-and-see approach regarding Shafer's future in early September.

Shafer said he had one season left on his contract on Nov. 12 and likely would have had to been extended or bought out for the program to recruit in 2016.

Shafer arrived at Syracuse in 2009 and spent four years working as defensive coordinator under Marrone. In 2010, his unit was one of the best in the country, ranking seventh in total defense, 10th in pass defense and 13th in scoring defense. He was aa logical replacement for Marrone who left unexpectedly.

Shafer had previous defensive coordinator stops at Michigan (2008), Stanford (2007), Western Michigan (2005-06) and Northern Illinois (2000-03). Shafer also served as defensive backs coach at WMU (2004) and NIU (1996-99) after breaking into the coaching ranks as the secondary coach at Rhode Island from 1993-95.

After playing quarterback at Division III Baldwin-Wallace University in Ohio, Shafer was a graduate assistant at Indiana from 1991-92.

The news of Shafer's firing was first reported by Thayer Evans of Sports Illustrated. Contact Stephen Bailey anytime: Email | Twitter | 315-427-2168.

Syracuse over the years as we have portrayed in this book has had several great coaches and several who would have been even greater coaches if given time to mature with the program, or if they could have been convinced to stay.

Dino Babers was announced as the SU coach for 2016 onward. Babers has a great reputation and is a fine coach but so far, his record is poor. The most any of us have seen in the modern SU era is that SU accepts two years of poor records and then takes action or waits another year or at most two. Syracuse does want a winning team but after ten years, with some exceptions such as Ben Schwartzwalder, Dick MacPherson, Paul Pasqualoni and Doug Marrone.

The Institution's history shows that they do not appear to know how to attract great coaches or to keep a great coach when they get one. All Syracuse fans, including yours truly are hoping for an outstanding performance from Dino Babers team in 2018. We wish him the best.

Let's now take a look at where we stand from Coach Babers two years of experience with the Syracuse Orange.

Chapter 19 Coach Dino BabersFrom 2016 to ????

Coach Scott Shafer # 28

Year	Coach	Record	Conf
2016	Dino Babers	4-8	ACC (2-6)
2017	Dino Babers	4-8	ACC (2-6)
2018	Dino Babers	0-0	ACC (0-0

SU Football Coach Dino Babers with the team

2016 Dino Babers Coach # 29

The 2016 Syracuse Orange football team competed in their one hundred-twenty-seventh season of intercollegiate football. They were led by Dino Babers, in his first season as head coach of the Syracuse Orange. The Orange had a losing record this year at 4-8; the same record as in Scott Shafer's last year at the helm. The team was 2-6 in the ACC. They were not selected to play in a bowl game in 2016.

On Sept 2, SU played its season opener and home opener against Colgate, ranked #21 ranked in FCS). The game was played in the Carrier Dome, on the campus of Syracuse University in Syracuse, NY. SU won the match (W 33-7) before 31,336. On Sept 9, at home, Louisville defeated the Orange L (28–62) before 32,184. On Sept 17 at home, South Florida beat the Orange L (20–45) before 32,288. In its first road game of the season, on Sept 24, Syracuse defeated Connecticut in Rentschler Field, East Hartford, CT W (31–24) before 31,899. On Oct 1, in a home game played at MetLife Stadium, East Rutherford, NJ, SU was defeated by Notre Dame L (33–50) before 62,794.

Back on the road, SU traveled on Oct 8 to Wake Forest's BB&T Field in Winston-Salem, NC and were defeated by the Demon Deacons L (9–28) before 25,162. On Oct 15 at home, SU beat the #17 ranked Hokies of Virginia Tech W (31-17) before 33,838. Then, on Oct 22 at Boston College's Alumni Stadium in Chestnut Hill, MA, Syracuse won its second game in a row, W (28–20) before 34,647. On Nov 5, playing against #3 ranked Clemson, soon to be National Champions, led by Heisman candidate Desean Watson, Syracuse lost in a blowout-shutout at Clemson Memorial Stadium L (0–54) before 80,609 fans.

On Nov 12 at home, Syracuse lost to the Wolfpack of NC State L (20–35) before 34,842. Again, at home, SU was defeated by Florida State L (14-45) before 32,340. Then in one of the highest scoring games of all time on Nov 26, at major rival Pittsburgh's Heinz Field in Pittsburgh, PA, neither defense showed up and Pittsburgh won the game with a huge score of L (61–76) before 34,049.

2017 Dino Babers Coach # 29

The 2017 Syracuse Orange football team competed in their one hundred-twenty-eighth season of intercollegiate football. They were led by Dino Babers in his second season as head coach of the Syracuse Orange. The Orange had a losing record this year of 4-8; the same exact record as in the last two seasons. The team was 2-6 in the ACC. They were not selected to play in a bowl game in 2016.

On Sept 1, SU played its season and home opener against Central Connecticut. The game was played in the Dome, on the campus of Syracuse University in Syracuse, NY. SU won the match W (50-7) before 31,336. On Sept 9, at home, the Orange lost to Middle Tennessee L (23-30 Before 29,731. SU got its second win of the season on Sept 16 at home against Central Michigan W (41-17) before 33,004.

On Sept 23 at #25 LSU in Tiger Stadium, Baton Rouge, Louisiana, the Orange put up a good fight but lost to the Tigers L (26–35) before a huge crowd of 96,044. Then in the final September game, Sept 30 at NC State's Carter–Finley Stadium in Raleigh, North Carolina, the Orange lost to the Wolfpack L (25–33) before 56,197

For its third win of the season, Syracuse beat rival Pittsburgh at home in the Carrier Dome on Oct 6, in a close match W (27–24) before 33,290.

Highlight SU Defeats Defending Champion Clemson

In the greatest game for the Syracuse Orange in decades, if not centuries, SU defeated the reigning National Champions, #2 ranked Clemson at home in the Carrier Dome in a hard-fought close match on Oct 13 W (27–24) before 42,475.

When you create a list of the best games SU has ever played so you can show them as highlights in a book about Great Moments in Syracuse Football, October. 13, 2017 is a must-game for that list. My list would show the Friday win as the biggest for Syracuse since the Donovan McNabb era if not well before that.

Night game v Clemson at the Dome

The 27-24 win over No. 2 Clemson marked Syracuse's second win over a team ranked among the top two in football. Cole Murphy's 30-yard field goal with 9:41 remaining was the winning score. Quarterback Eric Dungey led the Orange with 278 yards passing and 61 yards rushing. BTW, I predict All-American in 2018 for Eric Dungey unless the NCAA sopped being able to spell Sceeerrrokuze.

A bit more detail:

Dungey on target. His 3 TD passes blows out #2 Clemson in a close match, 27-24

You bet the Syracuse Orange, who played like the vaunted Syracuse Orangemen from the Jim Brown days had a huge celebration in the SU locker room that could be heard through all of Syracuse. Finally, a great game from a team that is getting ready to be great.

Coach Dabo Swinney had a tough time believing what happened as this would not be a perfect season and Desean Watson would not bring back the Tigers. Syracuse under their collective breaths were singing Hold that Tiger the whole game.

Eric Dungey was well, and he threw for 278 yards and three touchdowns, Cole Murphy kicked a tiebreaking field goal in the fourth quarter, and Syracuse put a weird face on #2 Clemson 27-24 on this Friday night as the Tigers had to digest what it meant for their chances to repeat as national champions.

Clemson had won 12 consecutive games on the opponent's home field, the longest streak in Clemson history and they had tied for the second longest active streak in the nation. None of that mattered to the Orange-men who simply wanted to kick the opponents butts back to South Carolina. It's a football thing!

Dabo Swinney is a fine coach and he said: "It wasn't our night tonight. They were better than us," Swinney said. "There's nothing we're going to fix now. We're not going to be 12-0, that's for sure. That's not going to happen. This is going to hurt, but you move forward."

The Orangemen were (4-3, 2-1) are were 3-6 against the previous year's national champion, having also beaten Penn State in 1987 and Michigan in 1998. This was the program's first win in 13 tries against the No. 2 team in the nation. It was sweet.

SU Coach was elated. "This is truly one of the moments that you coach for. This is really special," said Syracuse coach Dino Babers, in his second year with the Orange. "This is big."
The Tigers took a big blow when quarterback Kelly Bryant suffered a concussion in the final minute of the first half. He was knocked down hard by defensive tackle Chris Slayton and lay on the turf for a couple of minutes before being helped to the locker room. Slowed after spraining his left ankle last week against Wake Forest, Bryant passed for 116 yards and ran for minus-8 yards.

"They came ready to play," Clemson defensive end Clelin Ferrell said. "They came out, they saw blood, they saw they had a definite chance to win the game and we just didn't capitalize on the opportunities we had to make a comeback."

Bryant, who watched the second half from the sideline, entered the game averaging 277 yards of total offense, but noticeably favored an injured ankle as Syracuse gained a surprising 17-14 halftime lead.

Zerrick Cooper replaced Bryant to start the second half and guided the Tigers to a tying field goal.

The Tigers tried a trick play with time winding down, but Will Spiers threw an incompletion on a fake punt.

The Syracuse defense limited the Tigers to 2 of 11 on third down, none more critical than Cooper's overthrow on third down before the fake.

Syracuse used big plays to stun the Tigers, hitting six for 20 yards or more as the Orange outgained Clemson 440-317. Dungey hit Dontae Strickland for a 23-yard score to open the game and also hit Ervin Philips for 66 yards in the first quarter and Steve Ishmael for 30 in the third to break a 17-17 tie.

In post-season interviews Eric Dungey had some fun: "Quick show of hands. Who thought we were going to win tonight?" Dungey asked in the postgame interviews. "That's exactly what we've been saying. It's just us. Nobody believes in us except us."

The Orange defense emulated the plays in Clemson's playbook. The Tigers were among just three teams in the nation averaging at least 230 yards rushing and 230 yards passing (Ohio State and Oregon are the others). The Tigers managed just 39 yards rushing in the first half and 113 total and finished with 204 passing. SU had its game faces on the whole game.

There were two big plays for Clemson but it in your mind you can subtract those two long runs and the rest of the night the Tigers gained 24 yards on 23 carries. Syracuse can do it when they are ready to do it.

The hometown fans stormed the field afterward as next to Mohammed Ali, this was the greatest.

"It was kind of surreal," Syracuse linebacker Parris Bennett said.

Syracuse's fabled Orangemen once again proved that they can play with the big boys. Syracuse had upset No. 17 Virginia Tech last October. If only the med staff can keep Dungey healthy, 2018 is going to be a year of possibilities and probabilities. Go Orange-----men!

Rest of SU 2017 games coming up

On Oct 21 at #8 Miami (FL) in Hard Rock Stadium, Miami Gardens, Florida SU put up a great fight against the Hurricanes losing by just 8 points L (19–27) before 56,158. On Nov4, at Florida State's Doak Campbell Stadium in Tallahassee, Florida, the Orange almost got an upset but lost L (24-27) before 71,805.

Then, on Nov 11 at home SU was beaten by Wake Forest at the Carrier Dome L (43–64) before 38,539. The Orange then traveled to Louisville on Nov 18 to Papa John's Cardinal Stadium in Louisville, Kentucky and lost the game in a blowout L (10–56) before 34,265. In the rivalry game at home on Nov 25 at 12:20 p.m. SU lost to Boston College L (14-42) in the Carrier Dome before 30,202.

The two close losses after Clemson--Miami and then Florida State last year would have been blowouts. This year they were just losses. That is a definite improvement. Not good for the spirit but not bad like last year. The last three games seem to be because of the defense; but I think it was as much the fact that offensive star, QB Eric Dungey was injured and then in the BC game, running back Dontae Strickland could not play either. The defense rarely got a break. SU also lost other starters earlier this fall. Many coaches will tell us all that you can't win without your best players or at least almost equal replacements. Syracuse in 2017 had neither.

Almost All-American Eric Dungey 2015-2017

Senior Eric Dungey is coming back to QB the Orange in 2018. A three-year starter known for his toughness and playmaking ability, Dungey is back and motivated as ever to turn in a winning season.

After having his third straight campaign cut short due to injury, the Oregon native is up six pounds to 228, was referred to by teammate Aaron Roberts as looking like a "gladiator" in the weight room this winter and has been medically cleared from offseason foot surgery.

Dungey's in line to have an improved offensive line, and in turn, possibly backfield. But his competition at quarterback is better, too— Tommy DeVito

Eric Dungey played in 26 games with 25 starts. He missed parts of each of his first three seasons due to injury. Dungey holds a school-record nine career 300-yard passing games and two 400-yard passing performances. He accounted for three or more touchdowns in 12 of his 25 first-string appearances. He owns or shares 12 school records.

In addition to holding the Syracuse record for most 300-yard passing games, Dungey is SU's career leader in passing yards per game (248.9), total offense yards per game (296.6) and rushing touchdowns by a quarterback (20) He is among the top 10 in program history in 10 additional career categories:

- Completion percentage (2nd - 61.7),
- Completions (3rd - 560),
- Pass attempts (4th - 908),

- Passing yards (4th - 6,472),
- Total offense plays (4th - 1,267),
- Yards of total offense (4th - 7,711),
- Touchdown passes (5th - 40),
- Touchdowns responsible for (5th - 60),
- Pass efficiency rating (6th - 131.46)
- Most yards of total offense per play (6th - 6.1)

He is one of six quarterbacks in team history to rush for at least 1,000 yards. Eric Dungey and Donovan McNabb are the only quarterbacks in program history with 6,000+ passing yards and 1,000+ rushing yards.

He has six career games with 400+ yards of total offense. He is a two-time CoSIDA Academic All-District selection and just one of 15 true freshmen to play for the Orange in 2015

2018 Dino Babers Coach # 29

The 2018 Syracuse Orange football team is preparing for their one hundred-twenty-ninth season of intercollegiate football. They are led by Dino Babers in his third season as head coach of the Syracuse Orange. The Orange have a losing record under Babers of 8-16 in two years but the margin of loss to some very powerful teams is much smaller than in prior years. Thus, there is great hope for the Syracuse Orange in the Fall 2018.

The recruiting class for 2018 also offers encouragement. Dino Babers brought in the best class in a decade and to top that, there are several big-name transfers that are on their way to play in Orange Country

Here's how SU stacks up nationally in the class of 2018

- National rank: 49
- 5 stars: 0
- 4 stars: 1
- 3 stars: 17

The 2018 Schedule is as follows:

Date	Opponent	Site
September 1, 2018	at Western Michigan*	Waldo Stadium Kalamazoo, MI
September 8, 2018	Wagner*	Carrier Dome Syracuse, NY
September 15, 2018	Florida State	Carrier Dome Syracuse, NY
September 22, 2018	Connecticut*	Carrier Dome Syracuse, NY
September 29, 2018	at Clemson	Memorial Stadium Clemson, SC
October 6, 2018	at Pittsburgh	Heinz Field Pittsburgh, PA (Rivalry)
October 20, 2018	North Carolina	Carrier Dome Syracuse, NY
October 27, 2018	NC State	Carrier Dome Syracuse, NY
November 3, 2018	at Wake Forest	BB&T Field Winston-Salem, NC
November 9, 2018	Louisville	Carrier Dome Syracuse, NY
November 17, 2018	vs. Notre Dame*	Yankee Stadium Bronx, NY
November 24, 2018	at Boston College	Alumni Stadium Chestnut Hill, MA

*Non-conference game. All times are in Eastern Time.

At syracusefan.com, this post from mlbball99 Scout Team offers great encouragement for 2018:

A couple of thoughts here:

Dino Babers is 56 years old. He is at a big school in a power six conference competing in arguably the best conference. He has embraced what the Carrier Dome can be. The football renovations have been done - practice facility, locker rooms, etc.

In his presser last night Dino raved about living in Syracuse and said how happy he was. Again, Dino is 56 years old. I do see schools trying to poach him after this year, but I think Dino has found a long-term home. I don't believe he wants to go try to rebuild something again at his age.

Wildhack and Dino have a fantastic relationship. Wildhack will play him ASAP.

We are so close to being a legit contender. We are a few plays away from being 7-0. Dungey is a legit Heisman candidate next year. The nation has noticed.

Also, do not forget, we have a 4-star QB grooming. Two 4-star OL on their way in.   Let's GO.

The Daily Orange Student Newspaper offers its thoughts on the probabilities of a Syracuse football turnaround

By Tomer Langer
SENIOR STAFF WRITER
UPDATED: Sept. 25, 2017 at 3:36 a.m.

When he was introduced as Syracuse's head coach on Dec. 5, 2015, Dino Babers asked for faith.

Belief without evidence, as he likes to specify. He said his goal is to make Syracuse a program that's "consistently good, not occasionally great." He didn't see any reason why SU couldn't reach the top of the Atlantic Coast Conference.

Babers has leaned on those mantras repeatedly since he arrived, asking for patience. He overhauled the offensive and defensive schemes and alluded to successful "cakes" the Orange would "bake," saying that SU was still working on the batter.

He also provided a timeline, saying that his system would be fully installed in the second year between the fourth and sixth games. On Monday, after beating Central Michigan, Babers stuck with his forecast.

"I think based off of the last game, it's probably about right," Babers said. "Again, I don't know, when you talk about the newness and guys being hurt and not being here the entire first year. But I'm not going to back away from a statement. This is when we normally get going, it just happens to be some of the toughest games on the schedule and that's how they fall so we have to see how we do."

The Orange (2-2) came close to proving Babers a soothsayer last night but fell, 35-26, to No. 25 Louisiana State (3-1, 0-1 Southeastern) in Baton Rouge, Louisiana. Some chalked it up to a likely blowout loss in the preseason, but several missed opportunities were the only things in the way of a Syracuse victory.

The steady performance of SU's defense and second-half offense highlighted the many reasons there are to believe that Babers can turn around the program.

But after dropping what could have been a signature win for the program, it's increasingly apparent the turnaround will take longer than expected.

Babers projected the timeline for SU because of the tangible results he'd had at previous coaching stops. He began coaching as a graduate assistant in 1984 and had a pair of two-year head coaching stints before he arrived at SU. At both Eastern Illinois and Bowling Green, his teams improved in the second year.

There have been clear areas of growth since Babers' arrival. A once-anemic offense stuffed the record books a year ago. The defense gave up more than 500 yards per game last year, but it has already shown vast improvements in Year 2.
In training camp, senior captain Zaire Franklin said the defense wasn't fully adjusted to the new Tampa-2 scheme being run in 2016. Though he said he felt the entire unit was much more prepared after a full year in the system.

"It would mean a lot to us," Franklin said last Tuesday about potentially getting a win at LSU, "to kind of start the Coach Babers era off the right way, the way it was supposed to."

Jimmy Garoppolo, the high-profile backup quarterback for the New England Patriots, was a junior starter when Babers' started at EIU. He also felt the difference between the first and second year. One play in particular, a 63-yard touchdown in the third game of the second season against Illinois State, sticks out for Garoppolo as the time when the offense fully clicked in the new system. The Panthers finished 12-2, compared to 7-5 the previous year and two 2-9 stints before Babers arrival.

"It fits his personality very well." Garoppolo said of Babers turning programs around. "He believes in what he's saying, and he has a way in making other people around him believe the same thing. That's what you need in a head coach. He does a great job of having guys buy in to the program. The coaches all buy in, and it makes for, in the words that he would say, it makes for a good 'La Familia.'"

There have been flashes of SU success but no concrete semblance of consistency. Last year's win over then-No. 17 Virginia Tech stands out as a high point that SU hadn't had since a 2013 bowl victory. Giving up 76 points in last year's season finale loss to Pittsburgh and blowing a home game against Middle Tennessee State this year are among the times SU has not performed.

Consistent moments escaped Syracuse on Saturday. Eric Dungey's first pass was picked off by top corner Greedy Williams and returned to the SU one-yard line. LSU scored on the next play. In the second quarter, wide receiver Sean Riley dropped a pass in the end zone while he was wide open, costing SU the go-ahead touchdown.

"We didn't get it done and that's the bottom line," senior wide receiver Ervin Philips said. "People can look at the game and say that we played well. But at the end of the day it's about getting it done, it's about winning."

If anything, the LSU loss showed that it would be foolish to count Syracuse out of any game moving forward. SU has three more games against opponents currently ranked inside the Top 25. Another high-caliber opponent, Florida State, lost to North Carolina State and fell out of the rankings. Syracuse faces the Wolfpack next week. The Orange could win its next two games and take the next step toward bowl eligibility.

Neither of those wins would make as much of a statement as the one SU let slip away Saturday night. Not against a Top 25 team in the SEC at what Babers called "one of the top five venues in America when it comes to college football."

Babers stressed postgame that he was disappointed, not upset. He wanted his players to have that one memorable win that they could tell their kids and grandkids about.

"They don't realize how close they were," Babers said, "and I'm disappointed they didn't get it right now at this time."
Based on his previous stops, Babers expected his team to get that win. Despite how close the Orange got, Babers' timeline will face a minor delay.

Another 2018 perspective

5 things to know about Syracuse football 2018 schedule
Updated Jan 17; Posted Jan 17

By Nate Mink
nmink@syracuse.com,
syracuse.com

> Syracuse football is entering its third year under head coach Dino Babers and the team and fans and alums are looking to improve upon back-to-back 4-8 seasons.(*Dennis Nett | dnett@syracuse.com*)

Dino Babers doing his job

Syracuse, N.Y. -- Syracuse football's complete 2018 schedule was released Wednesday with announcement of the ACC slate.

[The schedule is shown above.]

The Orange is entering its third year under head coach Dino Babers and is looking to improve upon back-to-back 4-8 seasons. This year's schedule carries the familiar national powers of previous years: Clemson, Florida State and Notre Dame are on it.

And, while the ACC has improved its overall health in recent years, making no game any small task, there is reason to believe this season's slate of games won't be as challenging as last year's.

There are seven teams on this year's schedule that played in a bowl game last season (Western Michigan was bowl eligible with six wins but was not invited to a bowl).

To put that in perspective, 10 of the 12 teams Syracuse faced last season went to a bowl.

Here are four more thoughts on the schedule:

1. The opener will tell us something

Syracuse for the past four seasons has opened against an FCS opponent that was mostly overmatched from the opening kick. The Orange felt good about itself, but it really didn't know how it would respond against any semblance of resistance.

Syracuse goes on the road in Week 1 at a healthy Mid-American conference opponent that has staff familiar with some of SU's veteran personnel.

2. Syracuse will get ACC heavyweights in September

Getting Florida State and Clemson in September should give SU a chance at the conference heavyweights with its roster intact. FSU will be playing its first road game under new coach Willie Taggart, who defeated Babers when he coached at South Florida two seasons ago.

Clemson will be carrying a loaded roster and will be seeking revenge for last season's loss at the Carrier Dome.

Depth is always a concern for Syracuse, so the health of its roster will be vitally important heading into October, which looks like the month where progress will or will not reveal itself.

3. Louisville a Friday night upset?

Nobody forgot what happened the last time an ACC opponent came to the Carrier Dome on a Friday night, when Syracuse handed Clemson a stunning, 27-24 loss.

For the second time in three years, Louisville is coming to the Dome on a Friday night (this time, without star quarterback Lamar Jackson).

Dino Babers and his team have pulled off stunning victories in each of his first two seasons.

Scalping Florida State at home or Notre Dame at Yankee Stadium would also make for another memorable moment.

4. October will reveal program progress

Syracuse will play three opponents in October that will go a long way toward deciding whether the program is able to take a step forward.

Games at Pittsburgh and at home against North Carolina and North Carolina State are three perfect examples of the kinds of wins the program needs to snare if it wants to continue to build momentum on the recruiting trail.

One is against a Northeast rival, and the other two are home games against good but not overwhelming rosters.

Take it another step forward, and the Nov. 3 contest at Wake Forest provides another opportunity for SU to show it can consistently defeat peer programs or programs with slightly better talent than SU.

Contact Nate Mink anytime: 315-430-8253.

Chapter 20: What Is the Future of Syracuse Football?

Packed House Will Be the Order of the Day at a New 100000 + Comfort Seat Stadium

Would it not be nice to find SU administration officials and the board getting behind a football revitalization program that begins with a brand new 150,000 seat stadium. Why not make it the "Big SU Dome" or some other creative name given to the world by SU students.

Just like crowds swarm to be in the huge Beaver Stadium or the Big House, or the OU "Horseshoe" in Ohio, would it not be nice to see some huge lines at the new "Orange Humunga Dome" or whatever we choose to call it. Why lines? Because 150,000 should not be enough to contain the new fan base when Syracuse University again chooses to highlight its football prowess.

"If we build it, they will come." You can take that to the bank. Perhaps 50,000 of the seats should be indoor with huge projections screens and huge mirrors showing the games in natural light. Nobody has ever done that! Why not be the best in College Football once a revitalization movement affects the Board? Why settle for #2?

In the whole time that I have been writing this book, I've been haunted by the endless cavalcade of excuses from commentators and "experts" of all stripes given to justify Syracuse's unnecessarily lackluster football record—most especially in the last decade. The most common rationalization I hear is that because Syracuse University is a small private school without the expansive resources of its larger colleagues in the Atlantic Coast Conference, the performance deficit is unexceptional, or worse, even predestined.

As a dedicated Syracuse football fan for over forty years, I found these conclusions disheartening and decided to embark on a voyage of examination to determine whether these explanations might be exaggerated in their pessimism or whether they truly were immutable forecasts of defeat.

I was hopeful that a comprehensive evaluation of empirical data might offer a more hopeful insight than what I hoped would turn out to be simply subjective prognostications based on anecdote or sentiment. Gladly, the undue focus on revenue and enrollment obscured a richer history with brighter possibility for this cherished football program, which I am happy to have the opportunity to present for your enjoyment. Additionally, I've recognized some potential areas of improvement that do indeed exist, several of which I share below.

Syracuse needs a problem solver on board

I worked at IBM for twenty-three years and for much of that time, my title was: Senior Systems Engineer. Chiefly, among my roles, I was a troubleshooter and a problem solver. As I began to see the pattern of poor performance results that arose from several intermittent coaches, I sensed there was no dedicated attempt by administration officials to help correct the underlying issues. As such, I began to think of options that I would employ if given the opportunity.

In my off time from writing, I began to think of what could be done with the once majestic Syracuse football program while at the same time, I was researching and writing season summaries for weeks on end. Eventually the summaries, alternating between both admirable and dismal, inspired me to imagine the implementations one could take to drive Syracuse to a more winning record if given the opportunity.

I immediately ruled out increased spending on football and soon recognized that verdict might have been premature. Although mostly every article I came across had dismissed further spending as impossible, I became concerned that a great deal of these conclusions appeared to be based on hearsay and conjecture. The university's resources were being constantly bad-mouthed and further investment in its football program was presented as mathematically foreclosed.

Nonetheless as I looked at the situation more closely and compared it to my experiences in researching six other universities, my first thought was that the problem was a simple matter of the school not recognizing the potential for investing in the program. With most historical documents taking the side that there were insufficient funds in such a small school, finding a solution had the potential to be elusive.

Comments ranged from disparaging the school's "small size," to its corresponding lower sports budget, and to acknowledging the fact that it lies in the shadow of the profitable basketball division. There was so much negativity I found even I was beginning to absorb it by osmosis. I began to believe that the university did not have even enough resources to rub two nickels together, let alone a pair of dimes or silver dollars.

But how then could I explain the long periods of winning? Infused with the doubts borne by the popular commentary, I started to think that perhaps even the most enduring winning streaks had simply occurred because of luck, despite the odds. I also never could deliver a satisfactory reason why Ben Schwartzwalder chose to become a coach at Syracuse. Was it for social reasons, financial, or the sheer thrill of the challenge? Whatever the reason, for Syracuse, it has certainly worked out. The same is true for Dick MacPherson and Paul Pasqualoni.

Luck and Schwartzwalder

Ben Schwartzwalder stayed at Syracuse for twenty-five years and delivered its finest hours in SU football history. He produced 22 straight years of non-losing records, took the Orange to seven bowls, and won the National Championship in 1959. He developed some of the most impressive running backs the game has ever seen - Jim Brown, Ernie Davis, Jim Nance, Floyd Little and Larry Csonka. Orange teams outrushed opponents by more than 22,000 yards under his direction. For 22 years, Ben Schwartzwalder made Syracuse Football something special. Based on his results, I surely would have recommended him for the job, but I was so young at the time, having been born in 1948, that I could not even speak in 1949.

But even Ben Schwartzwalder had his issues at the end of his career at Syracuse. Schwartzwalder's coaching career came to an end at Syracuse in the wake of racial tension and a boycott of spring football practice by black players in 1970. In a 1970 news conference, it was charged that black players had been the victims of racial epithets and unequal treatment and that money was given illegally to white players.

The boycott ended with Schwartzwalder suspending seven players and one leaving the team. He refused to take them back. In the ensuing controversy surrounding the boycott, Syracuse's performance on the field suffered. Schwartzwalder's teams managed only an 18-24-1 record from 1970 to 1973.

Schwartzwalder was forced to retire after the 1973 season, but he remained close to the Syracuse football program until he died of a heart attack in St. Petersburg. He is buried at the Onondaga County Veterans Memorial Cemetery in New York. For me, as I looked at Schwartzwalder moving on under duress and Maloney coming in, I felt sorry for Maloney.

In IBM management school, we learned that the worst management situation is one in which we inherit the position from one in which the predecessor was successful and well liked. Contrary to any assumption that as time passes, a more welcome openness to the new manager might materialize, rose-colored memory syndrome kicks in and instead, the older manager's flaws no longer are remembered making the comparison gap even steeper.

As case in point, the pundits predictably soon began to suggest that Frank Maloney, Syracuse University's replacement for Ben Schwartzwalder, was entirely unworthy to tie his forerunner's shoelaces. At their most charitable, they would comment that Maloney's tenure at Syracuse was marked by "inconsistency." As expected, the fan base quickly turned against him as the Orange failed to achieve the national status they had previously enjoyed under Schwartzwalder. It was difficult to accept that Ben was an outlying sui generis rather than a common standard to which all following coaches would aspire. Indeed, he was one of the greatest coaches of all time.

True to the theory of increasingly selective memory, the fans disremembered their impatience with Ben's last few seasons which were quite mediocre with respect to his earlier successes. He had only one winning season in his last five, a failure that would have at the time made him seem unworthy of his mantle. Yet it was unforeseeable that the team's success would have been so invariably tied to his stewardship as it eventually became clear during the tenure of his successors.

Syracuse had been spoiled by Schwartzwalder's achievements making Maloney seem excessively dismal in direct contrast. Further exacerbating things were limitations beyond Maloney's control, such as deteriorating facilities, particularly the archaic Archbold Stadium, home field since 1907, then in dire need of replacement. In all fairness, Maloney did recruit a number of future NFL stars such as Joe Morris and Pro Football Hall of Fame member Art Monk. But nothing stood up to the towering success of his predecessor and even his intermittent victories were made to feel as they had resulted from sheer luck rather than discipline, competence, and excellence.

Maloney became the subject of widespread criticism, not only from the fans and alumni, but also from the 1959 National Championship team. Its members even went so far as to initiate a campaign calling for his ouster, ironically enough during the year that turned out to be his best season, 1979. That year, the Orangemen qualified for the

Independence Bowl, and ultimately won, beating out McNeese State.

After coaching the Orangemen for seven seasons and presiding over the opening of a new stadium, the Carrier Dome in 1980 and with a decent overall record, Maloney was fired and replaced by Dick MacPherson seemingly out of nowhere. Where did Macpherson come from? Was he another lucky horseshoe grab? Time would tell and to this day there is evidence that may have been the case.

After a decade of tough going at Syracuse, MacPherson coached 10 seasons from 1981 to 1990. He beat the No. 1 team in 1984. He was undefeated in 1987. He coached in bowl games in four of his last five seasons, returning respect to the program. His success at both Syracuse University and prior success and at the University of Massachusetts earned him induction into the College Football Hall of Fame.

Along with strong coaching skills, MacPherson's larger-than-life personality was the prime reason Syracuse attracted a world-class staff during his decade at SU and he was able to keep top recruits such as Don McPherson in New York. This was not accidental. Before he came along by luck, in ten years, the Syracuse football program had gone 44-66.

By the time MacPherson left for the NFL's New England Patriots after the 1990 season, Syracuse was again a national powerhouse, delivering an undefeated season, a Sugar Bowl appearance in 1987, and bowl games in his final four seasons. Perhaps even more importantly MacPherson left behind 14 more years of prosperity. He left behind a deep-rooted coaching tree, including Paul Pasqualoni, that maintained the strength of the program for well more than a decade.

MacPherson enjoyed much of that next decade from the radio booth, watching his former assistant Paul Pasqualoni lead the Orangemen to many victories. By the time he left in 1990, MacPherson had compiled a 66-46-4 record, departing as the school's second best overall coach. Pasqualoni would later surpass his record with 107 wins.

I may not know the degree of the luck quotient's influence on the coaches preceding Paul Pasqualoni but his must have been apparent, serving as defensive coordinator for Mac and ready at age 32 (born August 16, 1949) to take over the chief coaching duties for the Syracuse Orangemen. This was a great stroke of luck for Syracuse indeed since no intensive search for recruiting a replacement was required. Pasqualoni was and is a famously great coach who now serves as Defensive Coordinator for the Detroit Lions.

Pasqualoni just happened to be an assistant at Syracuse from 1987 until 1991 when MacPherson left unexpectedly. Without the proper investment the university was in fact more than capable of making, such serendipity must also be attributed to dumb luck. The Orange (known then as the "Orangemen") enjoyed many successful years with Pasqualoni at the helm. The team won the Fiesta Bowl over Colorado in 1992 and defeated Clemson 41–0 in the Gator Bowl in 1995, Donovan McNabb's freshman year. The team had a 6–3 record in bowl games under Coach Pasqualoni, a feat even Ben Schwartzwalder had found challenging.

Pasqualoni's 14-year record with Syracuse ended at 107–59–1. He is second in wins only to Ben Schwartzwalder. Pasqualoni's only losing season was in 2002 where he finished with a 4–8 record. Most seasons of his tenure saw Syracuse competing as a Top 25 in the country. A new Athletic Director only 11 days into his job fired Pasqualoni following the 51–14 loss at the Champs Sports Bowl.

Though the loss was an embarrassment for the school, the blame did not lie squarely on its coach who. At only 45 years old, and having served very well, Pasqualoni was not to be mistreated as an obsolete relic to be put out to pasture. Despite that, new Athletic Director Daryl Gross, who himself was recently fired, terminated Pasqualoni this 14-year successful coach on December 29, 2004.

This action was taken in direct contradiction to the public statement issued by Syracuse's president Nancy Cantor promising to fans that Pasqualoni would be on the sidelines during the next season. Scant fortune has shone upon the program ever since. The day SU abandoned Pasqualoni was certainly among its unluckiest.

Right from the start, the damage was severe. During the 2005 season, the team's first without Pasqualoni, Syracuse posted a record of 1–10, the worst in its 117-year history. The University's disregard for its great coaches speaks for itself. Then there is Doug Marrone, now an outstanding head coach for the Jacksonville Jaguars who was just one playoff game away from the Super Bowl last year. In permitting Marrone's departure, Syracuse squandered yet another opportunity for success that many still excuse by insisting its football program is only a loss-leader.

Now I may be 100% Irish, but I am not a leprechaun. Wrongly convinced that SU had achieved its greatest years—not because the intelligent planning and investment by its administrators, but by happenstance, it appeared impossible to reliably replicate its golden era with anything short of a bowl of pixie dust or golden pot at the end of a rainbow—if that's what it takes to locate a great football coach and wisely maintain them, once found.

Having wrongly assumed Syracuse could not afford to invest in elevating its program, I had convinced myself that Syracuse could not afford the likes of Brian Kelly from Notre Dame, Nick Saban from Alabama, or Dabo Swinney from Clemson, if any of them would even consider Syracuse. So I had to think creatively if financial support was necessarily limited and luck would be as elusive as ever. There might not be another Paul Pasqualoni hanging around on the SU sidelines waiting to be discovered. Ultimately, I concluded that an investment by the school would be preferable and examined assumptions underlying the idea that it was inconceivable. What I found was surprising and encouraging.

So, what next?

In 2003, the Syracuse Orange team spent $7.5 million to get out of the Big East and join the ACC. For the past four years since Scott Shafer was the head football coach in 2003, the university has been playing football as a member of the Atlantic Coast Conference.

The ACC is a National Collegiate Athletic Association (NCAA) Division I conference that is part of the Football Bowl Subdivision (FBS). The ACC is an elite conference and the FBS is its elite crop division. Syracuse invested the resources to play football with the best teams in the nation yet ironically, it has not devoted the resources needed to compete well ever since Paul Pasqualoni was fired. Wins are a scarce commodity at Syracuse and playing in the ACC makes them even tougher to achieve. I began to consider that perhaps the FBS brand of football was too tough for Syracuse's ability to invest in its football program as it would need to do to compete well.

I began to think about Colgate. Until sixty years ago while both Syracuse and Colgate were independent, the Raiders of Colgate would frequently slap around the Orangemen. They would often be the only mar on an otherwise perfect SU season. Colgate was often the one team that separated the Orangemen from a flawless run.

As schools began to invest more in football programs, smaller schools such as Colgate (less than 3000 students) could not keep up and so they formed leagues with other smaller schools—such as the Patriot League in which Colgate plays today. The last Syracuse v. Colgate game was in 2016. Colgate, only a hop, skip, and a jump away from Syracuse in Hamilton NY, packed the house. The two teams have met 67 times over the years and despite Colgate not recording a victory since 1950, the overall series is now tied at 31–31–5. And just this year, the Raiders tied for the championship in the Patriot League. I'm confident the fans in Hamilton NY were proud of that for sure. It has been a long time since the fans and alumni of Syracuse were able to share the same pride.

But why am I talking about Colgate, a school whose total enrollment is less than 3000? Before taking an objective look at the facts, I had come to believe that any team that could beat SU so consistently for so many years must have been of comparable size. I couldn't have been more wrong as Syracuse enrolls just about 20,000 students, making its student body more than six times greater than Colgate's. It was logical to wonder why Syracuse would remain in the ACC and attempt to compete on the field with FBS teams when it supposedly could not afford the requisite responsibilities in preparation. Perhaps the university should have downgraded its program like Colgate? According to the mythology inhering in popular articles on topic, the putatively cash-strapped university would then be making better use of its profits raised solely from its basketball division.

As we have discussed briefly, my lack of proper research in my earlier thoughts about what was best for the program were unduly influenced by my deep belief that SU could not afford what it takes to compete in the ACC. Actually, as we will discuss shortly, this is not true. Syracuse has a lot of money, but it has clearly chosen not to spend its cash on football. The idea that the University is anywhere close to broke is a canard. Perhaps it was me, but I never saw any suggestions by SU officials that they were inclined to provide the infusion of funds necessary to make the program fly. But, I saw a lot of poor-mouthing, Or so I came to believe.

Syracuse University boasts a beautiful physical campus. It is regal, attractive, and situated in a highly lively town. The contagious perception that Syracuse University cannot afford the rigors necessary to compete at the highest levels is inaccurate and serves as self-fulfilling prophecy by restraining its football fans from pressing the university to improve the program substantially.

My father had a saying that applies here. Stating it verbatim may be too vulgar, but the sanitized version is: Stop wasting time and get on with something. That something of course is to bolster the program by endowing the necessary capital to prime the team for victory. The alternative of doing nothing would perpetuate a cycle of dross and mediocrity. And if nothing is to be done, a forthright acknowledgment of that wouldn't hurt as it would lower expectations that lead to such disappointment. Fans would be less disillusioned with dead-end performances once they were demystified by an admission of disinterest at the highest levels.

A decision needs to be made to spend the resources to start packing the Carrier Dome for fantastic seasons, which do indeed exist in copious amounts, or to downgrade the program by exiting the ACC and FBS. It doesn't make sense to commit only halfway, spending enough to gain access to the highest levels but not enough to compete meaningfully within them. Playing at lower levels at least would have the benefit of meeting fans' expectations of winning regularly despite not competing against the best teams in the nation.

This approach places Syracuse as the big fish in a small pond. After so many years of struggling with nothing to show but losses, it is high time for Syracuse to decide to win, wherever those victories can be achieved. A less attractive option that hopefully would never be chosen would be to exit football completely, like Gonzaga, the basketball powerhouse who left when acquiring football players during World War II was all but impossible. Gonzaga admitted they could not compete in football and they pulled out.

What about a SUNY Merger?

Problem solving most often finds alternatives that are obvious. Downgrading to the FCS is the natural answer to the adage: If you can't stand the heat, then get out of the kitchen. It is that simple.

My mission in this project is to write a book about the great moments in Syracuse Football. In so doing I gained empathy for the plight of the fans, the coaches, the players, and the alumni of Syracuse university having to live with a depressingly awful football program for far too many years. If Syracuse University officials believe they do not have the resources to fund a competent team, then why are they still competing? A downgrade to FCS from FBS might seem like a good deal for a school that would rather disparage its programs than invest in them.

Another nonobvious solution exists that merits exploring. There is always the possibility of merging with another school to combine the resources necessary to afford a first-class ACC team.

I am familiar with Central New York and have been for years. For two years, long before I was going to Syracuse games regularly, I worked for IBM in Utica, New York, just up from Hamilton NY on Route 12, and just over the Thruway from Syracuse. As a College Professor at Marywood University at the turn of the century, I teamed up with a former faculty member at State University of New York (SUNY), Binghamton to help build an IT program. I gained an acquaintanceship with SUNY's size and resources and have since learned it boasts three Division I football programs throughout its many locales.

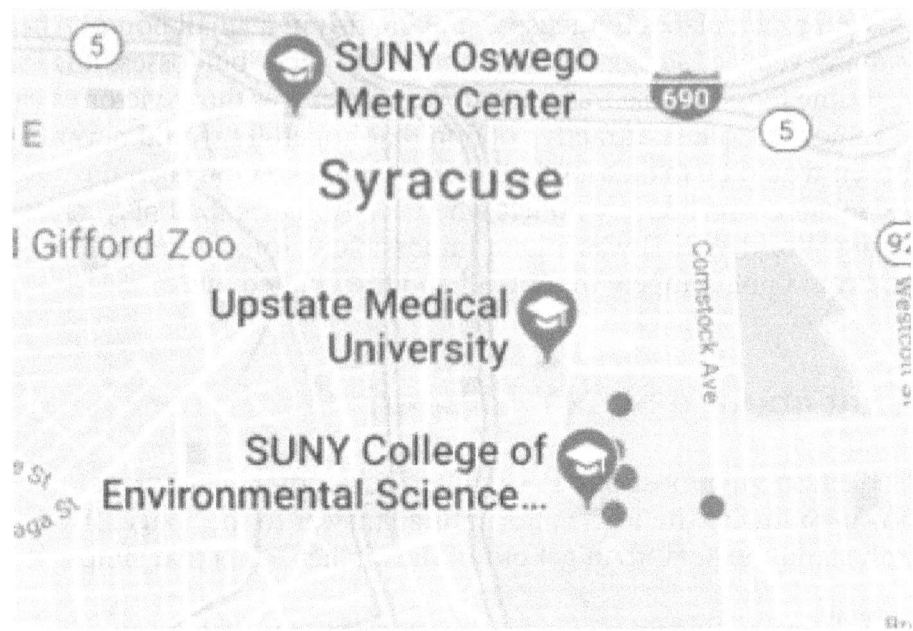

The three SUNY campuses in which Division I football is played are Albany in the Northeast, Buffalo in the Northwest, and Stony Brook on the East Coast. SUNY and Syracuse even share some programs taught on the Syracuse campus and in the surrounding areas, including The SUNY College of Environmental Science and Forestry; SUNY Oswego Metro Center; and the Upstate Medical University.

The troubleshooter in me kicked-in when I noticed that Syracuse seemed to be doing well as a small school but not doing well as in the big leagues. An alternative to downgrading that would maintain the grander status and identity would be to mergy Syracuse into the SUNY System.

As I described its beginnings in early chapters of this book, I made sure that we all knew that Syracuse is a very poor independent private institution. Now, I realize that I am wrong but to get to this point with the readers feeling similarly to myself, I did not change the earlier text. SUNY is an enormous, rich, taxpayer funded institution comprised of 64 campuses across New York State. A merger could make Syracuse a New York powerhouse that could mow down any other football power.

With Buffalo on the West, and Albany and Stony Brook on the East, Syracuse's football program would be the Central location. All football programs could feed into it, even while Syracuse outside of its sports division maintains its fully independent status as a university. With such a commanding joining of resources, great football again would once again thrive on the Syracuse campus. Perhaps a new field could be constructed by Manley or Skytop to handle parking and a 100,000+ seat stadium.

Show me the money!

Then again, just maybe Syracuse does not need any help from SUNY if it really wants to become an ACC powerhouse. But, the Administration can't be kidding or pulling a ploy. Otherwise, attendance at the Dome will quickly plummet to four figures before the first win. Moreover, if it is detected that this is an administration ruse, those in such a sparse attendance scenario will be hurrying out of the stadium with their mustard laden Dome Dogs and cool ones long before the Band hits the artificial turf at halftime. And they won't be scanning the radio stations for results.

Enrollment numbers for Syracuse come in anywhere from 19,000 to 21,000 with undergraduates representing about 16,000. Tuition and fees at Syracuse University are $43,318 USD without financial aid. With room, board, and other fees combined, total cost of attendance is $61,242 USD.

As I write this part of the book, looking for a solution to bolster the number of wins per year at this great football university, my earlier suspicions that the university's officials simply chose not to invest well in football have been affirmed. It was not particularly difficult to find some financials on the athletic programs including football and basketball. Before I offered a definitive recommendation about whether to start spending, downgrade to FCS, or merge with SUNY, I researched the popular financial conclusions commentators have expressed far too casually. The reality I discovered is that Syracuse is neither small nor poor and its football program generates a lot of revenue.

College athletics at the school level are primarily driven by decisions about money. When high paying jobs are threatened because a football team is losing continually, still other factors come into play. It comes as no surprise looking at the USA Today financial report on Division I programs in the NCAA for the years I have before me, 2014-2015, that I see massive revenues reported for universities.

The top revenue earner was Texas A&M with a whopping $192,608,876. Each of the top 25 universities within the database that was analyzed generated over $100,000,000 in revenue for the year. This begged the question: how much revenue does Syracuse Athletics generate in a given year?

While this data is not as readily available in the USA Today database, reports still exist in other publicly available data. For instance, the U.S. Department of Education office of postsecondary education for example, offers an "Equity in Athletics Data Analysis Cutting Tool." As the name suggests, the database compares funds spent and earned by men's sports compared with those of women's at the specified universities.

Don't lose heart, we can know the numbers without having to rely on innuendo as I had before I made a project and a chapter out of this. These numbers not only show the comparison of money spent and earned for men's programs versus women's programs, but also finances as a whole for the sports as well.

The numbers in the report show that from July 1, 2014 until June 30, 2015, Syracuse University generated $87,175,761 in total revenue from its athletic department. Syracuse would rank 35th in the NCAA, right behind the likes of West Virginia, North Carolina, Indiana, and Mississippi. It hardly matches the pauper image used by commentators to justify its lack of investment.

In the same database we see that Syracuse incurred $67,391,194 in expenses related to the teams during the time reported. This nets the University a gain of $19,784,567, which is a higher profit margin than nine of the top ten revenue generating public universities in the ACC. Boston College for example has net revenue of zero so Syracuse is miles ahead by contrast. Let's examine the chart below:

Team	Revenue	Expenses	Profit
Notre Dame	$121,260,381	$100,035,458	$21,224,923
Florida State	$120,822,522	$111,386,681	$9,435,841
Louisville	$104,325,207	$101,624,437	$2,700,770
Duke	$91,688,202	$91,174,723	$513,479
Virginia	$91,256,772	$91,345,925	$-89,153
North Carolina	$89,128,256	$89,080,843	$47,413
Syracuse	$87,175,761	$67,391,194	$19,784,567
Clemson	$83,534,371	$82,855,674	$678,697
Virginia Tech	$80,230,095	$77,679,721	$2,550,374
Miami	$77,724,833	$76,495,820	$1,229,013
Georgia Tech	$77,202,758	$74,979,077	$2,223,681
NC State	$76,834,603	$73,074,396	$3,760,207
Boston College	$69,300,736	$69,300,736	$0
Wake Forest	$58,672,116	$57,865,117	$806,999

Unsurprisingly, Notre Dame leads the pack in revenue and profit. Syracuse has twice the enrollment of Notre Dame, so we can hardly pretend it qualifies as a "small" school. It bears noting that reported numbers for Virginia and Boston College are confoundingly dismal. Boston gains zero profit while Virginia garners even less than that.

The data evinces the fact that contrary to popular misconception, Syracuse's athletic department is extremely healthy, and that they could probably provide cushioned seats in its bleachers for fans with season tickets without batting an eye. And who wouldn't like a Dome Dog on the house?

Comparing Syracuse University to Notre Dame, we see:

School	Academic Ranking
Notre Dame	#18
Syracuse University	#135

Here are some other quick facts in this comparison:

- **Syracuse, Much Larger School:** (21,789 vs. 12,292 Total Students)
- **Notre Dame, More Difficult to Get In:** (19.8% vs. 48.3% Acceptance Rate)
- **Syracuse, Slightly Cheaper Tuition:** ($43,318 USD vs. $47,929 USD Tuition)
- **Syracuse, Slightly Better Freshmen Financial Aid:** (73% vs. 66%)
- **Notre Dame Students Produces More Graduates After 6 Years**: (95% vs. 81% Grad. Rate)
- **Notre Dame Students Earn More:** ($70,100 USD vs. $56,600 USD Median Salary)
- **Notre Dame Has Much Smaller Class Sizes:** (10:1 vs. 16:1 Student-Teacher Ratio)
- **Syracuse, Slightly Warmer Summer Weather:** (70 vs. 70 Fahrenheit)
- **Notre Dame. Slightly Colder Winter Weather:** (26 degrees vs. 27 degrees Fahrenheit)

There is no lying to the government, the source of these stats.

Further elucidating the vitality of Syracuse's football program, another list was recently published in the Wall Street Journal, valuing it at a robust $120.9 million dollars, making it fifty-seventh in the nation. The list is too large to include in this chapter.

The numbers are impressive as well as the possibilities for expanded investment. These are illustrated by Ohio State, the nation's most valuable program at $1.5 billion, a number that drew critics of the amateur system that colleges have set forth a one that perhaps take away from academics.

This argument has never won where logic prevails. Football in many ways for a university is like advertising. If your football product is excellent, chances are a student can get a pretty good education at your university because you care about things. .

According to The Journal, the study "broke down each program's most recently available revenues and expenses, from 2016, making cash-flow adjustments, risk assessments and growth projections." Syracuse ranked ahead of famously healthy programs like Pittsburgh, Baylor, Brigham Young, West Virginia, Rutgers, Boston College, Duke and Wake Forest.

In this total valuation study, Florida State was valued the highest among ACC programs at $385.3 million. Notre Dame, which is still an independent in football, was valued seventh at $856.9. The last opponent I saw Syracuse face, Louisiana State, was valued fifth at $910.9 million. Syracuse dropped 11 spots in the calculations from last year at $130.5 million. It's not clear why the Orange's valuation declined so sharply but the most obvious reasons for even minor shifts are some changes in revenue and expenses that generate less of a surplus.

In its most recent filing with the federal government through the Equity in Athletics Disclosure Act, Syracuse reported making $38.1 million from its football program in 2015-16, while spending $23.2 million on football in 2015-16. There sure seems to be a lot leftover for a great coach and whatever else the football team needs. The question is: Is Syracuse University willing to spend the time, the resources, and the cash to help assure more inning seasons. If so, the next steps are obvious. If not, after this analysis, the next steps are just as obvious.

My recommendation would be to choose an option and commit fully to it. If Syracuse wants to maintain its football program, it needs to rectify the problem of constant demoralizing losses, either via downgrade, investment, or merger so that these terrible seasons become bad memories we can all one day selectively discard.

Amen!

Other books by Brian Kelly: (amazon.com, & Kindle)

Boost Social Security Now! Hey Buddy Can You Spare a Dime?
The Birth of American Football. From the first college game in 1869 to the last Super Bowl
Obamacare: A One-Line Repeal Congress must get this done.
A Wilkes-Barre Christmas Story A wonderful town makes Christmas all the better
A Boy, A Bike, A Train, and a Christmas Miracle A Christmas story that will melt your heart
Pay-to-Go   America-First Immigration Fix
Legalizing Illegal Aliens Via Resident Visas Americans-first plan saves $Trillions. Learn how!
60 Million Illegal Aliens in America!!! A simple, America-first solution.
The Bill of Rights By Founder James Madison Refresh *your knowledge of the specific rights for all*
Great Players in Army Football Great Army Football played by great players..
Great Coaches in Army Football Army's coaches are all great.
Great Moments in Army Football Army Football at its best.
Great Moments in Florida Gators Football Gators Football from the start. This is the book.
Great Moments in Clemson Football CU Football at its best. This is the book.
Great Moments in Florida Gators Football Gators Football from the start. This is the book.
The Constitution Companion. A Guide to Reading and Comprehending the Constitution
The Constitution by Hamilton, Jefferson, & Madison – Big type and in English
PATERNO: The Dark Days After Win # 409. Sky began to fall within days of win # 409.
JoePa 409 Victories: Say No More! Winningest Division I-A football coach ever
American College Football: The Beginning From before day one football was played.
Great Coaches in Alabama Football Challenging the coaches of every other program!
Great Coaches in Penn State Football the Best Coaches in PSU's football program
Great Players in Penn State Football The best players in PSU's football program
Great Players in Notre Dame Football The best players in ND's football program
Great Coaches in Notre Dame Football The best coaches in any football program
Great Players in Alabama Football from Quarterbacks to offensive Linemen Greats!
Great Moments in Alabama Football AU Football from the start. This is the book.
Great Moments in Penn State Football PSU Football, start--games, coaches, players,
Great Moments in Notre Dame Football ND Football, start, games, coaches, players
Cross Country With the Parents A great trip from East Coast to West with the kids
Seniors, Social Security & the Minimum Wage. Things seniors need to know.
How to Write Your First Book and Publish It with CreateSpace
The US Immigration Fix--It's all in here. Finally, an answer.
I had a Dream IBM Could be #1 Again The title is self-explanatory
WineDiets.Com Presents The Wine Diet Learn how to lose weight while having fun.
Wilkes-Barre, PA; Return to Glory Wilkes-Barre City's return to glory
Geoffrey Parsons' Epoch... The Land of Fair Play Better than the original.
The Bill of Rights 4 Dummmies! This is the best book to learn about your rights.
Sol Bloom's Epoch …Story of the Constitution The best book to learn the Constitution
America 4 Dummmies! All Americans should read to learn about this great country.
The Electoral College 4 Dummmies! How does it really work?
The All-Everything Machine Story about IBM's finest computer server.
ThankYou IBM! This book explains how IBM was beaten in the computer marketplace by neophytes

Brian has written 146 books in total. Other books can be found at amazon.com/author/brianwkelly

www.ingramcontent.com/pod-product-compliance
Lightning Source LLC
Chambersburg PA
CBHW060449170426
43199CB00011B/1139